The Hitler Trial

before the People's Court in Munich

The Hitler Trial

before the People's Court in Munich

Translation by
H. Francis Freniere
Lucie Karcic
Philip Fandek

Introduction by
Harold J. Gordon, Jr.
University of Massachusetts/Amherst

Volume One

UNIVERSITY PUBLICATIONS OF AMERICA, INC.

1976

Contents

INTRODUCTION

I.

The pressures which led to the Beer Hall Putsch and the Hitler Trial began to develop during the Revolution in Bavaria in 1918-1919 and grew steadily in the succeeding years. Finally, they were brought to a boil by the events and frustrations of the bitter year 1923. Therefore to understand what happened in the Putsch and what happened at the Trial it is necessary to go back to root causes. Taken out of context, it is very hard to understand why the players acted as they did. In context, the entire drama becomes plausible and the players real men rather than chessmen.

On 7 November 1918 Kurt Eisner, one of the circle of foreign—that is, non-Bavarian—artists and writers which made the Schwabing Ward of the City of Munich a glittering, dissident, turbulent, disenchanted and disunited island in the Bavarian sea of the city, began the Revolution in defiance of the leaders of the Majority Social Democratic Party (SPD) as well as of the royal authorities. He and his following, made up largely of rebellious soldiers laced with workers and radical peasants, made themselves masters of Munich in the absence of any attempt to defend the old order. By dawn of 9 November the Revolution had triumphed in the Bavarian capital.

Like most revolutions, the Bavarian Revolution was really a number of revolutions rolled into one. First, it was the revolution of the intellectuals of the radical Left against the old regime and the trade union leaders and the moderate Socialists. It was also the revolution of the peasants, who were frightened, bewildered and resentful of a war which dragged on and on without apparent rhyme or reason and was clearly lost despite all of the promises of their national and Bavarian leaders. They had seen their sons lost or maimed, their freedom and prosperity reduced by wartime

i

economic controls. Now they wanted an end to it all. It was the revolution of the ordinary man in the city streets who had suffered for years under shortages and grey, grinding work, borne up by the hope of victory. He too had lost sons and had seen the rich flaunting money, food and drink, while his own rations shrank. It was the revolution of the rear echelon soldier and sailor who had endured all the petty, chafing restraints of military life and the arrogance of his officers, often half-baked, half-trained reservists, without any of the shared risks and passions and excitement that made front line duty a national crucible in which young men of all classes and ranks faced a common fate and struggled in the mud with a common and tangible enemy. Most of all, it was the revolution of all who wanted peace and security once again and who seized upon Wilson's flamboyant promises as a life-preserver in a sea of despair. Even so, like all revolutions, it was the work of a small, activist minority, leading less active sympathizers and supporters and watched by the great uncommitted masses of the citizenry.

After its initial triumph, the Bavarian Revolution passed rapidly into ever more radical phases, particularly after Kurt Eisner was assassinated. This swift progress to the left resulted in the rapid demise of the brief harmony among the various revolutionary elements. Very few peasants or members of the middle classes were prepared to follow the path marked out by men who were dominating the Munich regimes, especially since the most spectacular of these leaders were not Bavarians or even not Germans. Worse still, in the eyes of many people in an area where emotional antisemitism was a strong social force, several of the most violent revolutionaries were Jewish.

The revolutionaries in Munich, on the other hand, supported by the mobs of soldiers who were resisting discharge into the ranks of the unemployed and by armed workers, were determined not only to hold their ground but to extend their power over the entire state of Bavaria.

The result was a polarization of politics. Bavarians had to choose between the uneasy coalition of anarchists, syndicalists, Communists, Independent Socialists (USPD) and unaffiliated radicals dominating Munich or the right wing Socialist Government, which had been elected by the Bavarian Legislature (Diet/Landtag) on the basis of the election of January 1919, which had been based on universal manhood suffrage. After its flight from Munich, the elected Government of Prime Minister Johannes Hoffman controlled Northern Bavaria from Bamberg. The Republic of Councils (Räterepublik) in Munich dominated Southern Bavaria by means of the city's traditional primacy, its size, and through loose coordination with other radical regimes in the larger cities and towns of the countryside supplemented by occasional armed excursions from the capital. Generally speaking, extreme leftists favored the Munich leadership, left-leaning Socialists wavered, and the rest of the political spectrum took up a stand with more or less enthusiasm behind Hoffman.

The existing situation was scarcely one which could endure. In the long run neither regime could or would tolerate the other. Nevertheless, paralyzed by internal conflicts and lacking an effective striking force, the Munich faction let the initiative slip from its hands—which it could not afford to do. It is axiomatic that unless it maintains its initial momentum and swiftly crushes the opposing forces while surprise is on its side, a revolutionary government has little prospect of victory unless the overwhelming majority of the population is at least passively on its side. In this case, the dice were very heavily weighted in the other direction, since the democratically elected German federal government in Berlin had meanwhile established itself firmly throughout the rest of the nation by military and political means and was now prepared to aid the Bamberg Government. Hoffman and his Cabinet, who were almost all Socialists, although the coalition which had elected them to office was largely non-Socialist,[1] did not want federal assistance because they wished to maintain the Bavarian state's rights within the new Germany and because they disliked and distrusted the regular Army officers who commanded the federal forces.

Therefore Hoffmann feverishly attempted to glue together a force which could free Munich. In view of his attempt to form an army on the basis of elected leaders and soldiers' councils and of the speed with which this force was raised, it is not surprising

---

[1] The SPD received approximately 33 percent of the total popular vote. Middle Class and Peasant parties received approximately 65 percent of the total vote. The radical left Independent Social Democratic Party (Eisner) received a trace over two and one-half percent.

iii

that it had indifferent success even against the equally haphazardly led and organized forces of the Munich Red Army. The result was that within weeks Hoffmann abandoned his attempt to go it alone, called for the formation of Bavarian Freikorps on the federal model, and invited Berlin to send in troops.

Once the federal forces marched into Bavaria and the Bavarian Freikorps were assembled in force, there was no question regarding the outcome from a military viewpoint. Munich was surrounded in the last days of April 1919 and on 1 May a general attack began spontaneously when some of the troops marched into the city in response to a rumor that the "Reds" were massacring their foes. Despite strong resistance by small pockets of Red Army forces, the attackers were in complete control of the city within thirty-six hours, at a very moderate cost in casualties. They were greeted with wild enthusiasm by the bulk of the population, who were clearly sick of the radical experiment, and this enthusiasm was only slightly dampened by the murder of a number of Catholic apprentices by soldiers of a Bavarian Freikorps who thought that they were supporters of the Räterepublik.

While the memory of the Catholic youths lived on—ironically, primarily in the propaganda of left and liberal groups whose enthusiasm for them in life would have been minimal—a number of impromptu executions of prisoners by the Red forces became a major political factor in Bavaria throughout the Weimar period. The "hostage murder" (Geiselmord), as the deaths of a group of military and political hostages slain at the Luitpold Gymnasium came to be known, enraged the victors in Munich much as the slaying of the Archbishop of Paris had inflamed the hatred of the victorious French government forces against the Communards in Paris in 1871. The hostage murders made for harsh treatment of the defeated leaders and later became a byword and an enduring memory keeping alive fear and hatred of the Republic of Councils in Bavaria.

A number of the leaders of the Republic of Councils were tried and executed. Some of the Russian prisoners of war who had fought for the Reds were slain. Many other men who had been active in the Councils or in the Red Army were sentenced to long terms of imprisonment—although few, if any, served more than a few years. So the Left as well as the Right had its martyrs, and they sought to make the most of them. Although the surviving Left radicals were in fact too weak to do anything

iv

more than threaten revenge, this they did in strident tones. Thus they kept alive the fear of revolution and reenforced the popular belief both in their power and their villainy.

However, much more to the point was the fact that the Republic of Councils led to the development of counter-forces and to the rise of a new generation of anti-Red leaders of whom the most immediately imposing was perhaps Colonel Franz Ritter von Epp, while the truly crucial figure in this wave was the still insignificant Adolf Hitler. Colonel von Epp came to the fore as the "Saviour of Munich" because his was one of the few Bavarian Freikorps led by a senior officer young enough to have a serious future in the new Reichswehr and to cut a dashing figure in a situation where Bavarians were desperate to find a native hero to match the Prussian and Württemberg leaders of the federal forces. Epp, who never lost a chance to advertise himself, became an idol of University and Gymnasium students and a patron of Right Radicals of all shades and hues. Hitler, still a simple corporal whose amazing powers as a rabble-rouser, schemer and juggler of men were completely unawakened at the onset of the Revolution, came swiftly into his own in the succeeding months. He first called attention to himself by attacking the Republic of Councils in the barracks with sufficient vehemence that he would have been arrested had he not outfaced his would-be captors over the sights of a rifle, if he is to be believed. Next he became a lecturer on political subjects in the Provisional Reichswehr, the interim army which served as a bridge from the old army to the new. However, the official National Socialist claim that he became an "education officer" greatly exaggerates his status, since the official records still carry him as a corporal. Still, his post led him into undercover political work through which he came into contact with the miniscule German Workers Party. Recognizing his spiritual home at once, Hitler left the Army and became first a leader and then the leader of this organization, which he soon renamed the National Socialist German Workers Party. From that point forward he never looked back. The would-be artist turned soldier had found his métier at last.

Two other men who were to play crucial roles in the Beer Hall Putsch and the Hitler Trial also found their political feet in the aftermath of the Revolution. Gustav von Kahr, a Bavarian civil official who had followed in his father's footsteps up the ladder of bureaucratic success, suddenly became a political figure to reckon with and a patron of conservatives and Right Radicals, and he moved into a central position on the political scene. Meanwhile, Ernst Pöhner, hitherto a judge, a reserve officer and a prison official, emerged from the revolutionary chaos as Police President of Munich and an enthusiastic friend of right extremism. Out of the caldron of Revolution these men who had entered it as politically passive figures emerged as men with a mission.

Nor were they alone in their revulsion against the Revolution. Even many of its early supporters had turned away from it or even against it. An extreme example was Count Anton von Arco auf Valley, the man who assassinated Kurt Eisner. According to his own statement and supporting evidence, he had fallen under Eisner's spell at the beginning of the Revolution, only to decide that his former idol was an evil genius and the Revolution an abomination. Anton Ritter von Bolz, an early National Socialist paramilitary leader, briefly joined the SPD before swinging right again, while Herman Esser, a confidant and deputy of Hitler's had been a Socialist newspaper editor in Kempten during the Revolution. Naturally only a small number of Bavarians made such a wide pendulum sweep, but a great number shifted clearly to the right, as the results of the elections of June 1920 illustrate. The total vote of the Marxist parties declined sharply and the parties of the right grew much more than those in the middle, while within the reduced Marxist block parties of the extreme Left grew dramatically at the expense of the moderate SPD. Essentially the elections indicated a growing lack of confidence in the parties most closely associated with the Weimar Republic, an ominous augury for its future.

The reasons for this change are still a matter of dispute, but it is quite clear that a considerable number of complex and sometimes contradictory factors operated to create this result. First of all, the results of the Revolution were not what great numbers of Bavarians had expected or desired. In fact, some of them were not desired by many people on any side of the political fence. The extreme Left did not get the dictatorship of the proletariat. The moderate Socialists did not get the popular mandate they desired for the creation of a Marxist state based on democracy. The liberal middle class voters found themselves very much in a minority. The bulk of the Bavarian peasantry and the politically minded Catholics found that their Bavarian Peoples Party had a plurality but was far from a majority. The more radical peasants were in a hopeless minority position. Conservatives and the radical Right, still not formally divorced, nevertheless found each other very uneasy bedmates and were still too weak to enjoy real power although their vote was growing.

Further, it is clear that one of the major aims of the majority of the supporters of the original Revolution and the hope of the many who had stood by and watched its success was the achievement of peace—by which they meant peace on more or less acceptable terms and the return of what they considered to be normal conditions of peacetime life. They had listened to the siren song of President Wilson only to find that the Fourteen Points comprised a typical political platform—something to run on, not to stand on! It is true that informed observers should have realized that the Allies were never likely to carry out this program, which would have meant a Germany stronger than that of 1914.[2] However, very few Germans, and probably proportionately fewer Bavarians, were or could have been well-informed regarding events in Allied countries during the war. After all, even today, in an era of saturation journalism, one must make an effort to get more than spasmodic coverage of home news from even important foreign lands. Most of all, Wilson said what a lot of Bavarians wanted to believe, and they believed it. When the Treaty of Versailles made it clear that the cloud cuckooland was as far away as ever, much of the popular resentment spilled over on the government and the "system" which had accepted the Treaty,[3] even though the great majority of the critics were not prepared to go to war to resist the Allies. Political leaders are usually blamed for anything that goes wrong and credited with

---

[2] Self-determination of peoples would have meant the addition of the German borderlands of Czechoslovakia and Austria, including the South Tyrol, to the Reich, which would also have retained at least the Saar Basin and all of Upper Silesia, as subsequent elections have shown. Even the fate of Alsace could not be predicted with certainty, as is indicated by the flat French refusal to permit a plebiscite.

[3] Attacks on the "system" are by no means a recent development. The National Socialists, for example, were always denouncing the "system" and even referred to the Weimar Republic as the System Times (Systemazeit).

anything that goes right during their time in office, whether or not they had any responsibility for such developments. Every Allied demand and every German concession brought a fresh storm of resentment and made new foes for Weimar Berlin, since the Reich, not Bavaria, was responsible for foreign policy.

Further, for complex reasons closely associated with the war and the terms of peace, the return of technical "peace" did not bring with it those social and economic conditions which Germans, including Bavarians, associated with that term. At least as late as the middle of the 1920's, when people talked of "peacetime" they were usually referring to the period before 1914. If the loss of Germany's great power status, of territory and of wealth, was deeply resented, the loss of prosperity and economic progress cut right to the bone, hitting people in their everyday lives. Large-scale unemployment, growing taxation, and inflation with its reduced purchasing power all led to mute resentment and growing agitation, which was to result in dangerous explosions of violence in the coming years. On this front, the Bavarian authorities bore a share of the blame in the public eye, but the bulk of it was directed against the federal government which had become in 1919 the primary economic power in Germany, as was made painfully clear to every citizen through decrees and taxes. A government which delivers or presides over relative prosperity can normally count on complacency on the part of a great majority of its citizenry, even though a minority may complain of its alliance with mammon and some may even turn against it violently. A government which does not deliver such economic benefits is likely to find itself in ever deeper trouble. After all, one of the primary functions of any modern government is the creation of a situation which permits the great bulk of its citizens to obtain the basic necessities of life—a concept which varies from place to place and time to time, but usually rests on a regional concensus. The survival prospects of any government, and especially of a democratic one, dim rapidly when it fails to meet economic expectations.

Thirdly, law and order broke down with increasing frequency, largely because of the above considerations. Here again is a major function of any modern government. Although governments are at times blamed for being over-zealous in pursuing these ends, especially in democracies, since some diminution of individual freedom is always implied in the execution of this function, throughout historic times whenever a regime fails lamentably and consistently to maintain law and order and to protect its citizens from criminal or political violence, its chances for survival are sharply reduced. No matter who is at fault, it is the official government which is blamed by most people when it fails to protect them. This is axiomatic and is one of the bases for the operations of most modern guerrillas and rebels. This means that a government which fails to meet the level of expectations in this sphere is likely to find the population either transferring its loyalty to other persons or groups whom they expect to function more satisfactorily, or going over to the foes of the government in search of protection or creating self-defense forces. Any or all of these reactions undermine the strength and effectiveness of the government in question and can easily lead to its destruction. In Bavaria all three reactions were to be observed in the years following the Revolution.

Last of all, and far more important than it is in the United States, came the problems of Bavaria's relationship to the federal government and to its neighbors. The nearest parallel we find in the U.S. are the still not entirely extinguished mutual hostilities which poison the relations of the northern and southern states. In Germany such factors were and are much deeper-seated and had a much longer history of political, religious and popular conflicts and prejudices behind them than in America. To understand the problem represented by this complex of hostility, it is necessary to examine some of the most important components which formed it. On the purely legal and political level there was the question of the rights of the federal and the state governments. This question was particularly acute because the new Weimar Constitution had overset the old balance of powers, giving far more authority to the federal government than it had enjoyed before the Revolution. This reduction of state power was resented to a greater or lesser extent by all of the German states, but particularly by Bavaria, which had been the most reluctant to give up its independence and which had been permitted to retain even more autonomy than the other states under the Bismarckian system.

Throughout the Weimar period, every Bavarian government, including that of Eisner—who believed in centralism in theory—sought to redress the new balance in favor of greater Bavarian rights, privileges and powers. This struggle was not primarily an empty clash over titles and pomp, although these

ix

considerations played a role in it, but was focused on such central questions as control of the armed forces, ownership of railroads and, above all, the right to tax and the division of tax monies.

This legal and formal political conflict was greatly intensified by the fact that after 1 May 1919 the Bavarian government was consistently well to the right of the government of the Reich during the 1920's. As a result, deep mutual suspicion of "Red Berlin" and "Reactionary Munich" beclouded and troubled relations between the two capitals. Nor was this suspicion reduced by the fact that Berlin was also the capital of Prussia, much the largest German state and one which was ruled during almost the entire Weimar period by a coalition in which the Majority Socialists were the dominant element. Neither side made any very serious effort to prevent bitter press outbursts against the other, and even official needle-pricks were frequent. For example, in 1922 the Bavarians learned that the Reich and Prussia alike had sent intelligence agents in Bavaria (and other states), while the Bavarians flatly refused to cooperate with federal legal authorities seeking to enforce the Law for the Defense of the Republic, which was extremely unpopular with the majority of Bavarians. This political gap did much to reduce faith and confidence in the good will of the other side in all negotiations.

Also very important, if harder to pin down, was the pervasive and unfortunate influence of the mutual disrespect and suspicion with which the various German "tribes" regarded one another. Even today, a bad driver in Munich is likely to be called a "Prussian Pig" if he has a northern licenseplate, although there has been no Prussia these thirty years. Even an Oriental who aroused the hostility of a boothholder at the farmers' market in Munich was called "a Chinese Prussian Pig." On the other hand, Prussians and especially Berliners were inclined to look down upon all other Germans with a cool and assured insolence which enraged Bavarians. Even Kurt Tucholsky, a left liberal writer who liked to puncture pomposity and prejudice and to act as a champion of the underdog, could remark: "Besides human beings there are also Saxons and Americans, but we do not deal with Zoology this semester." Hindenburg, similarly, expressed his initial contempt for Hitler by referring to him as a "Bohemian corporal." To be a corporal was bad enough—but to be a Bohemian one was certainly beyond the pale. Such prejudices were bred in the bone and were likely to surface at the most unfortunate moments. More significantly, they lay always just within the circle of vision of the conscious mind and were rooted deeply in the subconscious so that even self-criticism was often phrased in such terms, as when a Bavarian Minister of War, bitter at the stupidity of his countrymen, remarked, "It is a real blessing for us Bavarians that the Tyrolese exist!" This tribalism played its role in the tragicomedy that led to the Hitler Trial, and therefore should not be overlooked.

Religion was another factor that soured Reich-Bavarian relations. Bavaria was essentially and militantly Catholic despite the existence of a Protestant enclave in Franconia. Berlin and Prussia—with which the Bavarians tended to equate the Reich— were primarily Protestant, and this carried its burden of suspicion, mutual contempt and deepseated resentments. Germans were no longer prepared to fight one another over their religious differences, but they were quite prepared to discriminate against one another on this basis. Too, since Catholics tended to possess a good deal less than their proportionate share of the national wealth, social and economic resentments gave added edge to religious differences.

And beyond these overtones of economic resentment associated with the religious question there were crucial economic problems and attitudes separating Bavarians from North Germans and especially Prussians. Big Industry and Commerce and Big Finance and Agriculture were all centered in Prussia. Bavaria was essentially a land of small business and industry and of peasant farms. Bavarians of the Right as well as the Left were frequently hostile to what the National Socialists were later to call "international finance and industry" or, falsely, "Jewish finance and industry." The small farm owners, although often prepared to side with the great estate owners against the hated urban and industrial forces, were at times prepared to attack the great landlord. They certainly often viewed him with suspicion. Many commentators have seen this Bavarian attitude as being "bad"—an attack on modernism and progress. However, our generation is beginning to have belated second thoughts about the natural rightness, wisdom and inevitability of ever expanding industrialism. Whether it is "good" or "bad" is not, however, the question at issue here. What matters is the fact that this issue divided Berlin and Munich. Certainly Bavarian suspicion of and opposition to big business and big government was based not only on emotionalism and a blind traditionalism but on solid self interest and intellectual conviction. Bavarians believed themselves to be defending their way of life and their ability to exist, both of which were threatened by forces emanating from the North.

Next came the difference between Republicanism and Monarchism. The men who ruled in Berlin, like those who ruled in Munich, had in many cases served the Kaiser or other German monarchs in official posts and at least some of them were admittedly still monarchists at heart. However they had turned away from the past and were serving the Republic as Germany's legal government. General von Seeckt put it succinctly: "Do not ever strive to bring the dead to life. We must build anew . . . ." On the other hand, the men who held power in Munich were avowed monarchists who had not given up the idea of a restoration— although there are hints that they might prefer to delay the day until they were no longer in office—and represented voters who approved and expected such views from them. This difference of perspective, recognized by both sides, tended to enhance suspicion and coolness at high levels and open hostility at lower ones.

Catholicism and Monarchism together helped to create another barrier to Bavarian-Reich cooperation—Separatism. Throughout the early 1920's there were Bavarians who seriously thought of the temporary or permanent separation of Bavaria from the Reich. Frequently this idea was coupled with a scheme for the fashioning of a new German monarchy, a project that was always encouraged by the French, which gave it a greater plausibility in the eyes of friends and foes alike. It is very clear now that the great majority of Bavarians had no interest in such schemes, but it was not so certain at the time; and constant rumors, a badly botched Putsch attempt,[4] and the activities of

---

[4]   Two unlikely conspirators, a dramatist and theater critic, named Georg Fuchs and Hugo Machhaus, the latter a former National Socialist editor and musician, attempted in 1922-23 to carry out a separatist revolt in Bavaria financed by French money. Their scheme was nipped in the bud. Fuchs was sentenced to 12 years imprisonment while Machhaus committed suicide in his cell awaiting trial. There seems to have been no serious danger to the state, but the affair was a nine days wonder in the press.

French agents kept the pot boiling. The result was strong suspicion of Bavarian loyalty in the North and even among the other Southerners, Bavarian resentment against these suspicions, and sharp clashes between nationalists and state's righters in Bavaria.

Last but not least, more or less intangible differences in culture and tone exacerbated the relations between Bavarians and Prussians. The Prussian upper classes placed great emphasis upon the maintenance of a cool and placid exterior under all circumstances, looked upon reason as being superior to emotion, and cultivated understatement and at least the appearance of humility. This credo is well exemplified by the motto of the Prussian General Staff: "Be more than you seem!" Needless to say, many Prussians did not attain these ideals, but they colored Prussian life and especially Prussian evaluation of other individuals and groups. Bavarians, on the other hand, valued their reputation of being warm, spontaneous, and happy people. They cultivated hearty appetites of all sorts and saw nothing amiss in letting emotions have free rein. The result was that Prussians were inclined to see Bavarians as coarse, boastful semi-barbarians, while Bavarians saw Prussians as dried-up, humorless, sour Puritans. A typical expression of this difference of tone from the Prussian viewpoint is Peter von Heydebreck's description of the difference in character between himself and Hermann Göring: "He, the typical Bavarian, exuding power and uncouth; I, rooted entirely in the old Prussian tradition, reserved and acid." A political cartoonist of the time expressed the outward reflection of the cultural gap far less kindly but with admirable impartiality: "Here waterhead, there beerhead!" Such differences in personal values and in perceptions of their opposite numbers were not likely to make understanding and compromise very easy where Prussian and Bavarian faced each other with pen or telephone in hand, or, even worse, face to face.

All of these factors made for stubborn adherence of the majority of Bavarians to a course divergent to that steered by the helmsmen of the Reich and to a hardening of attitudes on both sides of the white-blue border posts. In turn, this cleavage between Berlin and Munich was very important in developing the atmosphere in which the Beer Hall Putsch would occur.

The years 1921-1922 widened the gap despite the sincere but intermittent efforts by responsible leaders on both sides to reach a viable compromise in the face of opposition of irreconcilables in their own camps. Naturally these efforts were sabotaged openly by extremists of all shades who saw them as surrender to the evil forces of the foe, while the stresses of day to day friction and the rising economic and social problems afflicting Germany resulted in ever sharper divisions among Germans on all political issues. More and more people abandoned the political middle for the extremes of Left and Right and the voices of the extremists grew ever shriller and their hopes ever higher as they gained more and more adherents and whipped themselves into literal frenzies of political passion and hope. In Bavaria, in particular, voices were even more strident than elsewhere and hands more ready to reach—if sometimes unsteadily—for weapons. And weapons were at hand, especially for the Right, but to a lesser extent also for the Left, smuggled in from sympathizers further North.

The Conservative governments of 1921-1922 held firmly to their views, buttressed on a broad and stubbornly loyal majority based on the peasantry, Catholics, and the middle classes. Their majorities were eroded to some extent, but they remained safe majorities even under the worst of circumstances, as is shown by the elections of 1924, when the enemies of the coalition reached their highest tide until the 1930's. Brought into power with a clear mandate to hold down Marxism, they naturally kept the Left, both moderate and radical, on a very tight rein, while treating the Right Radicals as slighly naughty children. These leaders were not, however, unaware of the problems which these Right Radicals posed and the difficulties of solving it without alienating many of their own followers who could not see beyond similarities of rhetoric and enemies in evaluating the extreme Right and without losing the possibility of winning many followers of the radicals back into the governmental fold. Their dilemma was perhaps best expressed by Minister President Eugene von Knilling, always a shrewd and cold observer, in 1923: "The enemy is on the Left, the danger on the Right."

The Marxist Left, hopelessly outnumbered, increasingly aware that their more successful comrades elsewhere in the Reich could give them very little effective aid, suffered from all of the problems likely to develop in such a situation. First of all, it was bitterly and fratricidally divided against itself by violent quarrels among the various parties and among the factions within the parties or on their fringes, so that little energy remained for fighting the class enemies. The Communists saw the destruction of the Social Democrats as the necessary prelude to ultimate political victory, but were deflected from even this limited goal by violent struggles over tactics. Yet at the same time, spurred on by Russian planners who still believed in the dogma that the world revolution was just around the corner, they expressed their frustrations and hopes in planning a violent revolution in the near future.

The Independent Socialists snapped wildly at both Majority Socialists and Communists, but soon fell victim to the hard fact that there was really no doctrinal or tactical room for a party sandwiched between the other two. Voters who found the Communists too violent, too irresponsible, too unwilling to compromise or too divorced from reality were unlikely to join the USPD, which was only fractionally removed from the KPD. Instead they passed to the SPD. In the same way those Germans to whom the USPD program appealed usually soon realized that they could get bigger and better doses of the same medicine right across the political street and joined the KPD. By 1922 the USPD was dead everywhere except in parliaments where diehards lingered on until the next election swept them out. The bulk of their followers went to the KPD, while a minority and the majority of the leaders returned to the SPD, bringing with them little if any political strength but introducing radical rhetoric which was not only at odds with the general views and objectives of the Party, but which made it unnecessary enemies.

The SPD fought a hard defensive battle on both flanks, against the USPD-KPD and against the non-Marxist parties. It was not strong enough to make policy or even to force the ruling coalition to listen seriously to its views, and it was unwilling to enter the coalition as a junior partner or to endorse the policies which such a coalition would pursue. To be in a futile minority position was a bitter pill for the party which considered itself to be the true voice of the German masses, but there was nothing that could be done about the situation as long as the SPD held to its program without making concessions which would make it more palatable to Bavarian tastes.

At the other end of the political spectrum a similar situation existed. The Middle Party, a middle class conservative coalition between two parties (German Nationalist Peoples Party— DNVP—and the German Peoples Party—DVP) which operated independently in other portions of the Reich, occupied the same position vis-a-vis the Right Radicals as the SPD did towards the

Communists. In each case personal ties and political hopes of winning over the misguided prevented a really effective stand against the radicals, who were troubled by no such scruples in their attacks on the moderates.

Yet the position of the Right Radicals was really no more enviable than that of the Communists and Independent Socialists. These groups, which formed a loose and mutually suspicious coalition of splinter organizations, had a vague agreement on general principles and prejudices to attract them to one another but differed widely on specific tenets of political doctrine and were often led by men whose ambitions far outweighed their capabilities. All of them were strongly German nationalist in outlook and hated Separatists as well as Marxists. They were thoroughly contemptuous of parliamentary democracy, which they saw as ineffectual and cowardly by nature. They also shared a general chauvinistic hatred of foreigners, which embraced anti-semitism, since they did not accept Jews as Germans.

By far the largest of these organizations and the most important until the Beer Hall Putsch was Bund Bayern und Reich, which bore all of the usual stigmata of the Racist Movement (Völkische Bewegung), as these groups named themselves. However, it had them in a relatively moderate form. Despite activist elements and occasional waves of general activism, the Bund was more interested in maintaining the status quo and preventing any shift to the left than it was in revolutionary change, although it certainly lobbied vigorously and called for a more "völkisch" policy on the part of the government of Bavaria.

At the other extreme of the Movement was the NSDAP, straddling the line between political parties and parliamentary organizations, but representing a clear, radical, revolutionary, and vigorously völkisch position. Its members were generally younger and far less ready to compromise on any issue than were those of Bayern und Reich, and its leaders despised the very idea of compromise. Its program called for the elimination of foreign (read Jewish and Slavic) influences in Germany, the crushing of Marxism, and then the reorganization of Germany to win back the place in the sun of which World War I had robbed her.

Scattered between these poles were a large number of other organizations (Verbände) which fought for survival among themselves and allied themselves with others in continually shifting formations. Multiple membership was common in the Movement and groups were formed, reformed or dissolved at frequent intervals. Here were all of the elements of a strong and dynamic political and paramilitary force, but its manifold energies and the talents of its leaders were to a large extent dissipated in petty squabbles and disorganized action.

Until the end of 1922, the Bavarian authorities were able to keep at least some sort of order in the Movement and some control over it through the interest of the great bulk of the Völkisch groups in paramilitary activities. General Arnold Ritter von Möhl, the tough-minded Commanding General of the Bavarian Reichswehr—a post in which he was primarily responsible to Berlin but secondarily to the Bavarian government—refused to deal with or provide money for any organization which was not affiliated with Bayern und Reich. However, at the end of 1922 Möhl was "kicked upstairs" to a less sensitive and powerful but more honorific post outside Bavaria, and his successor was neither wise enough nor strong enough to maintain this policy. The result was truly chaotic.

And chaos was particularly dangerous at this time, when all of the problems of the early Weimar years were coming to a head. Not only were foreign policy and economic problems gigantic, but the more radical elements of the Racist Movement, led by Adolf Hitler of the NSDAP, Dr. Friedrich Weber (a veterinarian) of Bund Oberland, and Adolf Heiss of Reichsflagge (a former Reichswehr officer), were increasingly frustrated by the refusal of the Bavarian government to follow their suggestions or bow to their demands, and the Communists were attempting to fish in troubled waters.

II.

1923, a year of disaster for Germany, was ushered in by the French invasion of the Ruhr Valley, Germany's chief industrial area, on the grounds that German reparations shipments fell short of the assigned total. Very briefly this action seemed a blessing in disguise, for it brought Germany a brief unity. Every political party from the SPD on the left to the German Nationalists on the right agreed to the formation of a national front against the French aggressors. Only the National Socialists and the Communists were absent from the mass demonstrations which swept Germany, and neither of these parties loved the French. Their abstention was tactical. Hitler took the prophetic view that the loudly trumpeted defiance and the cooperation of the parties was mere wind and self-deception. There was no use in trying to face France down until Germany was united and strong. Settle with the internal enemies first. Then the story would be far different. The Communists refused to cooperate because they would not ally themselves with the class enemy and insisted that only the destruction of the capitalist system in Germany could lead to a reckoning with the French exploiters, who were in any case hand in glove with the German industrialists.

In the seething excitement a federal government which stood well to the right of any previous Weimar regime was elected under the leadership of Chancellor Wilhelm Cuno. It soon became clear, however, that Cuno was considerably less effective as a politician than as a businessman, and that he was facing almost insuperable obstacles. The overriding problem was the economic one, which exaggerated all existing difficulties and quarrels and soon created new ones. Germany had already been experiencing that most frightening and exasperating of economic phenomena, a mixture of depression and inflation which had been progressing at a rapid rate, placing a serious burden on the individual, the economy, and the nation. Now this inflation made a quantum jump, entering a new dimension. It rushed along at a speed that was crippling and terrifying. Germany was cut off from her industrial heartland by French bayonets and from the money which poured into the national economy and the treasury from heavy industry. Even had the French not been determined to cut the Ruhr off from the rest of Germany as a step in their scheme of partition, the passive resistance in the Ruhr, which initially found the full support of the great masses at every level of the population, meant that industry lay idle and that the German government, which had called for the resistance, had to pay the idle workers and officials from badly depleted resources. The result was the printing of ever increasing amounts of paper money without any additional wealth to back it up. This is always the easy, politically safe, short-term solution to a shortage of funds. However, since it is a form of involuntary borrowing from the entire population, the long-term impact is highly inflationary and can easily lead to national bankruptcy if practiced on a large scale.

The French retaliated against the passive resistance measures of the Germans by arresting large numbers of people and by removing many officials from their posts and banishing them from the occupied area. These stern measures in turn led to active resistance to the French by means of sabotage carried out by unofficial groups of activists (including National Socialists despite Hitler's stand against *passive* resistance), as well as by others who were secretly sponsored by the German federal government, despite public disavowals. Deaths of a number of Germans at French hands, coupled with the sponsorship of abortive separatist movements, kept the pot boiling at fever heat. The economic upshot was that both the German and French currencies collapsed and the German inflation became spectacular in its extent, causing massive losses to all classes of the population. Business and industry, especially small and medium concerns, were ruined or forced to suspend operations, throwing their workers into the streets. The private savings of the great bulk of the thrifty were wiped out. Many of those who had anything to lose were ruined, while those who had already lost were threatened with starvation. Only the giants could roll with the punch since they had overseas connections and investments and since their deeper purses could not be sucked dry so swiftly, but their very survival made them unpopular, even though the poor would have been far worse off had these firms also been crushed. This wave of emotional anticapitalism aided those parties such as the Communists and the NSDAP which had long seen the giant corporations as villains.

The federal government knew what had to be done in the end, but since the surgery required was drastic and would be most unpopular, no one wanted to take the knife in hand if he could possibly avoid it. Further, after the fall of the Cuno cabinet in August 1923 the new Stresemann Government included Social Democrats, which multiplied the problems involved in ending inflation because they were as determined that the middle classes should bear the great bulk of the sacrifices which reestablishment of a firm currency would entail as their middle class colleagues were that the workers should bear a very good proportion of the economic burden. One way or another, week followed week and month followed month and there was no sign of an end to the melting away of the value of German money. Workers carried home a day's pay in wheelbarrows. Students found that the allowances telegraphed to them had lost half of their value overnight. In Munich in early November 1923 a light lunch cost well over a billion marks. An

American in Germany at that time could buy a good watch for a dollar or two. Unscrupulous traders, both German and foreign, speculated wildly. Banks used their favorable positions to protect themselves and often alienated many of their employees in so doing, even though these men would otherwise have lost their jobs. Everywhere fright was turning to despair and panic, and many people who had never known poverty were penniless and desperate. Yet not until after the Beer Hall Putsch did the federal government devaluate the old currency and introduce a new one—thus ending the inflation and wiping out the bulk of any wealth invested in currency.

Everywhere, confidence in the government declined with the value of the mark. Even ministers of the Republic expected that it would soon collapse and be succeeded by a dictatorship of some kind. Increasingly often the call was raised for a strong man to save Germany. As even many of the Republic's previous adherents melted away like snow in the March sun, fears, hatred, hope and desperation grew far faster among the many who distrusted, disliked or hated the Weimar Republic. Radicals of the Left and the Right alike saw it as their duty as well as their pleasure to take advantage of their new popularity to overthrow the system and rescue Germany by applying their own exclusive political elixir.

And there were forces available to be used to achieve their ends. On the right there were the so-called self-defense bands and other paramilitary orgnizations, and on the left there were the "Proletarian" or "Workers" Hundreds, and the unruly, violent mobs of the unemployed. All of these groups were armed to the best of their abilities and they frequently clashed with their rivals in defiance of the police and the duly constituted authorities. More and more frequently they fought with the police directly.

In Bavaria the growth of these organizations had been particularly promoted, not merely by the official patronage of rightist organizations desired as a form of militia, but by the policy of the government with regard to meetings and assemblies. If a meeting became unruly, the police dissolved it instead of reestablishing order. This was a policy which saved money and reduced police casualties, but it positively encouraged aggression by giving an advantage to any organization which could disrupt its rivals' meetings—and also forced even quite pacific organizations to form defense forces to maintain order in their assemblies. By 1923 left and right paramilitary organizations regularly attacked each other and fought pitched battles.

Naturally the federal and state governments attempted to hold these paramilitary forces in check, even in cases when they sympathized with or even supported some of them. But even the friendly ones were often unruly, and the hostile ones were slippery as well. They could be banned and dissolved, but they soon reappeared under other names but with much the same personnel. If leaders were jailed, their subordinates took their places, and it was very difficult to keep political prisoners behind bars for any extended period. One thing that the Reichstag and the state legislatures could usually agree on was the need for amnesties for political prisoners. Even more important, it was very hard to build up a case which would stand up in court against such offenders. Democracies with their careful protection of individual rights are at a great disadvantage when they face completely unscrupulous foes who fight them vigorously and then, when captured, turn the democracy's own legal machinery to their advantage.

Also important in the paramilitary question was the matter of national defense. In view of the French occupation of the Ruhr and threats to move deeper into Germany, the armed forces were not anxious to alienate completely the members of nationalist paramilitary organizations, since they might need these men to flesh out the Army's ranks should the federal government order a defensive war. Throughout the Reich, preliminary mobilization measures were undertaken although they were illegal under the Treaty of Versailles.[5] Nowhere did these measures go as far as in Bavaria, where the idea of a war of revenge against France was highly popular—especially with those who had very little understanding of the practical problems involved. General Otto von Lossow, the new Reichswehr Commander in Munich, and the Bavarian Government of Minister President von Knilling encouraged the Rightist Verbände to prepare themselves for possible action, either against rebels in Germany or against the foreign foe. At the same time, they used these preparations to give them greater control of the Verbände, to influence them and

---

[5] The Reich Government took, in secret, the view that France had violated the Versailles Treaty by taking action not covered by that document and therefore considered itself no longer morally bound.

their leaders and, most of all, to bring the bulk of their arms, especially heavy weapons, into official custody. Individuals who wished to be considered for use in case of mobilization—a powerful drawing-card in view of the mass unemployment—had to swear allegiance to the Government of Bavaria through the Reichswehr. For this reason Hitler and some other radical chieftains would not cooperate in the mobilization plans, let alone surrender their weapons.

The situation in Bavaria became even more difficult when Socialist-Communist coalitions came to power in Saxony and Thuringia. These regimes tolerated or encouraged the formation of Workers Hundreds and there was much wild talk of revolution, as well as serious Communist plans to this end. Too, laws were adopted which were clearly aimed against the middle classes, crimes against employers were more or less ignored, and Right Radicals were outlawed and in many cases forced to flee from either legal or mob action—usually to Bavaria, where they spread exaggerated tales of leftist atrocities. There were minor incursions into Bavarian territory by Hundreds or by policemen. Even though, at the last moment, the planned Communist insurrection was cancelled in October,[6] the situation remained volatile until the federal government reluctantly ordered the Reichswehr into both states to reestablish order and enforce federal laws.

In Bavaria the government and the mass of the population were both incensed and frightened by the Red menace on their borders. The government therefore ordered the establishment of a border defense force consisting of members of the Verbände and controlled by the Landespolizei, the Bavarian Green (paramilitary) Police, which was used to handle riots, insurrections, natural catastrophes and other problems which were beyond the capabilities of the regular (Blue) police. Many of the groups making up the Border Defense Force persuaded themselves that their presence on the border was in preparation for a revolution against "Red Berlin," but the mass of the evidence indicates that, as so often is the case, the wish was father to the thought. However, since the belief that there would be a revolution led by

---

[6]

Except in Hamburg where the Communists did not get the change of orders in time to prevent them from acting. The result was a short but bloody clash with the police before it could be suppressed.

Bavaria was widespread both in North and South, the danger of an explosion was increased still further.

Meanwhile the most extreme Racist faction dominated by Hitler organized itself into a loose coalition in early September. A roof organization called the Kampfbund was formed which included originally the Storm Troops (S.A.) of the NSDAP (but not the Party itself, which retained its independence of action); Adolf Heiss' Reichsflagge (National Flag), which was primarily active in Nuremberg and Northern Bavaria but had a small branch in the Munich area; and Weber's Bund Oberland. Later, as trouble developed between the Bavarian Government and Hitler, Heiss withdrew under pressure from his patrons in the Nuremberg business community. This move resulted in a split in the organization. The North Bavarian Reichsflagge remained loyal to Heiss and kept the old name. The Munich area elements took the name Reichskriegsflagge (National War Flag) and was held in the Kampfbund by its leader, Captain Ernst Röhm, who was in the process of leaving the Reichswehr under pressure because of his political activities. Finally, Kampfbund München, a small organization which had broken off from a rather sedentary Munich paramilitary organization of very formidable size, the Vaterländische Bezirksvereine Münchens (VBM), followed its leader, Alfred Zeller, into the Kampfbund. The Kampfbund was now the spearhead of the Right Radical movement and was increasingly steering a collision course with the authorities both in Bavaria and the Reich.

The first serious clash with Knilling's Government came at the end of September. The official abandonment of passive resistance against the French in the Ruhr had brought about a new surge of violent protests from the entire political Right. Hitler was only too glad to exploit this situation, despite having earlier denounced the resistance policy. His objective was the domination of the Bavarian Government and control of the police. To effect their program, the Nazis demanded the ouster of the strongly anti-Nazi Minister of the Interior, Franz Schweyer; the appointment of an economic tsar to fight inflation, profiteers, high prices and shortages of consumer goods; and appointment of a man friendly to the Verbände as Police President of Munich. To show their strength and force the hands of the authorities, Hitler and his friends planned fourteen massive political rallies for the night of 27 September and one of his closest lieutenants, the Baltic German Max von Scheubner-Richter, specifically admitted that if a Putsch developed out of these meetings, the National Socialists would place themselves at its head. Knilling found himself facing a new and much more powerful Eisner from a different political camp.

The Bavarian Government of 1923 was not, however, paralyzed by defeat and defeatism. It was certainly frightened and its hand was forced, but not in the direction which the Kampfbund had desired. Gustav von Kahr was appointed General State Commissioner with dictatorial powers in security matters, although the legitimate Government retained the power of review and veto over his actions—which was often forgotten by observers at the time as well as later. Knilling, who strongly disliked Kahr, had originally opposed the choice, but then apparently came to realize its advantages. Kahr was the man whose appointment was most likely to divide the Verbände against themselves and to prevent the more moderate ones from going over to Hitler, and it was also probable that the appointment would destroy Kahr as a serious political figure since it was very unlikely that he would be able to solve Bavaria's problems. Thus a united front of the Verbände against the Government could be prevented and the most important one, Bayern und Reich, swung behind Kahr, its Honorary President. The stage was therefore set for a showdown between Kahr and the Kampfbund, especially since Kahr's first official act was to ban Hitler's fourteen assemblies.

Unfortunately, the federal government completely misread the situation in Bavaria. Hearing of Kahr's appointment accompanied by the proclamation of a State of Emergency under Article 48 of the federal constitution, the Cabinet saw it as a pro-Nazi move and declared its own State of Emergency to override the Bavarian one—but without cancelling the Bavarian order. This action put General von Lossow in an impossible position since he was selected as executor of the orders of both "dictators," Reichswehr Minister Dr. Gessler and Kahr. The result was a tug of war for his allegiance. Lossow, always moved by the nearest firm voice, chose to stand with Munich against Berlin with the result that a long, complicated and completely unnecessary struggle developed which threatened to divide the nation and the Army. This struggle still remained unresolved in early November and led directly to the Beer Hall Putsch.

Naturally the quarrel between Reich and Bavaria was welcome to the Kampfbund, although it stood them on their heads where doctrine was concerned. Fanatic believers in a strong and unitary Reich, they found themselves defending and supporting a state's rights rebellion by men they suspected of being traitors. However, Lieutenant Colonel (Retired) Hermann Kriebel, the military leader, and Adolf Hitler, the political one, hoped to be able to edge the Bavarian authorities into an armed conflict with Berlin which they could transform into a national crusade which would bring them to the helm of Germany.

Kahr, who soon began to follow a policy of his own without directly defying the Knilling Cabinet, allied himself with Lossow and with Colonel Hans Ritter von Seisser, the de facto Commander of the Landespolizei. This triumvirate wanted a national revolution or at least a sharp turn to the right in Berlin, but they were not prepared to take the lead in any such venture. They therefore worked with groups in the North who hoped to set up a Steering Committee with dictatorial powers, which would contain General von Seeckt, the senior commander of the Reichswehr and even, if possible, the Social Democratic Reichspräsident, Frederich Ebert. Only at the beginning of November, when they were desperately trying to fend off Hitler and his friends and feared that the opportunity to bring an acceptable government to power would be lost, did Kahr and his colleagues agree to take any action themselves. Even this offer was carefully tied to sharing power (and responsibility) with a group of suitable Northerners, Reichswehr support for the action, and a firm program acceptable to all concerned. None of these conditions was likely to be met, but the entire project was still up in the air when the Putsch broke out.

At the same time, the triumvirate had negotiated with Hitler, Weber, and Kriebel, each seeking to use the other side for its own purposes and neither making any serious progress. In many ways this situation suited Kahr, the man of "eternal preparations," but it did not suit Hitler at all, who was becoming both impatient and desperate, since he was under very heavy pressure from his followers to take action. Sooner or later a revolutionary must cross his Rubicon or cease to be credible. Hitler was at this point and he knew it. He therefore turned from words to action with the aid of his usual circle and an uncertain and unpredictable ally in General Erich Ludendorff, the active member of the Hindenburg-Ludendorff team which had directed the German war effort in the last years of World War I. Ludendorff was, despite or because of his defeat, clothed in the same sort of legend as General Robert E. Lee was in the South after the Civil War, and therefore brought great prestige to the cause. However, he was also already in the grip of the mental illness which was increasingly to becloud his last years. As a symbol he was invaluable. As a colleague he was dangerous, but Hitler was a master at using dangerous men and did so in this instance. Together these men planned a revolt to force Kahr into the action they were now sure he would never take on his own.

III.

The night of 8 November was chosen because it was one which seemed to offer an excellent opportunity to paralyze the Bavarian governmental apparatus and to capture it. It also seemed peculiarly auspicious because it was the eve of the official anniversary of the November Revolution of 1918. Kahr was to deliver a speech on his program to an audience of distinguished citizens at the Bürgerbräukeller, one of the largest beer halls in Munich. The Putschists gathered their forces together at other beer halls, especially the Löwenbräukeller, and sent parties to seize the Reichswehr barracks and obtain ammunition and additional weapons.

At first everything seemed to go well. Kahr, Lossow, Seisser, Knilling and most of the other top echelon leadership were captured. Kahr, Lossow and Seisser were bullied into agreeing to go along with the "national revolution." The crowd in the beer hall, overwhelmed by Hitler's oratory and the excitement of the occasion (and possibly softened up by the good beer inside them) roared their approval. The conquest of Bavaria seemed assured. However, this appearance was treacherous and it is even possible that the Putschists would have been better off had the triumvirate been left free, since they might well have hesitated and hampered the preparations for putting down the rising, which would have been quite in character for Kahr and Lossow. As it was, even though they soon talked their way out of the beer hall, the die was cast before they stepped out into the cold, rainy night. Lossow's subordinate generals had already acted in his absence. One of Kahr's key assistants, Karl Freiherr von Freyberg, had begun issuing orders for police reenforcements as had Christian Pirner, a senior police official in the Ministry of the Interior. Commanders of military installations and duty officers, although they disposed of only a handful of men—the others were out on the town—managed to hold off the Putschists until their men and officers returned. When the triumvirate reached their offices, they simply rubber-stamped the arrangements made. The Putsch was doomed, even though the Green Police, left without orders, took only passive defense measures until Seisser showed his hand.

Meanwhile the Putschists, ignoring the need for speed in exploiting their successes, frittered away the night in talk or senseless small sorties from their bases. In the morning they found themselves in danger of being defeated piecemeal by the rapidly assembling government forces. Hitler, Ludendorff, and Kriebel then debated their next action. Ludendorff, the professional soldier, wanted to withdraw to the countryside, which meant the beginning of a civil war. Hitler, the political soldier, refused to let his movement "die in the dust of a country road" and insisted upon a propaganda march into the city. No precise plans seem to have been made. Hitler in a tight situation tended to favor improvisation, a reason for both his successes and failures. Judging by fragmentary reports, the preparations and actions of the Putschists, and the course of events, they seem to have been prepared to demonstrate and win support from the populace but also to try to fight their way to victory if the enemy's defenses seemed weak enough. Their precise objective remains unclear but there was talk of trying to relieve Röhm, who was beseiged with Reichskriegsflagge and Kampfbund München forces in the Military District Headquarters on the Ludwigstrasse.

The Reichswehr and Landespolizei garrisons of Munich, continually reenforced by troops from outside the city, formed a cordon around the government quarter and prepared to assault the Military District Headquarters. Their preparations were slow and methodical, since they wanted to have overwhelming forces available to prevent any possibility of a reversal and to prevent bloodshed by making clear to the rebels what little chance they had. Another column was being prepared to attack the Bürgerbräukeller. Röhm, surrounded but defiant, planned to fight but in the end he surrendered after Ludendorff gave his permission, but not before two of his men had been slain by mistake by a Reichswehr machinegunner.

Even before the surrender at the Ludwigstrasse, Hitler's

column, after pushing aside a small guard on the Ludwigs-brücke, marched through the heart of the city, surrounded and followed by a cheering and excited crowd. Finally, at the Feld-herrnhalle, a memorial to Bavaria's greatest generals, the column crashed into a covering force of Landespolizei in a classic demonstration situation. The crowded Putschists, marching twelve abreast, pushed against the police cordon. The police shoved back. Someone fired a shot and then a crackle of gunfire rang across the square and down the narrow Residenzstrasse. The Putschist banners fell. Dead and wounded men covered the street—and the Putsch was over, after less than a minute's fighting. All that remained to do was pick up the pieces.

IV.

Once the Putsch was suppressed and most of the key leaders captured, the question of how they were to be handled arose. The first question was: Should they be tried? If so, when, where, and under what circumstances? It was immediately clear that there was little sentiment in official circles in favor of avoiding a trial and even less belief that this was feasible. Kahr hoped for a pro forma trial at which the prisoners would plead guilty and the prosecution would admit that they had acted from patriotic motives, whereupon the convicted men would receive sentences in consonance with their cooperation. Apparently some of the accused were interested, but Ludendorff absolutely refused to consider such a solution.

The federal government and Dr. Matt, the Bavarian Kultus-minister (Religion and Education) wished to have a trial with closed sessions in view of the danger of the revelation of prelimi-nary mobilization activities and possible wild accusations by the accused. The ultimate decision was that the trial should be public but that when sensitive matters were discussed the court would go into secret session, a system that did not work very well, since it was to the advantage of the defendants to make as many accusations against the authorities as possible and it was helpful to them to be able to refuse to give details supporting their allegations on the grounds that these would be classified data. Then in the secret sessions they rarely provided much serious evidence. The result was that they got all of the advantages of creating suspicion in the public mind without having to present solid evidence to support it.

The Bavarian Cabinet, aside from the Minister of Justice, Franz Gürtner, who alternately flirted with and frowned upon the National Socialist leader whose Justice Minister he was destined to become, wanted the trial to be held outside of Munich. The judges, the legislature, and the defense attorneys wanted it to be held in Munich and won the day, at least partially because the defense attorneys claimed that their other legal business held them in the city. In the end it was decided, ironically, to hold the trial in the buildings of the former Reichswehr Infantry School, which had been dissolved by General von Seeckt because the great bulk of the cadets had joined the Putsch under the misapprehension that the Bavarian Reichswehr also supported it. So the buildings on the Blutenburgstrasse which had witnessed one of the few successes of the Putschists now was the scene of their trial.

Other minor questions which arose were quickly and easily solved. Departing from its usual practice, the Bavarian Government gave all of the officials involved permission to testify freely without reference to the maintenance of official secrecy, although it rejected a proposal for a blanket exemption. The Reichswehr similarly freed its officers.

Meanwhile torrents of demands that Hitler be freed were aired in every conceivable manner. The Government ignored them except to give orders for a tightened security in Munich since the depth and extent of partisan feeling on their behalf might well lead to the sort of senseless violence which had flared up in the first days after the Putsch. These measures were impressive but proved to be unnecessary. The intelligence network of the police was alerted to seek information regarding dangers during the trial period. Extra units of the Landespolizei were brought in to strengthen the powerful normal garrison. Reichswehr troops in other garrisons were also alerted to the possible need to send troops to Munich. Sentries were reenforced and special precautions adopted at high points in the proceedings. For example, the Reichswehr's Munich garrison was placed on alert on the day of the sentencing of the convicted Putschists. [7] Schools were closed for the day. Soldiers were forbidden to

---

[7] There were also several separate trials of lesser Putschists for specific offenses, but none of them roused much public interest.

enter the city alone if in uniform. Posters showing the sentences were banned and assemblies forbidden. Yet in the end there was no trouble beyond the occasional shouts of supporters of the defendants within the courtroom.

There were other problems over which the Government had no control, however. The trial was clearly a hot potato politically and many people wanted to disassociate themselves from it as much as possible. For instance, in the preparation of the prosecution's case, the first and second prosecutors stayed as much in the background as possible, leaving the junior prosecutor, Dr. Hans Ehard, who was to be Minister President of Bavaria after World War II, to bear far more of the burden than was normal in such a major case. On the other hand, in the trial itself they limited his freedom as much as possible when he proved aggressive and effective. The problems regarding the prosecutors were, however, minor compared with those posed by the judges. Stenglein just wished to stay out of trouble, but Presiding Judge Georg Neithardt made it very clear even before the trial that he had no intention of finding Ludendorff guilty under any circumstances. His conduct of the trial conformed to his prejudices and made it clear that his sympathy for the defendants extended considerably farther than Ludendorff. For example, he let Hitler rant for hours unchecked even when he roamed far from the subject. He forced Ehard to question Ludendorff again when the General's first testimony was clearly self-incriminating, insisting on a second and "laundered" version. Neithardt and the prosecutors also carefully did not call upon many of the key figures with knowledge of the Putsch to testify at the trial, although their pretrial testimony had often been clearly crucial. Examples are: Lieutenant Colonel Endres, Lossow's Operations Officer, who was expelled from the trial because he was a witness and then was never called; Freiherr Hubert von und zu Aufsess and Freiherr von Freyberg, both close friends and key lieutenants of Kahr; Majors von Hösslin, Doehla, and Hunglinger were others who should have been heard and were not. Neithardt also allowed Lieutenant Wagner, one of the accused, to call General von Lossow a scoundrel without serious rebuff and then fined Lossow for marching out of the court in protest. Yet the lay judges were far more prejudiced in favor of the defendants than was Neithardt.[8] Therefore the chance of impartial administra-

---

[8]   The Putschists were tried before an extraordinary (Volksgericht) to handle political crimes, which was about to go out of

tion of justice was very poor.

The Bavarian Cabinet was, once more aside from Gürtner, who tended to defend the presiding judge, enraged at the manner in which the trial was conducted but could exercise no influence on the court in view of judicial independence. General Friedrich Kress von Kressenstein, Lossow's former Artillery Commander and successor, was also furious at Neithardt's willingness to allow the defendants to abuse Army officers without rebuke.

Taken together, the prejudices of the judges and the timidity of the senior prosecutors goes a long way to explain Hitler's success in making the Trial into a major propaganda triumph which more than counterbalanced his defeat on the streets of Munich.

Another problem which weakened the case of the prosecution in the public mind was the fact that one of the very few effective moves the rebels had made during the Putsch was in the field of propaganda. They had succeeded in getting their version of the events of the evening of 8 November into the press before the Government could present theirs, with the result that a good many minds were made up before the counterblasts came. The first impression can be very important in such situations. Too, the Kampfbund leaders managed to secrete and later destroyed many documents which would have been highly incriminating. Franz Xaver Schwarz, the long-time treasurer of the NSDAP, later admitted destroying many documents, and Captain Röhm boasted in his memoirs that all through the Trial highly incriminating documents were sitting in a safe where he had hidden them in the Military District Headquarters.

One way or another the Trial was not a great triumph for either truth or justice, but it was a most important example of political legerdemain and a goldmine of data regarding facts, theory, and attitudes of all concerned in Bavarian political life. However, as in the case of mining in general, it is most important to separate the gold from the dross.

------

[8] (cont.)

existence. This "Peoples Court" included both professional judges who were legally trained and laymen without legal training.

V.

The great bulk of the manuscript which follows is based on the contemporary version of the minutes of the open sessions of the Trial published and edited by Knorr & Hirth, the firm which also published the most important Munich newspaper, *die Münchener Neueste Nachrichten*. This version was selected because it had been carefully prepared, corrected, and proofread by persons well versed in the Munich political situation. However, where the secret sessions of the Trial are concerned, the official transcript of the Trial made by court stenographers is the exclusive source. Further, this official version has been used throughout as a control on the accuracy and completeness of the Knorr & Hirth material.

The official manuscript is a difficult one for general use, since it consists of the uncorrected and unedited typescript of the court reporters' minutes. There are a good number of misspellings of proper names and other minor blemishes which reduce its readability and accuracy. However, it is vital as a check on the unofficial version and as the only source of the proceedings in the secret sessions.

Six copies of the original official transcript were typed up by the State Institute for Shorthand. They were distributed as follows: one to the Bavarian Ministry of the Interior; one to the Court; one to the Prosecutor's Office; one temporarily to the Institute for Shorthand (later disposition unclear); and two to the Ministry of Justice, one of which was to be handed on to the Ministry for Foreign Affairs (which also served as the Minister President's staff.)[9] Of these copies, two are known to have survived. One is in the *Abteilung II (Geheimes Archiv)* of the *Bayerisches Hauptstaatsarchiv* in Munich. The other was among the captured documents in Washington and was then returned to Germany, where it was deposited in the collection of the *Bundesarchiv* in Koblenz. A microfilm copy was made by the National Archives of the United States and is available there; and — much earlier — another was made by the author and is in his possession.

---

[9] BHSA, II, MA 103479, No. 10911G.

Because it is a German procedure to keep the indictment and the verdict together and separate from the transcript of the proceedings of a trial, these portions of the present manuscript stem exclusively from the published version. However, since these are the portions of the proceedings which are a matter of public record, a double check is scarcely needed here.

The reader must be very careful in using the minutes of the Trial, which constitute a very important historical document. He must remember that their importance lies as much or more in the presentation of what the various participants wish one to believe took place as for coverage of the events themselves. Further, the minutes enable the reader to judge for himself how well or how fairly the Trial was conducted. They enable the reader to evaluate the major Putschists and their opponents on the basis of what they said and how they said it. However, one should never forget that being glib and effective, or bumbling and ineffective does not equate in any way with being truthful or untruthful. Further, even when the speakers are being, according to their lights, entirely truthful, their memories may not be entirely accurate. Too, the accused and their attorneys, in particular, were far more interested in getting off lightly, in making a good case for their cause, and in blackening the reputations of their foes than they were in presenting the objective truth for the observer. Therefore when one wishes to get as close to the truth regarding the events and people dealt with by the Trial, it is necessary to supplement the Trial record by as much material dating from the actual events themselves or the period immediately subsequent to them, together with the memoirs of those who were involved in the drama, and then to analyze these often conflicting materials carefully before coming to a conclusion in the Ranke sense: the determination of the situation as it really was—or as near to that as one can get in this uncertain world.

Here is a very important document, but like any other historical document it only has meaning in its proper context.

Harold J. Gordon, Jr.
University of Massachusetts / Amherst

THE FIRST DAY, February 26, 1924

—MORNING SESSION—

The site of the hearings lies in the western part of the city on Blutenburgstrasse, parallel to Nymphenburgerstrasse. The short stretch running from Maröfeld to Adamstrasse is cordoned off. Mounted Police and barbed wire bar the way to vehicles; only pedestrians are allowed access. The single entrance is under strict surveillance by military guards and a security team.

This morning there is quite a bit of activity in this normally sedate street, although one can scarcely speak of tumultuous crowds or even clusters of curiosity-seekers. The public realized that there was nothing to see because the defendants are under arrest and have taken up quarters in the old Infantry School which has been altered to handle the voluminous business of the trial.

One is thoroughly searched before entering; even then, without identification and a specially stamped pass with a photograph affixed, there can be no entry past the outer barriers. Guards are stationed at the main entrance, in the corridors, and even in front of the door to the courtroom. Plainclothes police officials make one last spot-check for weapons. There is no question about formalities; there is even a special room where policewomen undertake a thorough search of all females. Officers of the Landespolizei and special security busy themselves with surveillance procedures.

As the defendants are led through the long corridor and into the huge courtroom at around 8:30 a.m., the doors off the corridor are closed as a security precaution. Just previously, the corridor had been cleared of people.

1

Soon, every last seat in the hall is occupied. The defendants sit with their attorneys before the tribunal. Members of the press from every sovereign nation work at benches that span the courtroom. In particular, one hears the sound of English. A special press room has been created for the occasion, and here typewriters clack incessantly as messengers run back and forth.

Besides Judge Neithardt, the presiding Judge, the tribunal consists of one assessor and three lay judges. In order to prevent protracted delays in the trial due to illness, replacement judges have been selected. Also seated at the judges' table with Judge Neithardt, are Supreme Court Councillor Simmerding; District Court Councillor Leyendecker; Herr Herrmann, an insurance official; Herr Beck, the proprietor of a stationary store; Herr Zimmerman, an insurance inspector; and Herr Brauneis, a tobacconist.

The Trial begins with the summoning of the defendants. As the names are called out, Judge Neithardt asks Pöhner if his health has improved enough to be able to follow the proceedings. Pöhner answers, "Yes, Your Honor."

Dr. Weber wishes to add to the record that he is an assistant at the School of Veterinary Medicine at the University of Munich.

JUDGE NEITHARDT: The witnesses have been scheduled for a later date. I would now ask the prosecutor to read the indictment.

Basis for Indictment

HERR STENGLEIN: On November 8 of the previous year, in the Bürgerbräukeller in Munich, a meeting of members of patriotic bands, working men of all classes, and specially invited guests allegedly took place. Generalstaatskommissar von Kahr had announced he would give a prepared speech. The assembly was to begin at 7:30 p.m. Before the appointed hour, however, the hall was so full that police had to bar entry for safety reasons. Many people were turned away at the door.

Shortly after 8:00 p.m., Kahr appeared in the hall, accompanied by General Lossow and Colonel Seisser. Von Kahr mounted the podium upon which Kommerzienrat Zentz had installed himself as moderator. Von Lossow and Seisser found seats close to the stage. Zentz opened the meeting with a few words of introduction; then Kahr began to speak.

2

At about 8:45 p.m. he was interrupted. A disturbance was originating from the entrance to the hall. Hitler spearheaded a group of armed men and stormed his way through the crowd and onto the stage. His accomplices carried revolvers and machine guns; Hitler himself clutched a small pistol. Simultaneously, members of Hitler's shock troops seized the entrance. These men had rifles, pistols, and machine guns which they trained on the audience. In the middle of the entrance, they set up a machine gun nest and aimed it at the crowd.

The security force guarding the main entrance to the Bürgerbräukeller were forcibly removed and armed men occupied the other entry, the Rosenheimerstrasse, and the side exits into the beer garden, and they manned the windows from outside. Inside the hall guards were posted at telephones, and no one was allowed to use them other than Hitler's troops. Hitler climbed on a chair by the stage and shouted for silence. To lend emphasis to his command, he fired a shot to the ceiling. Thereupon, he jumped off the chair. When Major Hunglinger stepped in his way, Hitler held the gun at Hunglinger's chest until a bystander pushed his arm away. Hitler then jumped on the stage and shouted roughly the following:

"The national revolution has begun. The hall has been occupied by 600 men, heavily armed. No one may leave. If there isn't order immediately, I'll train a machine gun on the gallery.

"The Bavarian government is deposed. The government is out. A provisional German national government is being formed. The Reichswehr and Landespolizei barracks have been occupied, and these men are advancing under the banner of the swastika."

Hitler then demanded that Kahr, Lossow, and Seisser leave the auditorium to confer with him. The men acquiesced and, guarded by heavily armed men, accompanied Hitler into a small room across from the coatroom. Before the door stood numerous followers of Hitler, also armed.

In the back room, then, were Kahr, Lossow, and Seisser, as well as Hitler himself and three armed followers of Hitler. Major Hunglinger also succeeded in easing his way into the room, but Lossow's guards were prevented from entering. When the leaders were in place, Hitler ordered, "No one leaves this room alive without my permission!"

He then turned to Kahr and said, approximately, "The Reich government has been formed; the Bavarian government has been abolished. Bavaria is the springboard for the Reich government. We must have officers. Pöhner will be president with the full power of a dictator, and you will be governor. I will lead the Reich government; Ludendorff, the national army; and Seisser, the police." When Hitler discovered Major Hunglinger, he ordered him from the room. Hunglinger obeyed at the request of Seisser.

Then Hitler, waving his pistol wildly, continued, "I know this comes as a shock to you, but someone must take the first step and someone must make it easy for you to take that step. Everyone must accept the lot he has been assigned. If you do not, you forfeit your right to live. You'll have to struggle with me and suceed with me, or die with me if this thing goes wrong. I have four bullets in my pistol—three for my compatriots and the last one for me."

At that, he pointed the gun at his temple. Thereupon, Kahr said to Hitler, "You can hold me against my will, you can have me shot, you can even shoot me yourself. To die or not to die is not important." Hitler then turned to Seisser, who reproached him for not keeping his promise that there would be no putsch. Hitler replied, "I did; but forgive me, for the sake of the Fatherland." When asked by Lossow, "What is Ludendorff's position?", Hitler answered, "Ludendorff is ready and will be here presently."

The whole scene may have lasted ten minutes. All during this time, the behavior of Hitler and his accomplices left no doubt that they were prepared to back up their demands with force if necessary. Kahr, Lossow, and Seisser were prevented from speaking with one another. At no time did Hitler receive any encouragement or assent from these gentlemen. As Hitler exited from the room, Dr. Weber entered. All but one of the armed guards had left the room. Dr. Weber led Kahr, Lossow, and Seisser to believe that they could speak freely to one another. At Seisser's request, Major Hunglinger was also called back into the room.

Meanwhile, Hitler was giving a second address in which he stated, among other things, "The Knilling cabinet has been dissolved. A Bavarian cabinet will be formed around a governor and a president with full powers of a dictator. I propose Herr Kahr as governor, and Herr Pöhner as president. I hereby declare the government of the November criminals in Berlin dissolved; Ebert is hereby deposed. A new German national government is born today in Bavaria, here in Munich. We will form a German national army at once. I therefore propose that until the final reckoning with the criminals in Berlin—the criminals that are destroying Germany—I will assume the leadership of the provisional German national government. His Excellency Ludendorff will head the German national army; General Lossow will become Minister of the Reichswehr; and Colonel Seisser will be Minister of the Reich police. The task of our provisional German national government is to march on that sinful Babylon, Berlin, and with the massed strength of this land and every German to save our people.

"I ask you now: Outside are three men—Kahr, Lossow and Seisser. It was a bitter pill for them to swallow. Are you in accord with this solution to the German problem? You can see what leads us. It isn't selfishness. It isn't vanity. It is the eleventh-hour struggle for our own German Fatherland that we desire. We want to build that kind of united state where the common man receives what is rightfully his.

"Be still! The hall is sealed off by the German Kampfbund. Morning will find either a new German national government—or our dead bodies."

Hitler returned to the small room and spoke of how his second speech in the hall had created such jubilation. He continued to apply pressure to Kahr, Lossow, and Seisser. Suddenly, the military command "Attention!" was heard, as well as cries of greeting. Ludendorff entered the room in civilian clothes. Herr Scheubner-Richter and two others had picked him up and, on the drive to the Bürgerbräukeller, had informed him of the present state of affairs. He was greeted at the door to the back room by Hitler, who confirmed what Scheubner-Richter had told him. Ludendorff then stepped up to Kahr, Lossow, and Seisser and said, without asking or answering questions, "Gentlemen, I am just as surprised as you; but the step has been taken. This concerns the Fatherland, our great nation, our great people. I can only say: 'Come with us, do the same!' "

The atmosphere in the back room changed completely when Ludendorff appeared on the scene. The pistols disappeared and, from this point on, threats were replaced by coaxing. Yet Kahr, Lossow, and Seisser were not permitted to speak with one another. Shortly after Ludendorff, Pöhner entered. An urgent discussion began now among Hitler, Ludendorff, and Dr. Weber. Again and again Hitler would shout that there was "no turning back now." Finally, Lossow and Seisser gave their assent and a while later Kahr declared, "I am prepared to assume leadership of the Bavarian government as the King's Deputy." Hitler urged him to repeat this before the crowd. At first, Kahr resisted, but he finally gave in to Hitler's insistent admonitions.

Hitler then returned to the main hall with Kahr, Lossow, Seisser, Ludendorff, and Pöhner. There he proclaimed the formation of a new government and the willingness of these men to take their appointed offices. Hitler then went on, "Today we need not express our gratitude to His Excellency Kahr, because at this moment his name is etched in the history of the German people. President Pöhner has assured me of his readiness to take over the state government with His Excellency Kahr. I hereby announce the creation of the provisional German national government and that the leader and commander of the German national army will be His Excellency Ludendorff. And so, we have removed the mark of Cain from the brow of the German soldier. Furthermore, as Minister of German armed forces, General Lossow will organize the army—the army that will rid this land of those criminals who discredited us five years ago and had us slaughtered.

"As minister of Reich police, Colonel Seisser will coordinate actions to purge Germany of those elements which have brought about our present misfortune, and in the coming weeks and months I will fulfill the vow I made five years ago as I lay in a field hospital, a blind cripple: Not to seek peace or comfort until the criminals of November, 1918, have been destroyed; until a Germany of power and greatness, freedom and majesty, is resurrected from the ruins of today's misery. Amen. Long live the Bavarian government of Kahr and Pöhner! Long live the new German national government!"

General Ludendorff declared, "Seized and overcome by the greatness of the moment, I hereby place myself at the disposal of the new German national government. I shall strive to restore the black-white-red badge of old to its rightful place of honor, from which the revolution has taken it. Everything depends on us today. For a German man, there can be no hesitation at this hour, no obstacle to full devotion not only with his mind, but full devotion to our task with all his German heart. This hour marks a turning point in our history. Let us go forth in earnest, convinced of the awful weight of our undertaking, certain and aware of our grave responsibility. Let us go with the common man to our task. If we are pure of heart—men of Germany, I do not doubt it—surely God's blessing, which we beseech in this hour, will be with us. I am absolutely convinced and do not doubt it: The Lord in Heaven will be with us when He sees that finally there are real German men again."

Pöhner said, "Of course, I will not evade the call of duty to my Fatherland. I will faithfully assist Herr Kahr in the serious task he has before him. We have always worked together. His Excellency may rely on me."

Kahr declared, "In the Fatherland's darkest hour, I will head the Bavarian government as the deputy of the monarchy which was destroyed iniquitously five years ago. I do this with a heavy heart and, I hope, for the good of our beloved Bavaria and our great German Fatherland."

Lossow said, "I hope that the task of organizing an army—a task equal to the others established here—will be successful and that this army will carry our flag everywhere proudly."

Seisser added, "I will attempt to accomplish the task allotted to me; that is, to create a state police—for the whole Reich—which is prepared at all times to preserve domestic peace under the black, white, and red flag." At that, the meeting was adjourned.

Meanwhile, heavily armed men had marched on the scene and had taken up positions in front of the Bürgerbräukeller.

Kahr, Lossow, Seisser, Hitler, Ludendorff, and Pöhner returned to the back room. Here a number of leading personalities of the Kampfbund arrived presently. Hitler again asked for forgiveness for his behavior, adding that the dire need of the Fatherland made the step necessary. Kahr inquired after the safety of the arrested cabinet ministers and was informed that they were well taken care of and that their families had been notified. Pöhner informed Kahr that he intended to entrust the leadership of the police to Frick. He also wanted to discuss with Kahr the composition of the list of ministers. Ludendorff spoke with Lossow and Seisser about the next military moves which he thought necessary—communication with Reichswehr troops, formation of a national army, break-up of the Vaterländische Verbände and their absorption into the Reichswehr, and protection against General Seeckt. In the meantime, Ludendorff discussed various statements for the press with a Captain Weiss who served as Hitler's press secretary. Finally, Ludendorff and General Aechter spoke with Lossow about events in the Pioneer barracks, where an Oberland battalion was held by the Reichswehr. Ludendorff and Aechter were excited by this news.

Even while the first incidents in the back room were played out, President Knilling, Ministers of State Gürtner, Schweyer, and Wultzlhofer, Chief of Police Mantel, Counsel Bernreuther, and Count Soden were led from the hall and detained by armed guards in a room on an upper story of the Bürgerbräukeller. These men were later brought under cover to the villa of a publisher Lehmann on Holzkirchenerstrasse and remained there until they were freed the following evening.

Kahr, Lossow, and Seisser only pretended to agree to Hitler's demands in order to regain their freedom of movement. As soon as they were able—at approximately 10:30 a.m.—they left the Bürgerbräukeller, and straightaway laid plans for suppression of the putsch. On November 6, they had called the leaders of the Vaterländische Verbände, particularly the Kampfbund, to the Generalstaatskommissariat, and had most emphatically warned against putsches of any kind. At the same time, they disclosed that violent undertakings would be met with armed intervention.

Moreover, the Generalstaatskommissariat had inside information that the Kampfbund was preparing an action. Among other things, they had learned of a conversation of leaders of the Bavarian National Socialist Storm Troopers in Munich on October 23. In this conversation it was disclosed that the forceful establishment of a Hitler-Ludendorff dictatorship in Bavaria was in the offing and that an armed offensive would proceed from Bavaria against Berlin. In this connection the names of Kahr, Lossow, and Seisser were brought up. Additionally, the Generalstaatskommissariat had found, prior to November 6, a leaflet with the forged signature of General Lossow. The leaflet contained a bogus call on the Reichswehr by Lossow to begin the march on Berlin. Participating in the conversation of November 6 at the Generalstaatskommissariat were Lieutenant Colonel Kriebel, Dr. Weber, and General Aechter, all from the Kampfbund. In connection with the meeting, Kriebel composed and sent the following letter, dated November 7:

Deutscher Kampfbund
Bavarian District
The Military Commander
Correspondence No. 332

TO: Bund Bayern und Reich
       Ehrhardt's Wikingbund
       The Reichsflagge
       Jäger's Battalion
       Hermannsbund
       Lieutenant Colonel Willmer

The conversation of November 6 with the Generalstaatskommissar has shown that he is banking on the disunity of our members. The Generalstaatskommissar has expressed quite clearly and unambiguously through the Landeskommandant and Colonel Seisser that he is determined to use force against any group that attempts to bring about a violent change. As military commander of Kampfbund Bayern, I insist that differences of opinion—even if they are so serious that they render a concerted effort of individual groups impossible—cannot prevent me and the combined military might of the Kampfbund from casting our lot with any group that meets the force of the Reichswehr and Landespolizei with force.

Signed, Kriebel.

On November 7, Landeskommandant General Lossow gathered in Munich the military and civilian leaders of the area in order to make them aware of the gravity of the situation. On the morning of November 8, Colonel Seisser, Chief of the Landespolizeiamt, called together the chiefs of the Bavarian Landespolizei commanded for the same purpose. Lossow and Seisser advised their subordinates that there was a very real possibility that Hitler would attempt to lead a putsch. They directed that a putsch of any kind be suppressed with force of arms, if necessary.

The action on the evening of November 8 originated in the Kampfbund. Since September 1, 1923, decisive leadership had been supplied by Hitler and his National Socialist Party. Hitler and Lieutenant Colonel Kriebel formed the high command of the Kampfbund. Dr. Scheubner-Richter was managing director. The Kampfbund was composed of the National Socialist Storm Troopers, under Hitler and Captain Göring; Bund Oberland, under Dr. Weber and General Aechter; and Reichskriegsflagge under Captains Röhm and Sendel. Ludendorff had long since approached Hitler and the Kampfbund. He was now closely connected with Hitler. Since early 1923, Brückner had been in charge of the Munich Regiment of the Nazis, which comprised three battalions. Besides this regiment, the Munich Nazi Party had special Hitler Shock Troops composed of highly trained Party members under the charge of Lieutenant Berchtold. Nazi Storm Troopers were also found outside Munich. The leader of all of the Storm Troopers was Captain Göring.

On the afternoon of November 6, after the session at the Generalstaatskommissariat, and during the course of November 7, secret meetings were held among various leading members of the Kampfbund. Final plans for an armed action were formulated at these meetings. Two plans were considered.

The first plan was Hitler's and was actually carried out on November 8. The second plan ran as follows. On the night of November 11, a large night exercise would be planned for the Kampfbund. On the following morning, the Kampfbund would march into Munich and topple the government, thus allowing Kahr, Lossow, and Seisser to take over their new duties with the force of the consolidated Kampfbund to back them up. But Hitler's plan was finally chosen. Participating in the decisive discussions were Göring, Scheubner-Richter, Kriebel, Dr. Weber, Hitler, and Röhm. They then set about alerting members of the organizations belonging to the Kampfbund and making preparations for the action on November 8. The high command was headquartered at the Rheinischerhof. The leaders were Hitler and Kriebel. Again, on November 7, a meeting took place among military leaders of the Kampfbund at which details of the action were worked out.

On November 6, Brückner, as leader of the Munich Regiment of the Nazis, issued an order in which he directed, "On Thursday, November 8, at 8:00 p.m., a tactical instruction for all officers will take place. Attendance is absolutely mandatory. After the exercise, a meeting of leaders will be held. The battalions will stand at battle alert on Thursday, November 8, at 6:00 p.m., at their headquarters for possible action. More orders will be issued tomorrow."

Reichskriegsflagge was holding a private party at the Löwenbräukeller on Thursday, November 8, at 8:00 p.m. The teams not needed for Thursday could attend the party and would be determined by the Regiment.

On November 7, Brückner issued another regimental command. It reads, "The exercise for officers of the Regiment scheduled for Thursday evening at 8:00 has been cancelled due to the general alert. The battalions will receive further instructions for Thursday evening on Thursday afternoon between 3:00 and 4:00. Required dress for the Thursday alert is uniform, cap, and sidearm." At the latest, Brückner knew on the morning of November 8 of the plans for that evening. At the same time, he received orders pertaining to his subsequent conduct.

On November 8, between 6:00 and 7:00 p.m., the First Battalion of the Munich Regiment assembled in the Arzbergerkeller, and the Third Battalion partly in the Ambergerhof and partly in the Gärtnerplatz restaurant. At 7:30 p.m., Brückner had both battalions march to the Löwenbräukeller. He himself had already set out for the Löwenbräukeller, and here he awaited news of the success of the ambush in the Bürgerbräukeller. Then, after he had distributed weapons to his men, he marched both battalions to the Bürgerbräukeller, where he arrived at about 11:30 p.m. and placed himself at the disposal of the High Command.

The leader of the Second Battalion, Lieutenant Edmond Heines, ordered the men of his battalion to dress in full battle gear on the evening of November 7 and to assemble in their garrisons, there to march upon the Bürgerbräukeller at 7:00 p.m. This, in fact, occurred. The men received weapons at Rosenheimerstrasse and then joined in the encirclement of the Bürgerbräukeller, as well as blocking off the approach.

The Hitler Shock Troops gathered at the Torbräu on the evening of November 8 at 6:00. Lieutenant Berchtold here announced that that evening at about 9:00 the existing government would be overthrown and a new government would be proclaimed at the Bürgerbräukeller. He had his men swear an oath of allegiance to Hitler's government. The Shock Troops marched off in formation, obtained weapons on the way, and arrived at the Bürgerbräukeller at about 8:00. While part of the Shock Troops helped to surround and seal off the Bürgerbräukeller, the other part forced its way into the hall at about 8:45.

At around 8:00 that evening, a large number of men from the Kampfbund, particularly Nazis, entered the barracks of the Reichswehr Infantry, 19th Regiment, First Battalion. They claimed they had been ordered there. There were only a few Reichswehr soldiers present, among them an Officer Böhm. He succeeded in contacting a few officers and he assembled his few troops. At a little past 8:30, the Nazis made ready to arm themselves. The Reichswehr, however, prevented this and threw them out of the barracks.

On the evening of November 8 at 7:00, the leader of the Ingolstadt National Socialist Storm Troopers, Chief Inspector Kuffler, received a letter from the High Command in Munich. The letter contained the information that a new national government, headed by Kahr, Ludendorff, and Hitler, would be proclaimed that evening at 8:30. The Chairman of the Nazi Party cell in Ingolstadt had this message announced that evening at a gathering at 9:00. Following earlier instructions, Kuffler procured trucks, loaded his heavily armed Storm Troopers on them, and drove off into the night for Munich.

On November 7, the leader of the Lower Bavarian Nazi Storm Troopers, Gregor Strasser, a pharmacist in Landshut, received a telegram from the High Command ordering him immediately to Munich. Strasser reported to a business office at 39 Schellingstrasse on the morning of November 7. He was ordered to be in Freising on Thursday, November 8, at 8:00, with 150 men from Landshut in order to provide a security force for a Nazi gathering.

On the evening of November 8, Strasser and 150 armed Storm Troopers drove from Landshut to Freising and waited there in vain for the anticipated arrival of Hitler. Around midnight, a courier from Munich arrived by car bringing not only news of the fall of the government and the establishment of a Reich dictatorship, but also an order to come to Munich. Strasser hastened to his lorry, drove to Munich, and reported to the Bürgerbräukeller at 6:00 a.m. He later participated, under orders, in the seizure of the Wittelsbach Bridge.

In Regensburg, on the morning of November 7, Party Secretary Löser, leader of the Oberpfalz Nazi Storm Troopers, received his orders from Munich in a telegram: He must report to the High Command in Munich on the morning of Thursday, November 8. Löser reported to Göring at noon on November 8. Göring revealed that that same evening a national government would be called forth and the Berlin government deposed. Göring gave him further orders, especially to alert Regensburg and the surrounding area. He made him swear an oath not to tell anyone of the coming events. Löser drove back to Regensburg, alerted the Storm Troopers in Regensburg and outlying areas, and also alerted the Regensburg unit of the Bund Oberland.

Due to the intervention of Colonel Etzel and First Lieutenant Unruh of the Reichswehr battalion, it was possible to thwart the Regensburg plan, disarm the Nazis and Oberlanders, and apprehend Löser. Löser explained to Colonel Etzel that he was not subject to the commands of the Reichswehr because he had orders from the government; that is, Hitler.

After the course of action for November 8 had been decided, Dr. Weber made his way to the Rheinischerhof on the evening of November 7 at 6:00. There a meeting had been convened that included the military commander of Oberland, General Aechter, and officers of the Munich Battalion of the Bund Oberland, as well as representatives of outlying party units. In all probability, Dr. Weber had filled in the Munich leaders by this meeting as to the planned action. Certainly he left no doubt that a violent coup d'etat would take place in a few days, with their help, and that the military section of the Bund must be geared and ready for it. To a few of the distant commanders—in fact, to the commanders of Werdenfels (Pölk) and Seefeld (Rickmers)—Dr. Weber handed over alert orders in sealed envelopes with instructions to open them on the evening of November 8 at 8:30. The contents of the order was, roughly, "The national dictatorship of Kahr-Hitler-Ludendorff has just been called forth. You are to come to Munich with any and all men, as swiftly as possible, and report to Lieutenant Colonel Kriebel. Signed, Dr. Weber."

The Werdenfels and Seefeld groups were considered to be well trained. Therefore, the High Command thought it wise to have them come to Munich as soon as possible for the action.

The Munich Battalion from Oberland was also summoned for November 8. Sections of Oberland were immediately employed in surrounding the Bürgerbräukeller and then later used in carrying out specific tasks. Other sections of the Oberland Brigade took part in the attempted seizure of the Pioneer Barracks. At around 8:00 p.m., several hundred members of the Oberland gathered there under the leadership of Captain Müller. They demanded weapons and ammunition. When the ranking officer, Captain Cantzler, refused, they attempted to attain their objective first with threats, then with violence. When this failed, Captain Müller announced before the crowd the fall of the Reich government and the creation of the Hitler-Ludendorff dictatorship, thereby hoping to force Captain Cantzler to distribute arms and ammunition. But Captain Cantzler would have none of it. Finally, with the support of the few Pioneers in the barracks, he succeeded in detaining and disarming the Oberländer.

The Reichskriegsflagge had planned a brotherly celebration for members and friends of the Kampfbund in the Löwenbräukeller for November 8 at 7:30 p.m. The invitations had been publicly announced. The members of the Reichskriegsflagge, however, had been ordered to attend in uniform. Members from outlying areas were also invited; for example, Wilhelm Meister, Johann Sebastian Will, and Herbert Müller, all from Schongau. Their invitations contained, among other things, the information that space would be provided for them in the Pioneer Barracks. As late as the afternoon of November 8, a large number of party members were contacted by telephone or telegram. That evening, numerous other members of the Kampfbund besides the Reichskriegsflagge did in fact appear at the Löwenbräukeller, particularly large numbers of Oberländer.

Then, at 9:00, Röhm announced the formation of a new national government of Hitler-Ludendorff-Seisser and a new Bavarian regime of Kahr-Pöhner. Röhm assembled his men and led them to the Wehrkreiskommando of the Reichswehr. At Schönfeldstrasse, other factions of the Kampfbund joined the march. The Wehrkreiskommando was occupied shortly after 9:00. The few sentries of the Reichswehr were unable to mount any kind of resistance against this surging tide.

For quite a while, the Kampfbund had attempted to exert influence on the members of the Infantry School. In particular, Lieutenant Rossbach had labored with success since the beginning of October to infuse the younger soldiers with Hitlerian ideas of a nationalist movement and rebellion, carefully avoiding the staff officers. To this end, Rossbach was constantly in touch with the Infantry School cadets. He met them repeatedly at Hitler gatherings, at specially arranged beer parties, in public saloons, and behind closed doors. Hitler himself once spoke to a group of cadets about his political aims. Wagner quickly became an acquaintance of Rossbach and soon was regularly attending meetings.

Listening to Hitler and Rossbach, the Infantry School cadets got the impression that a great national revolution would occur very soon. Wagner also met Lieutenant Pernet, Ludendorff's stepson, at these meetings. Rossbach announced a visit of several gentlemen of the Infantry School to Ludendorff's residence on November 4. Wagner was also one of the visitors.

14

On this occasion, Ludendorff spoke of the Volk and of a nationalist revolution. He expressed the view that the idea of the Volk would win out very soon, and he spoke of Hitler's meritorious service, particularly in that he and his movement in the last three years had been able to hold down the White and Blue Peril. According to Hitler, the White and Blue—or Bavarian—Peril is the danger that the monarchy would be restored. Then, either Bavaria would leave the Reich or the leaders of the Reich would annex it and place itself over Prussia. When asked when this nationalist rebellion would take place, Ludendorff answered that the first step was already past—this was the outbreak of the Seeckt-Lossow conflict. Now, he thought, it was only a matter of weeks or months until necessity drove the masses to the ideas of the Volk.

Wagner lectured his followers on Ludendorff's ideas. The Infantry School cadets must have received the impression that Ludendorff stood behind Hitler and Rossbach completely and shared their views in all respects.

At noon on November 8, Pernet came to the Infantry School and ordered Wagner to accompany him to the Kampfbund High Command on Schellingstrasse. Wagner obeyed. At Kampfbund headquarters he was informed of the coming action by Rossbach and Göring and was supplied with appropriate directives. Returning to the School, Wagner reported his information to a few of his trusted comrades and made certain that the students would be called to a supposedly urgent meeting in the casino at 8:15 p.m. In the course of the afternoon, Wagner took a few others into his confidence and was responsible for keeping his superiors in the dark.

That evening at 8:30 both officer groups met in the mess hall and both cadet groups met in an auditorium. Wagner then declared, "At this moment, the nationalist government of Germany is stepping forward in the Bürgerbräukeller. Simultaneously, all over Germany the nationalist revolution is breaking out. Nationalist brigades are already marching on Berlin from all directions. Tomorrow Munich will march. Behind the movement stand Ludendorff and Lossow with the entire 7th Division, Pöhner and Colonel Seisser with the Bavarian Landespolizei, and Hitler and his Kampfbund. Ludendorff has ordered that the Infantry School place itself immediately under Rossbach's command and function as shock troops. Staff officers are to be excluded. That, however, is only temporary. Luden-dorff wants to lead the staff himself tomorrow. A Ludendorff Regiment is to be formed from the Infantry School and other formations."

Wagner also announced the disposition of troops and added that Ludendorff wanted to review the troops at once in the Bürgerbräukeller. Practically all of the cadets followed Wagner's orders and filled the parade ground armed with weapons and ammunition. Meanwhile, Rossbach appeared, and from this time on, Wagner served as Rossbach's adjutant and was never very far from him. Rossbach gave another speech, confirming all that Wagner had said. Swastika banners and armbands were given out, and then, at about 9:00 p.m., the Infantry School marched to the Bürgerbräukeller with Rossbach at the head.

Even after the departure of Kahr, Lossow, and Seisser from the Bürgerbräukeller on the evening of November 8, Hitler's cadre sought to continue the nascent undertaking, even at a time when they certainly knew that Kahr, Lossow, and Seisser were determined to quash the putsch with legal governmental forces. The following excerpts from the diverse occurrences on the night of November 8 and the morning of November 9 will serve as proof here.

The headquarters of Hitler's High Command was set up in the Bürgerbräukeller. Essentially, it was there that further action was discussed, decided, and initially implemented. It was there that the main part of the armed Kampfbund was concentrated.

The attempt to commandeer the Pioneer garrison and the 19th Regiment at the outset had failed. News of this filtered into the Bürgerbräukeller at about 10:00. General Aechter and Major Paul von Müller drove to the Pioneer garrison at the request of the High Command—Hitler, Ludendorff, and Kriebel—but there they were apprehended by the Reichswehr. General Aechter called out to his driver, Lorenz Hüter, who had driven up to the main gate, "My good man, I have been arrested." Hüter drove the empty car back to the Bürgerbräukeller. Hitler then drove with Dr. Weber to the Pioneer garrison and to the 19th Regiment's barracks and was convinced that the Reichswehr had secured both and that the organizations of the Kampfbund had encountered resistance. After his return to the Bürgerbräukeller, Hitler addressed the assembled troops of the Kampfbund.

In the meantime, Major Siry volunteered to get information

16

about the whereabouts of Lossow and the Reichswehr's attitude. On the orders of Hitler, Ludendorff, and Kriebel, the Major made his way to the Reichswehr garrison, but he was arrested there and was unable to return.

Between midnight and 1:00, the order went out to occupy the Generalstaatskommissariat on Maximilianstrasse. An Oberland brigade was dispatched. When they returned in defeat, the Infantry School—at Ludendorff's command—was ordered to occupy the Generalstaatskommissariat at all costs, and to smash the resistance with weapons. The Infantry School headed for the Maximilianstrasse under Rossbach's command.

Negotiations were carried on with a leader of the Landespolizei in front of the Generalstaatskommissariat. The students prepared to exchange fire with the police. Finally, however, Ludendorff's command rang out: "Pull back." The cadets, led by Rossbach, then marched to the train station and from there to the Infantry School. Here, the true position of Kahr, Lossow, and Seisser was made known. Rossbach, however, was able with Wagner's help to hold together a large number of cadets and lead them back to the Bürgerbräukeller.

Meanwhile, the Wehrkreiskommando was secured by the Kampfbund under Röhm. Röhm also commandeered all telephones and supervised all calls, and finally, in the course of the night, had the officers locked up to prevent them from reporting to their superiors. Between 10:00 and 11:00 Hitler appeared, gathered the men in a courtyard, and gave a speech in which he said, among other things, "Exactly five years after the November criminals took the helm, a day of liberation dawns on Germany. The Berlin government has been banished to the devil. In its place stands a national dictatorship with Ludendorff as Commander of the National Army, Lossow as Army Minister, Seisser as Minister of Police, and myself as political leader." Hitler thanked the brigades for their cooperation and bound them to honor future obligations. He also thanked Röhm in particular for his brotherhood under arms. Shortly thereafter, Hitler left.

After him, Röhm went to the Bürgerbräukeller. He soon reappeared with several armed men at the municipal command post, where he hoped to find Lossow and Seisser. He was refused entry. Between 10:00 and 11:00 at night, Röhm returned to the Wehrkreiskommando, and around 1:00 Ludendorff and Kriebel arrived. In the meantime, it had been learned that Passau Reichswehr Battalion had received orders from the Staatskommissariat to march on Munich; that the Oberland battalion had eventually been disarmed at the Pioneer garrison, that General Aechter was a prisoner of the Reichswehr, that all members of the Kampfbund had been ejected from the 19th Regiment's garrison, that the barracks were being defended by the Reichswehr, and, finally, that Lossow was with the 19th Regiment and that the headquarters of the Wehrkreiskommando had been moved there.

One by one, Hitler, Ludendorff, Röhm, Pöhner, Kriebel, Dr. Weber, and other leaders, including Major Hühnlein, took seats. At around 1:00 a.m., Reichswehr Lieutenant Rossmann appeared. Under orders from Battalion leader Major Schönhärl of the 19th Regiment, Rossmann was to ascertain the fate of the sentries at the post and determine whether the Kampfbund planned an attack on the Oberwiesenfeld garrison. Rossmann spoke with Röhm, Kriebel, and Ludendorff, and he told them that Lossow was at the Infantry barracks and that preparations were being made that left no doubt that Lossow opposed the revolution and would proceed against the Kampfbund. Rossmann then returned to the garrison and made his report.

Around 3:00 a.m. Ludendorff, Kriebel, and Röhm sent a Lieutenant Alois Hecker to Lossow requesting him to attend a meeting at the Wehrkreiskommando. At this point, Kriebel said to Hecker, "Hecker, you are our last hope. You must go to the garrison and see to it that Lossow comes to this meeting with Ludendorff. Everything depends on it. There seems to be several misunderstandings which must be cleared up immediately."

When Hecker went to the garrison, however, he was ordered by Lossow to remain there and not to return to the Wehrkreiskommando. Around 4:00 a.m. Major Hühnlein drove to the Infantry School on Ludendorff's orders to request Colonel Leupold to come to him at the Wehrkreiskommando. Leupold obeyed and was greeted by Hitler and Ludendorff at the Wehrkreiskommando at around 5:00 a.m.

In their conversation, Leupold told Ludendorff and Hitler the following: "Between 12:00 and 1:00 last night, I was instructed by General Lossow to tell you that Kahr, Lossow, and Seisser do not consider bound to their promise because this promise was exacted under duress and because the 7th Division does not endorse this undertaking. I personally spoke with Lossow at the 19th Regiment this morning between 2:00 and

18

3:00. I confirmed this message with him and I have heard that troops are being called up to use force if necessary to restore order." As he was taking leave of Ludendorff and Hitler, Leupold stated that he did not think Lossow would change his mind, and he added that the Division would follow orders even if the orders conflicted with individual conscience. He would come again if General Lossow deemed it necessary. At approximately 6:00 Leupold reported his conversation to General Lossow.

Leupold's report to the men at the Wehrkreiskommando had merely confirmed what they surely must have known hours before. Nonetheless, they decided to carry on the action. Hitler, in particular, recommended ruthless measures; he thought it necessary to try for everything. He ordered Pöhner to take charge of an Oberland battalion, occupy the police presidium, and call out the auxiliary police. Hitler was convinced that everything depended on the attitude of the masses—that the main thing now was propaganda. The Hitler troops would have to rule the city and pretend to have a larger force by constantly moving about. Everyone expressed the hope that the troops would not have to fight against the black, white, and red banner.

Hitler, Kriebel, Ludendorff, and their staff, because they no longer felt safe at the Wehrkreiskommando, returned to the Bürgerbräukeller between 6:00 and 7:00 in the morning. Only Röhm and his men, on Ludendorff's orders, remained at the Wehrkreiskommando to stop the Reichswehr. Pöhner set out for the Wehrkreiskommando between 6:00 and 7:00 that morning and went with Major Hühnlein to police headquarters. He intended to take over the police building with Kampfbund troops. Various brigades of the Kampfbund did in fact follow him. As soon as Pöhner and Hühnlein entered the building, however, they were arrested; the Kampfbund troops retreated empty-handed.

At 9:00 that morning, armed squads, following Hitler's orders, threatened the lives of the publishers Parcus and Mühltaler, confiscated large sums of money, and brought it back to the Bürgerbräukeller. In the course of the morning, the troops of the Kampfbund were paid with this money.

Brückner received an order during the morning from the High Command to barricade Ludwig Bridge, Cornelius Bridge, and Wittelsbach Bridge with heavily armed forces on the right bank of the Isar, facing the city. Brückner carried out the order. Almost immediately, Landespolizei appeared, blocked off the bridges on the other side, and allowed no weapons to cross into the heart of the city. Now there could be no doubt that the Landespolizei did not side with the Kampfbund.

Of all the Hitler troops, the Hitler Shock Troops distinguished themselves as the most violent and lawless. The Shock Troops went on a rampage at the offices of the newspaper *Münchener Post*, perpetrated a brutal house search upon Erhard Auer, the vice president of the Bavarian State Senate, and took a number of hostages. During the morning of November 9, members of the Hitler Shock Troops forced their way into City Hall and dragged Mayor Schmidt as well as the Socialist City Councilmen off to the Bürgerbräukeller, there to hold them hostage. Hitler and Ludendorff knew of these prisoners, and yet did nothing to expedite their release.

Around noon, the High Command conceded that they had lost. Therefore, after drawn-out conferences, they decided to organize a procession and march into the city. All of the members of the Kampfbund lined up in columns. These men were armed—they had rifles, submachine guns, revolvers, machineguns, bayonets, and even hand grenades. The Hitler Shock Troops were to serve as security guards and therefore had fixed bayonets. A large number of these men had loaded their guns. An auto was also driven in the procession, supposedly as an ambulance. Hitler and Ludendorff took places at the head of the procession under tricolor, swastika, and Oberland colors. The object of the procession was to gain support for the action among the populace and either to push back the Reichswehr and Landespolizei or to entice them to join their side.

At Ludwig Bridge the Landespolizei barred the way and ordered the oncoming crowd loudly and unambiguously to stop and turn around. These warnings were ignored. As the Landespolizei readied their weapons, a number of Shock Troopers forced them back with fixed bayonets and drawn guns, disarmed them, and led them off as captives to the Bürgerbräukeller. The Hitler march proceeded farther until it confronted a thick chain of Landespolizei on Residenzstrasse, not far from the Feldherrnhalle. The men in the procession again did not heed the orders to stop which the Landespolizei clearly expressed in word and action. The marchers tried the same tactics as at Ludwig Bridge. This time, however, the police stood fast and finally had to use their weapons.

Meanwhile, the Wehrkreiskommando had been completely

surrounded by the Reichswehr. The squad under Röhm eventually had to vacate the building and surrender their weapons. Thus the action was finally smashed.

The following is brought to your attention regarding the individual defendants:

Hitler

Hitler was the soul of the whole plot. He drew up its plan, took charge of its execution, and proclaimed the fall of the Reich government and the Bavarian government. He distributed new offices and claimed for himself the supreme leadership of Reich politics. He endeavored to initiate, extend, and then continue the action even when it must have been completely clear that he had no prospect whatsoever of gaining his ends.

Ludendorff

Long before November 8, Ludendorff had let it be known, by his conduct toward leading personalities of the Kampfbund and by his behavior towards the infantry cadets, that he would support with his name and with his person a violent, unconstitutional movement, should it take place on German soil. He would, moreover, place himself immediately at its disposal as soon as such a movement should present itself with a unified program for success. Ludendorff was also celebrated recently in the press— publicly and uncontestedly—as the chosen leader of the coming nationalist rebellion. It is our belief that Ludendorff had been thoroughly apprised of the action of November 8 beforehand. At the latest he learned of the violent, unconstitutional nature of this undertaking on the evening of November 8 when a car brought him to the Bürgerbräukeller. Once at the Bürgerbräukeller, Hitler confirmed what Ludendorff learned on the way. He knew at that time that Kahr, Lossow, and Seisser had made no statement of any kind as to their future positions. He didn't bother to ask them their intentions but immediately declared that he would collaborate, and he urged Kahr, Lossow, and Seisser to do the same. Thus he immediately joined the rebels. He also acted as commander of the newly formed army in that he discussed and issued orders concerning territorial integrity, dissolution of the Kampfverbände, absorption into the Reichswehr, and quartering of the troops. He hailed the cadets marching under the swastika after their arrival at the Bürgerbräukeller, and he took command. He gave orders to the cadets. Finally, he placed himself at the head of the march into the city to lend credence to the whole affair through the power of his name and personality and to influence the Reichswehr and Landespolizei improperly.

Pöhner

Pöhner's sentiments coincided with those of Hitler and the Kampfbund. On the morning of November 7 Hitler sought him out, informed him of the coming putsch, and asked him if he was prepared to assume the office of president of the new Bavarian government. Pöhner answered in the affirmative and did act as president. He went immediately to the chief of police after the Bürgerbräukeller meeting was over, transferred power in the police presidium to Frick, and issued a series of orders. That same night he held a press conference and then went with Frick to visit Kahr in order to discuss the recent ministerial reorganization and the issuance of public notices. He then participated in the deliberations of the High Command at the Wehrkreiskommando and finally attempted to commandeer the police building by shutting out the police.

Frick

A very restricted, friendly relationship existed between Pöhner and Frick in that it was based on mutually congenial political views. Frick was constantly in touch with Pöhner. He also had good relations with the leaders of the Kampfbund, in particular with Kriebel, Dr. Weber, and Röhm, as well as Hitler. In the upper echelons of the Kampfbund it was generally held that Frick would become Minister of Police in Munich if and when a popular revolution should occur. This happened with Frick's full knowledge and consent. From Frick's behavior it was clear that he would accept such an offer in the event of a putsch. As soon as Hitler's Shock Troops broke into the Bürgerbräukeller—even before the outcome of the ambush could be predicted—Frick was designated as new Minister of Police by leading members of the Kampfbund. A note pad which was confiscated from a Kampfbund file cabinet had the following written on its back: "Frick June 26, 80—head of intelligence Hofmann—chief of police's first message to Frick: safely delivered." With this last cue, the initiates knew that the surprise attack had been a success. Therefore, Frick must have known what would transpire on the evening of November 8. In fact, he was ready in his office at police headquarters and waiting for the call from the Bürgerbräukeller which indeed came. After he was informed of the ambush, he neglected, in dereliction of his duty, to alert Landespolizei and special security, and he neglected to contact the Reichswehr. He also failed in his duty to notify the duly appointed representative of the arrested chief of police, although he was in a position to do so. Finally, he immediately placed himself at the disposal of the new, unconstitutional regime, and up until the time of his arrest he issued orders which only the legal Minister of Police or his duly appointed representatives are empowered to issue.

Dr. Weber

Weber played a decisive role in planning the action of November 8. It was he who made the whole thing possible in that he was political leader of Bund Oberland and cast his decisive vote for the action. He immediately adjusted the military apparatus of Bund Oberland to suit the putsch, initiated the military leaders into the affair, and himself saw to the alert of outlying units. On the afternoon of November 8, he obtained assurance via telephone that Colonel Seisser would appear that evening at the Bürgerbräukeller, and he also made certain that the villa of his stepfather, Lehmann, would be in order for quartering the ministers and various other people arrested at the Bürgerbräukeller. During the early morning of the 9th, at police headquarters, he recommended that the most important buildings—post offices, telegraph office, main train station, and others—be seized by units of Bund Oberland and that police sentries be removed. He also looked after the feeding and quartering of outlying Oberland groups and participated in the deliberations of the High Command in the Bürgerbräukeller and at the Wehrkreiskommando, and he finally decided to join the march into the city although he knew the true disposition of Kahr, Lossow, and Seisser.

Röhm

Röhm was probably present at the decisive conference on November 8. At the latest, he learned of the planned putsch on the evening of November 7 and then participated in individual consultations on the course and scope of the action. The Reichskriegsflagge celebration scheduled for November 8 at the Löwenbräukeller presented him with an opportunity to inconspicuously aid and abet the action in the Bürgerbräukeller and to gather as large a striking force as possible. In any case, Röhm occupied the Wehrkreiskommando in the interest of and on the orders of the new rulers, and he made all the preparations to defend the building with guns against a Reichswehr attack. He continued this conduct although he certainly knew that he was offering open resistance to the legal governmental authority.

Brückner

Brückner arranged the mobilization of his National Socialist Munich Regiment in anticipation of the planned action. Supported by the people he had armed and led, he helped start and continue the action together with the new rulers. Above all, he and his men joined the march into Munich.

Wagner

With foreknowledge of the action, Wagner willingly cooperated with the other defendants to execute the coup and to inform the cadets of the action behind the backs of their superiors. Further, he was able to persuade the cadets to aid the Kampfbund without the knowledge of and against the will of their superiors.

Kriebel

Kriebel was military leader of the Kampfbund. He cooperated in the final decisions concerning the action of November 8, 1923, made preparations for military action, and gave orders for military performance in individual cases. He was responsible for the success of the take-over at the Bürgerbräukeller and the subsequent detainment of the ministers there, and the president and the head of Section 6 of the police. He directed the occupation of the Wehrkreiskommando by units of the Kampfbund. He made arrangements to transfer police headquarters, the executive office building, the main telegram office, and the main train station from the custody of the Landespolizei to the Kampfbund. After General Ludendorff had agreed to head the National Army, Kriebel served as Ludendorff's chief of staff and ordered a number of military measures, the object of which was to aid the action and to stiffen resistance to the legal governmental forces.

And so, among other things, he attended to the stationing, feeding, quartering, and payment of the Kampfbund troops, and he gave orders on the morning of November 9 to the men of the Kampfbund to seize the bridges on the Isar. He even had a few mortars wheeled up so that the Kampfbund might better defend itself against the police or Reichswehr. Kriebel certainly knew well before November 8 that the Generalstaatskommissar and his colleagues were determined to put down any putsch, using force as necessary. Kriebel's letter to various patriotic bands leaves no doubt in the matter. Kriebel would not be dissuaded. He continued to support the action even when he must have known that Kahr, Lossow, and Seisser did not consider their promise binding, even when he knew they were taking measures to suppress the putsch. Backed by the massed might of the Kampfbund and the Infantry School, Kriebel had undertaken the violent removal of the Bavarian and Reich governments. He had undertaken to violently change the Constitution of the German Reich and the Bavarian Free State and set up in its place an unconstitutional regime based on force of arms.

Pernet

Pernet was a member of the Nazi Party, knew well the leading personalities of the Kampfbund, and was familiar with and supported the attempts to topple the government. He participated in meetings with cadets and got to know Lieutenant Wagner. He also endeavored to have individual cadets present at the meeting with General Ludendorff on November 4. On the morning of November 7, he received an order from Dr. Scheubner-Richter to go to the Infantry School that day, or at the latest the next morning, and summon Lieutenant Wagner to come to the High Command on Schellingstrasse at noon on November 8. Pernet went to the Infantry School on the morning of November 8, conveyed Scheubner-Richter's message to Lieutenant Wagner, and accompanied Wagner to the High Command, where preparations for that evening's action were in full swing. On the evening of November 8, Pernet went to the Bürgerbräukeller in uniform. After witnessing the take-over by Hitler's Shock Troops, he went to the quarters of General Ludendorff with Ludendorff's servant, Neubauer, and with Scheubner-Richter's aide, Aigner, and brought him to the Bürgerbräukeller. Later, Pernet and Aigner drove into the city to find Captain Ehrhardt, tell him of the birth of the national government, and sound him out. At the end of the gathering at the Bürgerbräukeller, Pernet helped to guard the participants and, as a result, served as ordnance officer at the Kampfbund High Command. In particular, he directed arriving Kampfbund troops to their quarters, and, on the morning of November 9, he took the money confiscated from the Parcus and Mühltaler printing house on Hitler's orders, made up a receipt, and distributed the money among the individual organizations as wages for the men.

The Indictment

HERR STENGLEIN: With the exception of Pernet, all defendants are charged with the collective commission of the crime of high treason. Pernet is charged as an accessory to the crime of high treason.

Motion to Exclude the Public

HERR STENGLEIN: I move that we exclude the public because an open hearing of the matter would constitute a threat to national security and public order, as set forth in Article 14, Paragraph 3 of the Legal Code. I therefore make one stipulation: If certain individual sections of the proceeding can be held separately and be revealed to the public without harm to the State, then the hearing may be open to the public for such sessions.

It is obvious from the preliminary hearings that in the course of their defense, the accused will speak of matters whose public discussion would merely invite serious danger for the government, particularly as regards foreign policy. In the interests of the State, this danger must be avoided under any circumstances. First of all, I move that my motion be decided upon in private session.

HERR HOLL: I shall read this statement, signed by ten defense attorneys:

"The indictment itself touches upon areas, the open discussion of which can hardly be in the interest of the Fatherland. The defense must necessarily delve into these areas. We, the defense, hereby refuse responsibility for any and all consequences, foreign or domestic, resulting from such investigation."

JUDGE NEITHARDT: Does someone else wish to reply to the prosecution's motion?

HERR HOLL: We have not discussed it yet. In any case, I request the prosecution's proposal be denied on behalf of my clients. My clients and the other defendants welcome an open hearing. The defense knows quite well when testimony does not coincide with the interests of the Fatherland. We will warn the Court ahead of time whenever sensitive matters are to be mentioned, but I don't think it feasible to exclude the general public, from the outset.

HERR RODER: We must now come to a decision concerning the prosecution's first motion, and then concerning the motion to conduct the entire proceeding in private. Your Honor, there is nothing to stop the prosecution from making a court motion in private. Perhaps then, we will be able to make you understand what the defense has to say about the second motion. It is my opinion that the prosecution's second motion, in its present broad form, is prejudicial to the defendants. This motion will attract undue attention because, judging from statements of government authorities in just the past few weeks, the trial would be both open to the public and thoroughly revealing. Each of the defendants has always placed the Fatherland before himself, and so it is today also. None of the defendants would do harm to the Fatherland, and none would mention anything in public to harm the Fatherland. But it is two different things if the defendants must completely renounce their right to a defense in public, or if they may only publicly defend themselves insofar as the Fatherland's integrity is not compromised. I am of the opinion that it is to the Fatherland's advantage to allow the greater part of the hearings to be open to the public.

JUDGE NEITHARDT: According to Article 175, Paragraph 1 of the Legal Code, the Court must decide on the prosecution's motion in private session. Other considerations are, as yet, premature.

HERR KOHL: I wish to thank Your Honor for referring to Article 175 of the Legal Code. However, in contrast to my colleague, Dr. Holl, that the prosecution's motion doesn't surprise him at all—from the beginning I was afraid that such a motion would be made, contrary to all promises made by the Generalstaatskommissar. He was quoted in the press as saying

27

that all aspects of this case would be revealed. The defendants guarantee to notify the Court whenever they have something to say that may not coincide with the interests and welfare of the German Reich and the State of Bavaria. I therefore ask for the opportunity to enumerate our reasons in private session why these proceedings must be public.

HERR LUETGEBRUNE: The prosecutor's motion is flatly contradictory. If this motion to exclude the general public is to be granted, it should have been done before the reading of the indictments. Now that it has been before the public, I deem it the duty of the Court to see that these men get a fair trial in front of the public. Each of the defendants has served the Fatherland with life and limb in great wars; they know where to draw the line and will do their duty for the Fatherland in this Court.

The presiding Judge announces the Court's decision:

JUDGE NEITHARDT: The public is excluded from the discussion of the prosecution's motion. The following may remain: the heads of the Landgericht, the Oberlandesgericht, and the Oberstlandesgericht; two representatives each from the Justice Ministry, Interior Office, and Foreign Office; representatives of the Reichswehr Office and the Reich Justice Ministry; and the court stenographers. The admission of other State or Reich authorities will be decided on a case-by-case basis. At 11:45, the Court will readmit the public.

28

JUDGE NEITHARDT: The courtroom is empty. I would like to outline briefly my point of view in this matter. Naturally it is my wish, and I realize that it is in the interest of the defendants, to conduct the hearing, if possible, before a broad public. The Court will, of course, comply with this as far as possible. In any event, the Court will allow every one of the defendants ample opportunity to inform us exactly of his attitude and, naturally, of his motivations for the action. But we do expect that no subjects be mentioned which might hurt the country in the area of foreign policy. I cannot, of course, tell you what these subjects might be; essentially they will have to do with details about the Reichswehr, details about the Vaterländische Verbände, training, equipment, supply of arms.

Call: It is all in the indictment!

JUDGE NEITHARDT: These are just very cautious assumptions.

A defense attorney objects.

JUDGE NEITHARDT: Perhaps I may ask you to listen to my opinion. I shall then be glad to hear yours.

That is, to be considered are training, equipment, and weapons supplies of the Vaterländische Verbände, reinforcement of the Reichswehr, and so on. That is my opinion, and I expect that, in view of their patriotism, none of the defendants will make a mistake.

HERR STENGLEIN: Unfortunately, the indictment had to mention details, the discussion of which can, of course, be disadvantageous to the State. This was unavoidable because of the actions of the defendants on November 8 and 9. The points listed in the indictment refer only to those matters which were so well known and had been discussed immediately after the undertaking with such frankness and clarity that any attempt to keep them secret would have failed and been inappropriate. In the indictment, however, anything that might indicate participation of the Reich, and of the State, in the events in question, or that might offer positive proof that an involvement of State and Reich constitutes a violation of the conditions of the Versailles Treaty has been carefully avoided. The questions which cannot be discussed publicly are, as the Chairman already indicated, particularly the following: Were "black" weapons available; had secret mobilization plans been prepared; had there been connections of the Reichswehr to patriotic organizations, and to what degree? Also there are those questions which specifically concern the emergency police, the border guards who were formed temporarily in the north of Bavaria; furthermore, the discussions that were conducted with regard to the formation of a Reichsdirektorium. These matters, however, are so closely linked to the defense plea of most of the accused that they will be mentioned in the public session even with the best of intentions on the part of the defendants, which I do not doubt—at least they will be alluded to, or will appear implicitly, as obvious and recognizable gaps suggesting something that cannot be said outright, but can be derived from the context.

Because of these considerations, I uphold my position in the form in which I made it. I cannot imagine that an interrogation of, for instance, defendants Hitler or Pöhner, Kriebel or Ludendorff can be conducted to the extent to which the defendants wish to defend themselves, without touching upon these matters. This question is significant, especially since we are conducting the investigation before a huge public, which encompasses virtually the whole world, so that anything said here receives very special significance. I therefore think that, in order to conduct the thorough hearing intended by the prosecution, we can proceed only in the manner of my petition.

HERR KOHL: If I understand the words of the Prosecutor correctly, the final purpose is to exclude the public altogether; for the Prosecutor is afraid that one of the defendants, when defending his views, might discuss those matters which are to be discussed, according to the indictment. We are not willing—and

I think I can speak for all attorneys and defendants—to defend ourselves behind four walls. The act of the defendants does not have to shun the public; the public must come to realize that, in Germany, judgment is passed upon men whose only motivation for action was an unlimited and overwhelming patriotism. We want the public to be excluded in those instances in which a real interest of our country is at stake; and all the Chairman needs to do is to request the individual defendants, during the interrogation, not to discuss this or that question in public; that the defendant would be given the opportunity to discuss those questions in a non-public session. I agree with the point of view taken by the Chairman. I am convinced that the Judges, both the professional Judges and the lay Judges, will attempt, as much as we will, to elucidate the events of November 8 and 9, so that guilt and innocence can be determined; above all, (that they will attempt) to clarify, as much as possible, the reasons why those men who, according to public opinion, ought to appear as co-defendants will sit in the witness box.

I therefore request to reject, by all means, the petition of the Prosecutor. I want to emphasize, again: The entire parliament has requested a public investigation, and Generalstaatskommissar Dr. von Kahr has repeatedly promised the Bavarian people, through the press, that this investigation will provide the most thorough clarification. A clarification, however, is not possible if the public is excluded.

I conclude by stating that I expected the petition of the Prosecutor, but that I did not fear it. If today the Prosecution demands the exclusion of the public, it is more or less afraid of the accusations it has made.

HERR HOLL: I regret not to be able to agree completely with the statement of my colleagues. The reason may be that my colleague does not have as good an insight into the political implications as I do because of the information I received from my client. You know, or perhaps you don't, that for weeks various gentlemen have made the greatest effort to find a way out of the terrible conflict into which we have been forced; on the one hand, our clients whom we have to assist by word and deed and on whose behalf everything must be presented that can be of use; on the other hand, the interest which is perhaps foremost, i.e. the interest of our German Fatherland. A way must be found out of this dilemma. The way out suggested by the Prosecutor is

31

impossible. If you were to exclude the public generally, you would seriously prejudice the interest of the defendants; for after these people have been accused publicly of things which they can partly disprove, they have an interest in disproving these matters publicly. It does not do any harm at all if a number of questions are discussed before the entire public.

However—and this is the conflict—there are other questions of which this cannot be said. The defense will take the greater national interest into consideration. I do not speak for all my colleagues, but my client at least will have no objections if the public is excluded in some cases with reference to certain questions. If for instance—just to mention some examples—the public is excluded if we discuss the question of the connections between Reichswehr and Kampfbund—Do they exist? To what extent, degree? How were they trained, armed, etc.?—then we shall not object to excluding the public, at this point, because that is of no concern to the French. Also we shall not object if the public is to be excluded as soon as the secret orders of the Reichswehr—of which we have copies—are to be discussed. But if, for instance, those details concerning the march to Berlin are mentioned, then it is for us a matter of proving to you that the defendants here did what the State authorities—Kahr, Lossow, Seisser—wanted to do; and we want to prove that the gentlemen were convinced that they were providing the other gentlemen with a stepping stone which the latter had wanted and asked for. It is impossible to exclude the public on this subject because it contains the reason, the true reason for the action; because it presents the motive of the accused. In this case, too, a public investigation is not damaging; it does not matter if the French, the English know that there are people in Bavaria who are willing to clean up a Berlin pigsty; if only one does not fling into the face of the French what we may be able to achieve and to do with these people in the area of foreign policy. I consider it completely out of the question to exclude the public if, as the Prosecutor intends, the question of the Direktorium, the Reichs-direktorium is discussed; that can definitely be discussed before the public. It even must be discussed before the public because it, too, refers to incentives and motives for the actions of the men here. We must, and we will reveal the betrayal of the men before you that was committed by a certain group of people—I don't want to mention any names, yet. Not only we, but the entire Bavarian and German people are interested in enlightening the public, especially also with regard to the trip made to Berlin on November 2 by a witness who will appear later; only then will they (the Bavarian and German people) know what kind of men had led them and how they had acted.

HERR RODER: First of all, I agree with the view of Justizrat Kohl that the petition for a general exclusion of the public is unacceptable. I also agree with the general explanations of my colleague Dr. Holl that certain questions should not be discussed in public. The question now is: How is the investigation going to proceed?

At first there will be the questioning of the defendants. As you know, the defendants have not yet been able to speak. Only the Generalstaatskommissar and his press have spoken about November 9, 10, and the following days. Any other information was suppressed everywhere. Hence, the defendants have kept quiet until now, except for correcting some very rude charges which deeply insulted their honor; that was the case specifically in the public charge of breach of promise against Hitler. I believe it is the duty of the Court to give those defendants who could not talk, until now, permission to speak today in the most comprehensive terms before the entire public.

I definitely thought you would permit every single defendant to speak in public, and would trust the defendants to submit their requests of when to exclude the public, because now those questions would have to be discussed which, in the interest of the Fatherland, cannot be discussed in public. After you have questioned along these lines, it will then be a matter of determining the way in which the witnesses should be heard. In my opinion, the interrogation of witnesses should proceed in the same manner.

It will be impossible, either with the questioning of defendants or witnesses, simply to pick out certain parts—whether they refer to time or to place—and to discuss these before the public. In my judgment, the hearing must proceed in chronological order if the members of the Court are to receive a true picture. The entire development, the entire growth of the movement, must take on a definite shape before your eyes; you must experience what happened. Specifically, I feel that it would not be right first to discuss the events which took place in public on November 8th and 9th and only then to discuss the historical development.

I therefore request the gentlemen of the Court to reject the petition of the Prosecutor and not to exclude the public at all, but rather to question the defendants and the witnesses from the beginning and to be confident that the defendants will ask for the exclusion of the public. In the case of the witnesses, I shall leave it, of course, to the discretion of the Chairman whether or not to exclude the public. In any case, the defense will be able to speak in each single instance.

HERR ZEZSCHWITSCH: General Ludendorff, whom I also represent, has asked the attorneys to disregard completely his connections with the Army during the war. General Ludendorff does not want to take the slightest advantage of these connections for himself. Although we attorneys know that we shall observe General Ludendorff's directive, we also know that here another matter is at stake, a matter which must be kept in mind during the entire investigation, during the debate of the role of the public; that matter is not only the German people, nor is it the broadest public beyond the borders of Germany. All these people are definitely interested in hearing the counter-arguments of General Ludendorff, after the tremendous insults which have been made by semi-official persons in Munich against these men, and after the monstrous listing of charges in the indictment. Thanks to the administration of the People's Court, we had the opportunity yesterday to discuss the entire question of inclusion or exclusion of the public with all those accused and all the defense attorneys—with a few exceptions.

After a lengthy debate we decided on the statements presented by my colleagues Dr. Holl and Roder. It is quite clear to us that the answers given by Adolph Hitler, as well as those given by President Pöhner, can stand the full public light, except for a few details which Mr. Hitler will probably bring up beforehand but which we must present here in order not to interrupt the logical sequence. It goes without saying that he would like to see the public excluded for that brief span in his testimony. Apart from that, the testimony of our client, General Ludendorff, will not be given until Lieutenant Colonel Kriebel and Dr. Fritz Weber have been heard; parts of these testimonies will definitely have to be given here behind closed doors. When General Ludendorff speaks, he will no longer have to mention those things which have already been discussed behind closed doors; he can disregard this gap simply by pointing to the testimony of Kriebel and Dr. Weber; in his testimony which he has to give as a defendant, he will not mention anything that cannot be mentioned publicly. Therefore I would like to support the requests made by my colleagues Dr. Holl and Roder.

HERR SCHRAMM: Some of the defendants request the Chairman to determine on whose behalf Lieutenant Colonel Endres is present.

Call: As the representative of the Wehrkreiskommando.

JUDGE NEITHARDT: The Wehrkreiskommando is not mentioned in the resolution about the admission of certain persons to the secret session. The Wehrkreiskommando is out of the question. I must ask the gentlemen to leave, since this is an explicit resolution. I thought those were the delegates of the Reichswehrministerium.

Call: Captain Beck is from the Reichswehrministerium.

JUDGE NEITHARDT: Then I must ask Lieutenant Colonel Endres to leave the courtroom.

HERR SCHRAMM: I also would like to add the following to the remarks of my colleagues. You know that the defendants are extremely bitter about the fact that they, alone, are sitting today in the defendant's dock, while those three gentlemen who played along with them don't have to keep them company; rather, the defendants are simply to accept the fact that those gentlemen will face them as witnesses, or even as accusers. Do you want to intensify this feeling of bitterness by not granting the gentlemen who are sitting here the opportunity to explain their attitude to the broad public! This would most definitely arouse the bitter feeling in their hearts: Even in the courtroom we are not allowed to speak to the public. That must be avoided under any circumstances! Please remember what persons you have sitting before you; then you yourselves will agree with the defense attorneys.

May I point out that recently there appeared articles in some papers which sounded as if attempts would be made to make this trial become a comedy, that is, to conduct the trial in such a way that the matter at hand would not be discussed at all, or to conduct it in such a way that the public would not hear of it. By referring to these particular articles I want to say that it is extremely dangerous and most unwise if we were to discuss

35

the subject of the trial behind closed doors, because then we would play into the hands of those people who already maintain that this is going to be a trial comedy. The entire public is very much interested in seeing these trial matters discussed frankly and freely before the public. The entire Völkische movement, too, wants to know in what position they are. All the men who are behind the defendants want to know: Can I or can't I go along, heart and soul, with what these men are striving for? It would do great damage and injustice, especially with regard to this movement, if the public was not admitted, if the trial here would be conducted behind closed doors.

I definitely oppose the petition of the Prosecutor, and I must urge to discuss those matters which the public can stand, really, before the public. Not only can the gentlemen who are sitting here judge when the time has come, but they will really do it; they will tell the Chairman, at the proper time, that this is the point at which the public must be excluded. Therefore there is not the slightest danger that things might be brought up in public which the public cannot bear to hear.

I urgently request to reject the general petition of the Prosecutor, to admit the public as a general rule, and to leave it to the defendants and the attorneys to announce and to request, whenever the time has come, that the public be excluded, or that a resolution be made with regard to the exclusion of the public.

HERR GOETZ: As matters stand now, there are two contrary petitions: that of the prosecutor to exclude the public in general and only to admit them occasionally; on the part of the defendants, there is the petition for a completely public trial from which the public will occasionally be excluded. I need not discuss which of the two petitions is desirable to the defendants; the defendants who might face an exclusion of the public have already had their views presented.

I would like to say that Dr. Frick, whom I represent, cannot be among them. He would be one of those defendants whose defense can and must be dealt with before as broad a public as possible, because the events within the police building are so simple and so uncomplicated that no misgivings about the interest of the State can arise.

But I can see another danger: If I understood the Prosecutor correctly, I heard that the criterion for the exclusion of the public will be the importance of the patriotic, political, and national interests involved. In my opinion, the way in which this will be handled will be a stumbling block for the differing views. We attorneys cannot possibly accept the fact that the State authorities consider something which, in our view, is a purely personal act on the part of someone who happens to be in political life, a "political action" to be discussed behind closed doors, for reasons of State; rather, we maintain that only that which goes beyond the subject, especially in military matters, can be used as a reason.

Objections will be raised that the exclusion of the public will practically be left to the judgment of the defendants if we want to proceed according to the request made by the defense. My answer to this is: Otherwise, the exclusion will be up to the Prosecutor. Who of the two has a greater right and a claim to having his petition granted? That is a point I would like to make right now, because it involves a very logical idea. The defendants who, until now, have not denied their, if I may say so, pronounced patriotic activities, are themselves more than interested in not throwing overboard, in the few minutes in which part of their lives is discussed, that which they have done for years—I emphasize, "have done for years"—that for which they now may risk a considerable term in prison. That would not help them, and we should not assume that the defendants would enjoy watching everything be destroyed.

There is another point to be considered which also does not occur in normal trials; and that is, that the defendants are in a position to judge how far they can go in their statements. And there is a third point, which has not yet been mentioned; it just occurred to me. We must consider that the Prosecution can argue, when hearing the witnesses, that the witnesses are not able to judge how far they can go. But, a curb can be put on this, once we know to what degree the witnesses have been released from their oath of office; only such witnesses who really know something will hide, for the main part, behind their oath of office. Hence, the Court must comply with the request of the defendants, which is the most forceful one. I therefore request that the petition of my colleagues be granted.

HERR GADEMANN: On behalf of my client, Lieutenant Colonel Kriebel, I would like to object above all to the accusation by the First Prosecutor who stated that the reading of the indictment to the broad public was a consequence of the events. In my opinion, it would have been the duty of the First Prosecutor to submit his petition to the Court before the indictment was read, and not afterwards, as he did. What is the success and the purpose of this petition? The indictment was read before a broad public; many parts of it contain gross errors, as will be proven by the evidence, and is already noticeable. The impression received of the defendants is very unfavorable. There is no doubt that this impression will be kept up, artificially, if the public is now suddenly excluded.

The defendants must take a strong stand against that. In my opinion, it is monstrous to say that the defendants are to be blamed for the fact that these matters have been disclosed to the world before a broad public by the indictment. I believe that, from this point of view, the petition of my colleague, Dr. Holl, with whom I completely agree, is also to be taken into consideration.

HERR HEMMETER: The true reasons for the petition of the Prosecutor are probably twofold. One of them is the fact that anything which might hurt the reputation of our particular homeland—and I am saying, expressly, the "reputation"—is not to be discussed in front of the public. The other reason is that those matters which could harm our great Fatherland must be kept from public discussion, under any circumstances.

I can only agree wholeheartedly with the second reason, as being absolutely urgent and compelling; I object to the first one from the depth of my conviction. It cannot be a matter of sparing individual persons who, by some chance, may once have been in a position to determine the fate of Bavaria in a biased way. Rather, the question must be to maintain here that the men who are now the accused can, and must demand, in the interest of the Fatherland and in the interest of Bavaria, moral and intellectual redress through a public investigation before the world.

It all depends on what one understands to be the interests of the Fatherland and of Bavaria. I think it is in the interest of our homeland to establish the fact that there are no people in Bavaria or in Germany who have as profound and deserved a reputation as the defendants; but who still do things that can simply be called moral and real crimes. In this case, when asking for the motives, it cannot be avoided to take into consideration all the details listed in the indictment.

I do not agree with the First Prosecutor that the indictment, or rather the form in which the indictment was written and presented, was the result of those actions with which the defendants have been charged. It is not our fault—and I must establish that—that somewhere in the public someone can say: A German court has established the fact that there is a connection between the legal and illegal Verbände; that there were connections between responsible statesmen and certain organizations; that actually parts of illegal organizations were in the legal barracks. That is what the indictment says. I was shocked when I read the indictment for the first time. It was superfluous that it calls for a "public defense" and a "public discussion," because the impression is that here a group of some ambitious men—as it is said so beautifully in the famous quote, "ambitious and dishonorable men"—attempted something which, in itself, bore the stamp of a crime against the State and of insanity. Not only can we, but we must discuss these matters.

I therefore wholly support the petition of the defense attorneys, my colleagues. We must try to conduct the trial before the broadest public; and it must be left to the patriotic sensitivity of the defense, as well as of the defendants, to inform the Court, on time, if in the opinion of those men who are to speak, matters will be discussed which really cannot be touched upon in public.

Still a few words! They refer to my client, Lieutenant Wagner. If you do not give us the chance to speak about the attitude, about the motives which led the cadets to these doings, then the entire action is incomprehensible and without any foundation. It is utterly impossible to take issue with the statements of the prosecution in the indictment if we do not outline these things from which, as I must call it, this action had to be born with absolutely compelling and logical necessity. Those who are guilty of having created these conditions are to be found elsewhere. Of that, the public here is aware. To see it confirmed is the wish of the public and, I may perhaps say, of the entire country.

HERR LUDENDORFF: If I understood the Prosecutor correctly, he thinks that I intend to conduct my defense in such a way that I will speak about things which will endanger the security of the country. The Prosecutor knows how I intend to conduct my defense. I have expressly told the Second Prosecutor during my last interrogation that I am not going to talk about military matters. I was deeply shocked when I read the indictment, because what it says amounts to high treason. That is exactly what the French are looking for. They want the dissolution of the Verbände; they want the integration into the Reichswehr. The question of the exclusion of the public from the proceedings is an entirely different matter. If I were a prosecutor, I would act against the Prosecutor.

JUDGE NEITHARDT: You are going too far!

HERR BAUER: As the defense attorney of First Lieutenant Pernet, I would like to express my agreement with the statements of the last speaker. As far as the defense of the First Lieutenant is concerned, there are certainly no reasons to demand the exclusion of the public with regard to his statements. I believe this does not concern him at all; yet, for the general reasons already presented by my colleagues, I support their petition to include the public, by all means, if it is at all justifiable.

HERR HITLER: I only want to mention one thing here. I ask the gentlemen of the Court not to assume that we who for four years have kept these secrets in our hearts cannot do justice to the matter. After all, for four years we have kept to ourselves all these arms matters and everything else, and not a word has come out. I think we can expect that much confidence; that here, too, not a word will be heard in public, beforehand, about those things which might actually hurt Germany. We do not intend to conduct our defense in such a way that Germany might be harmed. But there is a difference between doing harm to Germany, and doing harm to some men who, by their behavior, have harmed Germany in a most serious way. We will not hurt Germany! Those things that for four years we have kept secret will not get to the public. However, I beg of you, we must be able to invalidate publicly those crimes with which we have been charged publicly. I ask that this request be recognized.

HERR STENGLEIN: I realize that the defendants would like to defend themselves publicly against the indictment. I also realize that there is a public interest in discussing the matter publicly, although the public interest, as it exists, is to a great extent a desire for sensations.

An objection is raised.

40

HERR STENGLEIN: I said, "to a great extent." I am not saying that the public interest is nothing but a need for sensations. In this case, the public is huge; and nobody will argue that among the many people who are interested in the trial there are quite a few whose main motivation is a need for sensation, curiosity, and so on. But I definitely recognize, as I said before, that there is also a justified public interest. These interests, however, must be balanced against each other; and the question is, which of the interests deserve more protection: those which I mentioned, namely to avoid damage to Reich and Land by discussing things which can become very dangerous; or, those other interests I have indicated just now. I think there can be no doubt that the Fatherland has the highest priority.

By the way, I did not set up my petition in such a way that the public was to be entirely excluded; rather, I made the specific reservation that those parts of the evidence which could be discussed publicly would be discussed publicly. Hence, according to my petition, the defendants are also given the opportunity to make those statements with which they want to justify themselves before the public without damaging patriotic interests. I was only guided in my petition by duty and conscience; I have already conducted the investigation for three and a half months; and I alone carry the burden and responsibility of this difficult investigation. I also have the courage to defend the allegations I have made, and to defend them in public; and I must decisively reject the charge that I would be afraid to defend the indictment in public.

I also must reject the reproach made by His Excellency Ludendorff against the First Prosecutor when he spoke about "high treason." I wonder how it is possible to make such an allegation here. The indictment was written in such a way that the mentioning of those things which might be used against Germany was avoided where it could possibly be avoided; but it is impossible to keep silent about those things which are simply obvious, which have been discussed again and again in public, and the mentioning of which was indispensable to lay down the facts. However, we have carefully avoided anything which might somehow be construed as a reliable indication, a hint to those matters which could be harmful to Reich and State.

I uphold my petition in the way in which I have submitted it.

HERR KOHL: The statements of the Prosecutor call for another brief reply. He said that our petition for a public discussion was motivated by a certain need for sensationalism.

HERR STENGLEIN: I must interrupt you. What I said did not apply to your petition. Far be it from me to maintain that the wish of the defense to conduct the discussion in public was based on a need for sensationalism. I would never make such an absurd assumption.

HERR KOHL: I am glad that the Prosecutor immediately corrected my erroneous interpretation. I regret to have misunderstood the statements of the Prosecutor, and I do not at all hesitate to say I am sorry that I wanted to bring up the subject of sensationalism in general. I suppose that now this subject is settled in a way which satisfies both parties, for I have no reason at all to sharpen the atmosphere in the courtroom; and I hope that when this investigation is concluded, you will be able to attest that I discussed matters calmly.

The Prosecutor has furthermore indicated that he does not understand a statement by His Excellency von Ludendorff. I suppose His Excellency Ludendorff will reply to that himself.

In my opinion, it was not necessary to read the indictment before the public. According to judicial regulations, the petition to exclude the public could have been submitted at once; then we could have avoided all those questions which have now created a certain tension, and the public would not have had the impression that the position of the defendants has become more advantageous. If the indictment had been read when the public was excluded, it would have been possible to leave certain matters completely aside; but now it has happened, and we will have to discuss anything that is necessary to vindicate the defendants.

Incidentally, I also think that if the Prosecutor had begun his last statement with his concluding remarks, then we would have agreed much sooner. In the end he said that he did not generally object to the exclusion of the public, but rather that he wanted a public discussion, if the public safety of the State was not endangered. This is the desire of all of us who are here. We want to discuss those matters publicly which are already known to the public.

What, actually, is not known in this trial? In the Bavarian

Landtag, Dr. von Knilling has given a complete description of the circumstances. We can therefore discuss these matters publicly without any qualms; and, as soon as there are the slightest doubts that the safety of Germany or Bavaria is in danger, the defense will heed the advice of the Chairman and the request of the Prosecutor. We do not want to embarrass Germany; rather, we want justice to be done, if necessary with the exclusion of the public, and if possible before the public.

HERR HOLL: What actually is to be kept a secret from the public? If, for instance, the secret order Ia 800 is to be discussed, I can say that this order was already printed in big letters in a proclamation by the *Salzburger Volksblatt*. Of course, Paris has known it for a long time and, therefore, we may as well discuss the existence of this secret order.

JUDGE NEITHARDT: Even if a newspaper commits high treason, it should not be done again through the courtroom.

HERR HOLL: We could perhaps discuss the organization "Wicking," the assembly in Coburg and North Bavaria. The whole world, including Paris, knows about it. They don't have to be told details, officially; there are ways to avoid that. Furthermore, we can discuss the strength of the so-called "illegal Verbände"! Every child could see it by watching the funeral procession at the Armeemuseum. There they had all come together. One could see how many they were; and that all of them had a rifle on their shoulders was also visible. Photographs have been made. The end of the indictment states, very nicely, that Brückner, for instance, is the commander of the Regiment München, which consists of three battalions. The French cannot expect to know more.

So much has already come out that we may as well conduct the hearings in public; and I suggest, in spite of everything that is already known, to exclude the public from case to case so that things do not get out, officially, from the courtroom. However, we should determine, in general, in which areas and on which questions to exclude the public. My client is of the opinion—I don't know how the others think—that there are four points which require the exclusion of the public: (1) the discussion of military matters, of military secret orders; (2) the military formation of the so-called illegal Kampfbund; (3) the discussion of weapons and equipment of these Kampfbund; and (4) the question of connections between the Kampfbund and the Reichswehr and police. If these four areas are discussed secretly, then I think the interests of our country are fully preserved.

HERR SCHRAMM: I would like to point out, once again, that the present trial originates in the fact that on November 8 and 9 two philosophies (Weltanschauungen) collided: the Völkische Bewegung went into open combat against those groups which it has always fought. If we do not allow both Weltanschauungen to speak up, we are doing grave injustice to this spiritual struggle of the people. I want to emphasize, once again, especially this aspect.

HERR EHARD: I do not want to speak about the petition—it is not within my area of responsibility. I would like, however, to make a few remarks on behalf of the Prosecution with regard to the statement by General von Ludendorff. The First Prosecutor has already mentioned that the Prosecution here performs the duties of its office as it is required. I may assume that especially General Ludendorff, who for years has demanded of the German people the highest performance of their duties, will particularly understand this. I am surprised that he turns the performance of the duties of the Prosecution into a charge of high treason.

I would like to add a further remark—and I consider it important that this is done in secret session. If a collision similar to the one just caused by the General should occur in public between General Ludendorff as a defendant and the Prosecution, the Prosecution of course will, as a consequence, react in the sharpest way possible.

There is agitation among the defense.

HERR EHARD: —for the Prosecution does not intend to be accused of high treason; and I would regret very much if such collisions should occur.

JUDGE NEITHARDT: I really don't consider this debate necessary. There will probably be no more petitions with regard to the matter at hand.

HERR LUDENDORFF: I did not intend to accuse the Prosecution of a violation of their duties. I only objected to the reading of the indictment in a public session.

JUDGE NEITHARDT: There are no more petitions forthcoming. The Court will decide about the petition.
The Court issues the following:

Resolution

"Those present, including the defense attorneys, are ordered to remain silent about the discussions held in secret session, as far as they concern details of the Reichswehr, details of the patriotic Verbände, training, equipment, arms and employment of patriotic Verbände."

The order to remain silent is now actually known to the gentlemen; a violation of this order is punishable. I would like to add that I have been more cautious, when listing these points, than suggested by Attorney Holl.
The Court will now decide.

After a secret debate, the Chairman announced the following

Resolution

"The trial is to be public."
"The Court will decide, from case to case, whether the exclusion of the public is necessary."

At this time the public is readmitted to the hearing.

45

The Tribunal passes the following resolution: The trial will be conducted publicly. The Court will decide on individual cases as to the desirability of excluding the public.

The trial begins with the testimony of Herr Hitler.

Testimony of Herr Hitler

JUDGE NEITHARDT: Your home is in Linz, and you haven't obtained Bavarian citizenship?

HERR HITLER: No.

JUDGE NEITHARDT: You came to Munich in 1912 to receive training as a draftsman?

HERR HITLER: Not for training; I'd already completed that. I worked as draftsman just to support myself. I wanted to train to be a contractor and architect.

The Judge then ascertains that Hitler joined the Bavarian Army in 1914 as a recruit and had served the entire campaign with the 16th Reserve Infantry Regiment. The Judge reads from his record that Hitler has received several decorations including the Iron Cross First Class and the Service Order of Merit, as well as a regimental commendation for exceptional bravery in the face of the enemy. His service was characterized as "Very Good" in his military record. The Judge then reads from hospital records that Hitler was twice wounded.

HERR HITLER: Once I was hit by shrapnel and once I was seriously gassed.

Hitler remarks that on the night of October 14, 1918, he was overcome by German mustard gas. He was almost fatally poisoned and almost totally blinded. Three comrades who were with him died and others were blinded permanently. When Hitler left the field hospital, his eyesight had improved somewhat. For his occupation, he was considered at that time as a total cripple.

The Judge then notes that Hitler joined the 19th Riflemen Regiment as training officer in September, 1919, and that he was discharged from service on April 1, 1920. In July, 1919, Hitler joined the National Socialist German Workers Party and on July 29, 1921, was elected the party's first chairman.

JUDGE NEITHARDT: They say that you are also responsible for founding the Austrian NSDAP.

HERR HITLER: The party has been in existence in Austria for over 20 years.

Here the Court recesses for lunch.

—AFTERNOON SESSION—

The Presiding Judge opens the session at 2:30 p.m. and asks defendant Hitler if he wishes to explain how he became involved in the whole matter.

Hitler's Defense Speech

HERR HITLER: If it please the Court, Your Honor mentioned this morning that I received a rating of "Very Good" in my service record. It may seem peculiar that a man who had learned for four and a half years—six years, really—to obey his superiors, to contradict no one, to act blindly, would suddenly run headlong into a contradiction, the greatest contradiction that can exist in a country. Here I must reach back to my youth. At age sixteen and a half I was forced to fend for myself. I was barely seventeen when I came to Vienna, and for the first time I saw and understood the social problem—the incredible misery and the unfulfilled needs of large classes of people—and also the racial problem in the city where East meets West. In Vienna one could study the racial problem better than anywhere in Germany because it was in Vienna that the greatest foe of all Aryan humanity clearly showed himself, more than in Germany. Thirdly, I learned of the party and the movement that would affect the break-up of the Marxist movement. I left Vienna a staunch anti-Semite, a mortal enemy of Marxism and its trappings.

I went to Munich where I managed to survive. There was no question that I would serve the mobilization in those first days when the destiny of the nation was being wrought. I was convinced that the destiny of Germany and Austria would not be

48

formed in Austria but by the German Army, and therefore I enlisted. I will not say anything about the war; I just want to mention that I was absolutely convinced that, if Germany was unable to solve problems at home, if the government could not muster the resolve to throttle the Marxist problem, then Germany inevitably must lose the war and all our bloody sacrifices would be in vain. As a matter of fact, one could observe the first signs of the later decay, even below the surface, as early as the winter of 1916-1917. At that time, I was in the field hospital. A small incident will always remain rooted in my memory.

While we at the front still believed in absolute obedience at that time, it was practically nonexistent in the field hospitals. I was reading a book on military science in the hospital when the head doctor slammed the book shut and took it from me. Afterwards a Dr. Stettiner asked me, "What are you reading here? I thought you were smarter than that." I was completely dumfounded. Of course, Dr. Stettiner was a Jew. It struck me as odd that a man on active duty could say such a thing. There were many malingerers in the hospital. The hospital administration was either blind or they just didn't want to see how discipline and obedience had been buried. I then went out to the front and was able to see the consequences more clearly in 1917-1918.

On my second trip to the hospital, all I heard about was the coming revolution. On the night of November 5, even sailors came to us. I was a broken man and in terrible pain but I didn't report it at the time because I felt the collapse approaching. I couldn't believe it when I heard on November 7 that a revolution had broken out in Munich. I made up my mind on the night of November 9—on that night I decided which party I would turn to.

I searched for an opportunity to come to Munich, and a few weeks later I came here as a battalion reservist. I came in contact with the National Socialist Workers' Party, whose members numbered six at that point. I became the seventh. I converted to this movement in the conviction that the other parties had abandoned their responsibility to deal with the root of the German problem. In my opinion, the Marxist question is the basic problem of the German nation. Insofar as it places the many before the individual, mass before energy, the Marxist movement undermines the very foundations of civilization.

49

Wherever this movement succeeds, it spells the ruin of man's culture. Marxism works with two tools. On the one hand, there are mass propaganda and mass suggestion.

Hitler shows how youth is indoctrinated to Marxist ideas, first as an apprentice and then later as a union member where the spiritual dimension is called bourgeois. He explains that what is called Marxism represents a massive organization, a state within a state, a separate state that raises its clenched fist against the other state.

HERR HITLER: And so it becomes possible that a German considers his own blood brother a mortal enemy while he considers a racial alien—let us say a Hottentot—as his brother. The second tool of Marxism is indiscriminate terror. No movement has ever worked with such a thorough knowledge of the masses as Marxism. In place of Bourgeois irresolution, one uses brutality.

Hitler explains that he became acquainted with the two aspects of this movement in his early years. He therefore became a member of a youth organization which recognized that the elimination of Marxism was Germany's future.

HERR HITLER: Either Marxism will poison the people, or this poison will be bled off. Then Germany can recover, but not before. As far as we are concerned, Germany will be rescued when the last Marxist has been converted or annihilated. Germany has embraced the Marxist movement but the bourgeoisie has not.

And so that event which is known as the German revolution came to pass. The revolution was high treason, but high treason is punishable only when it fails. High treason is not punished when it succeeds in giving the people a new constitution. The events of November 8 and 9, 1918, did not constitute high treason, but rather a betrayal of the country. Betrayal of one's country can never be legalized. If our dead could rise and if they were asked if they would accept such a state of affairs, they would cry: "Never!" There can be no forgiveness for the acts of November 8 and 9. We consider this act to be a high crime, a stab in the nation's back. The National Socialist movement has established as its basic principle that the struggle against Marxism must proceed to its final consequences. Secondly, that the revolution can never be considered valid, as it is a consequence of an unspeakable crime. Thirdly, the National Socialist movement recognizes the problem of welding the German workers—the masses—into one nation again. This cannot come about through a negative educational process but only through a positive struggle against the corrupters. The multitudes that have served and are serving the Internationale are not even human. The racial problem is the most difficult and profound problem of the new age.

Hitler further declares that a majority is never able to make decisions; that the majority decision is always a weak one. In the end the one who wins is the one who knows how to manipulate the majority. Hitler explains that he didn't join the National Socialist movement for personal aggrandizement. Personally, it was very hard work creating a party numbering in the millions from a group of six men. The movement learned from its opponents. It used two tools.

HERR HITLER: Firstly, it has recognized that a massive, national demonstration of support is necessary. The movement knows the mood of the people—above all, they want respect. The party knew it could not buy the approval of the left by whining and moaning. We have not gone begging to the state for support. We stand fast on our conviction: For those who are willing to struggle with weapons of the intellect, we will lead the struggle with intellect; for those who are willing to fight, we have our fists. We have a propaganda machine and storm troopers. We saw that it is necessary to strike down with the sword anyone who would prevent the propagation of German ideals with the sword. The Storm Troopers had no military function; they had nothing to do with military affairs. Their task was to smash Leftist terror with greater terror tactics. That was their sole objective.

It remained their sole objective until 1923. In the first months of their existence, the Storm Troopers never lost sight of their objective. But in 1923 came the sad change. We had already recognized in 1922 that the Ruhr Valley would be lost. France's objective is to reduce Germany to a number of small states. When Upper Silesia was lost, they declared that the Germans must voluntarily disarm themselves. This disarmament practically sealed the fate of Upper Silesia. Naturally, each loss must lead to fresh losses. When we saw that the Ruhr Valley

51

would be lost, a rift was opened between our movement and the bourgeoisie. The National Socialist Party saw that the Ruhr would be lost unless the people awoke from their lethargy. Policy is not made with the palm branch, but with the sword.

France occupied the Ruhr in order to prevent Germany from ever offering any military resistance. Passive resistance makes sense only insofar as it is supported by an active front, even if the front is only the active will of the nation. At that time, a united front was called for. We favored a united front, but we wanted a front of homogeneous—not heterogeneous—elements. It was obvious that the Marxists would cooperate only until it became apparent that Germany would not be victorious. How could these people, totally devoted to the Internationale, prefer or want the national turmoil to overflow? At such moments a ruthless, rabid, brutal fanaticism is the only means to save a country from enslavement. But they organized a mercenary resistance in the Ruhr and degraded the national movement to a paid general strike. They forgot that one can't pray the enemy to death, nor can one stand about and await the enemy's demise. Millions were thrown into the insane passive resistance. And so bands of men were organized that later became the scourge known as Separatists. It was the government's curse that it did not really know how to ride this nationalist wave.

At that time, I went to His Excellency Lossow and explained that the development of this kind of resistance in the Ruhr would mean the end of the Ruhr. I told him that someone must stiffen the nationalists' resistance in the Ruhr. But the Reich must also be governed by nationalists. I also told Lossow that in a few months the Ruhr would be lost to us and that a time would come when one would not know whether Germany would ever be free again. I say this openly and I hope that Paris hears me: The only thing German youth thinks about is the day when we regain our freedom. Life would lose its meaning if we feared that this day could never come.

So we discussed these things. In the course of this conversation the arrangements which were outlined in the indictment were made. The development of the Ruhr conflict gave us justification. This state of affairs lasted until the money ran out. They threw away 4.5 billion marks while the military budget for 1912 amounted to scarcely 1.9 billion—1.9 billion in order to do something truly magnificent. The 4.5 billion marks were squandered on nothing, actually. The result was an incredible economic disaster and a complete devaluation of our currency.

On May 1, we attempted to prevent the parading of the banners of a foreign power, the Soviet Union, in Munich. The authorities took sides against us. They chose to protect those criminals who brought about the ruin of humanity in 1918 and committed serious acts of violence here. The authorities protected them from a counterrevolution. A few weeks later, the Ruhr rebellion broke out and with it went our agreement. Since then, I have not returned to the Wehrkreiskommando because I believe any further dialogue with them would be pointless. One could only hope that something would happen at the last minute. Something did finally happen, unfortunately, when Stresemann put down the Ruhr rebellion. I ask you to put yourself in my position.

Our movement was not founded to garner seats in parliament and collect dues; we founded our movement to apply ourselves to the fate of Germany in her eleventh-hour struggle. What does renunciation of the Ruhr Valley mean? In peacetime, if the German government had lost, say, Samoa, the Reichstag would have dissolved and the whole government would have resigned. An unparalleled catastrophe would have followed the loss of a single city. Now, for the past five years, region after region has been sacrificed. The country is being cut to pieces, and the end is not in sight. Yet the country is not the better for it; on the contrary, we are poorer than ever before. Millions of common people have been robbed of their property by deceitful money manipulators. The needs of the people grow more urgent every hour, and we sacrifice land necessary to feed millions of Germans. For what did our young men die? Why didn't they just line up for the slaughterhouse? You gave your lives for nothing. One doesn't die for big business; one dies in the belief that he is serving his country! Why are so many of our young men languishing needlessly in prison camps in southern France or North Africa?

A hostile press characterized the Ruhr debacle as the most shameless trick in history. If we had wanted to mount a massive propaganda campaign, we would have had German history and the present and future of Germany on our side. We had set up fourteen groups to organize a gigantic offensive all over Germany. Our cry was "Down with the Ruhr traitors!" We were prepared for everything except prohibition of this demonstration. On September 23, we heard the Generalstaatskommissar had

53

forbidden any demonstration. On the following day we received an official communique and also an invitation to participate in a session of the Generalstaatskommissariat to which representatives of other patriotic parties had been invited.

These are my impressions of the authorities. I thought of His Excellency Kahr as a pious, old, honorable official of the Crown—but enough of that. I met Herr Kahr a second time when the question of the Home Guard came up on the agenda. He assured me that he would never consent to disbanding the Home Guard. As you know, the Home Guard was disbanded a few days later. I spoke briefly once again with Herr Kahr in a private meeting, but that was the last time. I felt that at a time when the entire German nation called for a change in existing conditions, Herr Kahr was not the proper person to hold office. To have led an honorable and irreproachable life does not seem to be to a politician's advantage, but is rather a prerequisite for the post of the lowliest street sweeper. In my eyes it is a matter of course that a state official must have a clean record, and that used to be a prerequisite in the state. It was the revolution that made it possible for inmates of prisons to become ministers. Herr Kahr was of course above any such thing—he was an honest man. He did not, however, possess other qualities essential to a statesman. He may be the best administrator, but he does not possess the ability to rule with an iron fist. I was aware that he achieved great things when he had effective support from President Pöhner, for example.

As I have said, I did not think that Kahr was the man to fulfill the great expectations of the nation. I said immediately: I know Herr Kahr; he'll start the fight but he'll never finish it. He will get a good start, he will sound the call for a mass engagement, but the minute the fight begins he will collapse in fright. Scheubner told me of how Herr Kahr had said in an executive session that he controlled all the power—the Reichswehr and the Landespolizei are under his command and he can rely on them. Therefore he possessed true executive power. When we asked why our fourteen groups had been proscribed, no one could give any reason. I learned later that the groups were forbidden because of the danger of a putsch. Later, in prison, I heard a speech by Herr Knilling in which he said that the appointment of the Generalstaatskommissar was the result of a threat of a putsch on September 27; moreover, the putsch would have been the work of the fourteen groups.

Granted, at that time we would have had a plan for a putsch, and it would have been concealed from the police. In desperation, the State Ministry decided to appoint a Generalstaatskommissar to prevent this action. Naturally, one of the countless criminal officials would seek me out the next day to tell me, "You tried to foment a putsch yesterday. You are under arrest."

Herr Kahr introduced himself solemnly to the assembly, greeted my counsel, apologized profusely for not being able to meet me personally, and requested only a statement of our personal opinion of him. My counsel explained that he was not empowered to give such a statement; that I would do this myself. I gave a statement at noon and it read: "Our position regarding this government is no different from any other—it is subject to the rules of the Generalstaatskommissar. Our party was not created to serve as a support for the Generalstaatskommissar; it is devoted exclusively to the goal of saving the German people. As long as the Generalstaatskommissar acts to this end, he automatically has our support. And if he does not, then our party would have to oppose him, as it would any other government in this case."

Another odd thing occurred. Our meeting took place two days before—fourteen days before—the formation of the Generalstaatskommissariat was first announced. It was decreed that the entire patriotic movement was contained in two branches—a military and a civilian. Herr Kahr was tapped as head of the civilian branch. Thus, these people were chosen beforehand—I will speak further about this in a closed session—and so the reason for the prohibition of the fourteen groups could not be valid.

We really could not speak openly of the true reason. From the very beginning we were absolutely committed to the struggle against Berlin. I registered a complaint with Colonel Seisser about the ban on the groups. Herr Seisser did not say that the groups had been banned because of the fear of an imminent takeover; he said that the prohibition was the result of exceptional circumstances which the Generalstaatskommissariat was empowered to deal with. Of course, the ban would be lifted in a few days—one must be patient—it has nothing to do with us. Now I do not know who lied—Herr Kahr, Herr Knilling, or Colonel Seisser. I did not doubt for a moment that Herr Seisser was a trustworthy man.

A few days thereafter I had a conversation in Bayreuth with Captain Heiss of the Reichsflagge Nürnberg. He told me that it would be difficult to justify my reserved attitude toward the Generalstaatskommissariat since Herr Kahr was determined to settle the German problem—that is, to begin the march to the North. I said I did not think Herr Kahr was the right man, the kind of man who would take to the dusty highways and march on Berlin. I was more afraid that other factions might interpose as savior at the last minute.

When I explained, in due course, that *Dorten* is a dirty word among separatists, they told me that I would not be able to prove it in a courtroom. Events in the meantime have given us proof. I understand a federalist constitution to include an organization in which a large measure of cultural and economic independence is given to individual states. I cannot imagine federalism existing in this political sphere, particularly in power politics. If a nation of sixty million people is unable to fight for its sovereignty, then such an attempt by six or seven million is just a bluff. There is the danger, I said, that if Herr Kahr joins this battle, it may turn out that he is not the man to fight fire with fire; that he might capitulate in the end or seek outside help.

The economic situation at the time was so bad that people were crying for bread. When the people's needs are truly urgent, they discard their scruples about accepting help from all quarters. Austria is an example of this. The head of state in Austria, although his heritage is German, was not averse to traveling to Paris just when France was imposing a villainous treaty on Germany. Captain Heiss countered my reservations, saying that Herr Kahr was determined to take up the fight. And indeed the struggle began—decisions of the Reich court were ignored, arrests were not made, and so on. If that happened in another state, they would call it a coup d'etat, but we chose to call it defense against encroachments by the Marxist government in Berlin.

From the outset, I held the view that the fight against Berlin would never take the guise of defense of purely Bavarian rights. Bavaria represented common German law, and Bavaria would accomplish what its own people wanted in this struggle under the aegis of all Germany. I then explained to Herr Kahr that if he conceived of the campaign against Berlin as a purely Bavarian struggle, he would have the rest of Germany against him. We are not defending any special rights; we are seeking our rights in the form of common German law.

A second conversation with Captain Heiss eight days later strengthened my impression. Captain Heiss informed me that he was convinced Kahr, Lossow, and Seisser were indeed determined to take up the fight regardless of the consequences, and that all pertinent preparations had been made. I will reveal the preparations in closed session. All these preparations had to strengthen my conviction from day to day that an incident was inevitable. In for a penny, in for a pound. As may be seen from the exchange of telegrams, Herr Lossow refused to obey the Commander-in-Chief of the Reichswehr. It is naive to believe that there could be anything but an overthrow or a fight to the death. It is militarily unthinkable that there could be a pardon or compromise now. A military officer with extensive rights who rebels against his superiors must be firm in his resolve to either take the final step, or else he is a common mutineer and rebel who must be crushed.

I then said that I considered the affair extremely unfortunate because the people expected a massive national wave which would eliminate the Marxist government. I said that the people would take up the struggle against the November criminals with complete abandon and that a dictator would emerge from the gigantic national uprising. They were viewing the struggle as a purely Bavarian rejection of Berlin's authority instead of as a great national uprising. The people expect something more than a reduction in the price of beer, a stable milk price, or confiscation of butter. What genius must be consulted to propose those kinds of ridiculous actions at a time when every failure only increases the people's rage?

Lossow said: That's all well and good, but what's going to happen? I answered: You have begun the fight; either you must lead it to its conclusion, launch political and military offensives— you cannot fight like a snail that retreats into its shell and gets kicked around; or you do not fight, and there is capitulation; or a third way—outside help. I described this as the most shameful alternative there is. Lossow agreed with me that capitulation would be out of the question. Lossow candidly conceded that things could not go on this way, but what could *he* do? Now Kahr, on the other hand, would be the ideal person. I replied that I had always believed that a man belongs where he can do the most. Herr Kahr's position would legally belong to but one man, and that would be Pöhner. I had never met Pöhner, but it was common knowledge that he was the most energetic and competent man in Bavaria—certainly Herr Kahr wasn't.

I said further that, if they were serious, it would be ridiculous to oppose Berlin with volunteer brigades or the Bavarian military. The North German soldiers would never join us, if only because of sheer rivalry. This struggle had prospects for success only if it was led by an organization that could claim to be a German national army. The only general who could solve the German problem militarily would be His Excellency Ludendorff. I remember seeing him for the first time as a soldier in 1918 at a review of troops. I worshiped him as the only man of will in Germany, the only man who realized that nationality does not consist of men with muzzled weapons; that men must be driven by a fanatical will to victory, which must be the common characteristic of a nation. He realized that the battle must be fought not only at the front line but also at home; and if the people at home give up, then the general is not to blame. One must not make the mistake, attributed to the Carthaginians, of cursing their general for the sins they had committed.

Continuing his remarks, Hitler assures the Court that he had expressly stated that the purely political campaign must be left to him alone.

HERR HITLER: I must categorically state that I refuse to be modest about something that I know I can do. When a person believes that he is called to do something, he cannot escape it; he is obligated to fulfill his destiny. I discussed with His Excellency Lossow what I felt to be the best solution. When I finished, Lossow said that a showdown has to come; it is inevitable, and avoiding it is out of the question. Lossow added that he would have no objection to His Excellency Ludendorff—but Ludendorff alone is not enough. We must win over the men of North Germany, men of considerable repute, in order to make the whole plan work.

Lossow did not say a word about the question of a struggle; on the contrary, he stood in the middle of it. The struggle was unpleasant for him because it did not seem to have the support of many important figures. Lossow deemed it an important task to find such people. My second conversation with him heightened this impression. The motive for the struggle was apparently shifted to the background by the *Beobachter* incident, which was really only a small matter. The illusion was that Lossow's position was rendered more difficult by this controversy with the *Völkischer Beobachter*. For the first time I felt a human bond to him. I dispatched Herr Scheubner-Richter to Berlin to inquire why the *Beobachter* was banned. He was told it had been banned because of an article that claimed that General Seeckt consorted with a Jewess. I also spoke with a gentleman who told me that this was not true.

It was up to me to prevent this small conflict from getting any larger. I immediately ordered a retraction and a public apology for the insult, but the conflict by this time had blossomed even farther. At about this time I went again to see His Excellency Lossow. He was alone and very depressed. He said that once the struggle began, there would be no turning back. The battle must be waged, but how? All our conversations revolved around the question of "names." And Lossow stated here also that some "names" must be attracted. As Lossow sank dejectedly into his chair, I told him that I stood behind him, stood loyally behind him, and that I would do nothing contrary. I gave my word of honor to Lossow only, and to no one else. And even then, only in the sense that I would support him in the fight against Berlin. This decision was a bitter pill. Knowing Herr Kahr, I had to admit to myself that this struggle was doomed to failure.

Hitler then reveals that Count Reventlow warned him against pledging himself to Lossow and advised him to align himself rather with Seeckt.

HERR HITLER: Even a count exhorted me not to place myself behind Lossow, but to maintain neutrality in the conflict—which was impossible—or to join the other side. At that time I told Lossow that I supported him and that I would never attack him behind his back. That was the sense of my promise, and I kept it.

Regarding the Ruhr conflict, the future looked bleak to Lossow. Either resistance would take an active turn or it would break down completely. Each state, then, would have to see how it fared. Of course in that case the Reich would disintegrate. Inwardly, I was deeply shaken. Even if Germany went over to the Bolsheviks, I would rather be strung up from a Bolshevik lamp post than live under French domination. Lossow stated that if a battle could not be won, one must seek other ways and means to act.

Afraid that something like that might happen, I addressed Lossow and Seisser: "If events make it impossible for me to stand behind you, I am free and am responsible for my actions. If your actions make it impossible for me to support you, I will make my own platform." I never said a word to His Excellency Kahr, and I never empowered Lossow or Seisser to tell Kahr that I would back him up. Such a promise would have been madness, since I attacked Kahr every day.

Hitler then mentions the ban on Nazi gatherings and remarks that he learned just a few days later that they had predicted that he would support Herr Kahr at these gatherings for propaganda purposes. How would this position agree with his word of honor?

HERR HITLER: These gentlemen had an obligation to say, "Herr Hitler, that is not loyalty." They did not say it because no one interpreted the oath as anything but a genuine assurance that I would not turn on Lossow and Seisser in their struggle for existence. I did it—stupidly, but I did it. Lossow asked me if His Excellency Ludendorff was acquainted with my thought processes. I said that Ludendorff would generally judge Lossow's position as I would. Naturally as an old officer and quartermaster general he would have to say that there are two possibilities: Either Lossow fights to the end, or he must step down. Lossow said he would go to Ludendorff and speak with him personally.

Ludendorff received the first information from Lossow, not me. Lossow declared in his conversation with me, "I am determined to act, but I must be at least 51 percent sure of success." I was not in agreement with him. If someone is badly burned and he needs an operation, and if he values his life at all, he will undergo the operation even if there is only one-half of one percent of a chance for recovery. I told Lossow that strategy would be pointless if a field marshall always demanded a 51 percent guarantee from heaven. Furthermore, I said, "You should have told us that before you began the struggle against Berlin. Now there is just one question: You are either with us now, or you will have to find other means." Thereupon Lossow replied, "There is only one way—we must begin the struggle."

At the end of October, a shift in opinion appeared. A few

gentlemen from Berlin said that Seeckt was preoccupied with the same thought. A dictatorship was also being planned in Berlin. Lossow clutched at this straw, the dictatorship. Lossow said that if Seeckt took the helm then it would perhaps be better in the end if I got General Seeckt before he got me. I replied that as far as the second part is concerned, it didn't appear without prospects. But as far as the first part is concerned, I did not believe Seeckt would allow Lossow such an experiment. In any case, this small hope caused people to pursue threads of hope in Berlin.

The fact was that for that whole time Seisser and Kahr shared the same goal with us; namely, the removal of the Reich government in its present international, parliamentary attitude, and its replacement by an absolute, nationalistic, antiparliamentary government—a dictatorship. If they declare that they did not want to use force, that they did not want to force a coup d'etat but rather something like a coup d'etat just using pressure, I regret that I have no records, no information, on this kind of coup. Revolution is the destruction of a government by the former opposition; a coup is the disposal of a government by a former ruling group.

In brief, our conception was normal. It was natural for us if, for example, Seeckt or Lossow went to Herr Ebert with the friendly request: "Herr Ebert, here are our troop divisions. We won't use force, but they don't belong to you any more. Please step this way." That is called doing it without force or bloodshed. If in fact our whole undertaking was high treason, then Kahr, Lossow, and Seisser also must have committed high treason because for months on end they agitated for nothing other than that for which we sit in the dock.

Hitler then reports on two conversations that he had with Colonel Seisser at Dr. Weber's apartment.

HERR HITLER: Seisser held the view that action was necessary, but that time was needed in order to make preparations: "Only when these preparations have been made can we detonate the explosion. It's only a matter of a short time. The day of the explosion will come and it will be the explosion we've all been waiting for."

The conversation with Lossow was basically the same, except that Lossow's resolve was chipping away. Lossow was still obsessed with the idea of having two figures from the North

61

join the movement, possibly a pillar from the agricultural community and perhaps one from trade and industry. Lossow contended that the new ruling council could not survive without agriculture. I contradicted Lossow and told him that it was nonsense to believe that farmers would bring eggs into a city to please the ruling council. If a Bolshevik government came to power and paid with gold, the farmers would deliver eggs and butter to the market alright.

The behavior of the farmers during the reign of the General-staatskommissariat is also proof to Hitler of how little an agricultural contingent has to say.

HERR HITLER: But because Lossow wanted it, we said, "Good, these men should be included." The basic theme of these discussions was how to get more men into the ruling council. Lossow never said, "I won't do it." All that he had to do was say it. It would have been madness to do something if we did not know where the present ruling clique stood. Otherwise, how would we have been able to give the statement on the 8th at 8:30: The national government has just been called forth in Munich.

Colonel Seisser said to me, "Herr Hitler, have a little patience. I'm going to Berlin to talk to Seeckt; then I'll come back down." I said, "If a final decision isn't reached, I must sever my ties to the Generalstaatskommissariat and Lossow. If you are not determined to act, then say so. Then it's over for me." It was either-or for me. We were tired of being duped. Apparently that was the last time that I spoke with Seisser. He traveled to Berlin, returned in a few days, and did not talk to me. I had the feeling he was avoiding me. I said to myself that things can't go on this way. On the one hand, they had me believe they were ready to strike. Baron Aufsess said in a fiery speech that Kahr sat with the fuse in the powder keg. As for the importance of this man, one could not be absolutely certain that he was only the mouthpiece of his master, since the reverse was not readily assumed.

What did they think of our position? We did not have any recruits. Lossow could say to his officers, "Gentlemen, next week there will be a coup. Dismissed." We couldn't do that. We were not always able to inflame people with a clear policy. If the leaders had told us, "We don't want to be in it," then the matter would have been taken care of. But they expressed their will so clearly in the later stages that we had to conclude that they wanted it but that they lacked one thing—the nerve to take the plunge. What I heard, particularly from the session at the Generalstaatskommissariat on November 6, did nothing but confirm my conviction that these men wanted to—but, but!

Hitler continues his narrative. He remembers a similar situation in early 1920 when the Hoffmann government took to flight because a former lieutenant and twelve men appeared with unsheathed bayonets in front of the Landtag.

HERR HITLER: And Herr Kahr took the helm through the coup. The process was unconstitutional, but he had hence brought Bavaria many blessings. So it was then, and so it is now. How the Reich Chancellor who surrendered the Ruhr can still be Chancellor is something later generations will not comprehend. The Reichstag had to be sent home and the President had to go also. Thus is was quite obvious that the impetus had to come from outside because the result would otherwise elude itself.

I learned from my friend Dr. Scheubner that Lossow had spoken with two gentlemen from the North of late and had always stated unequivocally that he favored action. He could not understand why there was nothing afoot in the North and why the other generals did not attack. One must also note that the hope is there but that the will is weak. The last letter from Scheubner, who was dependability personified in this regard, read that Lossow had contacted different people lately in order to get men from the North down here. I learned that he asked Ludendorff to see to it that this happened. I also got the impression from a session on November 6 that Lossow, Seisser, and Kahr were in over their heads and must either strike or capitulate.

Lossow and Seisser stated that Knilling had nothing to say. It was their opinion that the Generalstaatskommissar was completely independent, holding all the executive power; and that Hitler supposed from Kahr's orders to the Justice Ministry, the Interior and Agricultural Ministries, that Kahr was the undisputed leader. This conviction would be strengthened if the parties of the entire nation should appear here. Kahr possessed state power and state authority. It was only natural that the impossible relationship between Kahr and Knilling could not exist for long. Seisser never left any doubt about it. He stressed that the Landtag would not meet again, and that Kahr would be in a position to attack us. For us, the situation was clear insofar as it concerned only one question: When do these men want to translate these frequent and lengthy discussions into action?

On November 6 they agreed that they were ready to act. Even in the speech to his officers, Lossow expressed similar sentiments. Their whole demeanor woke the belief in us that they were only waiting for an excuse. Then, the final point. Scheubner told me that His Excellency Lossow had expressed his opinion: If the North itself does not strike, then separation is practically unavoidable. I said to myself: If the North initiates the fight, then the whole affair is good; if they don't, the impetus will probably come from a quarter that will bungle the opportunity.

On the evening of November 6, I resolved with two men—I will not name them, they are dead—to set events in motion. I said that the time had come to end their irresolution. Otherwise we may see a catastrophe; otherwise the initiative could come from a quarter that did not have national German interests at heart. There was another conference on the following day. From the first moment, the position was taken that no one was to be informed who did not absolutely have to know. I could do that because what we were planning was anticipated by everyone.

The general mood of all the circles was that a savior must finally appear. I ordered that the older men should not be informed. As a result, even General Aechter was not told. Ludendorff may not have known anything. His attitude was apparent at any given moment. I did not inform a number of people in my own party. The whole organization was set up so that the military leaders did not even know why they raised the troops. Later, many people were wrongly locked up although they did not commit any crime comparable to the actions of Lossow, Seisser, and Kahr, who discussed the smallest details with us.

The date was finally set for the 8th. Since I had learned by chance that Kahr would be holding a meeting, that seemed to be the right time to bring off *fait accompli*. The hall would be surrounded and the three would be lured out on the pretext of a telephone call or something of that sort. The men were to be told that there was no turning back now, for them or for us. Things developed differently.

As a precaution, I asked for an audience with Kahr on the 8th. I was denied an interview. I was not really rejected; the interview would take place on the next day. On the 8th I learned from Scheubner that a discussion which I knew of had already had the same result, but the men were more decisive and much more energetic. If the men were determined to act, a pretext could only be welcomed. If I had known that they wanted to begin on the 12th, I would have refrained on the 8th.

I was determined to bring about a decision on that evening, come what may. Our entire military staff knew nothing. They were ordered to get ready to act as security for a rally and other purposes. When they realized what was to come, it is understandable how Kahr's announcement was interpreted as a proclamation of the revolution. It is entirely understandable that many people could have and must have said, "Today is the day of reckoning." There is circumstantial evidence to support, for example, the fact that Gerhard Auer, who is fine-tuned to such moods, left the city, as others did. Word of the coup was all over the city.

Now to the events proper. I entered the Bürgerbräukeller at 8:00 p.m. It was beseiged by hordes of people, and I thought at first that the plot had come to the attention of the police. I had to admit that it would be rough going for the first Storm Troopers arriving by car. In any case, I went in. The hall was packed to its limits. I knew at once that it would be impossible to call the men out of a crowd this size, and so I left the main hall with the feeling that things could get difficult under these circumstances.

I went into the foyer and asked Scheubner to inform Ludendorff at once. If Ludendorff would not join in, he should telephone. I placed a guard by the telephone. That Ludendorff might refuse was unthinkable. Scheubner returned directly and told me that there was a huge crowd outside. Everything looked black. I went out and asked a police official on the scene to clear the streets, otherwise it might cause a disturbance in the hall. The police official then had the streets cleared.

At 8:34 p.m. the Shock Troops arrived—scarcely a handful of men—and occupied the foyer. I unsheathed my revolver, since I couldn't go in clutching a palm branch, and told my aid Graf, "Make sure I don't get shot in the back." Of course I could not have trained my gun on Kahr all the time; I had to use fists and elbows to clear my path.

Hitler explains the direction of his revolver as the natural movement of a soldier when he goes through a crowd.

HERR HITLER: The fact that we did not take aim at Kahr clearly shows that Kahr did not appear to be the type of evildoer who can only be contained by pistols and the like. Kahr immediately retreated from the podium looking pale and shaken.

Hitler then relates how he created order in the hall and testifies that he knew exactly which method to use.

HERR HITLER: It was in the very nature of the affair that I had to fire my pistol and say something as briefly as possible. Only a man who reads speeches prepared for him couldn't comprehend such a thing. I wanted to get Kahr, Lossow, and Seisser alone. Then an officer barred my way. As was later established, it was Major Hunglinger, and he had his hand in his pocket. I held the gun to his head and said, "Take your hand out of your pocket." No one knocked my hand away. Hunglinger took his hand out. Then I asked the three to come out, and said that we would guarantee their personal safety. And I said—as these men concede—that nothing would happen to them. I had the foyer cleared and led the men in.

I have spoken at hundreds of gatherings and was always in command of my senses, and that night was no different. If they say I was waving a pistol wildly and doing a kind of St. Vitus's dance, then they are correct insofar as, for example, an alcoholic sees trees dancing. It is an inner, spiritual process with them.

Kahr was a broken man and I felt sorry for him. I was even sorrier for Lossow and Seisser. I was sorry to have to guard German officers, but there was no other way and so I apologized. I said, "Forgive my actions." What was publicized was willfully taken out of context and partially invented. So were Kahr's first remarks about living or dying. I must emphasize that Kahr had not struck any heroic pose. I assured him once again that he was in no physical danger. Then Kahr said, "I'm not afraid; to live or not to live is all the same to me." I said with a smile, "There are still five shots in my pistol—four for traitors and one for me if all is lost." Then I gave the gun to Graf to reload the one bullet I had fired. No one was threatened, and extracting a promise by force would not have made any sense since I couldn't always be looking over their shoulder and, anyway, they could renege on their word at any time. I did not threaten them; I only reminded them of what we had discussed all the time.

To be sure, I did say there was no turning back. If we were ruined, so were they. I meant that they would go to prison with us if we failed, an opinion that I must now revise. Kahr's objection was characteristic: "One must have an inner faith in the affair. Now, after this incident, the people won't believe that I am acting of my own free will. You didn't even let me finish my speech." "Pardon me," I said. "I was told you would end your speech at 8:30 on the dot, so I planned on 8:30." That was his only practical objection. Lossow's objection was, first: Is the same thing happening in the North? And second: Is Ludendorff ready? I explained that nothing had happened up North and that Ludendorff had been contacted and was due at any minute.

Dr. Weber and, later, Pöhner arrived not after, but before, Ludendorff. I went out to make sure that the Shock Troops had arrived, and I went back in. When Kahr protested that these events could be misinterpreted by the throng in the main hall, I said that I was ready to go out and speak in the hall. I told Dr. Kahr that I would propose that he agree to take office, and that I was convinced that this would evoke thunderous applause. If I had threatened him with the revolver, there would have been no need to go into the hall and deliver a speech.

I reentered the main hall and briefly explained that a decision was in the making in the back room as to whether Kahr would head the new government. "They are wrestling desperately with the decision and they need to know whether this gathering agrees with this solution." I proposed the solution and the applause nearly brought the house down. I went back and said, "Your Excellency, there's no need to be ashamed. You won't be reviled; they'll carry you on their shoulders."

In the meantime, Ludendorff came and asked whether these gentlemen had been informed of his coming. I said "yes." Ludendorff left no doubt that ultimate success was possible only with Kahr, Lossow, and Seisser. Now Ludendorff spoke with Lossow and Seisser. By the end, both men were deeply moved. Lossow shook hands with Ludendorff. Very impressed, Seisser also gave Ludendorff his hand. Then Kahr spoke up. "Good," he said, "now we're all monarchists. I shall assume regency for the king."

That problem didn't concern me; I wasn't concerned about whether a monarchy should be proclaimed, but whether the revolution of 1918 was recognized. The important thing was that

Kahr felt at last that he was the deputy and had the authority to make further decisions. We told Kahr that there was nothing in his way. I said also, "I will see that Crown Prince Rupprecht is informed that our movement is not directed against him, but has as its exclusive aim the squaring of accounts with the November criminals. The future may decide what happens after that."

Deeply moved, Kahr gave me both his hands and looked me long in the eyes. I said, "I have nothing personal against you," and Kahr's eyes clouded and he was unable to speak. I assured him that I would be as loyal as a dog to him.

Hitler then explains that his words in the main hall were accurately recorded in the Münchner Neuesten Nachrichten *with the exception of one passage which was altered in all probability due to foreign policy considerations. Hitler declares, "We were never so deeply moved." He takes offense at the remark about a "beer mug," and he emphasizes that he is almost a prohibitionist. To soak a throat, dry from speech-making at a beer hall, one drinks beer. Hitler further alleges that Kahr gave him his hand a second time on stage.*

HERR HITLER: At that moment I trusted him like a brother; it was the same for Ludendorff and Pöhner. If Kahr had said, "I won't do it," then I would have had no other choice but to accept the consequences. I would have taken the consequences for myself regardless, but that a man with whom I had spoken dozens of times could say at the crucial moment, "I won't do it," seemed to me a sheer impossibility.

I found out that the 19th Regiment had been held back. I drove out with Dr. Weber to judge the state of affairs for myself. After a visit at the Wehrkreiskommando, I returned to the Bürgerbräukeller. I wanted to advise Lossow that the officers of the 19th Regiment refused to recognize the new alignment. Lossow was to give them an ultimatum. I was convinced that these men would stand behind Lossow. In the meantime, however, Lossow, Seisser, and Kahr had driven away. Ludendorff did not have any qualms; a promise under such circumstances was a safer bet than a thousand hostages.

At this point our concern was not that the gentlemen had been killed but that they may have fallen into the hands of the enemy and were now, not as before, in actual danger. We were convinced that if the masses cast their vote, they would realize that this was a matter of manifesting the wishes of the people.

This action was the fulfillment of the will of the people, larger in scope than the Kurt Eisner campaign in 1918 which was only an assortment of rogues, deserters, and jailbirds. I must say that the officers under the charge of Herr Lossow, men who had been trained in wearing the cockade, were able to put on without hesitation the old cockade of honor—beneath which thousands had fought, which had been carried to Lithuania, Livonia, the Ukraine, and elsewhere—just as easily as they could take off the tarnished one. That was the reason why we hoped for a change.

I tried in vain to contact Kahr, Seisser, and Lossow. I drove out to the Wehrkreiskommando, and there we discussed the situation. Even there the feeling was prevalent that Kahr, Lossow, and Seisser had probably become victims of a violent assault. If I could not get an answer, fine. Pöhner could be a victim too, for all I cared, although Kahr should have had the decency to tell the compatriot with whom he sat and spoke a few hours before: "I can't bring it off," or "I won't do it to prevent an innocent man from heaping all kinds of crimes on himself." And actually he was innocent because he had not been present at the conversation with Kahr, Lossow, and Seisser.

In any case, it would have been Lossow's obligation to tell the quartermaster general of the World War, our last great German general, not the aging general but the Ludendorff of German history: "Your Excellency, I swear to you, I cannot and will not do it! We will see how everything goes." He must have known that His Excellency Ludendorff gave his word only because Lossow and Seisser were in on it. This was an unparalleled lack of principle—not informing him.

On another morning, Lieutenant Colonel Leupold made his report to the officers of the 19th Regiment about Lossow's remarks. We knew that these were the men who formed the opposition when Lossow had been in conflict with Berlin. How could we value his word when he sat between 20 Berlin officers bent on democracy? So this message only confirmed the view that Herr Lossow sat in a circle of men that would not let him out but placed him in an either-or situation. A struggle against the Reichswehr on Landespolizei was, from the beginning, out of the question. We wanted to bring about the change with them in the forefront. As long as we were not absolutely certain that Kahr, Lossow, and Seisser acted from inner conviction or that the people would reject us, we had an obligation to see this thing through; but certainly not just to satisfy Herr Ludendorff's ambition. This action could not make him any greater than he already is. In fact, he was the only one who had something to lose. Everyone else had something to gain.

So we weren't motivated by stupidity, but by our obligation to the people who stood up for us and who still stand up for us and who will continue to stand up for us, even after this trial. Our jail cells will become the beacon for the spirit of young Germany. We have to show the masters of Germany that if they remain set in their outlook they will clash head-on not with rogues, bums, and lackeys, but with the finest and noblest Germans in the land.

Thus, we couldn't turn back. We started the propaganda campaign from the Bürgerbräukeller to enlighten the people again and to win them over to our cause. I strictly forbade any allusions to treason because I thought that it would be devastating to offer this rebuke, if the officials themselves were victims of coercion. At 10:00, at 11:00 and 12:00, we still had not received any positive communication about the situation.

As we had said at countless meetings before, our leaders were not like the Communists who cringe at critical moments; they marched at the head of the columns. A group of civilians who had joined the march were ordered to step out. I no longer worried about the officials who were to blame for the misery of all Germans. In any other country they would not be in office but there (Gesturing) where a zealous prosecution would like to put us. I did not want any martyrs on my hands, so I had the officials released. On Ludendorff's right marched Weber; on his left, Scheubner-Richter, myself, and other men. At Ludwig Bridge the men at the barricades, deeply shaken and broken, let us through as the water stormed underneath. In the rear, people who had joined the march called out, "Let's beat their brains in." We called back that there was no reason to harm these people.

We marched to Marienplatz. Our guns were unloaded. Enthusiasm was at fever pitch. I said to myself: The people are behind us; they won't be mollified any more by ridiculous decrees. The people are ready to settle accounts with the November criminals. They still possess the desire for honor and human dignity, and not for slavery.

In front of the Residenz a weak line of police let us through. Then there was a confrontation and a shot rang out. I thought it sounded like a rifle or carbine, not a pistol. Then they let loose a volley. It felt like I had received a flesh wound in my left side. Scheubner-Richter went down and I with him. I twisted my arm when I fell and received a second injury.

I was stunned for a few seconds and then I attempted to pick myself up. Another shot was fired from the alley behind Preysing Palace. All around me lay dead men. The police were attacking in front of me; behind me stood armored cars. My men were 70 to 80 meters behind me. I was unable to see Ludendorff any more. A large man with a black coat lay on the ground, covered with blood. I was convinced that it was Ludendorff. A few more shots were fired from the Residenz building and from the alley behind Preysing Palace, and perhaps a few wayward bullets from our side. I was driven from the square near the Finance Office.

At nightfall I wanted to be taken back. A few days later, in Uffing, it was discovered that I had suffered wrist and collarbone fractures. At the time I was bedridden with physical and mental anguish because I thought that Ludendorff had been killed. In Landsberg I got my first look at the newspapers. I read the allegation that I had promised Herr Kahr not to do anything without notifying him, and that I had made this promise on the evening of November 6. I was portrayed as a totally unscrupulous bastard. It is absolutely brazen that men who worked with us the whole time now revile us with lies because we are unable to defend ourselves and are somewhat broken in spirit. I never made such a promise to Herr Kahr, nor to Herr Lossow, nor to Herr Seisser. I said that I would give them loyal support, that I would not take action against them. I said finally: "If you cannot decide, I will not consider myself bound to my resolution."

As the campaign of slander against me intensified in the course of the following few days, and, as one after another, men were sent to Landsberg Prison solely because they belonged to the movement, I resolved to defend and protect myself with my last breath. I did not come to this courtroom to disavow anything or escape responsibility. I protest that Herr Kriebel is assigned responsibility, even if only for military provisions. The responsibility is mine alone, but I say that I am not therefore a criminal and that I do not consider myself a criminal. I cannot plead guilty, but I do admit to the deed. There can be no "high treason" against the traitors of 1918.

In the second place, it is impossible that I committed high

treason, for high treason was not committed in the deeds of November 8 and 9, but rather in the whole conception and direction during all the months before. If I am really supposed to have committed high treason, then I am amazed not to see in the dock the officials whom the prosecution is obligated to indict since they strove for the same end. They discussed and planned it down to its details. This will be presented specifically in closed session. I do not consider myself a traitor. I consider myself a German who wishes only the best for his people.

JUDGE NEITHARDT: Cabinet ministers and police officials were also arrested. Were you aware of that fact?

HERR HITLER: Yes, Your Honor.

JUDGE NEITHARDT: Why did that happen?

HERR HITLER: To facilitate Herr Kahr's decision and to remove the difficulties surrounding the last deliberations.

JUDGE NEITHARDT: Did you order the vandalization of the *Münchener Post,* or did you have prior knowledge of it?

HERR HITLER: The police informed me of it that night. I said that I was ready to dispatch one or two carloads of men and to have two of our men to accompany every two policemen in order to prevent those kinds of incidents. In any case, I do not condemn my people. Quite the contrary. In a thousand years the *Münchener Post* could never make up for the crimes it has committed all these years against the German people, and what they had done to break our will to resist in the war.

JUDGE NEITHARDT: You had no knowledge of the search of Auer's rooms?

HERR HITLER: His stepson brought me the news and I said that as far as I was concerned he had been punished enough, and that we should let him go.

Hitler then answers the Judge's questions concerning whether he knew about the hostages, and if the hostages had been brought to him. Hitler answers that he could not bring about a change in their status because conditions were such that the hostages would have been slain immediately if they had been released.

JUDGE NEITHARDT: Did you organize the seizure of money at the home of Parcus?

HERR HITLER: Yes, Your Honor, as a reminder of the events of 1918; even more so as the next day the troops—well, I cannot say any more now.

HERR STENGLEIN: I believe that the prosecution has obtained today for the first time exhaustive testimony of Hitler's culpability. Up to now he has disavowed it and referred us to a memorandum we have never seen. Cross-examination of the witnesses will reveal more, particularly as regards the allegations against Kahr, Lossow, and Seisser.

The proceedings are recessed, to reconvene the following day.

THE SECOND DAY, February 27, 1924

—MORNING SESSION—

The defense opens the second day of the trial with several questions to Hitler. Attorney Luetgebrune asks Hitler if at any time during his conversations the subject of competition between the leadership factions of Hitler-Ludendorff and Kahr-Lossow was broached.

HERR HITLER: Not one word was ever spoken about a directorship as a bone of contention. If these gentlemen claim that, then they lied to us.

JUDGE NEITHARDT: You never spoke among yourselves of such a thing?

HERR HITLER: Never. Our conversations were structured around the idea that if Lossow and Kahr, the creators of the idea, wanted a dictatorship, then only His Excellency General Ludendorff could be considered as supreme commander of the national army.

HERR HOLL: Didn't you, Hitler, state that the national uprising could only succeed with the cooperation of the Reichswehr and the Landespolizei; that your own work was accomplished when the people had been incited to rebel?

HERR HITLER: In a meeting of representatives on October 6 or 7 in Nuremberg, I stated that we must carry on a national rebellion in cooperation with the Reichswehr and the Landespolizei. We never discussed any political reward for me.

74

HERR EHARD: I wish to ask Hitler if he did not claim the foremost position in Germany for himself on the evening of November 8?

HERR HITLER: I might mention that it was not possible to aspire to the foremost position in Germany at that time; it was more a question of establishing a secure base in Munich and Bavaria. I never said that I wanted the leading position, but I did want to lead the political struggle. As long as Ludendorff stood by my side, it would have been ludicrous to speak of the foremost position.

HERR STENGLEIN: You stated, "I will assume political leadership of the Reich."

HERR HITLER: I said that I would assume the foremost position in the political struggle.

Now the Court takes up the cross-examination of Dr. Weber. The Presiding Judge establishes the fact that Dr. Weber was in the field four and a half years, has aided struggles of liberation, has compaigned in the Ruhr Valley and Upper Silesia, and has been active in the patriotic insurgency movement for the last two years. Dr. Weber confirms the above.

JUDGE NEITHARDT: You are the president of the Bund Oberland?

HERR WEBER: Yes, Your Honor.

JUDGE NEITHARDT: The German Kampfbund to which Oberland belongs was founded in Nuremberg on September 1, 1923. Now, suddenly, the Kampfbund has achieved political notoriety. What was the reason?

In this connection, Dr. Weber asks permission to set forth how things were viewed by the Oberland. It was a revelation for him to see how all the classes and clans were united in the Oberland. Dr. Weber then describes what led him to attain the leadership of the Bund Oberland, and he then discusses the paradox in the patriotic movement which arose from one faction's wanting a return to the conditions of 1914 and a glossing over of what had occurred in the meantime.

HERR WEBER: It is our conviction that this is simply

impossible. When speaking of patriotic insurgency, one must differentiate between the popular revolutionary factions and the more reactionary factions. In 1923 this discord became more obvious. Then a bloc of five factions was founded, and on September 1, the alliance of the Reichskriegsflagge, the National Socialists, and Oberland took place. The three groups had a number of things in common: The youthful outlook of the leaders and members, rejection of outdated structures, disregard for questions of state organization, and an unshakable will to bring about the nation's freedom. The final objective was to smash the Treaty of Versailles—that infamous deed—at all costs. I believe that one can and may say openly that all our intentions and efforts were directed toward destroying these bonds and shackles.

Of all these factions, Oberland was perhaps the strongest politically oriented group against the Treaty of Versailles. Oberland's task was to break down class barriers and create a new and greater German Fatherland. Of course, such formulation of foreign policy naturally shaped our attitude toward domestic problems. Our experiences have taught us to look for the deadliest enemy in Marxism, in Jewry, and in a democratic-parliamentary system. It went without saying that if we wanted to march over the Rhine we would first have to establish a solid system of government in Germany that would remove the threat of a stab in the back, as happened to our fighting men in 1917.

Dr. Weber then describes the expansion of the Bund Oberland in Germany and in Alpine Austria. He emphasizes that the thrust of the Oberland was always the solution of the overall German problem, and not internal Bavarian affairs.

HERR WEBER: Oberland strove for a system of government in Germany which would harness the total national strength of Germany and that would begin to realize overall German goals. Our main task was to lead a crusade for spiritual and moral regeneration in ourselves, and through us, in all our people, because we were convinced that a new Germany could only become a reality through a spiritual and moral regeneration of its people.

It was only in the summer of 1923 that it became possible to have closer contact with the leader of the National Socialist movement, Hitler. This contact had to result in an alliance because we saw that at the head of the National Socialist movement stood a man whose inner convictions coincided with our demands and opinions.

Dr. Weber then tells how Oberland came in contact with General Ludendorff. When Oberland was fighting in Upper Silesia, it seemed perfectly natural to the commander of Oberland to approach His Excellency Ludendorff at the conclusion of hostilities. The association with Ludendorff stems from that time. When Oberland fell on hard times in 1922, Ludendorff was the only outsider who recognized and remained faithful to the principles of Oberland. Dr. Weber states that Oberland is perhaps the only group in the insurgency that is financially solvent, because it made great demands on its members' willingness to sacrifice.

JUDGE NEITHARDT: I believe that you should return to the question of the Kampfbund.

Dr. Weber replies that the Kampfbund did not publish any regulations; that a consensus simply materialized about what the Deutsche Kampfbund wanted.

Judge Simmerding reads the charter of the Kampfbund. The Presiding Judge then reads an affidavit, dated November 16, in which Dr. Weber had stated that the political leader of the Kampfbund was independent of other factional leaders in times of crisis. Dr. Weber calls what he said at this hearing correct; namely, that Hitler was convinced from the beginning that a new Reich government, a national dictatorship, should be set up in Bavaria, there to solve the national problem. He states that this idea found expression after the Generalstaatskommissariat had been set up in Bavaria.

HERR WEBER: The Generalstaatskommissariat came as quite a surprise to the general public, but a number of informed people, including myself, had known about it for weeks. The plan had already been mapped out for me by Dr. Pittinger, leader of Bund Bayern und Reich, in exhaustive discussions. I had many misgivings about the currency question, let alone the appointment of a Generalstaatskommissar. By the end of August, the same plan had been developed in the Ministry of Justice by competent authorities.

Dr. Weber then tells of a trip to Mittenwald to see President

Knilling, to whom he expressed forebodings about the proposed Generalstaatskommissar. At a later date, he also expressed his doubts about Kahr to another person whom he does not name.

HERR WEBER: From the start it was obvious to us in the Kampfbund that limiting the national dictatorship to Bavaria could not lead to the desired end—the internal liberation of all Germany. Hitler always insisted that restricting the dictatorship to Bavaria could be perilous. The impetus must come from Bavaria to solve the German problem and to liberate Germany from Marxism and from everything that the postwar revolution had imposed on us. I cannot go into what was discussed at the Wehrkreiskommando. We had to be convinced that the Generalstaatskommissar, the leader of the Bavarian Division Command, and the commandant of the Landespolizei were in complete agreement with us.

JUDGE NEITHARDT: At the preliminary hearing, you spoke of the conquest of the North by a national army.

HERR WEBER: The pressure on Berlin would be increased by the conscription of a national army. This also gained immediate approval in North Germany. If large blocs of legal officials in Bavaria had sworn allegiance to the new Reich government, if great segments of the North German Reichswehr followed suit because of Ludendorff, and if patriotic groups all over the country united, then there would be nothing for the Berlin government to do but yield to the pressure, pack it in, and disappear from the stage. We believed that a struggle with the North could be avoided. In my estimation, there would have been no armed resistance except from Socialist and Communist enclaves in Saxony and Thuringia.

JUDGE NEITHARDT: At your hearing, you also said that Hitler insisted that everything would work out someday because the situation was too desperate.

HERR WEBER: At a meeting on October 25, Colonel Seisser asked Hitler if he would move against the Landespolizei and the Reichswehr. Hitler answered, "Of course not"; he hadn't even thought about it. He felt bound not to act without Seisser's full knowledge. On November 1, after Hitler and Seisser were in complete mutual agreement on all points, Seisser declared that he was driving to Berlin to sample the mood there and to feel out

Seeckt. Final decisions would be based on these impressions of Berlin. Hitler said, "Act swiftly; if you aren't ready to take action when you return, then I'll make the leap for yourself, Kahr, and Lossow."

JUDGE NEITHARDT: You said earlier, "Economic necessity drives our people so that either we must take action or our country will swing over to the Communists. If you come back and don't do anything, I am forced to move independently."

Dr. Weber explains that as a result of the events of November 9, his memory is shakey as far as previous days are concerned. He doubts that the expression, "swing over to the Communists," was used. In any case, it should be mentioned that, after weeks of wrangling about the meaning of the march to Berlin by competent authorities in Bavaria, there had to come an explosion from below if no decision to act could be reached. Dr. Weber tells the Court about the meeting of November 6.

HERR WEBER: I was present as representative of the Bund Oberland. Dr. Kahr said that the normal channels to solve the German problem had been exhausted, and that the unconventional channel had to be tried by all means. There are certain financial, military, and food-rationing measures to be taken, and these will be taken. The context of the Generalstaatskommissar's directives was that he had decided to take the national problem by the horns, starting in Bavaria.

JUDGE NEITHARDT: It was allegedly said, "If one of the factions becomes restless, use force to keep it in line."

HERR WEBER: Dr. Kahr wanted to demonstrate that a faction which steps out of line would not have his support. More than anyone else, it concerned the Erhardt factions which had already been alerted. Herr Lossow stated that the Reichswehr stood behind the Generalstaatskommissar all the way, and that they were determined to follow every directive of the Generalstaatskommissar. Moreover, as Commandant of Bavaria, he was resolved to collaborate in any coup for the tricolor, provided it had a 51 percent chance of success.

Colonel Seisser spoke of the border patrol problem in North Bavaria. He said that Herr Kahr could rely on the Landespolizei unconditionally for support. That evening, on the basis of notes that I took, I informed Hitler that for the first time at a sizeable

79

gathering Herr Kahr had shown his complete agreement with Hitler's train of thought and his objectives, and that I would arrange a meeting as soon as possible between Hitler and Kahr. Hitler empowered me that same evening to petition His Excellency Ludendorff to facilitate the meeting. This I did. Why the meeting never took place is beyond me.

JUDGE NEITHARDT: On the basis of the conversation of November 6, then, you became convinced there existed complete agreement between the three men and the Kampfbund.

Dr. Weber affirms this, and also the next question of whether he knew of Lieutenant Colonel Kriebel's circular in which he declared on November 7 that he and the combined military might of the Kampfbund would band together to try and bring about an overthrow.

HERR WEBER: It could only be a matter of supporting the Erhardt group.

JUDGE NEITHARDT: Röhm was in charge of the Reichskriegsflagge. How is it that Röhm was not present at Lieutenant Colonel Kriebel's for the meeting of all of the leaders?

HERR WEBER: Röhm and Hitler were such good friends that I can say that Röhm would have been in complete agreement with this business. On the evening of November 7 at 6:00, a special meeting of the leaders of Bund Oberland was convened. After executing my daily duties about which I will have more to say later, I announced to the individual group leaders that I was certain the time was at hand for the first step toward realization of our aims.

JUDGE NEITHARDT: Was it expressly agreed at the meeting of November 7 not to inform Ludendorff, so that he would have a free hand? Is that correct?

HERR WEBER: That had been mentioned that morning or noon.

Concerning the events in the Bürgerbräukeller, Dr. Weber remarks, "That's correct—according to the original plans, Kahr, Lossow, and Seisser would be called to the telephone." Why another plan of action would be chosen was a mystery to him. When he entered the back room, Kahr was standing at the win-

dow, Lossow was smoking a cigar and leaning against a chair, and Seisser stood near the doors. Besides Hitler, only his body-guard was present. The allegation that guns were thrust through the windows and pointed into the room is not true. There were only two guards patrolling outside and they had shouldered their rifles. When Ludendorff requested General Lossow's assistance, Lossow placed both hands on his saber and said, "Your Excellency, your wish is my command." Seisser made a statement to the same effect.

HERR WEBER: General Lossow, the Generalstaatskommissar, and I, never had too much in common but I came into closer personal and political contact with Colonel Seisser. I can only say that when he spoke to General Ludendorff he was dead serious. There were doubtless tears in his eyes. Seisser pledged his assistance honestly and openly.

Dr. Weber made his way from the Bürgerbräukeller to the Pioneer barracks, where an Oberland battalion under Herr Müller was held in check.

HERR WEBER: Müller had opened his sealed envelope at 8:30, and his written orders were to guard the train station in order to maintain order and to prevent packs of Eastern Jews from escaping with bundles of stocks and bonds. I never dreamt of a change in the attitude of Kahr and Seisser on the night of November 8. At 2:00 I established a telephone connection between Ludendorff and Seisser. I also spoke a few words with Seisser. When Ludendorff asked what was happening with Lossow, Seisser explained that everything was in perfect order and he was just going to drive to the Pioneer barracks in order to coordinate the matter with Bund Oberland, and would then pick up Lossow at 19th Regiment headquarters. There could be no doubt about Lossow's promise. I believe that Herr Scheubner-Richter expressed his doubts that night and I remember how Ludendorff forbade that kind of talk. Lossow had given him his word. A German officer did not break his word.

In answer to the Presiding Judge's question, Dr. Weber answers that the wording of the speeches in the hall was correctly recorded in the Münchener Neusten Nachrichten. *As Dr. Gerlich told him on the night of November 9, only a few passages were deleted in view of foreign policy considerations.*

JUDGE NEITHARDT: You are supposed to have ordered Berchtold to cross the Isar south of the city if possible, because some segments of the Reichswehr were not yet reliable.

HERR WEBER: I don't remember that at all. If I said that, I probably meant incidents, like at the Pioneer barracks.

JUDGE NEITHARDT: When did you first receive a reliable report on the change of attitude in Kahr, Lossow, and Seisser?

HERR WEBER: I never got a reliable report. We found that out when they started shooting at us.

JUDGE NEITHARDT: But you read the proclamation before the shooting began.

HERR WEBER: I saw it for the first time as we were marching into the city. One of my men ran over and told me what was in it. It was true the order to unload the rifles was given beforehand. It was not my responsibility to see that it was carried out. The purpose of the march was to ascertain the mood of the city and to make propaganda. We wanted to carry the idea of a people's dictatorship into the city and to sample the atmosphere in the city.

Then Dr. Weber describes the approach to the Feldherrnhalle.

HERR WEBER: At the head of the column were National Socialist and Oberland flags. I see it all clearly now. An officer of the Landespolizei, subsequently identified as First Lieutenant Godin, wrenched a carbine from one of his men and poked it in the chest of one of the flag bearers, an Oberlander. He knocked the carbine away with the standard. I am positive that the gun went off, so this seems to have been the first shot. And I can still see clearly how a stocky, broad-shouldered Nazi jumped out and cried, "Don't shoot! His Excellency Ludendorff is coming!" In the next instant, he was hit and he crumpled to the ground. All of us were temporarily frozen. At once, a withering volley of fire was laid down by security police carbines. A few of them attacked with rifle butts. At the last moment I saw a group of Landespolizei swarm out onto the balcony of the Feldherrnhalle and commence shooting down on the wounded and the retreating men like they were wild animals. Even some of the dead and wounded were struck a second time. I threw myself on the ground.

When I regained my senses and the shooting stopped, I saw His Excellency Ludendorff go from the Odeonsplatz to the Residenz, accompanied by Major Streck. I caught up to Ludendorff and entered the Residenz with him. I was all broken up inside that something as unbelievable as this could happen in nationalistic Bavaria; that the supposedly nationally oriented Landespolizei would fire on our greatest German war hero. This was so unbearable for me that I was delirious for the next few hours and was overcome by convulsive sobs.

No one in the Bund Oberland had known about the action. It went without saying that they carried the orders contained in sealed envelopes. Any guilt or blame can never be laid to the other members of Bund Oberland. I would like to assert that when the plan for the 8th was submitted to me on the 7th, I immediately joined Hitler's side of my own free will, fully conscious of the consequences. It was my self-evident duty to join. There was no undue pressure exerted upon me. I would also like to emphasize that Kriebel is in no construable way responsible for these political decisions and resolutions.

JUDGE NEITHARDT: Herr Weber, how did you imagine things would later turn out?

HERR WEBER: On the basis of my knowledge of conditions in North Germany, I knew that many factions of the patriotic movement there wanted what we in Southern Bavaria wanted. I knew that perhaps too great a hope was placed on Bavaria—that the nation's cure would come from here. It was obvious to me that the impetus had to come from Bavaria. As I subsequently learned—Reichswehr Minister Gessler mentioned this in a speech in Württemberg—the events in Munich caused broad segments of people in North Germany to put out feelers in Bavaria concerning the thrust of this action at Berlin. If these three men had not played it so close to the vest, if they had not broken their promise in such a despicable manner, I am completely convinced that our goal in Germany would have been achieved. To me, the final goal of the action was to carry the tricolor high over the Rhine after settling domestic affairs.

JUDGE NEITHARDT: You were certain that the action could only succeed in union with the Reichswehr and the Landespolizei.

HERR WEBER: That was understood.

With that, Dr. Weber winds up his testimony. Now follows a series of questions from the defense and prosecution.

HERR HOLL: Did you order the occupation of the Pioneer barracks?

HERR WEBER: No, never.

HERR HOLL: Were you aware that, at the end of October, the directives of personnel in the Ministry of the Army simply were not carried out?

HERR WEBER: Yes, I was aware of it.

The defendant will introduce three instances as proof. He explains that since he and his friends had sworn an oath of loyalty to Bavaria, the Weimar Constitution automatically ceased to apply to Bavaria for them, and it was abrogated by the legal Bavarian statutes.

JUDGE NEITHARDT: Now, how do you square this with the remarks you made, at a hearing on November 16, that only a violent revision of the Reich Constitution could lead to your objective? You were convinced that the Reich Constitution was null and void.

HERR WEBER: Because it was null and void, it should be done away with by force.

Dr. Weber discloses, in response to a question by Herr Luetgebrune, that he had a "quid pro quo" discussion with Colonel Seisser. This discussion took place on the evening of November 1. The plan for assignation of portfolios called for Ludendorff as commander in chief of the national army, Kahr as regent of Bavaria, Lossow as Reichswehr Minister, Seisser as Minister of Reich police, and Hitler as leader of the struggle in the role of general supervisor, modeled after Lloyd George.

HERR HOLL: How was it that the arrested ministers were brought to the Lehmann villa?

JUDGE NEITHARDT: You are Lehmann's stepson?

HERR WEBER: That's correct. I believe that someone asked

84

Captain Göring: "Where do we take the prisoners into custody?" Tölz also mentioned them. I said, "If they're not to be taken far, perhaps you can take them to Grosshesselohe, to the Lehmann's villa." No one informed Herr Lehmann, either before or after. The Lehmann family, who had witnessed the proclamation in the Bürgerbräukeller, were extremely surprised by the quartering of the men there. I chose the villa because I knew that there were enough rooms available.

HERR STENGLEIN: When was this conversation with Göring?

HERR WEBER: In the Bürgerbräukeller, when Hitler was negotiating with the others.

JUDGE NEITHARDT: Did you know why Count Soden was arrested?

HERR WEBER: No.

The discussion continues, revolving chiefly around the November 6 session in the Generalstaatskommissariat. In response to Herr Kohl's question, Dr Weber explains he interpreted the threat offered there as a threat against the Erhardt troops. The Erhardt troops and the Bund Bayern und Reich were expressly warned that they no longer enjoyed the support of the Reichswehr or the Landespolizei.

JUDGE NEITHARDT: Lossow is supposed to have said that he would proceed against the bands *manu militari.*

HERR WEBER: I don't recall that expression.

Attorney Gademann asks Dr. Weber if he ever heard Lossow express that he wanted to march to Berlin himself, or that he would join any coup.

HERR WEBER: Yes, sir.

HERR GADEMANN: Did you know that patriotic bands from the other side had been invited to an assembly on November 11?

HERR WEBER: I only learned of that subsequently.

HERR GADEMANN: Were you aware from a conversation on November 8 that standing troops in North Germany would have nothing against a march on Berlin? Was the subject ever brought up in any meeting?

HERR WEBER: Yes, indeed. It was repeatedly mentioned in conversations with Colonel Seisser that the state's forces—above all, the Reichswehr—would surely not commit themselves if the action was taken under the tricolor, under a new Reich government with Ludendorff in charge. There would be a collision if the action was presented as a purely Bavarian affair. General Lossow also endorsed this view.

HERR SCHRAMM: Did the conversations in the back room of the Bürgerbräukeller impress you as being very cordial, or were they more in the nature of a dispute?

HERR WEBER: Well, I really couldn't call it a dispute. When a quarrel is in progress, one side does not offer the other cigars and cigarettes. When Colonel Seisser had finished a cigarette, I offered him another. Later, Lossow came up to me and said, "Have you got another cigarette?"

Laughter.

HERR WEBER: I had no idea that the three men were forbidden to speak with one another.

HERR SCHRAMM: It is alleged that in spite of your efforts to keep the men from speaking with one another, they succeeded in calling out the word "comedy." Wouldn't you have heard that?

HERR WEBER: I would have heard the word "comedy." In my opinion, the gentlemen could not have been thinking about playing games. Otherwise, Herr Kahr would not have grappled so long with his conscience and asked if we were monarchists.

In response to Herr Hemmeter's question, Dr. Weber states that in a conversation around October 20, at which representatives of patriotic bands were present, including Professor Bauer and Dr. Pittinger, it was pointed out that the time for preparations was over; that it was high time to move unless we wished to risk everything.

HERR HEMMETER: Was there anything mentioned in this connection about what office—in what capacity—Herr Pöhner would serve?

HERR WEBER: I had known since the middle of October that Herr Kahr had recommended Pöhner for the office of General-staatskommissar over Saxony and Thuringia at the beginning of the action. Pöhner retorted that things hadn't come so far that we could do this from Bavaria.

Herr Schramm states the November 6 session appears to be of extreme importance. He asks the Judge and the District Attorney whether they have the minutes of this session in their possession.

HERR SCHRAMM: If not, why hasn't the prosecution taken the effort to procure a copy? It certainly exists because it was later read.

JUDGE NEITHARDT: I am not aware of any transcript. Dr. Weber is supposed to have made stenographic notes, but none were found.

HERR SCHRAMM: At the time it was read, General Epp had it.

HERR ZEZSCHWITSCH: As far as I know, General Epp is present here.

Schramm requests permission to ask General Epp whether such a transcript exists.

JUDGE NEITHARDT: Please step forward, Herr General Epp. Do you know something about such a transcript?

HERR EPP: Who is supposed to have written the transcript?

HERR SCHRAMM: Didn't you invite a group of people to your home, where Herr Hörauf read the transcript?

General Epp states that he knows nothing about it. When Herr Schramm reminds him that witnesses are here, General Epp raises his booming voice to say that there is no cause to take him to task in public. Thereupon, General Epp makes his way to his seat.

HERR EHARD: Are you aware that the efforts in the Kampf-bund for this march on Berlin—this pressure—that these efforts to exert pressure and pursue your own ends had been made several months before the Generalstaatskommissariat had organized?

HERR WEBER: I reject the term "our ends." We always pursued German ends. That's correct; these efforts to pressure Berlin or to march on Berlin do extend far back. They go back to the time when the patriotic movement began.

HERR EHARD: I've had enough of this. By the way, you seem to be very testy because I said "our ends." You seem to believe that the Kampfbund alone can achieve national German ends.

HERR WEBER: It has pursued them most avidly.

HERR EHARD: Haven't you ever heard that General Ludendorff has very little sway in the Reichswehr, particularly in North Germany?

Commotion in the audience.

JUDGE NEITHARDT: I request that you direct your questions to me.

HERR EHARD: I wish to ask the question because it is crucial; namely, the question of whether the Reichswehr, even with Ludendorff in command, would use force?

HERR WEBER: On the basis of my knowledge of the North German Officers Corps, I must say that reverence predominates for the greatest German commander and general who ever graced Germany not only in the last War, but in all German history. Therefore, the possibility of such a situation is practically nil.

HERR EHARD: That's what I wanted to know.

HERR KOHL: That's what you didn't want to know. Your question was insulting to a German officer of such stature, and you ought to have received an answer like the one you just heard.

Applause in the audience. The Judge gavels order.

HERR EHARD: I remind you that there will be witnesses who will express similar views. I haven't expressed my own personal opinion.

Ehard then asks Dr. Weber whether he heard what was said between Major Hunglinger and Herr Lossow in the back room of the Bürgerbräukeller when Dr. Weber reminded the men that

88

they were forbidden to speak to one another.

HERR WEBER: The gentlemen did not speak with one another. Lossow called Hunglinger over, but I told Hunglinger to forget about talking to Lossow until the situation was cleared up.

HERR EHARD: Did you know that agreements had been reached that the march was to break through even if the police tried to stop it?

HERR WEBER: Of course we planned to break through. After the incident at the Ludwig Bridge, we didn't think about Landespolizei stopping us.

Herr Roder wants to ascertain the degree of freedom of movement of the men in the back room of the Bürgerbräukeller. He requests permission to ask whether the men moved freely. Dr. Weber replies in the affirmative. Only Herr Kahr sat for a long time at the table; later he stood up.

JUDGE NEITHARDT: A guard was posted at the door?

HERR WEBER: Outside the door.

JUDGE NEITHARDT: So that they couldn't leave the room.

Upon further questioning, Dr. Weber states that no attack was intended at all during the march, and that he did not observe that the Hitler Shock Troops had fixed bayonets. Hitler remarks that he did not know this either.

HERR KOHL: Was there an advance party in the march?

HERR WEBER: No, the flags constituted our advance party.

Herr Kohl then asks if Herr der Pfordten marched with them.

HERR WEBER: He marched with us out of the Bürgerbräukeller.

In reply to another question, Weber terms it physically impossible to have stopped or reversed the march when the Landespolizei ordered it.

HERR RODER: Is it correct to say that no action was taken when a crowd of civilians separated the leaders from other marchers so that the marchers couldn't have taken any action because there were people in between?

HERR WEBER: That is absolutely correct.

With that, the cross-examination ends. The examination of a few points is postponed for a closed session.
Hitler takes the stand again to elucidate his position on the well-known letter of Lieutenant Colonel Kriebel.

HERR HITLER: On the afternoon of the 7th, a letter from Captain Göring was handed to me. Göring explained that the letter was posted to obtain contact with Group C, the Erhardt organization. A few days before, I had had an inconclusive meeting with Erhardt. My military staff was convinced that it would be to our advantage to come to terms with Erhardt. This gesture would be the bridge to Group C. I approved the letter without a great deal of fuss. Its purpose was to assure the only organization which might be affected by the statement that we would support them and that unruly groups would not be supported.

JUDGE NEITHARDT: With what?

HERR HITLER: With our propaganda machine and public opinion.

HERR EHARD: The letter doesn't mention propaganda machines, but rather military power.

HERR HITLER: Because Lieutenant Colonel Kriebel wrote it.

At this point the hearing is recessed, to reconvene at 2:00 p.m., the same day.

Presiding Judge Neithardt opens the session at 2:00 o'clock with the observation that a rumor, which had reached his ears, was spreading about a remark that he had supposedly made yesterday—"Herr Hitler, I regret that I didn't meet you sooner." He wishes to emphasize that not one word is true.

Hitler remarks that he doesn't need to emphasize that; nothing was done by him to start the rumor.

The testimony of Herr Pöhner begins.

HERR PÖHNER: If I have played a role in this affair, then it can be understood from the viewpoint which evolved from my experiences of the events of 1918. After four years of service at the front lines, I returned to witness the collapse of the home front. I could see the forces at work—even on leave, unlike at the front lines—that strove for the ruin of the German Reich. When I came home from the field, I had to take a stand on the so-called "revolution." Or, more correctly, that crime not only of high treason and betrayal of country, but also betrayal of the people.

At that time I had been a royal judge and officer for 20 years. I watched in rage as racial aliens perpetrated traitorous acts against my people in the name of freemasonry. I watched in rage as officers changed their opinions with acrobatic agility and swiftness in this time of betrayal and how, after the November crime, they suddenly presented a face different from the one they had been wearing for the past 10 or 20 years. I was enraged to see how high officials prostrated themselves before such people as that Jew Kosmanowski, and called them "Excellency." I was enraged to see how General Staff officers ran around with red armbands in Munich, Nurnberg, and Würzburg. It was clear to me that I would never dishonor my oath to the flag and my oath as a judge. I never made a secret of my attitude. I always detested officials and officers who assured me, to a certain extent, under an oath of silence, that they too were monarchists and patriots.

I also expressed my basic opinions unreservedly in my later functions. After I had assumed my post again as Landgerichtsrat, I declared myself ready, at the behest of the Ministry of Justice, to take over the management of the Stadelheim maximum security prison. I repeat, "at the behest of the Justice Ministry." I was called out of the session then. I immediately declared that I naturally denied any responsibility to these new authorities, and would only heed the instructions of my superior, Oberststaatsanwalt Baron von Sartor, who was close to me. I knew him from the civil court and we held similar views. This was on January 10, 1919, when the resolution was still in full bloom. To this day, I am proud that my first act was to tear down the Red tatters. At that time, the prison was the only building without a Red flag. I persisted in my attitude up until the liberation of Munich, even during the Soviet period.

I did not deviate one inch from this, my belief, when I took over the function of police president. I did not force myself on this office; I accepted it at the behest of the Ministry of Justice. I was certain I would come into conflict with the authorities who were, after all, partly authors and partly beneficiaries of the November crime. The conflicts with Social Democracy are well-known.

My acquaintance with Herr von Kahr dates from this time. As President of Upper Bavaria, he was my immediate superior. I learned to respect him highly. He and I held the same belief, namely that what had transpired the previous November was a crime. He was a monarchial official of the old school and thus I got along very well with him. I sincerely respected him because he walked a straight line, and also he had the courage to cover me, during my orientation, with his own authority as Oberststaatsanwalt von Sartor had once done. I made no secret of my beliefs to my subordinates, either. Furthermore, I didn't when it was a question of reorganizing police headquarters, for its quality had suffered considerably in the past half year. For the most important post at police headquarters, head of the newly created Political Division, I chose Oberamtmann Dr. Frick, because I judged, from his behavior during the revolution, that he would make no secret of his convictions and that he would never be a "yes-man."

As Police President, I was, of course, in a position to meet many similarly minded people who were members of the patriotic movement which had lately sprung up and expressed itself in various forms and structures. I knew the people who were active in the Old Home Guard, Bund Oberland, later the National Socialist Party, and in other organizations from this time. And it was from this time on that the leaders of these organizations began to trust me, because I was an opponent of Marxism and because I supported any movement on behalf of the Fatherland. After my resignation as Police President, I kept in touch with these people although, at that time, there was no external reason for me to concern myself with the problems of the public—of political life. After returning to the judicial life, I had completely removed myself from political party machinations. I never even went to elections! I always considered the party system a cancer on our society. In 1922, Herr von Kahr and I became estranged, because I couldn't understand why he had failed to break with a party that had attacked him. During 1923, I met with Herr Kahr only twice. One time was in casual conversation with Herr Kahr and various men in January, just after the outbreak of the Ruhr conflict. I didn't meet him again until September 30, shortly before Kahr had been appointed Generalstaatskommissar.

Different sides demanded that I work with Herr Kahr again. I resisted because I harbored doubts about Herr Kahr's ability to make necessary decisions in difficult situations, and I wasn't sure he had the fortitude to persevere. I later told him so to his face. Nevertheless, I met him once more when a most authoritative figure expressed a desire that I might put aside personal differences and resume relations. The ulterior motive was stated at a meeting the day before that, through the offices of a certain Captain Erhardt.

This could probably be discussed better in secret session.

Luetgebrune requests exclusion of the public for this purpose.

HERR PÖHNER: So that I can tell my story *in continuo*, I will now omit anything that might endanger national interests, and reveal it in closed session. I was requested to grant Erhardt different concessions by some North German gentlemen whom Erhardt had brought from Austria, or wherever he was staying.

On the afternoon of September 24, I invited him to my home. On this occasion, Lieutenant Erhardt told me there were people who were serious about marching on Berlin, and that I might seek an accommodation with Herr von Kahr to this end because if he set about raising troops in North Bavaria, a lot would depend, strategically, on the North Bavarian area for troop deployment and communications to be secure. It must also be guaranteed, he said, that acts of sabotage, disruption of rail lines, and other such incidents can be prevented. On that same afternoon, Frick was visiting. I was unable to reject, out of hand, the proposals of Erhardt and his companions that it would be in the national interest to work with Kahr again. Erhardt suggested that I try to become Staatskommissar in order to obtain a mandate for North Bavaria. I called and made the appointment with Herr Kahr the next morning at 8:30 in his office on Maximilianstrasse.

At the same time, I contacted Lt. Col. Kriebel, since he was Chief of General Staff at Escherich and I was well acquainted with him. Herr Kriebel stopped frequently at my office; I knew he was the military leader of the Kampfbund and, therefore, I wanted to speak to him first. I intended to clear up a few political and military exigencies and eventualities with Frick and Kriebel so that the next day I could present Kahr with clearly worded and well-thought-out proposals. Kriebel also prevailed upon me to work in conjunction with Kahr, and I couldn't ignore this necessity, for the sake of the Fatherland.

Thus, it was to Kahr's advantage, then, as a source of power with dictatorial prerogatives, to win over the whole patriotic movement as one of his prospective tasks. However, I realized that he had failed since behind him he had only organizations like the Home Guard—organizations made up of elderly and immobile people who lacked resoluteness in their political convictions. By and large, these people were convinced that law and order was the highest principle in Bavaria and were devoid of any other political ideas. Herr Kahr was also unsuccessful in enlisting the support of other organizations, such as the National Socialist Storm Troopers, Bund Oberland, the Reichskriegs-flagge, and a majority of the students. The aforementioned had all united in the Kampfbund, who took a partly expectant, partly stand-offish and totally suspicious attitude towards Herr Kahr. This activist movement had a pronounced nationalistic character. These were people who had spent almost the entire war at the front. They weren't home fighters, and they weren't pack mules; they were front-line fighters. In their minds they saw not Herr Kahr, but Adolph Hitler as their natural leader.

I knew that the leaders of the popular organizations had great trust in me, from before. Thus, when Frick and Erhardt convinced me that I would be in a position to gather even the aloof factions—the activist groups—under the Kahr banner, I couldn't shirk my duty; and so I asked Kriebel to go with me to see Herr Kahr.

Herr Kahr objected to Herr Kriebel's presence, and asked if he came as leader of the Kampfbund. I said, no, he hadn't; I had asked him to accompany me as a sort of military expert. Thereupon, Herr Kahr dropped his reservations concerning Herr Kriebel's presence. At Herr Kahr's invitation, Colonel von Seisser was included in the discussion. After saying the North must be cleared out, Herr Kahr proposed that I take the mantle of civil governor of Saxony and Thuringia, if I was ready. The proposal took me somewhat by surprise. I explained that Erhardt thought it desirable for me to take over the Kommissariat for North Bavaria. Herr Kahr rejected this, saying he could not further transfer the authority conferred upon him, and that he was not empowered to do so. Then he repeated his proposal of my assuming the position as civil governor of Saxony and Thuringia.

Pöhner now defines why he didn't accept the offer; that, in particular, the relationship of the civil governor to the commander of the Reichswehr was very unclear. Kahr told Pöhner that his relationship to the Reichswehr commander would be defined in a manner similar to the way in which service regulations provided for the military in cases of disturbances.

HERR PÖHNER: In this way, said Kahr, Colonel von Seisser would be able to give me more information. The same relationship would exist, on a smaller scale, between me and the commander of the Reichswehr in Saxony and Thuringia, as between Kahr and Lossow in Bavaria.

Now Kahr's relationship to Lossow was equally unclear. I had come to the conclusion that it was just impossible to know who was master and who was manservant in Bavaria. I had very little inclination to get myself involved in such a nebulous affair, and I answered evasively. Herr Kahr was obviously anxious lest I react negatively. He said, "You need not make a final decision today. Discuss it further with Colonel Seisser. I dare say, you have not refused." The discussion went harmoniously, if uneventfully, which was what Erhardt and the others thought desirable. This was the second conversation I had with Herr Kahr, in a year.

The next day I met with Colonel von Seisser. Kriebel had arranged the conference. I discussed with Colonel von Seisser, once again, the particulars and modalities by which Herr Kahr expected me to cooperate. I reminded Colonel von Seisser that, under the circumstances, I was placing myself in a precarious position and that I would have to take on a large political responsibility and I again emphasized that I had no desire to put myself on the rack a second time. I told him I would have to be certain of the nature and extent of Herr Kahr's power and of the kind and composition of this force. I also expressed my fear that if the power to give orders remained with the Commander of the Reichswehr, I would bear the responsibility, in the end; and that should the commander of the Reichswehr be afraid to accept the responsibility for far-reaching decisions, I would be in a precarious position.

Colonel von Seisser told me that he would see to it that a cooperative man would be entrusted with the office. He mentioned General Danner's name; I agreed. I was merely voicing the concern that finding the right persons would not, by itself, be any guarantee. I asked him whether the Kampfbund troops might not be used; that if Lieutenant Colonel Kriebel were serving as leader of the Kampfbund, it was clear to me I would have the assistance of someone I could rely on under any circumstances. Colonel von Seisser said that this would be impossible; the troops wouldn't be content to stop in Saxony, they'd keep on marching. I made no secret of my doubts about their competence. I said to Colonel von Seisser that I was unable to overcome my fear that Herr Kahr would be able to make a good start, but that he would be unable to go forward and might be vulnerable to outside influences; and, if so, I would be in "hot water," so to speak. I couldn't make up my mind whether to accept the proposal or not.

That was the only conversation I had with Colonel von Seisser. I didn't meet with General von Lossow at all. I spoke with him, in March or April, for quite different reasons, but during that time I didn't see Lossow at all. For me, the affair had been decided by itself, and I personally had no interests whatever in trying to make it work.

Pöhner remarks that the political development of October 1923, with its ferment and serious economic plight, was well known. He further stated that there was mounting agitation in all quarters due to the disastrous economic policies pursued by the government.

HERR PÖHNER: Since I stood outside and had a "bird's-eye-view," so to speak, of the developing political situation, it was perfectly clear that sooner or later it would have to explode. I found my observations were confirmed by statements I occasionally heard from men in the Kampfbund. I spoke to Dr. Scheubner-Richter, whom I often met on my walks, and he stopped me long enough to give me very precise information from the mouth of Erhardt himself.

Erhardt visited me again about the middle of October. When I asked him how he liked Munich now, he replied that it was "the pits." I was somewhat surprised by this expression, for I had expected the exact opposite. There was a warrant for his arrest in Leipzig, and a wanted poster had been issued. I knew he had received safe conduct from Colonel von Seisser's police, and an I.D. card, according to which he was an auxiliary police-man for the Bavarian Government.

Erhardt explained to me that there had been no progress, and asked me to arrange a meeting with Hitler. I was aware that there was tension between the National Socialists and the Wickingbund. I set up the meeting, which was postponed once, and which finally took place on November 7. Erhardt called me the same day and told me the meeting had been fruitless—and that was the end of my involvement in the events that took place in September, October, and the beginning of November.

Now, naturally, it didn't escape me that the agitation of the action-oriented groups, particularly Oberland and the Erhardt Organization, could cause an explosion. I was also not entirely unaware that the same phenomenon had attracted notice. The signs were the same everywhere. I also knew that North Germany was in a state of turmoil.

This was the state of affairs when I visited Hitler on the morning of November 8—not the 7th, as stated in the indictment. Hitler informed me that it was now necessary to come to the aid of the men who had resolved to start the march on

97

Berlin—Kahr, Lossow, and Seisser—and remove the Reich government. They, themselves, could not afford to stoop to illegal action, but that they would put up with it if they were presented with a *fait accompli*, just as they put up with it in 1918. Hitler detailed to me how he saw the affair, and how he envisioned the initial phase—Hitler has already covered this ground in his testimony. He wanted to use the November 8 assembly as his stage through which he envisioned the "affair," if I may use that expression, progressing rapidly from here, and then the German problem would be brought to a boil, the forces set in motion, and a national uprising through all Germany would be accomplished.

I found Hitler's reflections thoroughly enlightening. I felt the explosion would be immediate. Inside, I was overjoyed that finally someone had come to the fore who possessed the courage to take the lead and force these men who lacked the strength to take the leap; someone who could create a new climate through which action can be taken. Hitler said that he would continue to produce propaganda, by himself, and that he wanted to feed a spiritual revolution within Germany, and that Excellency Ludendorff was destined to head a National Army which would have to be organized, at once.

Pöhner then mentions the well-known distribution of offices and testifies that Hitler had asked him if he was ready to take over the position of president, here in Bavaria.

HERR PÖHNER: Hitler made no secret of his conviction that Kahr was capable of prevailing as regent only if he had someone of competence supporting him. Hitler asked me if I was ready. The proposal itself took me by surprise, but I was satisfied, at this juncture, that here was someone, finally, who had the fortitude to act. I therefore answered, when asked, "Yes, I'm in." I gave Hitler my hand. I told him, again, that I didn't want the office; and that, as a judge, I would take a vacation so that I could help Herr Kahr find a safer position.

Hitler was with me for approximately one hour. I expressed my unconditional approval of his proposal. I felt the deciding factor was that inevitably as events began to climax, the position of Generalstaatskommissar would be precarious so long as the patriotic factions remained divided, and that I could be of valuable service as a liaison man between Hitler and Kahr since I was convinced I could persuade the whole nationalist movement to support Kahr. Therefore I replied affirmatively, without hesitation.

In the Bürgerbräukeller

I was at the assembly in the Bürgerbräukeller that evening—I probably don't need to relate what happened. I was sitting immediately below the podium, next to General Count von Bothmer.

During the time Herr Hitler was outside the hall, in the back room with the three men, a great disturbance erupted in the main hall. Count Bothmer had tried to reassure the crowd by saying that no one intended to harm Herr Kahr, but his voice was lost in the hubbub. Kommerzienrat Zentz asked me if I would say a few words to the assembly and assured me I would have a calming effect on the crowd. I therefore agreed to speak to the assembly since they had obviously gotten the wrong impression as to the purpose of the putsch. Thus, at Kommerzienrat Zentz's request, I mounted the podium in an effort to explain to the assembly what was happening.

I had scarcely begun to speak when an officer forced his way onto the stage and asked me to accompany him to the back room. In the cloak-room between the main and side hall, I encountered Dr. Weber. Herr Hitler was still in the back room and while I was talking to Dr. Weber, Hitler came out and went back into the main hall. Dr. Weber and I then went to the back room since we thought it best not to leave the three men alone, and we could keep them company. These men were distraught over the turn of events, which were totally contrary to their conception. As Dr. Weber was conversing with Colonel von Seisser, I turned to speak to Herr Kahr. I explained the situation to Kahr, and asked him if he would not join us. Herr Kahr, being extremely angry and very indignant about the whole episode, exclaimed that it was unheard of to shanghai him from a hall in the middle of his speech; he was so angry that he refused to do anything. I replied that this government of revolutionaries must finally be eradicated. Herr Kahr merely retorted, "Incredible, that they would shanghai me, like this!"—that was his main objection! He then proclaimed, "You must tell a person before you do something like that. You can't just kidnap someone like a brigand! You could have waited 8 or 10 days." He had sent his men to North Germany in order to secure an agreement with certain officials there.

99

While I was conversing with Herr Kahr, Excellency Ludendorff entered in the company of, I believe, Dr. Scheubner-Richter—however, he turned around at the door. Excellency Ludendorff greeted the three men; first Herr Kahr, then Lossow, then Seisser. He then returned to Herr Kahr to implore him not to refuse this call going out to him now, in this fateful hour of the German Reich; to do what we all were ardently expecting of him. Herr Kahr reacted negatively. Ludendorff then spoke with Lossow. The details of this conversation escaped me, because we had formed two groups. Ludendorff addressed Lossow in a hearty, comradely fashion. At first, Lossow kept a very neutral bearing. He neither rejected nor accepted. Lossow was visibly moved by Ludendorff's cordial talk.

Finally, Ludendorff said to Lossow: "Right, then, Lossow; come with us and let's shake on it!" Lossow, who at first stood there seemingly downcast and uncomprehending, regained his composure, snapped to attention, shook Ludendorff's hand and declared his approval. I cannot say in what form he gave his approval. Excellency Ludendorff was speaking loudly and clearly; Lossow softly. The long and short of it was that he gave his approval. It was our salvation that Ludendorff had succeeded in bringing about Lossow's collaboration. I was inwardly happy that the two soldiers had found a common ground for cooperation. Immediately thereafter, without the slightest objection, Seisser, of his own accord, stretched his hand out to Ludendorff and happily shook it. I had the impression—and I'm not mistaken—that Colonel Seisser had been waiting for Lossow to shake hands, and Colonel Seisser happily extended his hand, by himself.

In the meantime, Dr. Weber and I were speaking with Herr Kahr. We continued to press him for his consent, but we were still unsuccessful. Herr Kahr gave the impression that he was very angry and personally insulted by Hitler's actions. Ludendorff then turned to Kahr and spoke to him most cordially. He told Kahr that he could not deny the German people in this hour. Herr Kahr was timid—almost meek—and said the affair wasn't right; it would have to stop; that we had to wait; it could have been done 8 or 10 days from now. I banished that fear by saying that if it would work in 8 or 10 days, it would work now, and that everything wouldn't hinge on one or two people from North Germany. The names of Kahr and Ludendorff would be so attractive and would sound so good that if the movement were introduced under those two names, and if Herr Hitler who knows how to influence the masses were added, I had no doubt about the outcome of the matter.

Herr Kahr could not quite accept these considerations either. He suddenly raised a new objection: "I can't join in," he said, "because I'm a monarchist. I am the representative of the King here, and without the consent of the King I can't do anything." I replied to Herr Kahr, "Excellency, that is also my viewpoint. We have always worked together on this ground because we are both monarchists and royal officials; and, as such, you have an obligation now, when it is a matter of quelling a revolution, to show your true colors. We may not place ourselves behind the king, but in front of him; and we may not involve him in this intrigue. As officials of the Crown, we have a duty to prove ourselves, through action, as men who cherish the old traditions."

Herr Hitler, who had entered the conversation and practically begged Kahr, immediately refuted Kahr's objection and said: "Yes, Your Excellency, there has been a grave injustice to the monarchy, which was so shamelessly victimized by the criminals of 1918, and this must be corrected. If Your Excellency permits, I will drive immediately to His Majesty and inform him that the German uprising will repair the injustice inflicted upon His Majesty's late father." Herr Kahr could not resist these sentiments and thereupon pronounced his unconditional agreement and gave his consent. He said he would join with us but would only take the office of King's Deputy.

As we were about to leave the back room, Herr Kahr insisted that he didn't want to return to the assembly. He would be ashamed to return to a gathering from which he had been shanghaied. He would have his declaration given by proxy. I said that that was impossible. Hitler told him the people would hail him. Finally, Herr Kahr dropped his last defense. I don't need to relate further events since they were well publicized by the press and have already been the subject of the testimony here.

From the preceding events, as they played themselves out in the back room, I left with the impression that these three men had given their earnest approval and would not quibble or twist the meaning of it. I never dreamed that these men would have inner reservations and that they would only pretend to cooperate. I still today believe that to be absolutely impossible and out of the question. I continue to believe that it is impossible for Lossow to hold these beliefs, because it is unthinkable that a German general would give his hand to General Ludendorff while maintaining a secret reservation. I had the feeling that Colonel von Seisser—I'm not deceiving myself here; I know him well—was merely waiting for the ranking general to give the approval for which he desperately awaited. This corresponds to his Greater German orientation, which I always assumed he had. Inwardly, he was happy that the hour of salvation was at hand.

Concerning the actions of Herr Kahr—the man, of the three, I know best—I could understand his hesitation. I understood that it was a natural reaction to what he thought was a gross insult and indignity. However, the assertion that he held a reservation and only pretended to collaborate, or that he wanted to play games, this is absolutely untrue. And if Herr Kahr is claiming this, then he is perpetuating falsehoods, to his disavantage. I feel that such a representation is so inconsistent with his character that, official explanations to the contrary, I find the whole claim false.

Now, as to the events themselves in the hall, I don't need to say anything. Herr Kahr was received with frenetic joy. I had often witnessed how Kahr had been the object of applause at large gatherings, but I have never experienced such a spontaneous, intense, and frenetic storm of applause like the one received by Kahr that night. After the announcements, we returned to the back room. I asked Herr Kahr when he wanted to discuss the composition of the new cabinet with me. I proposed that we should do it immediately. He had relaxed, somewhat, and told me to meet him the next morning at 9:00 o'clock. It was his belief that the replacement of the Minister of Agriculture, and the problem of police authority were the most pressing issues. He confided that he had earlier considered Hubert von Schilcher, the large landowner, a good choice for Minister of Agriculture but that, unfortunately, he had died a few weeks ago. He then focused on the police problem and immediately said to me: "You will want to have Frick as Police President. He is probably your own choice." I had already thought of recommending Frick for this post and so I said, "I am grateful to His Excellency for anticipating my wish with his proposal." Then Kahr said, "Frick will probably be the best man for the job, since you have worked with him for years and he still shares many opinions with you." Herr Kahr also brought up the question for discussion of how the populace should be informed. At first he seemed to want to make the announcement himself. However, Hitler quickly asked Kahr to leave that task to him; he would take care of all propaganda activities himself. He felt it would be better if the populace heard the news from him rather than Kahr. Herr Kahr agreed and asked me to look him up the next day. I went to police headquarters. I met with Oberamtmann Frick, who had to be given an accurate account of the events that had taken place. I described to him the events which had taken place in the Bürgerbräukeller and informed him of Herr Kahr's decision to have him take over the Police Presidium.

Frick said that of course he wanted to take the job, but would assume the position only in an official capacity. While I was speaking with Frick, Colonel Banzer came over and asked me to get rid of an officer with a steel helmet, who was constantly following him. I asked Colonel Banzer, "Can I rely on you, unconditionally?" I knew that Colonel Banzer had been over at the Bürgerbräukeller and was overjoyed with the outcome. He said, "Yes, sir, unconditionally!" Then, he shook my hand. I ordered the officer to stop following him.

Frick reminded me that it would be necessary to notify the provinces. I drove with Frick to Herr Kahr's office where we had to wait 45 minutes. Herr Kahr apologized for keeping us waiting so long but, he explained, he had just spoken with Minister Matt. He didn't say whether Matt was here, or whether he had spoken with him on the telephone. Kahr informed us that he not only had notified the president, but that he had also issued a circular which would be going to all officials. The text of the telegram was: "I have the government in my hands as Regent of Bavaria." Herr Kahr was in high spirits. Frick also had the impression that Kahr had put aside his annoyance of a few hours ago. He was thoroughly changed. Both of us were firmly convinced that—this was around midnight—Kahr was absolutely committed to the affair. Kahr left the meeting in a most cordial manner and repeated his invitation to meet with us the next day, as previously arranged.

We then drove to police headquarters where members of the press had been waiting for some time. I gave these men information about the events at the Bürgerbräukeller and further disclosed that Herr Kahr had dispatched a circular to all authorities. While I was still at police headquarters, a telephone report

103

came in saying that General von Lossow was nowhere to be found. We made inquiries at a number of places, but were unable to get any information as to his whereabouts. Communication with the Wehrkreiskommando was repeatedly broken off; evasive answers were given. I drove home to try and get some sleep. At about 4:00 o'clock in the morning I was awakened by the telephone. The caller was the Executive Editor of the *Münchener Neueste Nachrichten*, Dr. Gerlich, with whom I had spoken at about 1:00 o'clock at police headquarters. He demanded, "What is this supposed to mean?"—he had just received word from the publisher of the *Münchener Zeitung* that printing and distribution of morning editions would be punishable by death, according to the Generalstaatskommissar. I replied that that was sheer nonsense and obviously a fabrication; "Who released this message?" I asked Dr. Gerlich to call and ask Director Buchner, and to let me know as soon as he got an answer to my question. Dr. Gerlich asked me if the order had been issued by my camp. Naturally, I replied, "No," and said it was impossible that Herr Kahr would issue such an order. Dr. Gerlich also informed me that about 30,000 copies had already been sent out by *MNN*. Approximately 20 minutes later the phone rang again. Dr. Gerlich told me that Buchner had discovered that the order for the newspaper ban had come from the Generalstaatskommissariat. It was immediately clear that someone was giving out unauthorized information; I wanted to relay this fact to Frick, but I was unable to reach him because they couldn't locate him at police headquarters. Next, Herr Scheubner-Richter came to my home and asked me to come to the Wehrkreiskommando. He said that differences of opinion and misunderstandings had occurred there and that no one could find Herr Lossow. I then drove with Herr Scheubner-Richter to the Wehrkreiskommando—this was around 5:00 o'clock —and met with Ludendorff, Hitler, Röhm, Kriebel, in addition to several other men. We were in agreement that there was someone trying to sabotage us and discussed the best plan of action. After several different proposals had been rejected as inexpedient, Hitler proposed that public opinion be manipulated in a grand fashion in order to win the masses over to the recently begun national revolt. He felt that if one of the men, for example Herr Lossow, were to waiver that favorable public opinion might compensate for such a loss. Hitler also said that, above all, we should be sure the Kampfbund could seize and secure the police headquarters. I agreed to this proposition and immediately went to police headquarters accompanied by Major Hühnlein.

I went there completely unaware of the events which, in the meantime, had taken place. I asked an officer to tell me where Frick could be found and he said he was with Colonel Banzer, at the moment, and offered to take me to him at once, which he did. Looking down-trodden and distraught, Colonel Banzer—who had said a few hours before that I could count on him—answered my question as to whether he had seen Frick, by saying he had orders from the Generalstaatskommissar to arrest me. That hit me like a hammer! I asked, "Who ordered that? The General-staatskommissar, personally?" He answered, "Yes, the order came to police headquarters from the Generalstaatskommissar." I will reserve judgment at this time on this point. I do not care to discuss, in public session, the next occurrences, nor a number of points which pertain to the relations between Herr Kahr, Seisser, and Lossow.

JUDGE NEITHARDT: Didn't you tell anyone—even Frick—about the communique which Hitler had sent on the morning of November 8?

HERR PÖHNER: No one. In the preliminary hearings, District Attorney Dresse tried to force a statement from me implicating Frick. I stated, at the first hearing, that I would answer frankly any question put to me, but I ask you not to ask questions which would implicate any other persons because of course I will refuse to answer them. Nevertheless, the prosecution again tried to trick me into implicating Frick by suggesting I had spoken with him. I didn't speak with anyone, neither in person, on the tele-phone, in writing, verbally through another person, nor in any other form. I spoke only with Hitler. I think it is rather improb-able that Frick had any knowledge of these events since he obviously would not have come to me had he known. By virtue of our cooperation over the years, our relationship was grounded on absolute trust.

JUDGE NEITHARDT: Naturally, you knew there would be arrests.

HERR PÖHNER: I did not "know," but I assumed there might be. If I had known, I would have prevented one or more arrests; for example, Count Soden's. I didn't worry at all about such details.

JUDGE NEITHARDT: Were you aware that the three men in the back room of the Bürgerbräukeller were kept separated on purpose?

HERR PÖHNER: The room is rather large. They were standing around, unrestricted, and conversing with one another. Kahr, however, was standing in a corner. I went over to him because he was near me. I didn't notice any intentional separation of the men.

JUDGE NEITHARDT: Did you have any knowledge of the vandalism at the *Münchener Post* or the house searches around the Theresien Meadows?

HERR PÖHNER: I heard about them at the police station and ordered them halted.

JUDGE NEITHARDT: Did Hitler say, at 8:00 o'clock the next morning, "The Bavarian Government must be deposed," or was that already understood?

HERR PÖHNER: That was understood.

During questioning by the Prosecutor it is established that Ludendorff had turned to Lossow, not Seisser, in the back room of the Bürgerbräukeller; and that the previously contrary allegation was based on hearsay. It is further established, through Pöhner's interrogation, that the meeting with Kahr on the night of November 9 took place at his home, rather than at the Generalstaatskommissariat.

HERR SCHRAMM: The Generalstaatskommissar refused to appoint Herr Pöhner Staatskommissar of North Bavaria because he was not considered to be fully qualified.

I would like to ask the defendant whether Herr Kahr explained where he had gotten the authority to confer on him the position of Staatskommissar of Thuringia and Saxony?

HERR PÖHNER: I didn't ask him about that. One can only have such authority if one has taken the necessary steps.

HERR SCHRAMM: Herr Kahr probably clearly understood that the movement would be extended beyond Saxony and Thuringia.

HERR PÖHNER: Of course.

HERR STENGLEIN: Was it a question of marching on Berlin, or, rather, of guarding Bavaria's borders against Communist agitation in Saxony and Thuringia?

HERR PÖHNER: I had the firm impression, based on the fact that Kahr and Erhardt stood in close relation, that it was a matter of greater magnitude than Bavarian border patrols. There was no question about this. Erhardt would hardly let himself be night-watchman for Bavaria, between Nürnberg and Hof.

HERR HOLL: Would you have taken over as civilian governor before, or after?

HERR PÖHNER: The question answers itself—Did a civil governor invade Belgium first, or did the troops? Kahr said the North must be cleaned up. It was quite clear what he meant.

In response to Herr Schramm's question, Pöhner answers:

HERR PÖHNER: On September 20, a meeting of the Reichs-kriegsflagge from all over Schwaben took place in Augsburg. There were 2,000 people there. Heiss declared, to thunderous applause, that now the pig-sty in Berlin would be cleaned up; and, that the Bavarian fist would create order in Berlin. The intent of the speech was quite clear in view of the mood which prevailed everywhere then. Even in pacifistic patriotic unions, or not-so-activist unions, the hue and cry was spreading, "To hell with Berlin!" The march on Berlin was being preached in all these federations as an official government program. This was also being clearly stated in the newspapers.

Herr Hemmeter wants answers to three questions which are signified by the following dates: March 13 and 14, 1920; 1921, shortly before Kahr's first departure; and the 1922 B.B. Affair. He asks whether Pöhner remembers that on the night of March 13, 1920, Dr. von Kahr decided to place himself in the custody of legal authorities while on the way to a so-called "dry putsch," and did so.

The Judge deems the question germane to the prosecution of the present trial.

HERR HEMMETER: Your agreement to the action is obvious. You had only to wait for the moment when you were summoned from your bed to make the leap.

JUDGE NEITHARDT: I think it would be prudent to discuss this question *in camera.*

HERR RODER: Exclusion of the public may take place only in the interests of national security. I find it simply incomprehensible how national security could be jeopardized by seeing that Dr. von Kahr did such wonderful things in 1920 and later years. This Court—which, until now, has led these hearings in a commendable and non-partisan manner—could only demean itself now by awakening the suspicions that protecting hands surrounded Kahr.

HERR ZEZSCHWITSCH: His client, Ludendorff, would be greatly interested in the answer to this question, because it will be of supreme importance to Ludendorff's participation.

HERR HEMMETER: My question is: Is Pöhner aware that on the night of March 13, 1920, the then-president of the Upper Bavarian Government, Dr. von Kahr, placed himself without hesitation in custody of the legal authorities, in a way that exactly resembles that of November 8, 1923? While others were working, he was sitting and waiting.

Also: When the "Security of the Republic" law caused a large outcry in Bavaria, that Dr. Kahr unflinchingly joined a movement which had as its goal the removal of the "legal" government—"legal" according to the Prosecution—using the same means? Namely, "pressure without pressure"?

HERR STENGLEIN: I do not accord these questions any essential importance to the determination of guilt or innocence.

HERR HEMMETER: Perhaps we will succeed in bringing evidence that Dr. von Kahr has committed, in the form of a continuing crime, what the District Attorney calls "high treason."

HERR RODER: Hitler came to the conclusion that he needed only to facilitate Kahr's leap because he knew Kahr's background. Therefore this background must be discussed.

HERR LUETGEBRUNE: Now it becomes a question of whether a conscious intent to use force can be attributed to the defendants. If it was made clear to them that it would be easy to get State authorities to collaborate, then certainly it can be seen that they couldn't have come to the conclusion that force would be needed to achieve their goals.

Herr Gademann stresses that an answer to the questions raised by Herr Hemmeter is also vital to his client, Kriebel.

Herr Kohl moves that the Court also rule on the charge against Captain Erhardt.

HERR HOLL: Dr. Weber also has an interest in clearing up this question so we can settle with Dr. Kahr concerning what he thinks is necessary in the interests of the Fatherland, since he was there at an officers' meeting in March 1920 and received a direct impression of what must be done.

JUDGE NEITHARDT: Is Herr Pöhner in a position to answer the questions?

HERR PÖHNER: I was present at the activities of the night of March 13, and of August, 1922. I was picked up by car at a holiday resort.

HERR RODER: The defendant Pöhner believes that Dr. von Kahr did not collaborate in the back room of the Bürgerbräukeller for form's sake and afterward change his mind. I request to ask this question: Did not Pöhner often observe that Kahr is the type of person given to changing his mind?

HERR LUETGEBRUNE: I request that the Court decide the following questions: First, whether the questions asked are relevant; second, whether they should be asked publicly. I request that both questions be answered affirmatively.

As counsel for defendant Pernet, Herr Bauer sides with the other defense attorneys.

The Court passes the following resolution: The decision on the questions raised is postponed until after Herr Kahr's testimony.

HERR HOLL: I have named Captain Erhardt as a witness. I must now take steps to bring this about by asking the Prosecution: Is it correct that the Prosecution had one of their officials, directly or indirectly, inform Erhardt that he would be arrested if he were summoned to appear as a witness for the defense?

HERR STENGLEIN (with raised voice): It is absolutely untrue that the prosecution had any such message prepared.

HERR HOLL: Then may I call the witness?

HERR GÖTZ: Can Herr Pöhner verify that Colonel Banzer and Major von Imhof offered their congratulations when he and Frick were with both men?

HERR PÖHNER: That's correct; both men congratulated me.

Herr Hemmeter asks Pöhner from which quarter the stimulus came to work with Kahr, and whether the invitation came from a particular quarter—a crucial point.

HERR PÖHNER: I already said the stimulus came to me from various quarters—important quarters—to collaborate with Herr Kahr. I do not care to discuss this question in open session.

HERR LUETGEBRUNE: How was it that Herr Kahr turned to Herr Pöhner with his misgivings about taking over the post of civil governor to Colonel von Seisser, the Commandant of State Police?

HERR PÖHNER: At the meeting, I thought that Herr Kahr had already discussed this and had agreed with the power brokers under his command—the commandant and the chief of police—concerning the conditions under which the actions of the Reichswehr, state police, nationalist groups, the Wicking Bund, and myself were to be taken. That is what I thought when the chief of the state police was also departmental head in the Generalstaatskommissariat. Those who were left were nothing but small-fries. Seisser was the only one of any importance.

Herr Luetgebrune then asks whether Pöhner noticed any signs of violence when he entered the back room on the evening of November 8.

HERR PÖHNER: Hitler had been in there about 10 minutes when Dr. Weber and I came in. From that moment on, while I was inside—I was always inside, uninterrupted, for a good 50 minutes—there was not the slightest hint of violence or threats. There was no possibility of yielding to a threat, either. They discussed everything quite calmly. They were simply being asked in a piercing, urgent manner. Only Graf, Hitler's bodyguard who stood at the door, had a weapon; he was nothing more than a decorative figure.

HERR LUETGEBRUNE: It occurs to me that during that long

conversation those gentlemen said nothing substantive about their objectives. How do you explain that?

HERR PÖHNER: We all agreed on the objective. We changed our ideas about the ways and means of execution but the objective always remained the same.

Herr Zezschwitsch would like to know, in reference to the plan to attract an agricultural dictator, whether Herr Kahr or someone else from his coterie had named certain persons for this job.

Pöhner says, "No, Herr Kahr didn't name any names."

Herr Zezschwitsch then asks why Kommerzienrat Zentz would ask Pöhner to restore order in the Bürgerbräukeller.

HERR PÖHNER: I was the closest man in reach. We knew each other and Kommerzienrat Zentz assumed that, as a well-known Munich personality, I would be in the best position to quiet the people.

In regard to the question of threats, Herr Hemmeter wants to hear from Pöhner whether Lossow and Seisser were in uniform.

HERR PÖHNER: Yes, they were.

HERR HEMMETER: The uniform of a German officer also includes a weapon?

HERR PÖHNER: I just wanted to establish that with regard to the question of threats.

Laughter.

Herr Gademann asks Pöhner if he really believes, as stunned as he had described them to be, that the three men would have had the presence of mind to be whispering to one another, "Put on an act."

HERR PÖHNER: The three gentlemen were obviously not masters of the situation, and were incapable of making decisions. I have never seen such incomprehension! I do not see how they could have whispered to one another; it does not correspond with their confused demeanor.

111

Herr Gademann asks Pöhner if Herr Kahr told him why he should go to see Herr Seisser—solely to learn what his position of Staatskommissar was to be; or also so that he could receive technical instructions?

HERR PÖHNER: Herr Kahr said that since we were there we might as well discuss the position of Staatskommissar with Colonel von Seisser. He didn't indicate a reason. However, Colonel von Seisser and I had previously spoken of other things at a meeting on October 2; due to its contents, I may not speak publicly about it.

Herr Hemmeter strenuously objects to Pöhner's remark about his collaboration with Herr Kahr repeatedly getting him into hot water, and asks the following:

HERR HEMMETER: When was the first time you got into hot water?

HERR PÖHNER: The first time was March 16, 1920, at 4:00 o'clock in the afternoon.

The Judge reminds Pöhner that he need not volunteer information; otherwise, he may be charged with more punishable acts.

HERR PÖHNER: I make no secret of my convictions. I told the Prosecutor that I have been fomenting what you call "high treason" for the last five years.

Herr Roder asks if Pöhner knew when he joined the police, either that Dr. Frick was a co-worker who was already won over, or that Frick knew nothing at all about the whole business.

HERR PÖHNER: Dr. Frick was very curious, very intent on learning something from me.

JUDGE NEITHARDT: That's not the answer to the question!

HERR RODER: Didn't Dr. Frick say immediately, "I have supported you as best I can"?

HERR PÖHNER: He did not. He could very easily have said it, in view of the mutual trust that existed between us.

HERR RODER: Dr. Frick was reproached for selecting Regierungsrat Balss as leader of the political division?

112

HERR PÖHNER: I recommended that Frick be entrusted to Herr Balss, a man I know to be absolutely reliable, with the position of leader of the political police.

HERR SCHRAMM: Did you think that it was possible that Herr Kahr would do the monarchy such a disservice by dragging it into a conspiracy through a casual promise, one he didn't intend to keep?

Pöhner explains that he first learned about Dr. Kahr's claim of the secret reservation from a newspaper after his arrest, and that it is completely incompatible with the monarchist orientation of Herr Kahr.

HERR PÖHNER: The monarchist persuasion is exactly what united us in 1919. For this reason, I refuse to believe that while Dr. Kahr called himself the monarchy's deputy, he acted with the reservation that he only did it for show. That repudiates the whole monarchist outlook!

HERR HOLL: Didn't Bund Bayern und Reich tell Herr Kahr at the end of October that if his dilatory policies didn't stop, their ties would be severed?

HERR PÖHNER: That is correct. Pittinger told me the same thing. Pittinger came to me at the end of October and bitterly complained that Herr Kahr could not be persuaded to act. On his account, strife had been rife in Bund Bayern und Reich and Pittinger wanted to have a parley with him. It never materialized. Consequently, Pittinger sent his deputy, Baron Auffers, with a four-point ultimatum detailing what was expected from the Generalstaatskommissar. I cannot remember the four individual points exactly. I remember that an active policy against Berlin was eagerly anticipated by Bund Bayern und Reich; if it did not receive attention and prompt action at the Generalstaatskommissariat, then the relationship between them would deteriorate. It must have been very tense then. Even Pittinger was angry about the passivity of Herr Kahr.

A discussion ensues as to whether the questions which are to be handled in closed session should be dealt with. The defense suggests that the questions are not for the public hearing and should be handled, in their totality, in secret session.

Pöhner's counsel requests that the session be adjourned out of consideration for Pöhner's health.

The proceedings are recessed, to reconvene the next day.

THE THIRD DAY, February 28, 1924

—MORNING SESSION—

The beginning of the session is delayed almost an hour and a quarter. The car that was supposed to bring General Ludendorff from Prinz-Ludwigshöhe broke down in the street. Therefore, the General had to take a train and arrived late in Munich—after 9:00 o'clock. A truck brought him from the train station to the courthouse. The Court has been notified by telephone of why he is late.

The moderator opens the session and announces the reason for the delay.

HERR KOHL: Before the next witness testifies, I must make a remark regarding the informative testimony of Herr General von Epp. The General responded negatively to the question concerning the appropriateness of reciting, in his presence, the minutes of a session on November 6, 1923, between Kahr and representatives of the Kampfbund. In the meantime, after making inquiries, I am in a position to raise the following claims. Probably, on November 12, 1923, General von Epp invited representatives of the university student body to the Graf Törring house. Attending were 100-150 students from all faculties. General von Epp recited the statements of the "Fähnriche" (youth clubs) concerning their participation on November 8, and Lieutenant Colonel Hörauf read the minutes. The responsibility lay with Herr Epp to swing the students in Munich behind Kahr. A segment of the representatives, notably the representatives of the Catholic student unions, affirmed Herr Epp's summons. One segment maintained a neutral attitude. The representatives of the Munich Burschenschaft (Student Association) declared that it was impossible for them to back a man who broke his word. It may be that perhaps the students' reasons escaped Herr General

115

von Epp's grasp; it was due to Lieutenant Colonel Hörauf's reading such a transcript. I cannot characterize his speech unfairly. I assume that it was due to an error or an oversight.

We, the defense, have learned that not all the summons were served on the prospective witnesses. I received a gentleman yesterday who, without a doubt, should be cross-examined at this trial, because he could give information about certain preparations—I cannot detail them in a public hearing—for November 8. I request that the advocates at least notify us which witnesses are to be summoned by the Court.

JUDGE NEITHARDT: For the next few days a few witnesses have been summoned for other testimony. I want to ask the defense counselors to tell me whether all the subpoenas will be enforced. In the course of the trial we will discover which witnesses to summon.

HERR KOHL: I concur completely. I tried to see if Captain Erhardt really lives at his given address. I discovered that he lives one story above Lieutenant Colonel Kriebel. Therefore, it probably would not have been too difficult for the prosecution to locate him.

HERR STENGLEIN: When Herr Pöhner wanted to see Lieutenant Commander Erhardt testify on the stand, the prosecution inquired after the address of the witness Erhardt, but was unable to locate his whereabouts at the time. Whether he is here or not is another question. The prosecution has established pertinent evidence through the testimony of Kahr and Seisser and now has no cause to search for the whereabouts of the other witness. The prosecution has no interest in his testimony and has not searched for his location.

HERR ZEZSCHWITSCH: I would have been satisfied with the Chief Prosecutor's argument if, by at least the beginning of December, a detailed memorandum in which a petition was made to take up legal proceedings against Kahr, Lossow, and Seisser had been sent to the Court with copies to the Ministry of Justice and the Attorney General. If these petitions were sent it is, in my opinion, an absolute mistake to confine ourselves to the prosecutor's depositions of these gentlemen and to arrange to call the witnesses accordingly.

HERR HOLL: I was told yesterday that my colleague, the

prosecutor, interpreted my question regarding Lieutenant Commander Erhardt as an "attack," so to speak. Far be it from me to attack the prosecution, because I expect that, by the end of the trial, the prosecutor will be for acquittal of all the defendants. I asked the question yesterday in order to get the answer I expected—namely, "no." Lieutenant Commander Erhardt was informed that if he was presented as a witness for the defense, he would be placed under arrest by the prosecution. Who is the culprit that misused the name and trifled with the reputation of the prosecution in such an irresponsible manner? Erhardt's word is above reproach. I will expose this culprit in the course of the hearings.

The Court then proceeds to the testimony of Lieutenant Colonel Kriebel.

Testimony of Herr Kriebel

HERR KRIEBEL: I will first give a brief sketch of my activities after the War. After the War, I was with the armistice mission at Spaa—not of my own free will—I was ordered to go. I participated in the shame and I had to endure it personally at the front where a ruthless, merciless foe stood, capable of every atrocity, while bands of traitors in the rear destroyed the only bulwark we had to blunt the will of the enemy. It was plain to me that there were enemies within as well as without. They had to be removed before we could work on the great problem for the sake of which I stand here. I had to negotiate with these people who, thanks to the crime of November, 1918, occupied their ministry offices by breaking their sworn oath to the Kaiser. I had to experience how these men could wantonly abandon and sacrifice the interests of our people; that was probably the most galling thing that an officer could experience after this War.

Nevertheless, the excellence of our people became so apparent that it will shine forever like a beacon in these dark hours. When the negotiations were over, where we were personally meted out the coarsest and most obscene abuse, I rebelled against the French violations and traveled in the Palatinate—my second home; I was born there, spent the best two years of my military career there, and was able to lead a Palatinate Company against the enemy—in uniform to see with my own eyes if there was any truth to the rumors that had reached us. I received shabby treatment from a so-called French officer, General de

Metz, who is branded as the most vicious successor to Melacs. I was unable to change this because our uniform had been disgraced by the November crime. We had no power behind us to give that swine what he deserved.

JUDGE NEITHARDT: I request that you modify your criticisms somewhat.

HERR KRIEBEL: On our departure from Spaa, we were treated like the Versailles Peace Mission. A drunken band of soldiers pelted us with rocks and heaped abuse on us. It was impossible for the French, Belgian, and English military authorities to intervene. When the train departed and there was a pause, I called to the Belgian band with a clenched fist from the window, "See you in a few years!" A storm of wrath was their answer—a renewed rock attack. I vowed not to rest or relax until I achieved what I had yelled to the Belgians. That is the basic premise from which all else derives. I returned home in September and was supposed to fill a position in the Peace Commission, serving in the Saar Border Commission. There, Forestry Superintendent Escherich offered me a position as chief of staff to organize the Erhardt Wikingbund. The Erhardt Wikingbund was not created on Herr Kahr's orders, but it arose out of the courage and bravery of various men—above all, Escherich himself, Kangler and others at home who dared to stand up with their lives against the Red traitors. Kahr was considered sponsor of the movement. As chief of staff of provincial administration, I participated in the upheaval of March, 1920. There I earned my coup d'etat spurs, so to speak. The high point of my activities for the Erhardt Wikingbund was the well known "Landesschiessen" with the celebration at Königsplatz which was the finest expression of gratitude for the work I had done up to then. I didn't appear in public; I left my share of the glory to Escherich and Kahr—those who deserved it. The success which the Wikingbund earned by putting Bavaria in order boosted its reputation beyond the boundaries of Bavaria. Soon, channels of communication were opened to organizations outside Bavaria, organizations who found expression in the Escherich Organization. This organization also took me to North Germany; therefore, I was in contact with all the men who were patriotically active in North Germany. I have had lasting contact with these men. Due to outside pressure, allegedly, to save Upper Silesia and the Ruhr Valley, Bavaria was ordered by the Reich

Government, to disband the Erhardt Wikingbund. It was clear that the loyal German men in the clever administration who, above all, exploited the North German press, were reluctant to defy the order to disband since, as it was artfully reported in the newspapers, Upper Silesia and the Ruhr Valley would be lost and the integrity of the Reich destroyed. It would have been impossible to allay those fears if the man who said: "I will stand and fall with the Home Guard!" had also had his say. In order to learn this fact, I went in May to Herr Kahr in order to give him a fresh outlook on the situation. I told him that it would be possible to oppose the treaty if we knew with certainty that he stood either behind or in front of the Erhardt Wikingbund. Kahr refused to give me an answer. And so the fate of the Wikingbund was sealed. I am to blame for telling my old friend Escherich that he wasn't to blame for the break-up, but that the guilt lies with another man whom I've previously named. It was clear that from that time on I radically modified my relationship with Herr Kahr whom I had respected up to then as a friend of the Fatherland. I recognized him as a back-door man who would not take the final consequences if it was at all possible to avoid making a decision. The dissolution took place. The Erhardt Wikingbund survived a bit longer, in men's clubs and hunting clubs. Our hope that it would be possible to continue such an organization secretly was not realized. On account of my connections with German-Austrian circles from my service in the Erhardt Wikingbund and the Escherich organization, I was forced to take a stand on the German-Austrian question. I am a "dyed-in-the-wool" Bavarian! The enlargement of my narrow Fatherland was always the goal of my desires.

I claimed the right for the Bavarian people to annex its former colony, now called Austria. My activities in the Erhardt Wikingbund were over at the end of 1921 because people said that it wanted to restore the Danube Monarchy to the throne. This reproach made me very angry. The first chapter of my patriotic activities was thus ended. In 1922, I worked in a different fashion but in a similar direction. I had long-standing ties to individual bands, later united in the Kampfbund—the first being the Reichskriegsflagge, of which I had been a member since 1921. It had become apparent that a certain difficulty lay in the union of young and old men in the Erhardt Wikingbund. The swelling ranks of youth in the bands and their attrition rate in the Erhardt Wikingbund convinced me that something was growing, something that bore watching. Through the Reichskriegsflagge, I also came in contact with other bands and eventually Hitler himself. I didn't come to Hitler because I had been influenced by his speeches. Before I had heard his speeches, I felt drawn to him for another reason. I joined the Kampfbund through my association with Hitler and my ties to the youth leagues. I later became military leader of the Kampfbund. This occupation has brought me to my present state. In consideration of law and order in the State, I request the opportunity to testify further in closed session.

Chief Prosecutor Stenglein moves for exclusion of the public.

After brief deliberation, the Presiding Judge announces the decision:

JUDGE NEITHARDT: The public will be excluded from hearing further testimony because their presence may constitute a risk to national security. The representatives of those authorities named on the occasion of the first closed session, plus Privy Councillor Döberl and Colonel Schraudenbach are permitted to remain. An oath of confidentiality is imposed upon all. The room will be cleared.

The hearing room is cleared and the closed session begins.

—SECRET SESSION—

HERR KRIEBEL: In accordance with my convictions which I expressed when leaving Spaa, I have conducted the affairs of the staff of the citizen guards from the following point of view: for me, it was to be a matter of reviving the manly virtues which Germany had displayed during the war until it bled to death; my leadership was directed towards arousing the people to a spirit of defensibility, and from there to the formation of a national army, and finally to a war of liberation. The significance this attitude has had for me, from the beginning until today, has been nothing else but (the duty) to serve the preparation of the great war of liberation which we will some day have to fight, whether or not we want to, or else we must go under. After the barest foundation for the citizen guards had been laid, after these single units had been merged and thus the foundation had been laid to form a center of orientation for the pride which, for so long, had been claimed by Bavaria—I soon began, going beyond this immediate goal, to prepare my actual task as I envisaged it.

In order to prevent a faslification of history, I would like to emphasize here that von Epp's assertions published in the newspaper shortly after November 9 are a falsification of history. In his article he says that the patriotic bands are greatly indebted to the Reichswehr and to the Landespolizei; as a matter of fact, the Reichswehr owes its development and the strength it has gained in Bavaria to the foundations laid by the citizen guards; and so does the Landespolizei. I would like to stress explicitly that when the Reichswehr was to be rebuilt, its new members were recruited mainly from the citizen guards since it (the Reichswehr) tried to hire able young men who were willing to serve again in the army. This is true, in my opinion, especially of Forstrat Escherich whose merit consists in having made Bavaria a center of order for a long time.

121

When training and organizing the citizen guards, I thought of the year 1813. In order to express this idea externally, I selected from the Army Museum the well-known white-blue armband of the citizen guards which the Bavarian militia had worn in 1814 when marching into the war of liberation. That has become known; I want to mention it only to prove that my attitude has not changed from the very beginning. To keep the youths from switching from the citizen guards to the youth band, I chose a flag from the Bavarian Army history; I found one in the so-called Landfahne which in the Middle Ages served to strengthen the regional enrollment of the then existing mercenary army. I did this because it was clear to me that it is impossible to fight a war with only older gentlemen; young men that have stood in the battlefield, above all young men in the process of growing up, are what we need. Everything was directed towards the future: to create, through the spirit of defensibility, the national army, the compulsory military service, and lastly the war of liberation.

Needless to say, one of the main conditions for reaching my goal was our supply of arms, and I would like to express here and now my gratitude to those innumerable brave young men, whom I do not know by name, for the work they have done in more than two, almost three years to maintain the supply of arms for our people. I also would like to thank those who had the courage to hide weapons despite the laws against the possession of arms which entailed penal servitude or fines—penalties which were actually imposed by the German governments. Those who were hiding weapons have not yet received any thanks; on the contrary, they have been persecuted. Today, they are sitting next to me in the prisoner's dock; a number of them are fugitives scattered across the country and pursued by the Prosecutor. Yet their only crime is that since the founding of the citizen guards they, without sparing themselves, have done nothing worse than hide and secure weapons for the people and our Fatherland, which is against the national laws. I would like to express my gratitude to them.

I would like to stress unequivocally that the Reichswehr cannot take credit for having secured weapons. They secured certain small quantities—black (illegal) stocks—for their own purposes, but those who actually secured arms were our people; the young fellows and decent chaps who are now being persecuted, disbanded, and punished because for four years they used to value the interest of the Fatherland more highly than the laws prescribed by a criminal government. That is what they were trained for. They have done it enthusiastically.

It was not easy. The men had to drive around in automobiles for days and for nights in order to carry the arms from one betrayed hiding place to another. In one castle, a huge quantity of gun powder had been stored in a wall. Then this wall had to be torn down, but no paid worker would have dared to put his chisel to a wall filled with gun powder to get it out. Our young people, risking their lives, took it out to save the Fatherland because the powder had to be stirred and dried on time so that it would not be lost. I want to emphasize this work. It was done against the Reichsregierung and against the order of the government, at the risk of losing their lives, their property, and their freedom.

JUDGE NEITHARDT: Lieutenant Colonel! You talked about a "criminal government." I cannot permit that.

HERR KRIEBEL: Yesterday, this expression was also used. I therefore thought I could use it, too. I have also found out that they have tried to establish connections with foreign states. Von Kahr conducted negotiations, specifically with Hungary, while I was present. The subject of the talks were arms shipments to Hungary in support of the so-called "awakening Hungary."

The situation which I previously described changed after the citizen guards were dissolved. Now the citizen guards continued to exist in a new band, a secret organization. Forstrat Escherich and I made the basic decisions. At the time, we asked Sanität-srat Pittinger to head this organization, since we did not want to burden this secret organization from its inception with our names. From this secret organization the now-existing organization, Bayern und Reich, has developed. At the time, Sanitätsrat Pittinger had taken charge of this organization as a trustee. Once he was in charge, he separated from Forstrat Escherich.

I am now going to discuss the question of the youth band. As far as I am concerned, I can claim to be one of the experts on the general ideology, on the hopes of the young people and on those in our nation who have patriotic feelings. Since September of 1919, I have done nothing but pursue this question. I have approached the matter with passion and have intended—at first intended—nothing else but the unity of all Verbände. That is what I was striving for; but as I realize now, my aspirations, until November 9, were based on incorrect knowledge. For a long time I have been the military leader of the V.V. München, where I recognized this division which ran through the organization. The reasons for this division I did not learn until November 9 and later. It is my opinion that a man's belief must be the right one for him and that someone who claims to have character cannot have two, but only one, correct view. I would like to emphasize this because yesterday the Prosecutor rebuked us for thinking that our belief is the only valid one. Quite naturally, I consider my views correct and the only ones that have any validity for me.

HERR EHARD: I made this remark only once.

JUDGE NEITHARDT: May I ask you not to talk simultaneously. You, Mr. Prosecutor, will have your chance to speak after the defendant.

HERR KRIEBEL: Drawing on my long experience, I must conclude its quintessence to be as follows: There has always been a certain difference in thinking and feeling between young men and older men. The young men have always wanted deeds, while the old men were supposed to give advice. This difference in the thinking and feeling of young and old men, however, was never as strong as after the War. It has become stronger through revolution and defeat to such an extent that it seems as if a generation had been skipped, as if grandfathers were facing grandsons and not fathers, their sons. The reason for this development is that all the young men have never known, as men, our Germany in its splendor and power and greatness; while we adults, before the War, knew our Fatherland as men and have before our eyes the past as an ideal for our patriotic aspirations. Naturally, any patriotism is directed towards the goal of rebuilding a more beautiful, a better Germany. It is also natural that the older men, knowing how things were in the past, are looking to the past; while the youth, not having known the past, feel only that they want to create a better and more beautiful Germany and look to something in the future. This is the essence of the division in the entire patriotic movement. Yet I would not think of reproaching those patriots who belong to the group that looks to the past nor (would I think) that their patriotism might be a little—even one iota—more passionate, warmer, or more honest than ours.

Still, I must say the youthful patriotic enthusiasm has

taken an entirely different direction. They want something new; that is the Völkische movement, in which especially the active members strive for a new, great, beautiful Germany, a country in which the State is the authority which would render the secret organizations superfluous, a country worth living in, a country which guarantees the integrity of all national actions. Many of these youth bands already existed at Jungebünde at the time of the citizen guards. Oberland already existed at that time, O. Erhardt existed, it was the time of volunteers, and I think there were some that I cannot remember at the present time. The fact that these youth bands spread so tremendously had to prove to every objective observer that here there was a new movement pushing for light, rising to the surface, no longer waiting to be suppressed by the others.

I, who thought only of the war of liberation, had no doubt whatsoever that we would not be able to fight a war of liberation without participation of the German workers, without the young German workers, the young patriots among the German workers who are willing to take up arms and to fight for their Fatherland, who want to be trained for this event, that is, who want to join the national organization. Nor (can we do) without the older workers who may be willing to produce the arms at the home front and to do all the work for the army at the front. No war of liberation can be fought without these workers.

But if we don't put our heads into the sand and look at the patriotic band and other parties who call themselves national, we can see clearly that none of the patriotic organizations had any sizeable constituency of workers until the youth band appeared and, above all, until the National Socialist Workers' Party was founded. On one occasion, when talking to the workers, I asked them: "If a conflict was to arise between the orders given by the command of the citizen guards and the orders given by your Party, what would you do?" The worker explained, "In a case like that I would follow the orders of my Party." That was the end of the Social Democrat Workers' membership in the citizen guards, because this man had not been converted to National Socialism. The same thing was true everywhere. The number of workers in any of the national parties is not worth mentioning; without the workers, we cannot fight a war of liberation. The way to freedom is possible only with (the participation of) the workers of the nation.

Up till now the only man who has been able to win over the

workers in sizable and ever growing numbers was Hitler. This is the reason why I joined Hitler. Later, I got to know him better. I know that this man is filled with sheer will and tremendous will power. I became his follower; because of the days of November 8 and 9, we are bound to each other in undying loyalty.

Through this, I became more and more part of the circle of the later Kampfbund. Gradually my position developed in a way which it did not before; it was built on the trust which these patriotic youth bands had in me. I consider it one of the most beautiful presents of my life. Through this trust, I attained a leading position in the youth bands. I have consolidated this position, never losing sight of my goal of how to further these splendid young people who wanted nothing else but to fight for their Fatherland, to be prepared for this struggle.

(I was thinking of) how I could use my connections to the officers of the Reichswehr and to the Landespolizei to facilitate their training as much as possible. Actually, such a great idea to train the young people who offer their services ought not to be burdened with problems, especially not those arising from trivial matters. But no, they employed the same chicanery, they made the same demands, et cetera, which had absolutely no other effort than to constantly irritate people.

Just imagine what it means for these young people, partly unemployed, partly students, partly workers, whose children and sons were often starving at home, who often hardly had sufficient food, to free themselves; for the students who also hardly ever knew how to feed themselves to take time from their studies in order to be trained for hours in the evening. Believe me, this requires an immense amount of enthusiasm, of loyalty which only decent young people could muster. They should have been treated by those concerned differently than they were. Allow me to mention the example of the Wehrkreiskommando. To me, their lack of understanding and their pettiness were virtually shocking. All they were thinking of was that, by no means, were their own positions to be endangered perhaps by having the leader of a Verband aiming for the top, a position of authority, or something of the kind. Those were the "great" ideas which guided their actions. I was deeply moved to see how much enthusiasm the young people brought along. There are other gentlemen here who have had the same experience as I had and who can confirm what these young people took upon themselves. First Lieutenant Brückner also knows about it, and so does Dr. Weber.

It was quite natural for an old soldier that the goal which I had before me in regard to the war of liberation and its organization could only be a real army, not an army consisting of volunteers only. But we could not see any other way to reach this goal which would have suited the young people. One can only hope to attain it by giving the following order: "As of tomorrow, there will be no more Verbände; rather, all the young people will simply be assigned to the Reichswehr batallions as volunteers." It is possible to give this order, but it will not be followed. Only gradually can one influence—also morally influence—these young men; then they will more and more begin to see the great goal, which is that they must represent a prepared army with the old military hierarchy at the very moment when we have to march against France. It must be the old German army as it existed before, built on subordination, discipline, and military chains of command. I can imagine that especially the kind gentlemen of the Wehrkrieskommando will reproach me for having seen myself as the Freikorps commander at the head of a great mass of men. (I can also imagine) the white-blue brochure writing in its pamphlet, *veni, vidi* about my ambition to ride at the head of the troops through the Brandenburg gate. My ambition, then, would have been to march at the head of a body of troops—whose size corresponds with my rank—across the Rhine and to throw out this pack of dogs who are treating my people from the Palatinate in such a way. I have received letters from troops telling me about the things that happen over there.

This is my ambition, my goal, and this is what I am fighting for all the time, not for a position. Whoever is petty cannot assume anything else from other people. Nobody looks behind the stove unless he himself has sat there. That is what is so contemptible! I have to defend an old name of old and good repute, and I want to hand the name down to my sons. I refuse to defend myself in public because I do not want the shame which has come over the Bavarian Officers' Corps because of November 9 and what followed, to be discussed by the wider public.

It is shocking, however, what contemptuous treatment we have received from that corner. The gentlemen are aware that a strictly confidential pamphlet was published by the Wehrkreiskommando and sent to all officers' bands, to the commanders, to be handed to all former officers. I can only call this pamphlet a lie. The way in which our honor has been dealt with is an infamy;

furthermore (it is) an attempt of the worst kind to influence the witnesses!

Machinations have also gone on against me personally. A document found in a box was confiscated. This was done by an authority whom I shall bring out into the open. They gave the documents to completely uninvolved persons asking them to let it be known in the officers' corps that I receive a huge salary. Isn't that an insult? And I am supposed simply to swallow all this. I shall defend my name once the trial is over and once I shall be free again; I am going to get those people. These villains in uniform and in civilian clothes who have smeared my good name are to suffer for it.

I shall now discuss the purely military activity. This is necessary in order to be able to understand the following statements by His Excellency Ludendorff: Ruhr struggle, passive resistance, preparation for the transition into active resistance. It is not true that we intended to prepare ourselves only in case the French should force us into a defensive fight; that is, in case they should march in and force us to defend ourselves. On the contrary, we wanted to get ahead of them in action. I am informed. I sat for General Epp as the confidential delegate for the Kampfbund in the Wehrkreiskommando. I have cooperated. Nothing more is required than the preparation to mobilize an army of volunteers until the army, established through compulsory military service, has been built up. Proof of the seriousness of this intention is a statement by General von Epp himself who says that in April they thought hostilities would break out in a few days and that, therefore, the preparations were to be accelerated as much as possible. Thus, it was serious. For this reason, we used all our energy in the Kampfbund to have the people trained. We tried to teach discipline to our young people who have no longer gone through the old army school. I am very well aware of the fact that this is actually prohibited in an organization in which the members are bound to absolute obedience to their leadership: the rule was, I believe, to unknown superiors. We did it because we told ourselves that we could not put our people as reservists into the army unless they had the basic concept of the military; that is, absolute subordination in their bones. We therefore had to proceed in accordance with the military concept of absolute obedience. There will be no arguments, only orders and obedience. This was not done to put ourselves on a high horse, but to be able to send people to the

Reichswehr who knew what obedience means.

This brings me to the question of guilt as far as the 8th or 9th of November is concerned. The State, who knew that we trained our people in such a way, even wanted this; the State authorities knew about it; (so did) Colonel von Seisser who helped in the training; and so did Herr Lossow. Even the now deceased Oberregierungsrat Stauffer had ordered that only that Verband which assumes the obligation to be at the disposal of either the Landespolizei as emergency police, or at the disposal of the Reichswehr as trainees, is considered loyal to the State and may retain arms.

Thus it was demanded of us that we train our young people in this way. I have therefore explicitly stressed in my testimony, and I uphold that statement, that the final military responsibility for all measures carried out—on orders by those second in command—rests with me. It is impossible to stop there. One cannot say, on the one hand, that the Verband has been trained militarily to obedience and order because we intended it to be a reserve for the new army and then say (on the other hand), you should have taken into consideration that the order cannot be executed. The machine gunner who had received the order to place his machine gun at the entrance of the hall had to do so, no matter what happened. One cannot go half way.

I would like to ask the Court that this great patriotic concept be maintained and that I especially cannot possibly put the responsibility on the shoulders of those people who did nothing but carry out the given order because they were trained with the knowledge of the State authorities to obey orders. One cannot rebuke them for that. I would consider it a personal insult if any man who did nothing but carry out his order in a way in which he has been trained by us for war is still in prison, pending investigation. I also have here an instruction from the Wehr-kreiskommando with regard to this training.

HERR GADEMANN: I request that this instruction, signed by Herr Lossow personally, be read to the Court.

The instruction is submitted.

HERR KRIEBEL: I had to touch briefly on this development until September 1. Owing to my position of trust, I had reached a certain station—not yet as a military leader, but as a military delegate. Gradually I became the military commander of the Kampf-bund; as such, I was in charge of all those matters discussed here. The division which has developed and runs through the entire national mòvement since November 9—the officers' Verbände and all others—this division which I had not recognized and hence my constant attempts to establish unity in the Verbände. When I realized that it was not possible, and since I had closer ties to the old officers, I turned to them to try at least to coordinate our great military task, which was to supply recruits for the army.

Since I myself enjoyed great loyalty among my comrades, it goes without saying that I gained a position of leadership in these attempts without striving for it. It was offered to me; it was a natural consequence. Therefore I settled various matters even-handedly, specifically those concerning the border guards vis-a-vis Thuringia and Saxony, both of which had become greater and greater Bolshevist threats.

At the end of August, I had a discussion with Pittinger, the strongest adversary of our patriotic movement, whom I consider the top man of that patriotic movement which looks to the past. I wanted to bring about a certain unification, and to accomplish this I had a discussion with him at the end of August. Major Fehm was also present. The idea of a Generalstaatskommissariat was expressed very clearly during this discussion with Sanitätsrat Pittinger. He had drawn up a long memorandum for himself in which he had appointed Oberstlandesgerichtsrat Pöhner as an obvious member to the board of directors which was to be established for Bavaria under the chairmanship of Kahr; (he had appointed) also Herr Hitler, a fact which I want to stress specifically. Kahr was supposed to head it. Furthermore, the general Bavarian tax strike was to be proclaimed immediately, while at the same time a Bavarian currency was to be introduced. It was because of this general tax strike that our unification negotiations failed.

After I had reported this plan to Herr Hitler and the other leaders of the Verbände which had merged in the Kampfbund, the plan was rejected. Since this tax strike had been made a certain condition for unification, the latter was dispensed with. I am not mentioning this to put the blame on someone, but I have to clarify the question as to why the attempts to unify finally failed. Hence the entire affair was based not so much on a strong separatist, but still on a purely Bavarian rescue action. Since those at the top did not simply begin an attack, we ourselves intended to proceed, first of all, with these two means: taxes and currency.

I also spoke with Sanitätsrat Pittinger about the person who was then to become Staatskommissar. Naturally, Kahr's name was mentioned. We discussed Kahr's personality, and I can only say that Sanitätsrat Pittinger had the same impression of him as the national leader of the patriotic movement. Sanitätsrat Pittinger said he gave him credit for anything; but a man of decision, he was not. Of this, Pittinger was convinced as all the other men—whether Erhardt, Captain Heiss, or anyone else. Also those who are not involved in the patriotic movement, high officials with whom I talked, shared this opinion: if it is a matter of decision-making, Kahr cannot be moved.

Now Sanitätsrat Pittinger felt that by placing energetic men at his side, this deficiency could be compensated for. We would then have: on the one hand, his popularity to create a large platform; on the other hand, this might induce him to make certain decisions and to give those orders which would accomplish what all of us, including Pittinger, wanted: to put an end to the pigsty up there and to begin the march to Berlin. This has been the topic of Professor Bauer's speeches, too. Nobody doubted that that was the goal, and, at this point, it is of no importance whether this, the march to Berlin, was meant in a figurative or a literal sense. But the view that things had to begin here prevailed everywhere in all patriotic organizations; there is no doubt about it.

Thus the result of this discussion was a failure to bring about a unification with the largest group we faced. Nothing had become of it. I have, however, never lost sight of these unification endeavors because I knew that, in the end, we would all have to join, especially when considering my idea of a war of liberation which was always on my mind. Here, too, I would like to state expressly that today, even after the split of November 9, I am still convinced that these people are on our side, even though on the surface they have now separated from us, having chosen to look to the past, while we are the others who appear to fight.

But as far as the inner development of our Reich, the creation of a great platform, the struggle for our new Fatherland is concerned, we are convinced that no other way is the right one, because I believe it is impossible to get any workers into a national band if we look back to November 7, 1918. Unfortunately, our present platform has become the arena of such fierce fighting between Catholics and Protestants, between the parties, between the single German regions, between the social classes, that I do not see a way for the unification of our people unless it is

131

on a most ideal platform—which is that of our admired Kühner—a goal which is still distant, the great German Reich which we want to erect!

Now to the border guards. In spite of the failure in our unification attempt, we still had cooperated closely with the Verbände. Now, in September, when the situation at the North Bavarian border became critical, we established contact with Lieutenant Colonel Scharz, with Kleinherz, and various other commanders. I told them that something had to be done. Some reports also appeared in the papers that now and then Red bands had penetrated into Bavaria. When investigating the matter, the following picture emerged: one border guard unit had been trained under the aegis of the Reichswehr and the Landespolizei Reich und Bayern had made preparations; the Reichsflagge had made preparations; the Jungdeutscher Orden made preparations; Erhardt made preparations; there were five or six units of border guards who had been prepared.

That, I said, is nonsense. We have to agree on a unified military and police procedure. Advancing from this position, I took the matter into my own hands and asked Lieutenant Colonel Breitner to help me with this task. He is an old friend of mine, who worked formerly for Bayern und Reich—when I asked him, he was no longer with them—but who also enjoyed the confidence of all patriotic bands and whom I considered an honest, steady, and decent man. He agreed to help me.

I believe it was the 9th of October when the decisive meeting took place in my office in the Rheinischer Hof, where the delegates of all the Verbände we have in Bavaria were present and agreed with this arrangement. It had been discussed beforehand between Herr Seisser and Breitner, the latter acting upon my request. At that time, it had been decided that the border guards were to be built up for a dual purpose: first, as a defense organization against Red attacks from the North; and secondly, as a security force for the assembly of troops that was to follow. In our plan, we had already designated the assembly areas for the entire North, for the northern border, the marching routes toward Berlin. I personally handed to Colonel von Seisser this map containing the drawings of the marching routes, the assembly areas, and the areas to be protected by the border guards. He completely agreed with me, and was quite satisfied with it; he approved it. There was never any doubt about the fact that here something was about to happen that was contrary to the will of the State; rather, it was done with the full approval of the man responsible for the emergency police, Colonel von Seisser, whom Kahr, meanwhile, had appointed chief of the department concerned with technical aspects of the defense.

The order went out on October 16 and became the basis for the whole idea which until then existed (only) as a thought: to begin the march on Berlin with the corps of volunteers only. They were to be followed by the actual military force of Landespolizei and Reichswehr, perhaps in echelon order to the right and to the left. In this way, outside attacks could be warded off as long as possible. This had been the idea: there was at that time no doubt whatsoever that we would march to Berlin. I mean it was so clear, everything so clear—as Professor Bauer has explained more than once—that it would happen. I only want to mention it since I believe it was simply self-evident.

Here is this order, the well-known border guards order, which I can also pass on to the Court. In order to demonstrate the co-operation with all patriotic organizations down to the smallest detail, I would like to state that some of the orders—a joint order had been issued—were signed by me for the Kampfbund and for those who leaned towards us—I believe, Wikingbund and Reichsflagge—and partly the orders were signed by Lieutenant Colonel Breitner himself, for those Verbände who had close ties neither to us nor to Bayern und Reich. Thus, the order went out as a common document of all patriotic bands, including the Landes-polizei, who had made themselves available as an emergency police force. This fact was well known to the Generalstaatskom-missariat and all pertinent authorities; for the emergency police was alerted by the Regierungspräsident of the two government factions concerned. The chiefs of the Landespolizei were the middlemen between us and the President.

Your Honor, would you now permit this order to be read aloud?

JUDGE NEITHARDT: Now? It would become the property of the Court.

HERR KRIEBEL: Before it is read, I would like to hand over this map with the areas marked. This will make it easier for the Court to follow the text of the order.

Herr Kriebel hands the map to Judge Neithardt who dis-cusses it with the Court and the attorneys.

HERR GADEMANN: First of all, I would like to make known excerpts of an original letter by Herr von Lossow of April 10, 1923. This letter confirms Kriebel's statement of the existence of a solid agreement that the great idea was to become reality by marching across the Rhine.

The letter is submitted.

HERR KRIEBEL: It was a suggestion I had made and which Herr Lossow took up. This has become the basis for all the later common decisions pertaining to the problem of national defense.

HERR STENGLEIN: Does this concern the mobilization which you mentioned before, the mobilization vis-a-vis foreign countries?

HERR KRIEBEL: And its preparation.

HERR EHARD: Who conceived the basic idea for the mobilization plan?

HERR KRIEBEL: It comes from Berlin.

HERR GADEMANN: And now to the order for the border guards. "The Military Commander, Munich, October 16, 1923, strictly confidential, only for the military leaders."

The order is submitted.

This is the order to the border guards of October 16, 1923, of which Colonel Seisser and the other authorities each received a copy.

HERR EHARD: It was stated that Colonel Seisser and others received a copy of this order. It strikes me as strange that Colonel Seisser did not express his opinion in writing on a matter as important as this one.

HERR KRIEBEL: That is not strange. Our cooperation has been complete. Colonel Breitner stayed with him all the time and kept me informed.

HERR EHARD: A written order does not exist?

HERR KRIEBEL: In line with the order, he called his men to his office and informed them of its content.

HERR WEBER: The chiefs of the Landespolizei in Northern Bavaria were informed of the order. The head of Bund Oberland went to see the chief of Würzburg on this matter and discussed the entire affair with him. Furthermore, he drove around the area to determine the military positions along with the military commander of Bund Oberland for the chief in charge of the Landespolizei in Würzburg.

HERR KOHL: May I ask whether any of the defendants are aware of the fact that hidden arms were transported to Munich and to Northern Bavaria as a result of this order?

HERR PÖHNER: Yesterday, I had to be deliberately careful with my statements. Later, I shall once again refer to the discussion, first with Ehrhardt on September 29, then with Herr Kahr on September 30, and thirdly with Seisser on October 2. In my testimony yesterday, I had to keep silent about several points because of the public's presence. I shall come back to these questions, but they have also been clarified by Lieutenant Colonel Seisser himself when he testified on October 2. His statements have confirmed what Ehrhardt had told me on September 29. I, along with Ehrhardt, had considered them to be a matter of course because of an agreement that had existed for years. I only want to mention one point since it characterizes the support of the State organizations and of the chief of the Technical Defense Department of the Generalstaatskommissariat. Ehrhardt told me already on September 29 that he and his organization had put themselves under the command of Mr. Kahr, and he was then in a position to set up his organization in Bavaria. Now, the organization Wikingbund consists mainly, perhaps up to 90 percent, of North Germans and, I believe, hardly 10 percent of Bavarians. Of course, Ehrhardt does not bring his North German men here to build up border guards. To those outside the group, the entire organization appeared as the Bavarian emergency police.

JUDGE NEITHARDT: Who said that?

HERR PÖHNER: Ehrhardt said so, and Seisser issued an identification card to him which was to protect him from police investigations because there was an arrest warrant, charging him with perjury and high treason, out (for him) from Leipzig. As I heard later, this ID card was actually—I never saw it myself—issued.

HERR FRICK: I saw it.

HERR PÖHNER: We agreed—and I don't deny it—that the title of Bavarian emergency police was to be a cover, to give it a legal coat, so that the backdoor could be kept open for the gentlemen. Von Kahr is the man who follows the principle of the open backdoor. I could name a number of examples for it—and Frick can confirm it—and I shall do so when facing Herr Kahr.

At that time, Ehrhardt already said—he had come the night before to talk to Seisser—that he was guarding the weapons well, that he was organizing Wikingbund excellently, that he had the best organization in Germany. All the soldiers had served on the front and were geared to strictest discipline. Wikingbund represented the best tradition of the (home) guards and the Navy. They certainly will not act as boarder guards here, as the night-watch for Herr Kahr. Whatever is said in that respect serves the purpose of the open backdoor. He who has ears to hear knows this full well; it does not require specifically sensitive ears. Already on September 29, Ehrhardt—he had come the night before—in that very night talked with Seisser for so many hours. He said he had been promised to get arms from the Bavarian Landespolizei—I couldn't say that yesterday. Seisser had already made this promise on September 29, that he would have the Landespolizei supply him with those arms to equip the so-called border guards. Already on October 2—that is, long before this discussion of October 16—Lieutenant Colonel von Seisser confirmed to me that Ehrhardt's statements were correct. He said that the Ehrhardt organization would now be equipped with weapons from the Landespolizei and that the arms transports were already on their way.

I only want to add this point—which has no relevance here as far as time is concerned—to my testimony of yesterday. Later, I shall discuss the other events. I think Dr. Weber also knows of them. I have said everything in my memorandum, Herr Prosecutor; everything can be read between the lines, and those who can read will be able to deduce it from my memorandum.

Call from the Court table: "I did, but I am warning against a public discussion of this subject."

HERR PÖHNER: That's quite right; I was not able to say it more explicitly.

JUDGE NEITHARDT: And because I could read, I thought yesterday that this question should not be raised; but it happened anyhow.

Herr Hitler, you wanted to say something to this point?

HERR HITLER: The training of our storm troops was begun for the first time because of the Ruhr conflict. Later it was discontinued on account of a new, initially oral, agreement of which Lieutenant Kriebel's order is actually only the final version. Now, training of our storm troops has been resumed in the barracks by the authorities, i.e. by the Landespolizei and the Reichswehr. Their new, highly intensified training dates back to this point in time. From the very first day, the troops were trained in the barracks, not as border guards or police, but from the very first day for the definite purpose of attack. The training was executed with two goals in mind: not only was the single man trained, but from the very first day the entire technical apparatus of training was aimed at the mobile war to the North.

This was one of the aspects which finally forced us to make a decision; it was impossible to keep the people who, night-by-night and morning-by-morning, had been imbued in the barracks with nothing but ideas of war, in suspense any longer. They were asking: When do we move? When will we finally start the battle to throw out that gang? We could no longer keep the men in suspense from week to week; and that was one of the reasons of our later operation, and hence one of the reasons which some day had to take effect.

JUDGE NEITHARDT: The men were trained in the barracks?

HERR HITLER: In the barracks, with the knowledge of the Reichswehr and the Landespolizei, and partly in the uniforms of the Reichswehr and the Landespolizei.

JUDGE NEITHARDT: By officers of the Reichswehr?

HERR HITLER: By officers of the Reichswehr.

JUDGE NEITHARDT: And that was not kept a secret? That was known?

HERR WEBER: Since the public has been excluded here, I would like to make a few remarks regarding the border guards. Immediately after the formation of the Generalstaatskommissariat, we too, were ordered to intensify as much as possible the training of our people; that, above all, the young people, many of whom in our ranks had never seen military combat, were to be subjected to the most intense and sharpest drills. Three times a week there was sharpshooting practice. And, week after week, both in and outside of Munich, drills were conducted under the supervision and the command of officers of the Reichswehr. Since there were relatively many of us, the rooms of the Reichswehr were not sufficient. Therefore, the Landespolizei also let us use their rooms, their officers and drill sergeants, everything under high pressure during the weeks of October.

Based on the order mentioned by Lieutenant Colonel Kriebel, I was asked how many arms we needed to equip our people in Northern Bavaria. Both the Reichswehr and the Landespolizei were, after all, fully aware of the fact that of all Verbände, Bund Oberland was perhaps best equipped with weapons. Our weapons, however, were partly stored south of the Danube, and now we were asked how many auto convoys we would need to load and transport our arms to our section in Northern Bavaria—that is, the eastern half of Lower Franconia. Loading had already begun. Furthermore, for this march to the North, we were asked whether we would also make available the heavy artillery which Bund Oberland still had since Reichswehr and Landespolizei apparently no longer had such arms.

JUDGE NEITHARDT: Who asked this question?

HERR WEBER: The Landespolizei; (they asked) whether our heavy artillery was ready for immediate use and whether we had provided for the horses that were to move our heavy artillery. If not, the Landespolizei would take care of it. Lieutenant Colonel Kriebel will be able to give more information. I, too, would request to add further explanations if this should be considered necessary.

HERR LUETGEBRUNE: I would like to ask who gave the order to continue training, "under the highest pressure possible"?

HERR KRIEBEL: These instructions came, first of all, from the Reichswehr—sometimes from the section commander, but also from the commandant and chief of the Landeskommando, Herr Lossow, and Lieutenant Colonel Berchem. Furthermore, Colonel von Seisser offered us the use of the barracks of the Landespolizei, along with the officers and corporals, for our training.

JUDGE NEITHARDT: You probably have this in writing?

HERR KRIEBEL: No, it was done orally.

HERR GADEMANN: It is appropriate here to discuss an order mentioned earlier, of which the Prosecutor wanted to know whether Mr. Seisser had been aware of it—

HERR EHARD: That was not my question. Please do not impute anything to me.

HERR GADEMANN: The evidence of this (Seisser's knowledge), is the fact that he himself—Colonel von Seisser—issued the known secret order 30107. I don't know whether it is known to the Prosecutor. I have it with me, if I could be permitted to read it aloud.

Call from the Judge's table: "Please!"

HERR GADEMANN: It is dated October 29 and reads as follows: "In the event of internal unrest within the German Reich," et cetera, et cetera.

The order is submitted.

HERR GADEMANN: This order was to be destroyed immediately after having been read; however, it was not destroyed or else it could not be here.

HERR EHARD: Upon receipt of the executory order, these preparations were to have been concluded. Hence it was a plan, not an active, actual mobilization.

HERR GADEMANN: Whether this was a plan or the real preparation for an active action, needs complementary information.

JUDGE NEITHARDT: I request the gentlemen to speak one after the other.

HERR KOHL: Let us get to the point. Yesterday I received a visit from an engineer by the name of Benedikt Jehle, formerly head of the Fliers' Organization Munich. He informed me that at the monthly meeting of October, 1923, of the aviators of the Munich district (Ortsgruppe), Captain Kirchner, a member of the Wehrkreiskommando, appeared there. He asked the members to vote on whether to join the Kampfbund as an aviators' organization. The members voted about it; the question was answered with a "yes." Now Engineer Jehle received an order, in strictest confidence, (to draw up) a plan: first of all, for the construction of an army airport; and, secondly, for the formation of a

139

unit of field aviators. The engineer did not consider the matter as important as it actually was—he was in no hurry to complete the plan—but then Captain Kirchner returned on November 5, 6, and 7, and asked him to speed up his work. Now Captain Kirchner has been transferred to Berlin.

HERR SCHRAMM: I request that Lieutenant Colonel Kriebel be asked whether he thinks it was necessary for the border guards at the Thuringian border to have three divisions and a stronger infantry; whether they needed heavy artillery only in order to keep a few Red bands from Saxony and Thuringia from penetrating into Bavaria. After all, at that time the Reichswehr had already marched into Saxony and Thruingia.

JUDGE NEITHARDT: Herr von Ludendorff?

HERR LUDENDORFF: Earlier the question of arms transport to Coburg was raised. There is Jensen, a clergyman from Herren-neustadt, near Coburg. He is the commander of the Ordens der Jungen Deutschen. He called on me and told me about it. I suggested to him that he be a witness. I can submit his notes, that upon the order of the Ehrhardt Brigade, considerable quantities of weapons were shipped to Coburg by the Landespolizei. A dispute arose between the Ehrhardt organization and the Jungdeutscher Orden on the one hand, and the Jungbayern on the other hand. Then Colonel von Seisser stated in a letter to the head of the Landespolizei in that area, Captain—

Call: "Bernhardt."

HERR LUDENDORFF: —that these weapons belonged to the Wikingbund, or rather to the Jungdeutscher Orden.

Call: When was that?

HERR LUDENDORFF: In October.
I would also like to draw attention to the quite unusual sequence of digits in the journal number of the order just mentioned by Attorney Kohl. The digits are ordered in such a way that anybody who is somewhat informed knows that there is something hidden there. The first journal number is 3107. The second, with which the password is given out, is not a higher number as one would expect, but rather 3018—that is, a lower number.

I would also like to remark on the Department of Technical Defense. For the Bavarian Generalstaatskommissariat of Herr Kahr, the Technical Defense Department, in my opinion, served the same purpose. How did the Generalstaatskommissariat get a Technical Defense Department? We know, after all, that at the very beginning this Department built an ammunition factory there.

HERR KRIEBEL: I want to mention that this order to the border guards and the order from the Reichswehr must be kept apart. They are two different matters. One is an order from the Landespolizei, the other an order from the Reichswehr. Naturally it would be a poor testimonial to the qualification of the Landespolizei if they were not strong enough to defend the Bavarian border against Red bands. This task did not require the mobilization of all the patriotic Verbände of Bavaria, with the addition of a North German organization—the Ehrhardt organization. The matter is quite clear. Preparations were made—I know it; I don't intend to wash my hands of it, and to implicate others; it simply was the way it was. We all cooperated quite properly and well, and we were all convinced that we all wanted the same thing.

So, everything falls completely into place. There is nothing artificial about it. Colonel von Seisser also wanted to do the job. This is simply the way things were. After all, it is almost a situation of war if a piece of Thuringia is cut off; that really means pushing matters too far.

In regard to the shipment of arms, Seisser told me when I expressed my reservations about the transporting of the arms which belonged to one of our Verbände: "No, the weapons don't belong to you—I am an old friend of his. They are the arms brought down by the Blücherbund in the Fuchs-Machhaas incident. They will return them." Blücher is also part of the Wiking group. I certainly used my power of persuasion with Lossow regarding these arms shipments, because a battery belonging to one of our Verbände had been positioned for O.C., or rather for the Blücherbund. This battery was held in high esteem because several people of the Verband were killed on it in Upper Silesia. This is why the troops attached such importance to their canons.

I am going to discuss briefly the matter concerning Herr Lossow and the question of arms. He had said in February, when it was a question of the Reichswehr taking over—simply taking away from us the weapons which we had collected for years—we were then told that this was done only in order to put them into good repair, which was something that was necessary and to which of course we agreed. Von Lossow literally said that it was because unrest, within the organizations, would develop against the Reichswehr since they were an army of the Reich; because the feeling is that when we Bavarians tell the Reichswehr that "there are so and so many canons and rifles in such and such a monastary," then sooner or later, because of the presence of North German officers in the Wehrkreiskommando, a secret or open report will go to the Reichswehrministerium. And since this idea of the government that these weapons belong to the State of Bavaria cannot be sustained, then the Reichswehr will suddenly receive an order to send these weapons to the North.

In order to stop this abuse of the Verbände, Lossow said: "My word must be sufficient that those weapons which the Verbände have handed over will be returned." When Colonel Lenz talked with Lossow on April 30, the latter said: "I don't care whether you consider me a perjury peasant, you will not get back the weapons." Of course I must add that the events of May 1 had some bearing on this. Still, I found that, for the future, this had cast some doubt on Herr Lossow's trustworthiness, because he never again considered it worth the trouble to refer to his "word of honor"—not with one single word, although I had written to him several times; this "word of honor," given by him in front of 30 officers, but apparently (not kept) for compelling political reasons. It still was not redeemed after this "political reason" no longer existed.

This has put a cloud over my relationship with Herr Lossow. It was a very painful matter and I often wondered whether I should not report it to the High Honor Council so that the matter could be investigated. But I did not want to compromise the chief of the Bavarian part of the Reichswehr, in which my old comrades serve; but now it must be done. At that time he simply broke his promise; so far he has not redeemed it. At that time, he made the battery available to the Landespolizei.

HERR HITLER: I request that Your Honor consider the following points when judging my later attitude after November 9. At that time, yes, before May 1, we also placed at the disposal of Lossow our arms, which our members had obtained under great hardship. We, too, got Lossow's word of honor that these weapons could be reclaimed by us at any time. When on April

30—they were requested to be returned on the 27th or 28th—Herr Lossow coldly declared that he could care less how he would be looked upon, I emphasized when talking to my gentlemen—they were terribly upset and wanted to submit this matter at once to the Honor Council—I said: "Please let us not be unjust this time. I oppose Herr Lossow's attitude in this case. Perhaps it is harsh; but, in this case, the fact is that, as the responsible commander, he perhaps has no other choice since he knows what finally might be done with these arms." At that time I protected His Excellency Lossow from (the consequences of) a breach of promise. I stood up for him—that same man who called me a man who was going back on his word! There you can see how greatly depressing this had to be for us, (to accuse) me, of all people, who at that time had defended him against everyone.

HERR EHARD: May I point out that this occurred immediately before May 1.

HERR HITLER: That is why I defended him; but one's word remains his word. If only he had, just once, said: "I cannot give you the arms," and then resigned, like a man, anything else would have been out of the question. I then still defended him because, I told myself, perhaps from the point of view of the State he had no other choice. I defended him before the officers, who took a strictly straight position, and especially from Captain Göring, who said: "That cannot be done. For an officer, there is no such thing as a breach of promise. If he does it, he must immediately bear the consequences and depart." Yet, I defended him.

Hence, I could have assumed that Herr Lossow himself would not attribute to me a word of honor which was intended to be nothing else than a declaration of loyalty for him and for me. I could not defend myself against his attempt to mark me a dishonorable man by breaking his word of honor.

HERR KRIEBEL: One could have expected an officer who knowingly breaks his word of honor to feel that a serious matter is at stake. But to say with a smile, "I don't care if you consider me a perjuring peasant," proves that this man has no idea of the meaning of a man's "word of honor." That is what has bothered me all along. Lossow committed this breach of promise by dispensing with the matter jokingly thinking that, as far as we were concerned, the matter was settled.

As for myself, it is not settled. Although I don't intend to stir up all the mud that appeared on November 8, especially in the officers' groups—for instance, the attitude toward the King, et cetera—I shall drag them before the tribunal later, when I shall be free again; there they will not get away from me, and Herr Lossow, too, will go there.

JUDGE NEITHARDT: I ask that the remonstrances against Herr Lossow not be repeated.

HERR KRIEBEL: Naturally he will have his chance before the Court of Honor.

JUDGE NEITHARDT: That is a different matter.

HERR EHARD: As far as we are concerned, these are the assertions of one party. We shall wait for the assertions of the other party. I believe it makes a very bad impression if an accused man, in his position as a defendant who is still an active officer, uses the expression, "villain," when referring to his superiors, or at least to those who were his superiors until recently.

JUDGE NEITHARDT: I did not hear that.

HERR EHARD: Defendant Wagner said it.

HERR WAGNER: Yes, I certainly did use the word "villain."

JUDGE NEITHARDT: I repeat: I didn't hear it. I reject it vehemently. You have no right to make such insults.
    Let us hear Herr Götz on this matter!

HERR GÖTZ: I must refer to a remark made in regard to the order. From listening to the Prosecutor, it seems to me—and I don't think I'm mistaken—that he imagines the order read before the Court to be the plan for an action which was to begin a little later. I don't know whether the Prosecutor is aware of the fact that in the military—of which I was an active officer for 14 years—we have one cautionary and one executory word of command. Both the cautionary and the executory commands are literally given in this order. It says, such and such is to be done upon such and such a code word, which the order cannot, of course, disclose. On the 12th or 13th, the code word is issued; then everyone who is familiar with the situation knows what this means. At this point, I firmly reject that the order might be interpreted as containing nothing more significant than a proposition for a race. For instance, an announcement of a race which is to take place later. The order was: You are going to do this now; and, as soon as I telegraph the word "fall maneuver" to you, you will attack.

JUDGE NEITHARDT: We shall discuss the fall maneuver of 1923.

HERR KOHL: My client Brückner feels that it is natural, when the name of Herr Lossow is mentioned, for the defendant's words to express a certain inner rebellion. The defendants have had to be silent for four months. They have had to let themselves be disparaged by the public—whoever opened his mouth was arrested by the public prosecutor. Yes, the Prosecutor should not be surprised if, under these circumstances, the defendant speaks the truth occasionally. If you, Herr Prosecutor, had not made so many arrests, they would have been able to talk more.

HERR STENGLEIN: Counselor, I did not arrest anyone for "opening their mouths," as you suggest. Apparently it has escaped you that the arrests were effected by the Generalstaatsanwalt. I firmly reject such a reproach.

HERR HEMMETER: I don't have to discuss the words of the Counselor; I intend to give the same answer. In view of the indignation which the arrest of the gentlemen has aroused, no one can blame them for, just once, wearing their hearts on their sleeves. I admit that I, too, have used the same expression here in the courtroom.

JUDGE NEITHARDT: Then I must censure you, Counselor; and I expect you to retract your words—for reasons of loyalty— just like Lieutenant Wagner.

Shouts.

JUDGE NEITHARDT: I mean, that you withdraw this expression.

HERR WAGNER: I would not think of it.

JUDGE NEITHARDT: All the more reason for me to reject both.

HERR HEMMETER: I, too, would not think of it. Perhaps I may continue?

Because of the fact that Herr Seisser's signature, under the order of Lieutenant Colonel Kriebel, is not legible, he was not truly suspected of having collaborated in this action. For certain reasons this notion must be nipped in the bud. It is wrong. At present those men who today are well-paid officials of the new Reich are not in a position to sign such orders personally and openly, even if they wanted to. I cannot now discuss this any further. These are unpleasant things which arouse the anger of every decent German—but it has to do with the economic conditions as they now exist. Thus, the hypothesis of the Prosecutor is wrong. It is the attempt to cover up the positions of Herrn Lossow and Seisser which is no longer tenable.

I also want to stress that legally the whole matter is of no significance. The paragraph of the penal code establishes very simple prerequisites for high treason. It does not require a signature at all. There are other actions which fully satisfy the provisions of paragraph 81.

HERR EHARD: It never occurred to me to establish a hypothesis. I only asked a question. If Attorney Hemmeter assails it as a hypothesis, he does something quite unnecessary.

JUDGE NEITHARDT: Is there anything that you, Lieutenant Colonel Kriebel, want to say to this point? If not, we can take a lunch break. I would like to hear from you for however long you might intend in order to defend yourself against my dispositions.

Herr Kriebel replies.

JUDGE NEITHARDT: The next hearing is scheduled for 2:30 this afternoon.

Whereupon, at 12:10 p.m., the hearing is adjourned to reconvene at 2:30 p.m., the same day.

—AFTERNOON SESSION—

The secret session continues, pursuant to the morning recess.

JUDGE NEITHARDT: The hearing continues.

HERR HEMMETER: In the name of my client I would like to state that my client and I deeply regret having used expressions in the morning session which should not have been used.

JUDGE NEITHARDT: Do you speak for your client, too?

HERR HEMMETER: Yes, I do.

JUDGE NEITHARDT: We shall now continue the interrogation of Lieutenant Colonel Kriebel.

HERR KRIEBEL: In summing up, I would like to state the following: The principal points of the order concerning the border guards were established in a meeting on October 9th by me and Lieutenant Colonel Breitner with the cooperation of all patriotic bands of Bavaria, including the Ehrhardt Organization. Lieutenant Colonel Breitner then discussed the order with Colonel von Seisser. It went out on the 16th, in its final form. Colonel von Seisser received a copy of the order.

Furthermore, I state that, in our opinion, everyone agreed unanimously that this was a preparation of a step which would eventually result in a march of Bavaria in the direction of Berlin. We never assumed a different purpose behind these things. One of the reasons why I never doubted this was due to the meeting I attended which had taken place earlier between Oberstlandesgerichtsrat Pöhner and Ehrhardt. I was also present at the discussion of September 30 which took place at the office of His Excellency von Kahr. The impression I gained from these discussions was the following:

It was planned, first of all, to appoint Oberstlandesgerichtsrat Pöhner the Staatskommissar of Saxony and Thuringia. I felt, as a soldier, that naturally this meant nothing else but the control of these areas of transit which, during the march to the

North, could not be left behind without having been pacified in a most rigid manner. This can also be gathered from a statement made by Reichswehrminister Gessler at the convention of the Democratic Party in Württemberg. On this occasion he said that he intended to send the Reichswehr into Thuringia and Saxony in order to get under his firm control the passageways separating the Bavarian organizations from those in East Prussia, Mecklenburg, Pomerania, and Westphalia, who were waiting in North Germany for the call from Bavaria. This purely military and obvious idea was also at the bottom of our thinking since it was quite clear that if one wanted to march on Berlin, then Saxony and Thuringia had to be brought under firm control. It was quite impossible to leave behind such areas—in the condition they were in—without using special precautionary measures.

This morning I spoke about the arms problems. I shall not talk about the merits of some of the young people in our organization. I would like to mention briefly that one of these men who applied all his energy to working in the interest of the Fatherland—the head of the V.V. München—has recently earned very little gratitude for his efforts. Nevertheless, I wish to particularly emphasize that that man who, after all, was in charge of this entire illegal weapons operation and who organized and personally protected it, (this man) is Captain Röhm who is now sitting next to me as a defendant.

I probably do not have to report on the topics of the discussion with His Excellency von Kahr. The precise testimony of Oberlandesgerichtsrat Pöhner has made the situation so clear that I have nothing to add. I have already mentioned this in my testimony, but if the Chairman would like me to—

JUDGE NEITHARDT: No, no. We already heard it.

HERR KRIEBEL: —he does not.

I shall now discuss the development of the situation. On October 22 the quarrel between Bavaria and the Reich had reached its peak. The 22nd of October is the day on which the pledge of allegiance was made by the Reichswehr to the Bavarian government. Without a doubt this meant a considerable worsening of the situation—a fact which became evident to even the blindest man. Those who were familiar with the situation—and I count myself and the other gentlemen among them—who, like I, worked in the patriotic movement and who were in constant touch with Colonel von Seisser—knew that the only purpose of the preparations was this conflict. And then there was this pledge of allegiance of the Reichswehr which was branded publicly by General von Seeckt in an ordinance as a breach of oath against the Reich.

It was quite clear that if, two days after this pledge of allegiance of the Bavarian Reichswehr to the Bavarian government, we as the representatives of all patriotic bands were called before His Excellency von Lossow to listen to a lecture about the situation and measures to be taken on account of it; and that if these measures consisted of the decision to fortify the Reichswehr under entirely changed conditions—in sharp contrast to and complete negation of any measures taken earlier in matters of foreign policy, an act which has already been alluded to in the order submitted today by the attorney—that then it would become clear that after the sharp conflict of October 22 and the order to take such steps, we could do nothing but assume that the preparations were meant as a reply to this conflict.

It is clear that the order received its special character from the introductory words of Herr Lossow. At least in the way in which he expressed himself, Lossow never left any doubt in our minds. It is difficult to repeat something like that; one can only repeat the impression. I cannot tell you the exact words, but the impression gained by all of those present was that the Reichswehr was to be strengthened for an interior conflict; after this strengthening, it would start its march to the North.

This is confirmed also by the fact that several organizations refused to participate in this undertaking, not because there was any actual conflict between them and the Reichswehr, but rather because they did not want their Verbände to be incorporated into the Reichswehr. They wanted them to be employed as Freikorps, besides the Reichswehr. Those Verbände who had refused to participate were Ehrhardt, Blücherbund, Reichsflagge, and Stahlhelm—while Kampfbund, Bayern und Reich, and the V.V. München, I believe, and one other organization made themselves available. Here one will raise the objection that this was only a defensive measure because we can count on the fact that suddenly General Reinhardt, who at first traveled peacefully through Bavaria with his Württemberg Reichswehr, would suddenly turn around and face Bavaria. I would like to invalidate such an opinion, from the start, by expressly stating that in view of the way Herr Lossow's order was introduced, we did not doubt that this was the order for the advance on Berlin, taking into account the conditions which had changed in the meantime. It was no longer a matter of simply pacifying the Freikorps in Saxony and Thuringia and then continuing the march, but, rather, of the other Reichswehr taking over this pacification.

There is no question that the pacification of Thuringia, as a passageway, was intended. This can be derived from a meeting I had with Colonel Seisser in which I said, with reference to the Freikorps, that it was my opinion, first of all, that we should march ahead and thoroughly clean up the pigsty up there. It was suggested that we, as an illegal organization, could do it with you, with your Green Police and Lossow with the Reichswehr coming behind us; and that they would see to it that this "illegal purge" became a legal State action. Seisser then told me: I have almost the same idea.

One must understand the position we were in. It is certainly possible to suddenly say it was meant in a different manner, but then should we not have been told so? I think that when the Landeskommandant calls all the patriotic bands together to effect a strengthening of the Reichswehr—and it is definitely nothing more than a defensive action—then I think we all know that in order to prevent misunderstandings, he must describe to us the exact defensive purpose. If he has not done so, he has no defensive purpose. He knew we were all in favor of an offensive, yet not a word was spoken classifying this as a fortification of the border guards against the North German Reichswehr. On the contrary, it was expressly stated that negotiations had been conducted with the North German Reichswehr, and so on. In any case, if Lossow had intended only to prepare the border guards, he should have said that it was no longer an offensive, as you with your Freikorps perhaps thought it to be; rather, it was to be a matter of protecting Bavaria from the threat of the Reich Executive. If he had said this, we would have known what was at stake. However, since he did not say so, but let us believe as we did, it was clear that he was thinking of other things.

One must assume, of a commander in charge who summons all the patriotic bands for assistance, that he would explain to them the purpose of their service; that he would state very clearly what he understands the job to be. None of us understood this to be a protective measure against the Reichswehr from Prussia and Württemberg.

150

Apart from that, perhaps I may now request that this order be read. I told Lossow I would immediately make a draft of the order to the Kampfbund and send him a copy as soon as it was written. Beforehand I want to state clearly that on October 27 I sent the final order of the fall maneuver to Herr Lossow, under his private address. Then on the 28th, there was the meeting with Lieutenant Colonel Diesterweg in which it was determined that he was only to be informed once it was accomplished that, on the one hand, the Kampfbund and all other patriotic bands including the Landespolizei had made themselves available on October 16; and, on the other hand, the Kampfbund (to) the Reichswehr on October 27. Before this order is read, I would like to ask Your Honor to inform the Court of the letter written by the Wanderamt of the Hochschulring München to His Excellency von Kahr on October 20.

Herr Gademann requests Herr Schramm to explain the organization Wanderamt.

HERR SCHRAMM: I am prepared to give information because there has been some misunderstanding. Oberland groups in North Germany were also called Wanderamt. Wanderamt was an organization working secretly, whose purpose it was to disregard the split between the various völkische Verbände in order to train the people in a purely military way—and without any political motivation—so that they might be prepared for the great day. At first I was the secretary, and a corps brother of mine was my superior; but then at the beginning of last summer's vacation when the head of the Reichswanderamt Ruhrgebiet had, de facto, been inactivated, I took over the management for the entire Reich—without any specific authorization. It was absolutely necessary since the Reichswehramt no longer had a leader and since my knowledge, especially regarding the march—after discussion with the leader of the Hermannbund which had most of the students, and of the Hochschulring—I took the liberty of sending the letter, which is about to be submitted, to the Generalstaatskommissariat.

Herr Gademann submits the letter to Herr Kahr of October 20, 1923. In addition, he submits the order I A 800 of the Wehrkreiskommando VII of October 26, 1923, (the so-called "fall maneuver.")

JUDGE NEITHARDT: To whom did this order go?

HERR GADEMANN: To the commander of the artillery unit VII.

Following this order, which got into the hands of the Deutsche Kampfbund, on October 26, 1923, the military commander issued a preparatory order to those Kampfverbände which formed the Kampfbund. This order, a copy of which went to the Wehrkreiskommando VII, was only intended for the military commanders. Also subsequent to this order by the chief of the Kampfbund, Bund Oberland issued an order on October 29, 1923.

Furthermore, various military units—referred to as "I 19"—issued the intermediary orders of November 2 and November 3. The order of I 19 of November 2, which refers expressly to the fall maneuver 23, states, among other things: "I request a report of how the ordered measures will be executed until November 8, 1923, at the latest. The medical checkup of those volunteers to be enlisted must be carried out at once."

In the order of I 19 of November 3, it says, under number 2: "There will be no general proclamation. Only absolutely reliable men are to be enlisted." Under number 7, it says: "Herewith the Verbände are instructed to send in the information of their strength until November 8, 1923."

The information on this order needs to be supplemented with the following details: The principal order I A 800, the general order of the Wehrkreiskommando VII, reads as follows—I have singled out these details to give a complete survey.

Herr Gademann submits the contents of order I A 800.

HERR GADEMANN: Subsequently, with reference to the oral discussion mentioned in order I A 800—

HERR LUETGEBRUNE: I wish to ask my colleague, Dr. Gademann, whether he doesn't have, and would like to read, appendix I, "Strategic Organization of War," which is attached to this order?

HERR SCHRAMM: This is dated November 3.

HERR GADEMANN: I don't have it here.

JUDGE NEITHARDT: The "War Organization" is not among the court documents. I must have it.

HERR KRIEBEL: Yes. Here it is. The Judge has the order.

JUDGE NEITHARDT: Yes, we already have the order.

HERR KRIEBEL: May I briefly add the following? The most important connection on the other side was Oberregierungsrat Stauffer of the Ministry of Justice. The Kampfbund order was issued following this oral discussion mentioned in the order. We did not receive the order; we were only informed orally. Upon the oral instruction by Herr Lossow, we then worked out the order which is yet to be submitted, while simultaneously this order was issued to the Reichswehr troops. That order we never received.

The assembly areas were mentioned here. This is the term for those areas where the troops were to be assembled to begin operations. Furthermore, reference is made to operations in the order issued by me. It went to the Reichskriegsflagge, the Oberkommando Hitler, Oberland, and Kampfbund München. A copy also went to the Wehrkreiskommando VII.

The order of October 26, 1923 is submitted.

HERR KRIEBEL: Concerning this order, I would like to say the following: If we refused to fight under the command of General Epp, we did so because Epp had made the most hostile remarks regarding our endeavors. He called us the "Komitatschi Bands." The same was true of Generals Ruith and Kress. Their reason for doing this was the fact that—and this is also characteristic of the attitude towards the Reichswehr—they had not supported Lossow in the pledge of allegiance to the Bavarian government. We expressly said that it was for this reason—because of their absolutely black-white-red, not black-red-gold views—too, that we did not want the two leaders to be entrusted with the command of a Verband in which our troops would fight. We knew that they were to be blamed for the fact that the pledge of allegiance had not been made to the Bavarian government; or for their reluctance to do so, because their attitude was black-red-"yellow," as we call it. We knew that Ruith was a friend of the Minister of Defense, Gessler, and that Kress had very strong ties over there. When I personally expressed my misgivings, nobody—neither Lossow nor Lieutenant Colonel Berchem—told me that such assumptions were incorrect; rather, they were noted and recorded in writing.

There are still some quite important orders to be mentioned. There is the order issued to the units—the executory order for the Reichswehr order, not for ours. Our executory order is the one from Bund Oberland. It is significant because later it became a target of attack in the meeting of November 6 where Berchem, Dr. Weber, and I were accused of disloyalty. I only would like to say, briefly, that on October 16 we had issued the order to our Verbände that as Freikorps they should be available to the Landespolizei for the march on Berlin. On October 24, we received the order that we were no longer to march as Freikorps, but rather as members of the Reichswehr. We simply cannot turn our troops around so quickly—to tell them, one day, that preparations are made for the Bund Oberland to be Freikorps; and then, the next day, that there is an order nullifying the first one and now you must become a company in the Reichswehr. Dr. Weber issued the order explaining this to our men. He used more explicit language than is customary, simply in order to make the people understand this turnabout.

JUDGE NEITHARDT: This order is also included in the court documents?

HERR KRIEBEL: It is the one dated October 29, 1923, in volume II, Appendix C to the testimony of General Lossow. I would like the order to be made known. The order is supposed to be a "disloyalty." The reasons cannot be discussed in a public hearing; perhaps Dr. Weber himself can read the order to the Court?

JUDGE NEITHARDT: Might it be sufficient to simply state its contents?

DR. WEBER: May I say, in advance, that as a matter of course all patriotic bands considered it an ideal—as the only goal worth striving for—that those Verbände who were closely knit with many ties, through military tradition, naturally should be sent into action as one unit; that is, as long as we had only to expect internal conflicts, and as long as there was no question of a national war. It had to be explained very carefully to the people second in command, as well as to our men that, of necessity, this was impossible—a fact which the leadership had realized.

154

Following the discussions which Kriebel had with the Landespolizei, instructions went out to our military units, in the middle of October, stating that we were to be employed as a close Verband in the eastern parts of Lower Franconia. Ten days later, this had to be reversed and it then had to be explained to our troops that, for the moment, we would not be proceeding in this way; that single companies from our Verband would and could be used. This is the reason for the confidential order of October 29, 1923.

This order is submitted to the Court, except for the ordering of positions.

HERR WEBER: I would like to say that, as far as I know, the reason for the remark in number 5 is due to a report made by Lossow to Ludendorff a few days earlier, that the Bund Oberland, a militarily able Verband, would probably be drawn together into a division if an extensive military involvement should develop, and also partly in the event of military operations against an external enemy.

We have the order I 19, which is an executory order to this Wehrkreiskommando order. It makes it quite clear that the matter is urgent, because it says: "The Verbände are requested to carry through the police investigation immediately. The Verbände"—that is, we—"are in charge of this matter."

Furthermore, it says: "I request information until November at the latest about the number of the other volunteers available." Then it also says: "The Verbände are asked to take along anything necessary... ."

There now follows what is already contained in the other order: "Any matters submitted to I 19 which concern Fall Maneuver 23 are to be sent, under cover, to an aide and are to contain detailed information about the success."

Hence, this is the executory order. This proves they worked hand in hand.

HERR GADEMANN: The order to the Verbände is dated November 2, 1923, and is entitled, "Infantry Battalion No. 6. Secret. Order of October 26, 1923. Fall Maneuver 23." The second order from I 19 is addressed to the troops and dated November 3, 1923. I shall submit a copy of it to the Court right away.

There is a third document which was issued outside of Munich, which proves that even outside Munich they worked on

155

the basis of I A 800. According to this, a strictly confidential discussion took place on October 31, 1923, at 5:00 p.m., between the commander of Regiment 20 and the representatives of the Wehr organizations in the District of Weiden—Northern Bavaria. The discussion is recorded in the document I have before me.

Dr. Gademann submits the report.

HERR GADEMANN: Here the code word, "Sunrise," is mentioned. This code word means the first day of mobilization.

HERR KRIEBEL: May I interject the following at this point? This is the executory order of the Weiden District, of the Bund "Bayern und Reich." It is characteristic of a certain attitude that "Bayern und Reich" already knew the code word, while we had not been informed of it until now.

HERR GADEMANN: The document is signed with "M. Hauptmann, M.D."

JUDGE NEITHARDT: What is the date of this order?

HERR GADEMANN: November 2, 1923.

HERR KRIEBEL: In general, I would like to say that we have, of course, revealed these matters only because the public was excluded. The matters were in absolutely safe hands, and we were too closely bound to each other to have made use of them otherwise.

HERR RODER: May I have the opportunity of reading a letter to the Court which has some significance here, and which contains a quite remarkable passage? It is an order S.A.N.A.B., Bezirkswehr Regensburg, Commander—the signature is illegible. The order carries the date: Regensburg, October 30, 1923. "Ref.: Mobilization. Secret. After due consideration." In this order, the first paragraph is typical and characteristic of the views of every gentleman here. It says: "There is complete agreement now between Hitler, Lossow, and Kahr. Mobilization is to be expected in the nearest future." What follows is generally the same as that which is said in the other order.

JUDGE NEITHARDT: Of which date is this order?

HERR RODER: Of October 30, 1923.

HERR LUDENDORFF: I believe what I wanted to say is appropriate at this point. The order I A 800 was issued on October 26. If it is read from a military point of view, there is no doubt as to its purpose.

Two days after the order was issued a communications center was set up in Leipzig. I have also invited to be a witness the gentleman who established the communications center. I don't know whether I am to reiterate his information; in any case, it would fit the context.

JUDGE NEITHARDT: Please. Please.

HERR LUDENDORFF: The gentlemen writes: "At the end of October I was expelled from Switzerland because of political activities. I took up residence in Munich."

This Herr Gresser was employed in Switzerland in the News Service of the German Reich. Somehow he came under suspicion there and was subsequently expelled. He then came to Munich. He happened to meet Polizeirat Bauer who, as far as I know, is also active in the News Service and to whom he reported his observations in Switzerland.

He goes on:

> "On October 28, 1923, I was ordered to come to the building of the Wehrkreiskommando VII at 11:00 o'clock in the morning. There I was received by Major Baumann, a major in the General Staff. Since I am a member of the Kampfbund and wanted to go to Saxony, I was asked by Major Baumann to forward information about the Saxon and non-Bavarian Reichswehr to the Wehrkreiskommando VII."

He was then given a questionnaire of the kind which, in my extensive military experience, is only prepared to get information about a hostile power—of course this is not meant maliciously. I only use this expression for the sake of clarity.

The questions run as follows:

> "1. What is the attitude of the non-Bavarian Reichswehr towards Bavaria?
> "2. Is the Reichswehr reinforced by black

(illegal) Reichswehr? To what extent?

"3. Of which organizations is the black Reichswehr composed?

"4. What is the attitude of the patriotic organizations towards Bavaria?

"5. Have the socialist organizations been called up to reinforce the Reichswehr?

"6. What is the attitude among the troops of the 5th Division stationed near Hof?

"7. Are there any troop transports? From where? To where?

"8. Is the security police being reinforced?

"9. Acts of sabotage?

"10. Number of personnel attached to telephone, telegraph, etc.?"

It may be interesting to hear how this Herr Gresser answered this questionnaire. The answer is dated November 1, 1923, and is addressed to Major Baumann.

Concerning the first question, "What is the attitude of the non-Bavarian Reichswehr towards Bavaria?", the gentleman in question answers: "All in all the attitude of the Reichswehr is national and not at all unfriendly toward Bavaria. The troops are partly behind Hitler. The Officers' Corps welcomes the actions of Bavaria as long as Bavaria remains black-white-red. According to one Lieutenant Colonel, an action of non-Bavarian Reichswehr against Bavaria is considered impossible here. Some of the older officers are opposed to any action directed against national circles."

Concerning question 2, "Is the Reichswehr reinforced by black Reichswehr? To what extent?", this gentleman answers: "Yes, 800 men in Leipzig."

His answer to question 3, "Of what organizations is the black Reichswehr composed?", is that there are 700 men from Bund Oberland, et cetera, here; 100 men are members of the Jungdeutscher Orden.

The answer to question 4, "What is the attitude of the patriotic organizations towards Bavaria?" is: "The majority of them are firmly behind Hitler; also, see my answer to question 1. The leaders of most national organizationss are Prussions, e.g., Bund Oberland, Stahlhelm, Jungdeutscher Orden."

Number five, "Are socialist organizations called up to reinforce the Reichswehr?" Answer: "No."

Number six, "What is the attitude of the 5th Division stationed near Hof?" Not answered.

Number seven, "Are there any troop transports?" Answer: "No. The battalion called off from Leipzig will be replaced by Battalion 11."

Number Eight, "Is the security police being reinforced?" "No. Attitude Jewish-democratic."

As far as the questionnaire is concerned, it is interesting to note the content of a questionnaire which was given to the same Herr Gresser by Bund Oberland. This is a questionnaire that refers only to the things which are so often asserted and which have to do with the entire action. Among other things, these questions refer to the activities of the Communist leaders and the strength of the Communist actions. Then it says: "Meeting places? Arms depots? Financial sources of the Communists? Acts of Sabotage? Mail, telephone, and telegraph circuits?" From these two questionnaires it can clearly be deduced that the first one is military, and the second one is political. That's what I wanted to say.

DR. WEBER: The attachment of the Oberländer to the Reichswehr of Central Germany was effected upon consultation with me, with my consent and upon my instructions. I am therefore completely informed of the mood and the attitude of the Reichswehr in Saxony and in Thuringia. I was also informed about the attitude of the Reichswehr towards Ludendorff. I may perhaps point out that I was also informed about the answers which were given to Major Baumann since the man in question was an Oberländer.

HERR LUDENDORFF: Herr Gresser took his leave on November 17. Ruith told him on November 30 that he no longer needed him. There are receipts for 2 trillions which he has received.

HERR KRIEBEL: As I said before, through my work for the Escherich organization I established connections with all national bands in North Germany. I still maintain friendly relations with many of them. From my acquaintances in North Germany I have known for a long time that all the men whom the North German bands made available to reinforce the Reichswehr had the order not to resist Bavaria in any way. Those are the instructions from the patriotic bands in North Germany. I cannot disclose any names since I cannot betray the people. After the chief of the Infantry School had gone to Berlin, a completely different policy was followed here. Those Bavarian

159

officers on leave, who originally had been discharged, were called back and, suddenly, it was maintained that Berlin and Munich wanted the same thing, that they had the same goal as Lossow. That happened in one and the same month.

I would like to inform the Court of one communication which I received from Lieutenant Colonel Heines. He had been a loyal colleague since 1923; and he was one of those who tried, day and night, to shift our arms from one betrayed arsenal to the other. He had made it the mission of his life to find and bring out into the open those traitors who had betrayed our arsenals to the Entente commissions. Through his activity, he had established close connections with the police, whose work at that time under the leadership of Herr Pöhner and Herr Frick, had a distinct national tendency. He also made acquaintances among the officers who worked in the area News Service in the Reichswehrkommando, besides this Major Baumann.

He writes me:

> "In the meantime, Württemberg troops had come to Thuringia, a fact which caused some consternation. I was asked to find out through my connections how these troops felt towards Bavaria, whether they were reinforced by black (illegal) Reichswehr, and to report anything worth knowing to the Wehrkreiskommando. I requested a questionnaire which I received immediately. It was duplicated and sent as quickly as possible to the individual command posts of the posts at the northern border of Bavaria. Furthermore, I was asked to report on the mood towards Herr Kahr and Lossow among the troops there—that is, the non-Bavarian troops. The Landespolizei had set up a communications center in Hof which gave continuous reports."

It all bears the same mark. I don't think I have to add anything. I have now come to the conclusion of those matters which I wanted to discuss while the public is excluded—there are still two things I wanted to mention as long as the public is excluded. They are not directly connected, but I still ask that I be permitted to state them in order to come to an end. One is the known preliminary order of November 7 which is among the documents and, consequently, I believe is an appendix to the indictment.

I believe it is clear to anyone, even if he is a complete lay-man in military matters, that from the beginning we were heading for war; that it was possible, at any moment, for our Verbände, in one way or other, to have to serve in action with the Reichswehr or the Landespolizei. It goes without saying that for this reason we accelerated our training of our people as far as possible, and that we also increased the training opportunities, if possible. A part of this training included the various exercises, as well as the night drills, which we ordered. As I said in my tes-timony, the measures we took for November 8 were not the result of a plan we had had for a long time and for which every-thing had been prepared; rather, they were a spontaneous decision put to us at the right opportunity. This opportunity was not just created, but had come with intensified training as the final result of the developing situation. This also goes for the night exercise from Saturday and Sunday and the march into the city.

I only wanted to say the following: From a purely military standpoint—and disregarding the completely different views we had while working, all the time, with the Reichswehr and the Landespolizei—those of us who knew how weak the Verbände were could not possibly have been thinking of attacking the others as laid down in the indictment, which says we intended to over-throw the government with the concentrated force of the Kampf-bund. We would never have committed such a foolish act. As a military leader, I would have called such a plan—which is abso-lutely unprofessional and downright ridiculous—complete non-sense. Hence, this preliminary order of November 7 for this night exercise was an instruction coming from Major Hühnlein, who is still in prison although it has been proved that he knew nothing about the whole matter.

I would like to emphasize, now that for once I can talk openly about the reason for the issuing of this order, that this order has nothing to do with the affair of November 8. The entire systematic intensification of training, and all these measures, continued without interruption. Lieutenant Brückner can con-firm that in the evening of November 8 the men were ordered to the barracks for a checkup. I categorically state, once again, that I should take my leave as a soldier if I had acted in such an idiotic manner, or if I had even thought of it. That would have been a stupid undertaking. Nobody could possibly believe that I, an old General Staff officer and experienced soldier, would be capable of such stupidity. I must reject, as vehemently as possible, this accusation because it is so unprofessional that, in the interest of my military reputation, I must defend myself against the thought that such a thing could even be used to indict me.

The second point I wanted to make is the following: The speech given by General Lossow and General Seisser has been rendered incorrectly in the indictment. At the end of their talk in the Bürgerbräukeller, both Lossow and Seisser stated expressly their hopes; that is, Lossow wanted to bring honor to the black-white-red cockade by leading the army against an external enemy, and Seisser said that after having destroyed the inner Reich with his police, he also wanted to lead his police against an external enemy. I was the one who prevented these two sentences from getting into the press, because I told myself it would be a catastrophe if phrases like these would be published now, because then, of course, everybody would march—even the Eskimos would come as an enemy and declare war on us, because of November 8. This is the way the two sentences were phrased. I would like to stress that expressly.

HERR PÖHNER: It is a matter of getting the facts straight. Whatever Kriebel said about the incongruity between the way in which the statements of Lossow and Seisser appeared in the *Münchener Neueste Nachrichten* and their actual phrasing, as it was done, was also the subject of a detailed discussion at the meeting of the chief editors in the Polizeidirektion between 12:00 and 1:00 o'clock at night. I could not say that yesterday. I appealed to the press to maintain national discipline. I pointed out to Dr. Gerlich of the *Münchener Neueste Nachrichten* that Lossow's and Seisser's concluding words about the black-white-red cockade and the external enemy had slipped out. Obviously, they would not have said these things if they had contemplated our political responsibility. I asked the gentlemen not to print these sentences, for reasons of national discipline. These things were uttered in a moment of enthusiasm by the two gentlemen who spoke the way they thought, especially Seisser who, if I may say so, in his thirst for war wore his heart on his sleeve. (I asked the editors) to prune the story, to trim it in consideration of the Entente who—although they know our views—might look for a pretext to act in some way on the basis of such careless statements.

Therefore, Dr. Gerlich and the other gentlemen—all the

chief editors were gathered in the Polizeidirektion—promised me to prune and trim the actual words by Herr Lossow and Herr Seisser. This is the way it happened; and this was the reason why, the next day, the press published something which did not correspond with the events in the Bürgerbräukeller.

HERR KOHL: May I make a brief statement? Last night my son saw Dr. Gerlich on another matter. On this occasion, Dr. Gerlich confirmed what Oberstlandesgerichtsrat Pöhner just said. He, fearing damage to the Reich if they should be published, intentionally omitted these sentences.

JUDGE NEITHARDT: That was one of the points which you said you would discuss later.

HERR SCHRAMM: In this context, I would like to add the following: General Lossow is supposed to have said, in the adjacent room in the Bürgerbräukeller, that he would prepare such a brew that Ludendorff would be delighted.

JUDGE NEITHARDT: I remember that Graf said that.

HERR SCHRAMM: Graf adds: "In this historical hour, this statement was one which made the deepest impression." In my opinion, this remark is of extraordinary importance. Nobody who is under "coercion" will make such a remark.

HERR PÖHNER: This would be a very interesting point. I myself did not hear this remark—at least I no longer remember it— because His Excellency Ludendorff was still with General Lossow, Lieutenant Colonel Kriebel, and Colonel von Seisser, later on. The gentlemen discussed certain matters. I could not hear the conversation because at this time I was talking with Herr Kahr about the transfer of the various ministries to certain individuals, and especially about the replacement of the Minister of Agriculture, of the Minister of Police, and so on. During this time, the officers negotiated with each other—but, now is the proper time to get the facts directly from the gentlemen present. All the gentlemen who participated, at the time, are here and perhaps someone can inform us of the form in which this remark was made.

HERR SCHRAMM: The pertinent document here is the Hitler document, Leaf 32: "Interrogation of the Witness Graf."

According to this, Lossow said:

> "The wish of Your Excellency is my command. I shall organize the army in a way in which Your Excellency needs it for an attack. I was especially touched by this scene, and I thought to myself: now nothing more can be amiss. The gentlemen were in a very good mood, etc., etc."

HERR PÖHNER: As I mentioned yesterday, I was not able to pay any attention to the talk between Generals Ludendorff and Lossow, and Colonel Seisser.

JUDGE NEITHARDT: Can His Excellency Ludendorff perhaps remember?

HERR LUDENDORFF: That was the essence of his answer. Whether those were the exact words, I cannot say, Your Honor.

HERR HITLER: I was present at that moment. I was perhaps 3 or 4 meters away when Herr Lossow made such a remark. However, I cannot give the exact words. I only know one thing: we all had the definite impression that Lossow was applying himself zealously to the task of carrying forward the plans we had agreed upon.

JUDGE NEITHARDT: Dr. Weber, were you not also present?

HERR WEBER: I cannot remember. It has eluded me. I know only that a remark was made by Lossow that he would organize the army as best as he could. I no longer remember whether this remark was made before or whether it was only after we had returned from the hall.

JUDGE NEITHARDT: May I ask Defendant Kriebel to continue?

HERR KRIEBEL: I knew that Kommerzienrat Zentz had invited the entire German and foreign press to the meeting in the Bürgerbräukeller. Zentz himself told me so. I therefore was aware of the danger that could arise if remarks such as those of Lossow and Seisser should get into the foreign press. I asked Herr Stolzing of the *Völkischer Beobachter* to see to it that this remark did not get into the press and that it was not published by the foreign press. How successful the attempt to tone down the foreign press has been, I don't know.

I said earlier that I could not name the men in North Germany from whom I received news. I would like to add something to this point. During my imprisonment I was visited by someone from East Prussia who told me the organizations there had been called up on November 9. On November 10 the battalion there was changed. This corresponds with the statement by Reichswehrminister Gessler that East Prussia, Pomerania, and Westphalia were also waiting for the signal from Bavaria to start marching. I did not want to say so in the public hearing so that no harm would come to the gentlemen from East Prussia where Severing is undertaking a so-called "purge."

Finally, I would like to say a few words about the so-called Oberkommando Hitler. In reading the indictment, one finds an "Oberkommando—one Oberkommando residing in the "Rheinischer Hof," one Oberkommando in the Schellingstrasse, one Oberkommando in the Bürgerbräukeller. Sometimes it is called Oberkommando Hitler. At other times it is called Göring. I would like to clarify this. Personally, I did not have an Oberkommand, but I was the military leader. As the military chief, I had my office in the "Rheinischer Hof."

The so-called Oberkommando Hitler, or Oberkommando as it was simply called, is the High Command of the National Socialist Storm Troops, with Captain Göring as its head. It was under the authority of Hitler—his "domestic army," so to speak—while I as the military chief was responsible to Hitler for the actions of the entire Kampfbund. Göring and I were responsible to Hitler; General Aechter, to Dr. Weber. The Reichskriegsflagge had a governing body. It is clear that, because of this dual subordination, I could not give any order that was not approved of by the political leader. That would have led to conflicts. In general, we were not organized to such a degree that important orders would have been given among the leaders. They were a circle of friends who had gathered to work together in the Kampfbund and who completely accepted the leadership of Adolf Hitler.

I can only repeat that I, alone, as military chief, am responsible for the military matters and actions; and, that my subordinates, down to the lowest rifle carrier, have acted only upon my orders. Thus I carry the full and sole responsibility. As I explained this morning, one cannot imprison any man for having carried out one of my orders. We have trained our people as much as we could to comply with the demands of the Reichswehr which wanted only highly disciplined companies.

I would request Your Honor's further permission to discuss those questions referring to the prohibited area, so that I may be able to conclude this part of my statement, and the public can be readmitted.

JUDGE NEITHARDT: I do not think it is necessary to discuss these matters again. They have been thoroughly dealt with.

HERR RODER: I would ask Lieutenant Colonel Kriebel whether, in his opinion, this fall maneuver 23 could have been directed against France?

HERR KRIEBEL: No.

HERR SCHRAMM: With reference to the same question, I would like to anticipate an objection which the prosecution would raise because of the wording of the order: "Fall Maneuver of October 23, 1923." It says in that order: "In case of internal unrest... ." I would like to establish, through Lieutenant Colonel Kriebel's statement, that it is impossible to determine the beginning of "internal unrest" in as exact a manner as is indicated in the order. For here, it seems as if it only required the pressing of a button and internal unrest would break out—not to mention the fact that on October 26, nobody talked of inner unrest.

All in all I have the impression that the passage dealing with "internal disorder" is not quite clear. Why is there suddenly this tremendous secrecy? Those were quite open matters. As a reminder, for the sake of completeness, I would like to state that with respect to the letter read earlier by my colleague—and by this I mean the letter of the Wanderamt to the Generalstaats-kommissariat—(the letter) is signed not only by the Wanderamt, but also by the Hochschulring and the Hermannsbund.

HERR KRIEBEL: I would like to respond to the question which Attorney Roder asked me. I have said before that the fall maneuver 23 could not have meant a war against France. That was out of the question. We had just prepared a separate mobilization for the war against France. That was the so-called "spring maneuver." We could not simply discard (the plans for) the spring maneuver which had just been completed. I think this is impossible, for internal reasons.

HERR LUETGEBRUNE: I would like to ask Herr Kriebel

166

whether "spring maneuver" is a technical term?

HERR KRIEBEL: "Spring maneuver" is an abbreviation of mine.

HERR HOLL: "Spring maneuver" simply means an operational exercise.

HERR KRIEBEL: I chose the expression to distinguish between several concepts. "Spring maneuver" means operational exercise; it means mobilization against the foreign enemy.

HERR HOLL: Before the public is readmitted, I would like to make known an order which nullifies order I A 800, or the order of the Landespolizei to enlist. The order is dated November 19, 1923, "Confidential, No. 3112," and reads: "The fall maneuver 23 is discontinued." Another order, canceling the fall maneuver, should be mentioned. We don't have it, but we do have a more recent order which, again, cancels the cancelation order, so that things have now been resumed. This order has the number 183 M; and "M" stands for mobilization. The order reads: "The discontinuation of our work is now over. Work is to be resumed in its entirety."

HERR LUDENDORFF: Here it says: "M.T.K." That means Mobilmachungsterminkalender (mobilization itinerary).

JUDGE NEITHARDT: What is the date of this order?

HERR HOLL: This order is dated December 15, 1923. At the end, it says: "19th Bavarian Infantry Regiment, 1st Battalion, signed: Schönhärl."

JUDGE NEITHARDT: I request that this document be handed over to the Court.

HERR HOLL: We have to question Major Schönhärl about it.

JUDGE NEITHARDT: It is doubtful whether he will be released from his oath of office.

HERR HOLL: Then we simply have to produce other witnesses for it.

JUDGE NEITHARDT: You can still hand over a copy of it.

HERR HOLL: I am handing both documents to the Court.

HERR LUDENDORFF: The two orders just submitted to the Court by Attorney Holl come under the same heading as the information I gave about the closing of the communications center in Leipzig. Thus, any preparations connected with fall maneuver 23 were discontinued.

HERR LUETGEBRUNE: For clarification in this matter, I would like Lieutenant Colonel Kriebel to answer another question. Is it possible that this operational exercise 23, and the fall maneuver 23 may be misinterpreted to mean actually nothing but a maneuver—that is, a trial mobilization, and so on?

HERR KRIEBEL: No; that is impossible. I myself have participated in the preparations for the operational exercise. At that time, I had been delegated to work at the Wehrkreiskommando and I know definitely that these preparations were serious. They were directed at converting the passive Ruhr struggle into an active one. That is also quite clear as far as the fall maneuver is concerned. I am fully informed.

HERR ZEZSCHWITSCH: You yourself stated—although not quite as plainly, I think—that the members of the Court might understand it that way. This important order was submitted to the Public Prosecutor in four copies, and an extra copy went to Oberregierungsrat Stauffer as the representative of the Gesamtministerium. I would like to add, as an explanation, that the entire fall maneuver undertaken with all the Kampfbund bands took place with the knowledge of the representatives of the Free State of Bavaria.

HERR LUDENDORFF: I wish to add that the expression "mixed units" is used on the page of the fall maneuver 23 which has been handed to the Judge. As far as I know, three units were formed in the mobilization plan. However, they were not "mixed units," but rather Verbände.

HERR HITLER: I can confirm Ludendorff's assumptions. At that time, during the spring, we conducted negotiations with Lossow with regard to the training of the Storm Troopers of the National Socialists. I stated in the open session that I could not say publicly why the former Storm Troops, which were intended only as a security force for meetings, all of a sudden became the

Kampfbund. This happened in January of 1923 during the Ruhr conflict. At that time, I went to Lossow and we decided, after long debates, that these Verbände, if they consisted of young men, were to receive military training. I also was in Berlin on a trip taken by Ludendorff during which I approached all patriotic bands and asked them if they would be prepared to make their young people available to the Reich for training. All of them were willing to do so, with the exception of one Verband who refused, for reasons which politically were, perhaps, very, very sound—that is, this Verband declared that one could not trust the leadership of the Reich; they might now train the men and, once the men were trained, they (the Reich) might not want to attack, but rather disband the Verbände because they were really trained. At that time I strongly opposed the gentlemen and emphatically stated that this seemed to me to be absolutely impossible. I considered it a duty to prepare the young men for the fight against France. I conducted the negotiations with Lossow in Munich, and the basic tenor was that it was out of the question to use these Verbände as closed Verbände, as closed companies of the National Socialists, and so on, for this purpose, i.e. for mobilization against a foreign country.

For this reason we also surrendered the arms. We were promised by word of honor that they were to remain our property. We handed over all our arms; they were repaired, stored in the barracks, and cleaned. In short, they were ready to be used, all for the purpose of mobilization. There were serious quarrels with the individual Verbände (who said) that in this case it would be absolutely out of the question that their former leaders would let themselves become battalion commanders. The express condition was that only those Verbände who on the day of mobilization were prepared to make available at once all their men as recruits—in this case as soldiers to be integrated into the army units—would be considered. Neither the individual nor the Verband has any right to interfere with the decisions concerning the individual men; that is an important difference to the training we received later in the second period.

When the Ruhr conflict was over, the training became less intensive. That is natural. Now the second training phase began. Here it was expressly permitted, as can be seen from all these orders, for the individual Verbände to form their own companies; even their commanders could remain, if they met the requirements. It is impossible to mistake the operational exercise—that is, the spring maneuver with the fall maneuver. The second preparation for the internal cleanup was directed at preserving the homogeneity of the individual units. Here we could not do without the cohesiveness of our Verbände because a Reichswehr whose men were more or less concerned with making a living did not seem as dependable in the fight against Communist and Pacifist elements. That was accepted without objections by our Verbände, whose concern was definitely political ideas.

This is why this last mobilization had only this one purpose. I am not talking about the manner of training. The commander of my München Regiment I (one) will be better qualified to speak about it. But as I have said earlier, there was in the entire set-up—and this was clear even to the most stupid man—the danger, in the long run, of not being able to constrain the people. If, day by day, these people heard nothing else but "When are we going to start?", and so on, then the day had to come when the affair was either called off or the attack begun. This was one of the motivating reasons which forced me to act.

HERR LUDENDORFF: Since he talked to me, I would like to confirm what Hitler has said. I have always maintained that this was to be the fight against the West. So did Dr. Weber. It was clear to the gentlemen of the Kampfbund that these troops were not suitable for external combat. Of course, it was my wish— since I had something to say in the matter—that those Verbände who through tradition consisted of really well trained people—as, for instance, Bund Oberland had proved in their fight against upper Silesia—that those Verbände should be allowed to form a company, and that they should stay together, if possible, to retain their proven spirit. This, however, should be done only to the extent that it was militarily defensible. It was quite clear that the responsibility was so heavy that nobody would think of sending untrained people to the front. The best bloc that Germany possessed was not to be sacrificed carelessly.

This is not the way it was. We complied with the wishes of the Reichswehr as much as possible when other things were at stake. The memo also says that I had advocated the dissolution of the Verbände. This is not true. I have always taken the attitude I am explaining here.

HERR HEMMETER: In this connection, an order I 19 of November 3, 1923, is still to be read here. It lists, in detail, from which Verbände the newly formed single-companies were to be

170

composed. The order, signed by Schönhärl, clearly states what has been said by Hitler: that at this time it was felt the men were to be incorporated as companies.

HERR BRÜCKNER: I would like to add the following to the statement of Lieutenant Colonel Kriebel. On October 1st I went to see Captain Hannecken who is General Staff Officer with Lossow, and I talked with him about these things. Later, I reported to my men what Hannecken had told me. He had said: "Accelerate the training of your men! The men must come out to the barracks for instruction, three times. We shall need troops ready for combat in the near future. We have instituted a number of special courses—the M. G. course, minethrower course, communications course." It was even planned to set up an officers' company to be trained three times a week. I had the impression that it was high time to have the men trained in the barracks, not only once or twice a week but possibly every day.

While training was going on—I was in the Pioneer and Infantry barracks every night and I spoke with the training officer—I had the definite impression that the men and the officers themselves were discontented because the march on Berlin had not started. I can remember talks with the gentlemen during which they said: "This Hitler is just as much of a liar as the others. You are not going to strike. It doesn't matter to us who is striking. We shall just march along. Now we have had enough of it." Every night the men waded through mud and snow; they tore their clothes during the drills and received no compensation. The men walked in snow and rain from Bogenhausen to the Eisembahn barracks; sometimes, as the commander, I felt like an idiot when the men came and asked: "When are we going to start?" I had to tell them, again and again, the time has not yet come. We must wait. We must wait.

This procrastination seemed to create hostilities which threatened to become dangerous. I also told Herr Hitler, personally: "The day will come when I can no longer keep the men in check. If something does not happen very soon, the men will take off." You must remember that there were many unemployed among them. Many men said: We are going to use our last suit, our last pair of shoes, our last dime for training. Things will start moving soon, then we will be enlisted in the Reichswehr and will be out of the whole mess.

If the indictment states that on the evening of November 8,

National Socialists had called on the Pioneers and I.R.19 to demand the handing over of arms and ammunition, this is not correct. The men went out by order of First Lieutenant Löwenmeier. The order said that the men were ordered to come for a police investigation on the evening of November 8. The police investigation is the last step in preparing for mobilization—that is, for the incorporation of the companies into the active army. It was known already, in peace-time, that once the examination was over the action would begin, within the next three days. This was the mood of the men. I regret to have to talk about it.

I went to the Deutscher Tag in Ingoldstadt. There the Pioneers of the Pioneer battalion E 7 were doing an exercise and I was invited to attend it. I had the impression that a Hitler meeting and the Pioneers at the Deutscher Tag are one and the same. The Pioneers had the swastika flag. Everything was done in such a way that one could say: These people are in complete accord with us. Captain Dostler reveled in his own patriotic words. One had the impression that he was already on fire; that he had to be let loose or else he would go to pieces. It was very strange that later this Mr. Dostler no longer remembered any of these incidents and the attitude he had displayed. I mean these are transformations from one day to the next which I cannot understand. The training and the whole atmosphere during the training were such that not only the leaders but also the men had to believe that action would soon begin. Every day they underwent high-pressure training. The men were separated. I visited the Pioneers out there for the last time on November 6. Then they were separated, according to their length of service, and so on. The men all felt that it could not take more than three or four days—at most a week—until action would begin. This was my impression.

HERR HOLL: Captain Cantzler of the Pioneer battalion had Captain von Müller from Bund Oberland for training. When Cantzler, the active officer of the Reichswehr, took over the training, he addressed his people in the following way:

> "I implore you not to treat this training lightly. The curriculum is so comprehensive that all your strength is needed to reach the required goal within a reasonable period of time. We are pressed for time. We don't know how long we can still continue training. It is impossible that we shall have to

come to a conclusion in the near future."

This is the testimony of Dr. Fuchs. I submit it to the Court.

HERR KOHL: Dr. Weber, you must be able to tell us that there were rooms in the Pioneer barracks which were exclusively used for the training of Bund Oberland people. Only the sergeant of the sleeping quarters and another corporal had a key to these rooms. But on November 8, the officer in charge—probably Cantzler—refused to admit the Bund Oberland men to the rooms assigned to them.

DR. WEBER: This is a point which I still intend to discuss in detail. At the time the mobilization orders were issued, the weapons for the companies of the 2nd Battalion, to be used in the action, were taken to the Pioneer barracks in accordance with an agreement between Captain von Müller and Captain Cantzler. This was done so that the men to be enlisted would have the weapons at once. The weapons were stored by our Verband in the Pioneer barracks. The key to the rooms was in the hands of a sergeant in charge of the sleeping quarters and several of the corporals who trained us. This was done because of an agreement between Müller and Cantzler.

I may, perhaps, add that the rifle practice which we conducted at Neufreimann was paid for by us since the Reichswehr told us they had no money. I distinctly remember that during sharpshooting practice, which was done under the supervision of Reichswehr officers, the leaders of the Reichswehr units asked our commanders repeatedly: "Are you the same braggarts"—and unfortunately I cannot repeat this expression because it is not parliamentary—"as Kahr and Lossow? Why doesn't he do something so that we can finally march together to Berlin?" In my opinion this, too, is proof of the close connection between the Reichswehr and our men. And by the way, the same impression was received in Bamberg, Nürnberg, and Würzburg.

HERR HITLER: I ask permission to make an explanatory statement which I could not make during the public hearing. The Judge asked me whether I had been responsible for seizing the money held by Parcus and Mühlthaler. Yes, I was. The agreement was—this is also stated in the order—that at the moment of mobilization our men were immediately to be paid by the Reichswehr. Our men were supposed to receive the same pay as their corresponding ranks in the Reichswehr.

Now as you know, the line to Lossow was blocked at 12:00 at night on November 8. It could not be reestablished until 3:00 in the morning. I was told by a gentleman that the Parcus company printed money. I did not have the scruples not to use immediately paper money, which had not one penny's worth of gold backing. In order to enable the men who had been hungry during the night to buy themselves a breakfast, at least on this one morning, we used it.

I was firmly convinced that the situation would become clear during the course of the day. That they could, after all the preparations, act against us—in the way in which they actually did—would have been so incomprehensible to any of us that we did not think of it at all. In addition, I thought I had to do it in order to prevent the same rioting that had occurred in the city, and of which I had received reports. There was a Kriminalkommissär Hermann who informed me, by telephone—this may have been between 12:00 and 1:00 o'clock—of the lootings committed in the city. I told the gentlemen that I would be prepared to immediately send a few trucks with men, and later to have the threatened areas patrolled by two policemen and two of our men to prevent such outbreaks. But if one did not provide the men with food, then naturally there was a definite chance that such incidents might receive a different impetus. Hence, from this point of view it was absolutely necessary to use the four and one half, seven and one-half thousand marks because they had not received what had been planned to be their regular pay.

Therefore, I gave the order—I take responsibility for it—to confiscate the money immediately. The money was delivered. I asked one of the officers—I think it was Herr Pernet—to make out a receipt and to distribute the money among the men. I hardly need to tell you that I myself did not take a penny of the money. Under normal conditions, our men would have had to be paid by the Reichswehr.

HERR LUDENDORFF: I would like to describe these Pioneer barracks. My servant, who was killed, was a sergeant with the Rossbach unit; to be specific, with Lieutenant Heines who is also under protective custody. My servant told me that he had to form two platoons from his Pioneer company which were to be incorporated into one of the existing, active Pioneer companies. He also talked about uniforms to be provided there. Upon my questioning concerning where the uniforms were coming from, he told me that Lieutenant Heines would know. I ask that Lieutenant Heines be heard on this point. I don't know whether the Judge has read the letter written by my servant shortly before his death. In it he mentioned, "shortly before 12," because of the preparations for the war. He was so certain the action would begin shortly that he wrote this letter to me. He was an enthusiastic man and did not believe he would have to give his life in the way in which it happened.

HERR BAUER: I would like to ask Hitler when he ordered the money to be confiscated. I am interested, since Pernet made out the receipt for the money.

HERR HITLER: The seizure was already ordered in the course of the night. I can no longer tell you the exact time. It was ordered upon the urgent appeals of a number of commanders of the troops who insisted that the problem of pay was the most imperative one because the men no longer had anything to eat. It had been their experience that those men who had been on duty all night and had not been able to sleep would be hungrier than anyone else. Those were large units. Furthermore, it was not practical for a single man to buy anything; he could not leave the group, and also the small stores in the neighborhood happened to be empty right then. They had to go shopping in large, closed groups. That prompted me to agree with the suggestion of the gentlemen. I cannot name any names.

I must admit that I had never thought of it before; but I could not act in any other way. I considered it a matter of course that, in a case like this, one does what is necessary. As far as I remember, the seizure itself did not take place, I think, until I had returned to the Wehrkreiskommando. I was there when the money was brought in, or rather when one of the gentlemen who had acted as an escort reported it to me. I asked the gentleman—I believe it was Pernet—to write a receipt for the money, immediately. I had no time to take care of it. Furthermore, I informed the regiment commanders to determine at once the amount, per head, which would be paid out justly. I would like to emphasize that Röhm may perhaps be able to explain to some extent why later the money could no longer be found.

I must stress that officers were in charge of the money in the Bürgerbräukeller, and I would not have asked for a statement of accounts because there were no thieves or swindlers among my officers. People who had sacrificed themselves for years and who had, day by day, endured personal hardship for a ridiculous salary; who had left their peace-time positions because of their passion for the military because they were born soldiers; who were not forced to wear a cockade, contrary of their views, which they did not want to wear—these people were no thieves. If these men had been thieves, they would not have risked their lives again and again. Who would have been in a position to control them? These people, who often literally rescued money from profiteers, did not sell anything illegally or illicitly. I had blind faith in my men. On November 9, the whole leadership put themselves at the head of the troops. People who were ready to die with the next hour would not steal an hour before.

HERR PERNET: I received the money between 8:00 and 9:00 o'clock. I have destroyed the receipts which I got from the units.

HERR RÖHM: I, too, proposed confiscation of the money by members of the Reichskriegsflagge, since it was necessary to give the men money so that they could buy themselves a breakfast. Furthermore, we had to pay the many volunteers who had enlisted. But the money did not arrive until an armistice had been made and after I had left the Wehrkreiskommando. The money was left in the office of the Chief of Staff, as I later found out. Our people did not receive any of this money. It could no longer be distributed. Three quarters of the money was stolen, and that by those troops who occupied the Wehrkreiskommando, Reichswehr, and Landespolizei. Witnesses will be named.

HERR BAUER: If I understood Hitler correctly, the order to confiscate the money was given at a time when nothing was known, as yet, about the fact that Kahr, Lossow, and Seisser would withdraw or desert us. This means that on the basis of what had happened before, Hitler could feel justified to claim this money for the men under his command.

HERR HITLER: It was getting grey. It was already dawning; I suppose it was probably between 7:00 and 8:00 o'clock. First of all, I could not get any connection with Lossow and Seisser. If I had been able to, I would immediately have talked with Lossow about what was being done to secure the pay for these men. However, since I was not able to do so, one of the gentlemen who knew that Parcus was printing money said there was only one way to get it since confiscation at the bank would be impossible because the money in a bank belonged to the people and they needed the money. The money which was seized, however, was nothing but pieces of paper, behind which there was practically no value of the Reich. I had not the slightest hesitation in agreeing with the request, out of a sense of responsibility, since after all the next day it would have been done on someone else's authority. I was convinced I was completely justified, as well, for the reasons I stated before concerning the lootings.

JUDGE NEITHARDT: Is there any other subject you wish to discuss which you could not talk about yesterday in the public session?

HERR EHARD: May I make a general suggestion? Would it be useful, perhaps, to discuss with regard to this the following question? What did the gentlemen here think about the feasibility of this march to Berlin?

It goes without saying that such an undertaking would have immediately caused the gravest international difficulties, as well as the gravest political difficulties at home. I request that you briefly discuss the availability of quarters, of the railroad connections, of horses for the columns, of army service corps, of food, clothing, and so on. On the left hand, to mention this briefly, the French with their allies; on the right, the Czechs, Poles, and the Reichswehr ready to march in.

HERR HITLER: I would appreciate it if I were given the opportunity to answer this question. I would like to discuss one point beforehand, i.e. the difficulties as far as foreign policy is concerned. I have to speak in rather broad terms. What were to be the practical reasons for international difficulties? The reason must be the fact that France would not tolerate a positive recovery of Germany; for if such an action would bring about the destruction of Germany, then the Prosecutor would probably not assume an intervention by France. Under both the most favorable and the worst of circumstances, France could only be expected to intervene if Paris was afraid that inner political events in Germany might cause the creation of a form of government which will categorically eliminate the politics of exploitation of the German Reich as they were conducted until now.

I must tell you one thing, Herr Prosecutor. If we had anticipated these international problems and made them the determining factor for an inner political German reorganization, we should have been much freer much sooner, for any change of mind with Germany which could lead us to the political freedom of Germany will be opposed by France no matter in what form it takes place. Any such change of attitude, which in Paris will be considered a change from the former German attitude of wretchedness, will of course be noted as such by France.

Today I cannot separate the French-German problem from the context of the European problem. If we look today at the European scales, we can see two great opposing forces. In 1914, England began the war against Germany for only one basic reason. It had always been England's principal political and great goal to maintain the so-called European equilibrium. Only a European equilibrium would be a guarantee for England to enable it to take care of its own world-policy problems. French politics, on the other hand—contrary to England—were determined for centuries by the idea of Balkanizing Germany. That is, to create within Germany a system of balancing forces. France wishes to Balkanize Germany. It wants to prevent any leading power in Germany from becoming a crystallizing point. France wants to pursue world politics, secured by a German Reich which is broken up into small states. Basically, England does not want the breaking up of Germany into small states; it wants to prevent a European hegemony. That European power which threatens to achieve a hegemony on the Continent is England's enemy. But, in the course of the centuries, this enemy has changed. At one time it was Spain; later, the Netherlands; then France, and now we are the ones. The animosity was over as soon as the Balkanization of Europe had been reestablished.

It is different in the case of France. France's intentions vis-a-vis Germany were and will always be the same. France does not want hegemony. France wants the shattering of Germany in order to achieve its own hegemony in Europe. If I consider the French problem of who today wants French hegemony in Europe, neither England nor Italy do. Neither nation is interested in supporting this French hegemony, whether it is in the area of economics, industry, or of the military.

When, five years ago at the writing of the peace treaty, England did not take a position against the excessive French demands, it became the antagonist of French power. The reason for this was the fact that in four and a half years the nation's passions had been aroused out of a need for self-preservation. Now the leading minister could not simply alter the attitude of his nation. Furthermore, Germany was the least (likely) of the powers even to attempt to change the situation. Because of the purely mechanistic German view of history and government, we thought that politics can be ordered: "left turn, right turn." The German delegates could have said, in Versailles: We are not going to sign the treaty! You can keep this piece of paper. That would have been the only thing to do.

The other opportunity came when England had been defrauded of its final goal of the war. Today, English interests no longer correspond with French interests. They are diametrically opposed. But this does not mean that England would act as a cat's paw for Germany. Oh, no! Germany is not in a position to be an ally until the German people realize their need for self-defense. A nation without a drive for self-preservation is not considered by a people accustomed to earning 90 percent and letting others earn only 10 percent. England would go along with Germany if Germany's political position was pro-England. However, that is not the case; and that was the reason why, at the beginning of the Ruhr conflict, England's position was actually pro-German; why England, at that time, did not want the Ruhrgebiet to become French. That was not in England's interest.

The Germany which tries, on its own, to imbue its paid-for general strike with the manifest will to active resistance will have a chance. However, a power with whom one cannot ally, such a power is a thing to be partitioned and will remain a thing to be partitioned just as Poland once used to be. Either the German Reich rallies to move up, or else it will go under. This rallying will not take place if one quietly waits and watches. It takes place only through greater activity — through a far greater effort. It has always been this way in the world, in the life of nations. A nation which has lost its economy, which has been robbed of its largest food-producing areas must not say: "Because the enemies do not want us to arise, we cannot attempt to achieve this rise; we must postpone it — postpone it forever."

Such a nation can only be saved if it lets the entire world know, unequivocally, that it has not yet given up; that it is not yet a colony, but can still be an ally. Nevertheless, this ally is expected to be ready for attack and to be prepared for the fight by instilling in the minds of its people the will to fight. This will to fight and to achieve victory is not displayed by the Berlin government. We were destroyed because of a lack of national

179

thinking. Not because of a lack of arms, but because of a lack of national pride. Today if we truly desire to put an end to the German misery, we must understand that as a result of that lack of will, we must now remedy that lack by an excess in these prerequisites for the education of a nation. We have always been convinced that the solution could never come from Berlin. It cannot come from Berlin, for there the general atmosphere is so polluted and confused that they always try to reverse the development.

I remind you of the examples we find in world history. Never in the history of the world has a nation whose capital was contaminated been able to rid itself of this contamination with the help of its capital. The classical example is here in Munich. We would never have freed ourselves from the Red Regime if health had not been restored by the healthier part of the people. The same goes for Hungary. And one can find the same example in the history of Antiquity. Again and again a better wave was carried into the heart of the Roman Empire, "to" Rome. And that is the deeper meaning of the crossing of the Rubicon. You see it in Turkey. The liberation could not come from its rotten center, from Constantinople. This city, just as in our case, was without any patriotism, polluted by democratic-pacifist, internationalist people who were no longer capable of deeds. It could only come from the rural areas. Do not tell me that conditions today are different than they were. Generally, the conditions of mankind are always the same—they must be the same, because the fundamental principles are the same and have been the same throughout the centuries.

We had witnessed the same phenomenon in recent times in Spain. A Catalonian general marched against Madrid, first with a brigade and then it became a division, finally, the whole country is at his feet. When he marches, the whole of Spain has not been won yet—Madrid is not Spain—but it is conquered.

You have another classic example in the Young Turkish revolution. Enver Pasha marched to Constantinople and there built a new nation; and a new spirit came over the totally contaminated capital. And, finally, the last—the most classical example—in Italy! The fascist wave came from the North and conquered Rome. The most grandiose example of history, however, is the founding of the German Reich. Vienna, the old German Imperial City, could no longer muster the strength to create a strong martial German Reich—no. From the little sandy province up there, from little Brandenburg, came the power that was to build a German Reich. Once a certain mentality has disappeared in an area, the liberation only comes from outside— can only come from outside.

Therefore, from the very first day we did not expect, and we still do not expect German deliverance from today's evil to be brought about in a peaceful way, in the way of a general reconciliation with the rest of Europe. No. We are convinced that the entire crime which the people committed against themselves in 1918 can only be atoned for through a tremendous, unheard-of effort; perhaps even through more and bitter suffering.

However, the question is: Do we want this upheaval? Or do we want to renounce the rise of the Germans? My position is that if peace for Germany can only be obtained through death, then I would rather die—die now! I say that if German freedom can be attained not with a 51 percent, but with a 1 percent probability, then I would risk the 1 percent rather than be responsible for letting the German nation perish in shame and misery.

That was our guiding idea. It was clear that we could not fight against the Reichswehr. Lossow and Lieutenant Colonel von Berchem thought it ridiculous to believe that they would not shoot at Ludendorff. Thus, whoever thinks, in a case such as this, of the conditions as they existed at the front where enemy stood against enemy, does not understand the underlying principles and currents of such a revolution.

I am convinced today—and it is quite clear to me—that the uprising would have swept throughout the rest of the Reich if General von Lossow had not turned around, and if Colonel Seisser had not retreated. If, instead, these gentlemen had driven through Munich, on the next day, and had hoisted the national flag of revolution, a tremendous rejoicing, a tremendous enthusiasm would have burst out in Munich, Nürnberg, Bayreuth, and the German Reich. If the first division of the German National Army would have left the last square meter of Bavarian soil and for the first time entered the Thuringian country, we would have experienced the rejoicing of the people over there. It would have been evident to the people that the German misery was over; that liberation could only come through an upheaval. The pacifist-defeatist, completely immoral government in Berlin would have had to retreat before attack. If one does not understand, first of all, that an internal change has to be brought about, and that a national government must come without considering the "majority" principle, then Germany shall never rise again.

Yesterday the question was asked of whether we felt we were justified in organizing the uprising, whether we thought we had the majority. Herr Prosecutor! If the right to venture upon such an undertaking for one's countrymen rested only with the majority, you would not sit here today as a German Prosecutor, because this German Fatherland was not founded by majorities but, rather, by the decisiveness of individual personalities who, often enough, were in opposition to the majorities. Above all, Germany itself is not the product of the majority. It is the product of a hero who, supported by means of power, wrenched his creation from the majorities in an unheard-of struggle.

I have said I cannot consider the revolution of 1918 a high treason. I said that for a definite reason: a coup d'etat and high treason were also once committed by Bismarck—as the people on the left think. The *Frankfurter Zeitung* called his actions, at the dissolution of the Prussian Parliament, "high treason, coup d'etat," et cetera. And yet this coup d'etat and high treason were approved of at the time. Why? As I said the day before yesterday, high treason is the only crime which can be punished only by failure. It will not be punished if it is successful. What do we mean by "success" of high treason? Success is considered as an improvement over the existing situation; an endeavor undertaken only in order to satisfy the ambition of a few, is not high treason, nor is it a coup d'etat, but either of them simply mean acts of treason.

That is what the people of November 1918 committed. None of us would be here if, since the year 1918, our German people had not visibly collapsed from month to month. The most obvious and clearest proof of this is that you, Herr Prosecutor, asked whether in consideration of the foreign policy situation we thought it possible to go through with the uprising. Isn't that a true characteristic of the misery of the German people, that we are not permitted to clean up our internal affairs because of the "foreign policy situation"? Isn't that proof of the fact that this "revolution," this "high treason," failed? Because if it had been successful, it would not have been sanctioned by France. If the high treason of 1918 had been a moral success, the opposite of what you said, Herr Prosecutor, ought to happen. Then France would not have to be afraid that a revolution against this high treason might take place. Rather, it ought to long for the revolution against this high treason because this new high treason would destroy the form of government so hated by France.

France praises the earlier high treason because it was treason against Germany. Bismarck's high treason was later legalized because, through the "high treason" of then-premier Otto von Bismarck, the German Reich was erected. This other "high treason" will never be legalized since nothing remains of the German Reich but German misery. You don't believe that such matters are justified reasons to stimulate the people to act? On the contrary, only the sign of a change of attitude inside Germany will cause the European world to take a different attitude towards France. I am convinced that in those days the German destiny would have begun to move. It finally failed because of such a small and trivial matter. It only shows that sometimes fate intervenes and that one does not know what is good and what is bad.

Do not think, Herr Prosecutor, that we, or I, believe we did something which now I ought not to have done. I can never be of this opinion. I have convinced myself that, of all my comrades sitting here, nobody knew anything in advance. Looking at the present development, I begin to think that it was, after all, perhaps good that another period went by; for do not think this trial will destroy us! Our prisons will be opened and the time will come when the accused of today will become the accusers. The time will come—perhaps only after centuries—but it will come and then one will be able to read in this history of the shame and disgrace, of the misery and distress, and they will be surprised that this was "high treason." We shall then all be justified. We shall not be the accused. We shall be the accusers. Our descendants will acquit us and they will say: Those were the only ones who had the courage to rebel against the continuous high treason.

It is not true that I stand here today penitent. I cannot do that. I have confessed everything. If I turned against the three adversaries, I did not do so for personal revenge, but because I am convinced that those who have destroyed German destiny ought to be destroyed. That has caused me to speak in this manner, not personal hate.

My position on the evening of November 8, and on the 9th, was to unite everybody—after Munich—and to incorporate them into the army. Here, too, we were able to proceed liberally because I knew the new army, under the command of Ludendorff, could have only one single purpose: that is, not to stop in Berlin but to continue marching with their eyes turned to the West. I could give him the last man without having to fear that he might say: "I am going to betray my principles." We were convinced that the Green Police and the Reichswehr were participants. And now you, Herr Prosecutor, assume the worst; that the North might actually have not been willing to join us. Even if that were the case, you must admit that the importance of a country having six or eight divisions at its disposal was different from that of a country which has none. I am convinced that the German Reichswehr would not have shot at Ludendorff, as the Prosecutor assumes. I don't derive this opinion from purely factual evidence. In this case it is not necessary. One cannot judge something like that purely on the basis of "material evidence." One must have a feeling for it. If Lossow had remained minister of the Reichswehr, a rivalry between the Reichswehr and Lossow would have been just as unthinkable as a rivalry between Seeckt and Ludendorff.

I must emphasize that I did not take this step carelessly and frivolously. It had been prepared for a long time by all concerned. I personally would never have gone so far if the Generalstaatskommissar, at that time, had not been appointed. After that, I had to say immediately: Now the great chance to bring together the German people, because of the loss of the Ruhrgebiet, is lost. I did not feel like a brother towards Kahr. I felt like a brother toward Pöhner. From the beginning, I thought if they want me to stand behind the Staatskommissariat, then the only man I would consider for that position is Pöhner. If he stands in this place, I personally have no further wishes. I know how he thinks and I don't have to hear anything else. It is entirely sufficient. If Kahr is in that position, I also know who is there. If, at a time like this, a man like Kahr is appointed, it is a catastrophe. He ought never to have been appointed. At a time like this, meetings should not have been prohibited. Rather, one should have seen to it that the people were being enlightened.

That is what I intended to do. I wanted to start a propaganda campaign of the kind that has never been seen before. I turned all the wheels towards Munich. Huge gatherings were already planned for all Bavarian cities and across the rest of Germany; and then there came this unlucky appointment of Kahr at a point in time when information of the masses was an absolute necessity, and such information was prohibited. An incompetent Prussian premier has coined the following phrase, after a lost battle: "The King has lost a battle; to keep the peace is the first duty of the citizen." That was the main reason for me turning away from Kahr.

HERR EHARD: I have tried to ask Hitler a calm and sober question.

HERR HITLER: I did not wish to insult you.

HERR EHARD: Please. I don't feel insulted, either. I only feel there was absolutely no need to choose a somewhat polemical form to the outside.

HERR HITLER: I did not intend to do so, but this is part of my nature—which is contrary to the nature of the Prosecutor.

HERR EHARD: This may be an advantage here.

JUDGE NEITHARDT: Herr Hitler, do you want to discuss any other subjects?

HERR HITLER: No.

HERR WEBER: I still have a number of points, but they should be discussed only after certain witnesses have been heard.

HERR KOHL: Unfortunately I think the closed session will have to be repeated when Herrn Kahr, Lossow, and Seisser are questioned, and reproached with this. Hence, there will still be an opportunity should any of the defendants forget anything.

JUDGE NEITHARDT: I am asking if there are still any subjects to be discussed here which have not yet been discussed.

HERR PÖHNER: I still have a request.

HERR HITLER: I am reminded that the Prosecutor asked me another question concerning food and clothing. In the spring of last year the people in Berlin thought themselves in a position to begin the fight against France. At that time they had been promised support. England, for one, was to give them substantial aid; and arms factories were to be set up in Sweden. England was to deliver heavy artillery, and so forth. However, the people—as could be derived from the general tone of public

185

opinion—did not have the will to fight. An example of this is that National Socialist locomotive engineers who brought in trains from the occupied area were arrested by Severing, and six comrades were extradited to the French. In Dortmund alone more than 300 persons—all of them members of our movement— were arrested by the Prussian police. Under these circumstances, of course it is natural that a state which does not have the will to fight cannot rise militarily.

The internal structure of the Reich makes this impossible. If weapons had actually arrived, they would at most have been sold illicitly. I am convinced that on the day on which Germany proves to have the will to resist, weapons will be of least importance. As we know, peoples have never been liberated through arms; it has been through will. We, too, had weapons at one time. If I think back to the time when, in 1914, I went to war without knapsack, without helmet, batteries, with eight or ten shots, and if I were to consider how we were equipped in 1918— why did we collapse? We had the weapons, but not the will. Once little Prussia was the place of rebirth and resistance. From this small germ cell of national reawakening, and of the idea of national resistance, there came the liberation of 1813. It is the same today.

HERR KRIEBEL: I only wanted to say briefly that since the year 1919, the study of the wars of liberation has become my special field of research. On the basis of serious study and observation, I can only say the following: The characteristic of wars of liberation has been that 90 percent of a nation considers an upheaval impossible; while only 10 percent venture it. The characteristic of a war of liberation consists in the fact that one nation is completely subjugated by another nation so that finally not only the will of the people is aroused, but the nation obtains their own weapons. Some people have perished in the process, but they perished with honor. However, the great nations have become great through wars of liberation. The essence and pre-requisite of every war of liberation is the will of the people—or the will of a minority of the people—to rebel and to fight. In the Spanish war of liberation those recruits who did not want to go to the army were bound in chains and brought to the regiments. And yet, even with such regiments, the Spanish chased the French out of the country.

I only wanted to make this brief remark.

JUDGE NEITHARDT: I think we shall continue the questioning of Herr Kriebel tomorrow. For today, the session is closed. We will continue tomorrow morning at 8:30 a.m.

Whereupon, at 5:36 p.m., the hearing was recessed, to reconvene at 8:30 a.m., the next day.

THE FOURTH DAY, February 29, 1924

—MORNING SESSION—

At 8:30 the public hearings are resumed.

Herr Schramm refers to an article in the München-Augsburger Abendzeitung *in which it was stated that the defendants have strained to avoid any danger to national security, but the same cannot be said for the defense attorneys. On behalf of the defense, Herr Schramm registers a very sharp protest.*

HERR SCHRAMM: All the defense attorneys are aware that we must stop when national security is in danger, even when this is in conflict with the perception of the interests of the defendants. The proverb *salus publica suprema lex* applies to the defense here. So, the defense refuses to take advice from any quarter.

Herr Schramm further refers to another article in the Volkischer Kurier *where two graphic artists show each other their drawings in a streetcar: a filthy caricature of a lay judge and a vulgar caricature of Ludendorff. Herr Schramm declares:*

HERR SCHRAMM: We have no reason to permit such people in the courtroom. I request that Your Honor take the appropriate action.

JUDGE NEITHARDT: The Court had no prior knowledge of this article. Necessary precautions have been taken. I don't think they are here anymore.

Herr Schramm remarks that vulgar caricatures have also appeared in other newspapers which refer to the defendants. Finally, Schramm remarks that a foreign newspaper has written that the defendants lack seriousness and that they are staging theater.

HERR SCHRAMM: On the contrary, the defendants are upright

German men who represent a sacred idea with the purest conscience. Of course they cannot be expected to step forward whining and gnashing their teeth. We must naturally enter a sharp protest against such remarks by a foreign paper here, in a German courtroom. We will not tolerate it!

Herr Stenglein mentions a remark in a newspaper that everyone in the courtroom had been very serious during Hitler's speech except for the Prosecutor who bore a contemptuous grin. The Prosecutor terms it incorrect that he manifested any behavior not befitting his position.

Herr Mayer emphasizes, in conjunction with an editorial, that it is not incumbent on the defense to show that Herr Kahr, Lossow, and Seisser also committed high treason.

HERR MAYER: It is incumbent on the defense to prove that all these people acted against encroachments by unlawful authorities. The questions are taken from a broad complex and should demonstrate that Germany has no constitutional government. A German Reich chancellor threatened that he would not side with constitutional forces in a civil war and another Reich chancellor has said that he would form the last constitutional government. The only articles of constitution left are 48 and 76.

The defense counsel terms Dr. von Kahr's situation unique and establishes, in response to a remark in a newspaper, that Dr. Weber is Bavarian.

JUDGE NEITHARDT: Now let us proceed to Lieutenant Colonel Kriebel's testimony. Lieutenant Colonel, we said yesterday that you are the military leader of the Kampfbund and that the Kampfbund aimed at a combination of the patriotic bands who stood on a Christian, nationalistic, and Greater Germany foundation.

HERR KRIEBEL: That is correct.
First, I would like to compare briefly the organizational relationships of my position as military leader to that of the political leader. In many bands, the position of military commander is identical to that of the political leader. In other bands, the political leader has a military colleague. Also, there are bands in which the military commander occupies a position equal to the political leader. So, for example, Bund Bayern und Reich has a political leader, Dr. Pittinger, and a military commander.

Let me illustrate how this develops in a practical example. Let us assume a situation in Bavaria similar to September or August, 1922. Let us say that Dr. Pittinger intended to overthrow the government in Lerchenfeld—of course with Herr Kahr's approval. Then Dr. Pittinger would make his decision and entrust the military commander with its execution; this is exactly how the situation developed with us. The political leader gave instructions for execution. I had both to translate them into military terms and to give the orders to carry them out. Responsibility for every military measure belonged to the military commander. In fact, all orders emanate from the supreme military commander and he must bear the responsibility.

The accused requests the Court to bear this fact in mind concerning the question of detention so that people aren't still in jail because they only carried out orders.

HERR KRIEBEL: I now come to the events themselves. After the Generalstaatskommissariat had been established on September 26, I was called by Colonel von Seisser on September 27. He informed me that on the following day there would be a meeting of Herr Kahr and all the leaders of the patriotic bands, including Hitler. He had been unable to reach Hitler, and asked me to extend the invitation; I agreed. I sent the invitation via Hitler's deputy and asked for an answer, since he was making a speech and I couldn't reach him. The answer came that Hitler wanted to come. Then Dr. Scheubner-Richter appeared for a talk.

And so, the aforementioned conversation of September 28 took place, and then the meeting with Kahr on the 30th. Herr Kahr asked what I wanted at the session. Due to Hitler's position towards him, he could not receive me as a representative of the Kampfbund. Only when Pöhner answered that I came solely as his confidant, did Herr Kahr agree to let me remain at the session. I would like to clearly establish that I was rejected by Herr Kahr, as the representative of the Kampfbund.

On October 9 there was a discussion at the Generalstaatskommissariat. I was personally invited by Herr Seisser. The meeting was called to discuss riot police matters, and the question of how we would react to a call-up of auxiliary police to maintain public law and order. I explained that, at the time, I wasn't there as Hitler's representative and that I couldn't deliver any definite statements since I had not been apprised beforehand of the subject of the discussion and would first have to obtain a statement from Hitler about his feelings on the matter.

Then the events mentioned yesterday—which I will not repeat—took place. I'll skip right to November, November 4, the day on which the funeral rites were heid; the day I was permitted to lead the Youth Squad of our Kampfbund before the King. Of all the judgments passed on the march, one is particularly clear in my memory. It ran, approximately: "The shocking thing about the parade was that at the head you had well-fed, well-clothed, and newly outfitted Reichswehr; at the rear came the boys in tattered uniforms and faces drawn with hunger and want that radiated enthusiasm."

On the morning of November 5, I was called by Kommerzienrat Zentz. He and I had known each other for a long time. He held a position of trust in the Home Guards and was closely allied to it from the beginning. He told me I should come to an important meeting that evening which would concern an assembly; I agreed. I arrived at the meeting too early, and so spent about 15 minutes alone with Kommerzienrat Zentz. He lectured me on the purpose of the assembly; it was identical to his later speech. Representatives from home industries, business, heavy industry, and trade from Munich and Bavaria were present, as well as representatives of the National Employee Organization (white collar), Dr. Hartmann from the nationalist bands representing the Vereinigte Vaterländische Verbände, and Dr. Kühner of the Munich chapter of Vereinigte Vaterländische Verbände (United Patriotic Bands). Kommerzienrat Zentz had named me representative of the Kampfbund. There was no doubt that the assembly was convened at the suggestion of the Generalstaatskommissariat. Kommerzienrat Zentz stated that the meeting had been planned at the request of Herr Kahr. Kahr wanted to give a prepared speech, the purpose of which was to declare the revolution over and to proclaim a new beginning for Germany. He felt it was essential that the main hall of the Burgerbräukeller was filled. He had invited the Vereinigte Vaterländische Verbände (V.V.V.) in order to fill the hall. It was added that, at the closing ovation, the assembly should take the lead and free beer would be given away by benevolent donors.

There was another discussion concerning participation of Jews in the assembly. Dr. Hartmann, from the Bavarian V.V.V., expressed his opinion that such participation would be unwise, in view of Herr Kahr's need for the support of the patriotic circles—to invite Jews to this celebration. This remark produced a storm of passion from the representatives of the various trade organizations. They said that they had so many Jews among their members—not to mention on executive boards—that it would be impossible to convey the invitation if the question of restricting Jews was even discussed. Kommerzienrat Zentz quieted this storm of passion and remarked that few Jews would come because, since the deportation of Eastern Jews began, they were not inclined to speak well of him.

Since the revolution broke out in Munich on the 7th and the 9th in the Reich, I asked why November 8 had been chosen for the end of the revolution. Zentz said he didn't know why, but November 8 was the express wish of the Generalstaatskommissariat. The date could not be altered; the hall had already been rented for this day; everything had been prepared. I told no one the result of this meeting on the evening of the 5th, but I decided to go out to the bands to ensure that their members would be invited to fill the hall. I emphasize that I was still preoccupied with the idea that a union between Kahr and Hitler, between the two factions, was internally possible. It was only on November 9 that I recognized the impossibility of such a union.

Next came the famous session held at 4:30 p.m., on November 7 with Herr Kahr. That morning, I had been called by Herr Seisser. He had asked me if I would come to a session with Herr Kahr. The purpose of the meeting and the participants were not mentioned. Dr. Weber was also personally invited to attend, besides Herr Kahr, General von Lossow, and Colonel von Berchem and Captain Rudel, Herr Seisser, Major Hunglinger, and a few civilians from the Generalstaatskommissariat. Representatives from the Patriotic Bands were present: from Bayern und Reich, there was Kühner, Mayerhofer, and Major Semmelmann—I did not see Pittinger himself; and from Stahlhelm, Major Waeninger, and others.

The group was welcomed by Herr Kahr. There was no doubt left that Herr Kahr was hotly opposed to a Stresemann Government—a non-nationalist government—and he strongly felt that this type of government had to be chased out of Bavaria. Thus, the two methods for accomplishing this goal—the usual and the unusual—were presented. It was explicitly mentioned that the usual way would not be parliamentary. It was stated that if, in considering which way to go, it appeared that success could not be attained by the usual methods, then the unusual way had to be chosen. All the arrangements for this had been made, and everything was all ready.

192

The main concern was the disposition of forces and the question of what kind of political clarity we wanted. It was particularly striking, here, that Kahr, characteristically, had made a sharp distinction between settling the German problem and creating a new Prussian government. He explicitly said it wasn't enough to have the men for Germany, but that a new Prussian government had to be prepared. However, negotiations for this had not yet been finalized. He demanded discipline; he would personally give the order to act, and any premature act would be costly, and he would also withdraw his support.

He stated that if he were deserted by the bands, he would rely on the Reichswehr and the Landespolizei alone. Herr Kahr in no way indicated that he would give orders to fire upon hostile bands; he simply stressed that he would withdraw his support.

It is also significant that Kahr stated that there were rumors being circulated that individual bands wanted to attack independently on November 9 or 15. He named, in this connection, the Wikingbund (Erhardt), Bayern und Reich, Reichkriegsflagge, and the National Socialists. He directed his warning at these four groups.

Lossow, speaking after Kahr, merely mentioned that in general he was in agreement with Kahr. Lossow also said that he would collaborate on anything that had prospects for success; he didn't want to join any Kapp-Putsch. He then remarked about the differences he had with individual bands. He referred to a forged leaflet which had been distributed in the Reichswehr and called it stupid, because while it sowed mistrust toward him in the North German Reichswehr, he strove for the exact opposite. Also, he emphasized that he would use force against any band that would lead him astray—to a Kapp-Putsch. From different signs, I realized that the blame for the leaflet was laid at my door.

After Lossow spoke, Seisser remarked that the Landespolizei stood loyally behind Kahr, and that they would carry out his every command. After these statements it was not possible to open a discussion and express one's own opinions, since the meeting was adjourned. At Dr. Weber's request I had a brief conversation with Lossow in which I explained how dire was our need in these times, and how dangerous it was to put our people in the mood for change, again and again, and then to have the action delayed. I explained that there was the danger soon an explosion would come spontaneously. Besides, it was not out of the question that there would be food riots and it would be impossible to ask our men, who by and large are from the starving middle class, to fire on their own people. If it came to that, I said, that the Reichswehr and Landespolizei had to fire on those people, it would be impossible to win them over again for a march on Berlin. Kahr could be the savior of the people if he would make the decision of which he was certain and yet continued to postpone day after day.

My words were not without their effect on Lossow, for he shouted agitatedly that he wanted to march, but that until he could count on a 51 percent probability of success, it would be impossible for him to march. As a soldier, I was absolutely shocked. If we had acted in this way during the War, we would have been forced to capitulate in August of 1914. That is why the letter was circulated among the bands, because of this expression, and in conjunction with my exasperation with the petty, mistrustful way in which Lieutenant Colonel von Berchem had spoken. Through the letter I wanted to tell the other bands: We don't have the ambition to do everything, alone; we are at his disposal, the one who finally makes the decision. I already had proof that spies, in the service of the Reichswehr, had infiltrated our bands. It is true that it may have been unwise to write something like that, but I did it as a soldier. I didn't show it to anyone before sending it. I told myself, "Now is the time when a man must shoulder some responsibility."

As far as the action of November 8 is concerned, it was nothing more than a matter of opening the door for the three procrastinators in order to kick them through and into the impending event. The decision wasn't formulated two or three weeks beforehand, and details weren't worked out long in advance; this wasn't necessary. We didn't want to have a revolution in Bavaria. If a revolution arose, then we would have to attack in all the cities. We only wanted to give the three men that were just standing there, a springboard and a little shove, since they didn't want to leap into the water. Now everything revolved around the consideration of what could be and what would be useful in the execution of the plan. How could we prevent a simple thing from developing into the blood-bath it would from incomplete comprehension on the part of the State bands? At the November 7 meeting we decided it would be best to act on the 8th. Kahr himself stated that it would be best to end the revolution of infamy. It wasn't difficult to make the

military preparations. The Nazi Storm Troopers in the Bürgerbräukeller, the Reichskriegsflagge, who were gathered at the
Löwenbräukeller for a Party celebration, and Bund Oberland,
who long ago had planned a night drill for that night, would be
used solely with the view toward facilitating the leap, aiding the
new government, and taking over the most important security
measures as front-line troops.

During the course of November 7, the arrest of the Cabinet
Ministers, as well as military preparations, were discussed
because it was obvious that the Bavarian Cabinet was to be
turned out. It was well known that the cabinet had prepared an
emergency hideout in Regensburg. Their escape had to be
prevented; otherwise, a conflict could erupt between Kahr and
the exile government. Besides, we knew from occasional, filtered
statements that the Generalstaatskommissariat intended to free
itself from the bonds of the Cabinet and Landtag anyway.

The selection of ministers to be detained was determined
according to rank and was contingent upon the persons who
would be present in the hall. It was assumed that if Kahr was
giving an important prepared speech, the majority of the Cabinet
Ministers would come. We had great trust in Excellency von
Knilling. We were sorry that Knilling had not become Generalstaatskommissar instead of Kahr. We wanted to nominate him
for the Council of Honor of the Kampfbund, but he had declined
in order to ponder whether it might or might not put him in a
different position. For our part, we had a confidential relationship with him. It was clear, however, that he had to be taken
into custody. Very serious charges had been raised by all the
patriotic bands against Ministers Wutzlhofer and Schweyer. In
the name of the patriotic bands, Professor Bauer had petitioned
the President at least three times to get rid of Schweyer, once
and for all. We knew that we would be making allowances for the
mood of the people, if Wutzlhofer and Schweyer were removed.
My particular efforts were directed towards preventing
bloodshed between our men and the Blue and Green Police. If
the Police President and his chief advisors were also taken into
custody, probably Dr. Frick, as ranking official, would take over
the police affairs.

In any case, it was a relief to know that Frick was at Police
Headquarters in order to prevent bloodshed. Bund Oberland was
chosen to occupy the train station and the main telegraph office.
The march into the city was to be accompanied by music in order

to arouse the people and to create a sensation. The occupation of the train station was planned to prevent all the Jews with their stocks and bonds from catching night express trains to Berlin and Frankfurt, and so on. The occupation of the telegraph office was to prevent wild rumors from being telegraphed out of the city. From the very beginning, it was planned that our people would be relieved as soon as possible by the Green Police. This is proof that, naturally, we didn't want to act against the Green Police, but with them.

Lieutenant Colonel Kriebel then tells the Court about the necessity of covering the train station. He had learned from an acquaintance—an automobile dealer—that it was striking how automobiles were being bought up recently by certain classes and races.

HERR KRIEBEL: The nicest and most expensive autos were suddenly being sold. That strengthened my conviction that it was necessary to prevent the other poor Jews from fleeing the city.

The Reichskriegsflagge was in the Löwenbräukeller. Its leader was to be informed that as soon as Lossow had taken over the post of a Reichswehr minister, the Reichskriegsflagge would march into the Wehrkreiskommando and there act as an honor guard for Lossow. This show would also be an outward display of proof that we had placed ourselves under his command.

Lieutenant Colonel Kriebel then offers testimony that only the absolutely necessary people were informed of the plot so that no one would have responsibility unless it was necessary.

HERR KRIEBEL: That was the reason we didn't notify Röhm or Major Hühnlein. Although both of them had inwardly broken with the Reichswehr, outwardly they had not yet received their discharge. It was important to avoid individuals with such inner conflicts. Thus, that was the reason why we did not fully brief them. Today, although nothing can be attributed to him, Major Hühnlein sits in detention.

Now it has been charged that a note pad with various telephone numbers on it—a message that Frick was the first to be notified and the phrase "safely delivered," was found among my papers. The phrase, "safely delivered," was selected because that was the impression I got of the difficulties of making a decision, which had beset these three men. The phrase was for me, alone, and had no other meaning. I wrote the note to notify Frick first, in order that he not forget the most important point—namely, that bloodshed was to be averted. In the indictment I am charged with committing the crime of high treason with full knowledge of the Weimar and Bavarian constitutions.

JUDGE NEITHARDT: I would like to interrupt you. Not only were the words, "first report to Frick, 'successfully delivered,' " written, but also, "Löwenbräukeller." According to the latter, one might conclude that the report was to be made not only to Frick, but also to the Löwenbräukeller. Was the Löwenbräukeller telephoned?

HERR KRIEBEL: No.

JUDGE NEITHARDT: That is incorrect. The prosecution has revealed that a Lieutenant Reiner telephoned the Löwenbräukeller by using this password. Thus we can conclude that the remark, "safely delivered," was not for you alone.

HERR KRIEBEL: If that is common knowledge, then I will admit that I stationed a man who had been initiated in the Löwenbräukeller. The reason I didn't say that was because I didn't want to implicate anyone.

JUDGE NEITHARDT: Was it Captain Röhm?

HERR KRIEBEL: No.

JUDGE NEITHARDT: Was Frick also telephoned using this password?

HERR KRIEBEL: No.
    I know neither the Weimar nor the Bavarian Constitution. As I have testified, at that time I was still with the Armistice Commission. I did not read it afterwards, either—that is beside the point. The Bavarian countryside, the patriotic representatives, all the Cabinet Ministers, Excellency von Kahr, too, all called out: "Struggle against the Weimar Constitution!" And so I said in my simple soldier's spirit, "If everybody and everything screams, 'Struggle against the Weimar Constitution!', then why shouldn't I fight?" The same is true for the Bavarian Constitution. The Bavarian Constitution doesn't appear to be so perfect. The *Bayerische Volks-Partei Korrespondenz* itself says we must fight the Bavarian Constitution because it is born of the spirit of the revolution.

Lieutenant Colonel Kriebel also mentions the popular desire to modify the constitution.

HERR KRIEBEL: If I am convinced that something must be fought, then one must fight it not only with one's words, but also with one's deeds.

The execution of our action on November 8 took place just as planned. During the assembly I was sitting at a small table in the hall and attended the event as a spectator. From my seat I could see how Hitler came in. I could not see that a man with a machine gun stood at the entrance. I was occupied with quieting my neighbors and telling them to be patient. After the entrance into the hall had succeeded and Hitler had taken the three men into the back room, I felt that our action had been successful. I later left the room, and once the three men had given their assent, it was clear to me: Now we have succeeded. I was convinced that it was only a matter of putting these people into a position where they could pretend to give their assent to our plans. I calmed representatives of the press in the cloakroom and, in the confusion, tried to clear suitable places for them. Subsequently, when the Ministers were arrested, I tried to provide the medium for informing a representative of the President, a high official of the Foreign Ministry who requested that His Excellency's wife be informed of the events which had taken place.

After the three men had assented, a man came up to Major von Hoeslin and demanded that he take that mistake from his cap and put on the black-white-red cockade. Major von Hoeslin was angered by this demand and sent the man away. When the speeches had been concluded, I returned to the back room where I met Excellency von Kahr, just as he was leaving. I did not see Excellency Ludendorff's arrival. A short time later, Kahr left the back room to drive away. Then Lossow and Seisser also wanted to drive away. The news then arrived that the Bund Oberland Battalion had been detained in the barracks and, I believe, that its leader was under arrest. I went to Lossow and stated that now that he had taken over as Minister of the Reichswehr, would he send out the order to free the battalion? Lossow dodged the question. Then General Aechter, the military commander of Bund Oberland, came over and I said to Lossow, "Excellency, permit General Aechter to drive out and give your order." Lossow said, "It's all right with me if he drives out and gives the order to free the battalion." The men then drove off.

I was alone for a moment with Excellency Ludendorff. I asked him privately to pass me over for any particular role, because I didn't want to have any extra privileges as a result of this affair. I asked him to make me a battalion, or regimental commander, according to my rank, in the new national army. I stated that I wanted to show that a person can be involved in a movement without receiving any personal gain. Excellency von Ludendorff replied that he would consider it. He asked me to stay with him, because he had no staff whatsoever, and that was my position with Ludendorff during the whole night and the whole day. I felt like a bodyguard. The allegation in the indictment that I was Chief of General Staff is not true. I did not make such a statement. I simply said I was "sort of" Chief of General Staff. One could hardly expect Ludendorff to give such orders as "buy wurst," or "take care of rations," to a band. This is what I meant.

Now came the report that the Infantry School was on the march. I personally had nothing to do with enlisting the support of the War College. I knew only that Rossbach had friends and ties in the War College—but Rossbach was under Göring's command, not mine. Ludendorff then returned to the back room where it was again decided to drive to the Wehrkreiskommando. Lossow, for one, declared that he would go over there in order to give orders to his troops. Seisser said that he would drive to the Generalstaatskommissariat and then on to the Wehrkreiskommando. Lossow told Ludendorff that he was going to the Generalstaatskommissariat. I had absolutely no reason to think that a Bavarian General, who had specifically told Ludendorff that he was going to the Wehrkreiskommando and would wait for him there, could possibly not keep his word. Thus, we waited with the assurance that the gentlemen would arrive in due time. However, we were aware—from March, 1920—that on such occasions things often do not happen without some delays, and that there were always long deliberations and discussions.

On the night of March 13, 1920, there had been, in my hallway, also 20 to 30 men—Reichswehr officers: Kahr, Escherich, Pöhner—who had discussed how to win over General Möhl. There were also infinite hemmings and hawings. So I thought to myself, this could be happening with the other men. Kahr will hopefully be bringing these men around and will be telling them why he's doing it. There will be a few anxious souls who are against it. Nevertheless, word then reached us that an

199

order had been issued to bring up the Passauer Battalion. Now this eventuality had not been considered since I knew the Passauer Battalion was the support for the Wehrkreiskommando. That did not influence my conviction that a General, a Colonel, a statesman with clean hands—all who had declared themselves in support of the uprising in front of several thousand people—would not suddenly change their minds.

In my opinion, the Prosecutors do the gentlemen a disservice when they claim that I must have been convinced that men whom I knew and respected as honorable men, could commit a betrayal like that. More than once, a reasonable doubt would creep into my mind that the men had broken their word; but my nobler emotions rebelled against ideas like that. The fact that I was uninformed is not important. But I find it quite unbelievable that these three men, who claim to be honorable men and who pledged with a hand shake their loyalty to Ludendorff, didn't even have the courage to say: "Excellency, we are forced to change our position," because of this or that; or, "The situation is such that we ask you to make a decision to avert a catastrophe." Ludendorff will always tower over this morass of lies, deception, and broken promises. No pearls fell from his crown because he conspired with thieves. I don't care if I sit here and am locked up. It is enough for me that I cooperated in the affair—and it will be an honor for the rest of my life.

It is unbelievable how they treated this man. I am almost ashamed to have worn the same uniform as those men. I have continued to admire how Excellency Ludendorff, right to the end, did not utter one word of accusation or condemnation because of the breach of their promise to him. If those men were afraid during the night, and didn't feel they had sufficient strength to last—if they feared an ambush—they should have at least had the courage, during the day, to issue an official communique. I can prove that when we heard that Ludendorff had marched at the head of the column towards the Landespolizei and that he had fallen—which was false, thank God—one Captain Rüdel at the Wehrkreiskommando made the unbelievable statement, "That is the best solution."

Shouts of disapproval in the courtroom. The Judge gavels for order.

HERR KRIEBEL: I will call the man who heard this remark as a witness.

HERR STENGLEIN: One must not forget that we are being presented with a completely one-sided presentation here which contains the most serious personal attacks on these three gentlemen. I believe one must also be permitted to hear the other side before one publicly disparages people's character in this fashion. I am saying that such overtly acrimonious statements against Herr Kahr, Lossow, and Seisser must, at least, be censured since no opportunity has been given to refute them. Contrary to the reproach that Excellency Ludendorff was kept completely in the dark by the three men, the fact is that at about 5:00 o'clock in the morning Colonel Leupold came to the Wehrkreiskommando and announced that Lossow had decided he could not collaborate.

JUDGE NEITHARDT: That was more in the nature of a plea than an objection. Incidentally, it is not the business of the prosecution to reprimand the Presiding Judge for the conduct of the hearing. I have found no cause to interrupt the accused because he has the right to defend himself and I must admit he has made use of it within the permissible limits.

HERR STENGLEIN: I did not intend to reprimand Your Honor. I only wished to suggest that a censure might be in order.

JUDGE NEITHARDT: But that is an indirect reprimand.

HERR LUETGEBRUNE: The defendant absolutely must be permitted to vent his anger and indignation that such perfidy has brought a man like Excellency Ludendorff into the dock. It is incorrect that Colonel Leupold was sent by Lossow; Ludendorff sent for Leupold to obtain clarification about what was really happening.

HERR KOHL: The defendant Kriebel's verdict on Herr Kahr, Lossow, and Seisser's behavior—i.e. inexcusable for not informing the men with whom they had worked communally—is the verdict of all decent men in Germany. And I assume that the Chief Prosecutor also counts himself as a decent man!

JUDGE NEITHARDT: That is going too far! I cannot tolerate such a personal attack.

HERR KOHL: The Chief Prosecutor is fulfilling an obligation

which must be very onerous to him. Surely, since he was trained in the basic principles of German cadets, he cannot approve of such dealings.

HERR STENGLEIN: The prosecution is not here to hold a shield over these three gentlemen. I have not said I approve or disapprove of their behavior. I have only stated that one must first hear the other side before one condemns them. I said that Colonel Leupold gave the message at 5:00 o'clock in the morning. I didn't assert that Colonel Leupold was sent by Lossow.

HERR KRIEBEL: It was odd that General Aechter did not return from seeing Lossow; and, that after he had promised to beforehand, to come to the Wehrkreiskommando, Lossow could not be reached by phone. I am familiar with a similar case which occurred on the night of March 13, 1920. A former Reichswehr officer offered me the position of Chief of Staff of the Home Guard if I would collaborate in the downfall of Möhl. In this case, he cooperated. After Herr Ruith and Herr Kress had been installed, it was not impossible that both of them, who enjoyed Gessler's confidence, arrested Lossow and that General Aechter also had been arrested. Major Siry was also dispatched to inquire about the Reichswehr. He did not return. Lieutenant Hecker didn't come back either. We believe that these men weren't important enough to merit an answer. Therefore, Ludendorff said to Leupold: "Go out to Lossow and ask him how things stand, and bring me his answer." Leupold said that probably Lossow had changed his mind, but he also said he would bring the answer. This answer never came. Then, after a meeting with Herr Kahr, Pöhner said that Herr Kahr was happy and in good spirits; and, also, that he had made a long-distance call. That removed our doubts about why the aforementioned men had not returned.

As military leader of the Kampfbund, naturally I had to assess the situation and address the question of how we would proceed if Kahr changed his mind and we were attacked. I then drew up orders for the men. The first line read: "Lossow has gone back on his word." However, not even an outline was given out and even Excellency Ludendorff was not made aware of it.

Lieutenant Colonel Kriebel then alleges that Ludendorff reached Seisser on the telephone, but the connection was suddenly broken off.

HERR KRIEBEL: Ludendorff then sent a letter to Seisser requesting that he report to him, but when the messenger was unable to find Seisser, the letter was returned.

In the meantime, news arrived that Seisser had said he was coming to the Wehrkreiskommando. Röhm was ordered to organize the Reichskreigsflagge as an honor guard in order to execute the proper salute to Seisser, now the Minister of Police. If we had been against Seisser, we hardly would have prepared to "prepare arms." We would have, rather, prepared to "fix bayonets."

Concerning the march of the Infantry School Cadets who were to relieve the Landespolizei at the Generalstaatskommissariat, the accused remarks that an embarrassing scene took place there because Frick didn't arrive on time to inform the Landespolizei that they were to be relieved.

HERR KRIEBEL: I received a report that Seisser stood there and refused to intervene in the conflict—he merely looked on. We didn't interpret this to mean he was hostile to us; we assumed that the new instructions had not arrived.

In all our patriotic bands, regardless of their persuasion, the resolution was passed that immediately after the planned action against Berlin had started, the first decree that had to be issued was: "Any looters will be summarily shot." As a result of the generally prevailing serious economic deprivation, the danger that people would be carried away and start to plunder had to be squarely faced. As far as the reproaches leveled at the National Socialist Storm Troopers go, it must be said that they were not a gentleman's club. The Storm Troopers consist of young, nationalistic workers who are accustomed to settling differences of opinion with their fists; not with grandiloquence nor with appeals to a Court of Honor. It is obvious that a few excesses could have occurred. In any case, it was our firm resolve to take steps against all such transgressions with all the means at our disposal. We didn't want such actions to disgrace what we had begun with pure hearts and hands.

At this point, there is a recess in the hearing.

After resumption of the hearing, Lieutenant Colonel Kriebel continues his defense speech.

HERR KRIEBEL: I don't think that I've forgotten anything

substantial. On the morning of November 9, various delegations, individuals, and several people from the Landespolizei—and later, at around 11:30, Major Hartlmeier and a Captain—came for discussions. I came away from them with the general impression, mainly taken from the Landespolizei sergeants' statements, that the mood of the Landespolizei among its sergeants and men was such that I couldn't decide whether they wanted to oppose us or even use their weapons against us. The fact that around 10:00 o'clock a major of the Wehrkreiskommando, who was ignorant of Lossow's position, appeared—now I know why he was ignorant—he gave us no clue as to the mood. Major von Hartlmeier spoke first with Excellency Ludendorff. I was standing in their vicinity, but I didn't hear what was said. Then, as he was leaving, he spoke a few words to me. What he told me agreed with what Excellency Ludendorff told me he said to him. Hartlmeier said that he didn't know what the mood was and that he intended to clear up what was happening. He wanted to prevent the unthinkable, i.e. the Reichswehr and the Landespolizei, the organs of State power, from firing upon the nationalist bands that should go hand in hand with them. Every clear-headed officer must have known that this possibility existed and that history would hardly impose a more infamous burden on a unit, if it wrote that the troops fired on Excellency Ludendorff. I thought that every officer on the other side must know that—or so I thought. And so all morning I believed that although the Landespolizei had occupied the Ludwigsbrücke, a decision had not yet been reached because I naturally anticipated an official report. Of course I gave orders to prevent a surprise attack. After all, I was military commander. We couldn't allow ourselves to be caught like mice in a trap. The precaution was just a maneuver which, as a soldier, I naturally considered—as long as we had weapons—to prevent myself from being captured. I am blamed for wheeling up two mortars to the bridge. They were old spoils from Upper Silesia. I don't believe that they were in any condition to serve—they were stage props. I don't believe that the Landespolizei were "routed" by these two field pieces either. I don't assign any special significance to this business.

Anyway, our leader was ordered to come to terms with his rival in the Landespolizei to avert bloodshed. I believe that it is confirmed in a witness's testimony that an agreement was in fact reached between Captain Göring and a commander of the Landespolizei. We weren't about to open the hostilities! Also, a crowd of people appeared among us and told us about the mood in the city. Most said the mood of the populace was favorable. The papers, spreading the joyfully received news that finally what everybody was waiting for had arrived, did their part in the morning. Perhaps a few blemishes appeared, but everything that occurs in history produces blemishes, more or less. The general mood was such that no one except those people with briefcases stuffed with stocks had anything to fear. Someone told us we should put the alleged hostages—the preventive arrestees—at the head of the column and hold them before the Landespolizei in order to free Pöhner and Frick. This idea was rejected, particularly by Dr. Weber. This matter did not even come to the attention of Hitler or Excellency Ludendorff. I only want to say this in order to reveal the various influences and reports that affected us.

In the course of the morning, it became apparent that we were in an untenable position. The proper amount of time we allotted to our opponent for a clarification of his position had expired. One cannot set a certain time for it; one must act on one's intuition. The opposition must have had enough troops gathered to attack us and earn a clear-cut victory. For reasons which I will elucidate later in closed session, I proposed that we should withdraw to the Rosenheim area. This proposal was rejected. Fortunately, I had thought to create a buffer zone between the two parties so that we would have the ability to decide without the danger of coercion. There was still another possibility: to try, once more, to obtain clarification. The people that we had sent as messengers to our opponents all appeared to be under arrest, or had otherwise been prevented from returning.

Thus, only one way was left open to obtain clarification: to march into the city and assess the situation ourselves; and this proposal was accepted. When I was asked about the route, I proposed that we should march to Marienplatz and then return to the Bürgerbräukeller. I chose this route to the Rathaus because, in the meantime, the black-white-red flag had been hoisted and because several gentlemen, belonging to the Red, Redder, Reddest Party, had entered the Bürgerbräukeller at the same time as we had visited the Rathaus.

I would like to mention one more thing. Two policemen were brought to the Bürgerbräukeller. Dr. von Scheubner-Richter told me about this. They were arrested because they had ripped down our posters. I said to Scheubner-Richter: "Be a kind of 'information officer,' interrogate them, and then release them," which is what he did. The same procedure was ordered for arriving hostages. At the time, it was only the armed intervention of our men that prevented our city fathers from being lynched by the furious mob. They owe their lives to our men. On Dr. Scheubner-Richter's instructions, they were interrogated. He had orders to release them, so I don't know why he didn't release them. I had no time to worry about such details.

It was decided, therefore, to have a march. I gave the command that the bands in the Bürgerbräukeller should report in front of the building that faced the city. The main idea for the parade was to have a demonstration, with music and flags flying; and, more importantly, to sample for ourselves the mood of the populace. Three orders were given: unload weapons, no shooting, and "all commanders up front!" In the meantime, though, the musicians had moved off. They had been sent to the front, but someone there had sent them back. The music would have had a much more military effect. The parade was organized in a two-group column—on the left, the National Socialists and on the right, Bund Oberland. At the front of the National Socialists, the reduced Hitler Shock Troops marched; after them came a few Hitlerite bands.

In anticipation, the Hitler Shock Troops had fixed bayonets, but had shouldered arms. On the other hand, the other bands in the march had rifles unslung, no bayonets, and unloaded weapons. Later, the columns of the march increased twofold. The leaders, without weapons, partly in civilian clothes, partly in officers' uniforms or band uniforms, formed a broad strip. In the second section, generally, there were friends of our movement, including Oberstgerichtsrat von der Pfordten who made the march solely out of loyal friendship to Pöhner. Of his own volition, he went to the police to inquire about Pöhner. He couldn't have been absolutely sure, but he thought that he saw his friend at the window. Von der Pfordten was crushed! He joined the march out of loyalty to his friend. He sealed his loyalty to his friend with his death.

The parade came to Ludwigs Bridge. We saw about eight or ten men posted on the other side. Now the German national anthem was struck up. When parade columns, 16 men across, sing, it is obvious that it's so loud that individual commands can't be heard. I knew when the Landespolizei received the order to load. When we shouted that they should come with us, that Hitler and Ludendorff were in the parade, the Landespolizei separated, left and right, and we marched on.

Meanwhile, to the right and left of us, a mob who accompanied the parade had gathered like a swarm of bees. The crowd at the Rathaus was like the crowd with us: they wanted to take the Rathaus and they were far more bitter towards the Landespolizei than we were. In any case, we gave no order to arrest the Landespolizei. We knew that they were following orders and were doing their duty with a heavy heart. That is how we regarded them. Even the commanding officer didn't give the order to shoot. At least I didn't hear him. We were greeted with jubilation at Marienplatz. Everyone shouted, "Hail!" The parade veered to the right and I thought it would take the route that I had proposed. When I saw the parade marching on, I thought to myself that since Ludendorff is marching with us, we will of course march with him. If we clash, at least he won't be the only victim. Friends don't desert one another in a situation like this. If events should repeat themselves, we will all still be at Ludendorff's side even if we all have to pay with our lives.

Obviously we couldn't march back down the Maximillianstrasse. The Generalstaatskommissariat and the bridge by the Maximilianeum were occupied. On Residenzstrasse I saw before me a weak chain of Landespolizei stretched across the street. We shouted, "Hey! Don't shoot! You can't shoot at Ludendorff!" The chain of Landespolizei broke and we marched on. We were at the heights of the facade of the Feldherrnhalle when a dense group of Landespolizei ran up from the direction of Theatinerstrasse. There seemed to be an officer at the front. Their cluster was so thick I was forced to stop. This officer fascinated me. I cannot exactly say what happened next. He charged with the carbine high over his head.

Later, I was stunned to learn that an officer, who I had assumed had been doing his duty with a heavy heart, would boast of his behavior in a newspaper. He said that he had perceived that the time for a decision was at hand. When this officer broke loose and began dealing out blows, the first shot was fired, as true as I stand here, from above by the Landespolizei. The shot passed between Hitler and me. It wasn't a pistol shot. The shot was the formal signal. Then they began an insane shootout. The officer wrote in the scandal sheet that he testified he saw men with rifles ready in front of him. I don't know who was carrying rifles. In the front row there were unarmed leaders, some in uniform, some not. Ludendorff was in civilian clothes, as was Hitler. I was shocked by the picture I saw and instinctively realized that it wasn't practical to stop here. Behind me, our people stood; in front of me, the Landespolizei were shooting. I thought, "If this develops into a shootout, I'm right in the middle of it." Therefore, I took cover by the foreside of the Feldherrnhalle.

I don't know whether our people returned the fire, but I can say one thing: The Hitler Storm Troopers were all tough, battle-tested, brave soldiers. It's understandable that they refused to let themselves be shot at like sheep. If I had been there, I would have grabbed a gun, loaded it, and fired. It is also obvious that we didn't want to have a shootout. If we had wanted to start the fight against the Reichswehr, we would have marched in a different formation. You may safely assume that we old soldiers wouldn't have marched in that formation with unloaded rifles.

I observed other things from my niche. I saw a member of the Landespolizei fire three shots, in rapid succession into a man lying on the ground—it was either Hitler's or Ludendorff's body-guard; each shot jerked the man's body into the air. Four shots were fired at me from a window of the Residenz. The bullets were buried in the wall of the Feldherrnhalle to the right and left of me. I thought to myself, if he continues to shoot, he'll get me, eventually, so I decided to fall down as if I had been hit. Then they stopped firing at me. I didn't have a weapon and had already changed from my uniform that morning—I didn't think the grand uniform and patent leathers would be the proper attire if we had to turn back to Rosenheim.

Everyone present today can probably imagine what sort of feelings coursed through me. I saw a man in a dark brown overcoat on the ground and thought, "It's Ludendorff." Luckily, it wasn't true; but, to my great sorrow, it was Oberstlandes-gerichtsrat von der Pfordten. Among the dead, I saw Dr. Scheubner-Richter and a group of young people. Both of the flags which had been carried at the front now covered two corpses. I shouted at several Landespolizei to stop shooting; I got into an argument with them. I wasn't afraid to yell, "Go to hell!", either. I then tried to get the Landespolizei to at least send for a doctor and medical personnel to save the wounded. After taking one last look at my dead friends, I slowly went home. If it's true what they told me—that Captain von Schrauth of the Landespolizei died trying to prevent the shooting—then I, even as an officer from the other side, will honor his memory, as we all should. I then attempted to prevent the arrested Cabinet Ministers from being harmed by our people after they had heard what happened and an understandable anger took possession of them. I also attempted to warn the squad at the bridge to go back. I was unable to phone the Lehmann Villa, or the Bürgerbräukeller. Therefore, I went out to the bridge, where I discovered that the squad on the other side had already disappeared.

I decided to get out of Munich in order to record, in peace and quiet, what had happened. That was on the night of November 10. Early on the morning of November 11, I drove back to Munich to find out what had happened at the Lehmann Villa, and to turn myself in. It was a joy and solace to me that the business with the Ministers had been settled properly. On the advice of my attorney, I did not turn myself in; instead, I drove out again. My counsel had told me that it would serve no purpose to let myself be locked up for weeks or months on end. When the date of the trial was imminent, there would be plenty of time. I turned myself in on January 16, and here I am today.

In conclusion, I can only say that I harbor no regret that I collaborated in the matter. I am proud to have participated in it, because I have always been disgusted with men who constantly complain about what should be done, but never actually try to implement a solution. As I have already mentioned, it has been and will always be an honor, for the rest of my life, to have sat here beside Ludendorff, Hitler, Pöhner, and my other friends.

In response to the Judge's question about the accused's thoughts on his position, Lieutenant Colonel Kriebel states that he had imagined, after the three men had joined them, that he would cease to be military commander of the Kampfbund which was breaking up into other bands. Consequently, he now only receives orders and is only the middleman until the individual bands align themselves.

HERR GADEMANN: A stenographic report of the November 6 session has come into my possession. In view of this report, I wish to ask the defendant the following: Didn't Excellency von Kahr describe the immediate establishment of a Reich government as the most urgent priority?

HERR KRIEBEL: Yes, that was said in his opening remarks to the meeting.

HERR GADEMANN: Didn't Herr Kahr also state, at this meeting, that you would work and proceed according to a carefully prepared and well-thought-out plan?

HERR KRIEBEL: Yes. The gist of it was that we just couldn't play it by ear; we had to have everything prepared, down to the finest details.

HERR GADEMANN: Did Herr Kahr also discuss at this meeting the financing, feeding, and marshalling the reserves? And did he emphasize that there would be a clear, unified, and concentric action?

HERR KRIEBEL: I don't remember the phrase "concentric action." The others fall within the sphere of the exact preparations. I believe that that was the topic of discussion.

HERR GADEMANN: Did Herr Kahr say that the preparations in this sense had been initiated and that General von Lossow had the entire military command?

HERR KRIEBEL: That's correct. Excellency von Lossow was to be in command.

HERR GADEMANN: Did Excellency von Lossow emphasize that the Bavarian Division was ready to support any Reich dictatorship if the affair had any chance of success? And did he want to march on Berlin?

HERR KRIEBEL: There was a remark made that the Bavarian Division would join in any action, except a Kapp-putsch.

Herr Gademann remarks that the about-face of Herr Kahr, Lossow, and Seisser is explicable, in his opinion, because after the events in the Bürgerbräukeller, the men realized that they weren't capable of the deed and also that they were afraid of losing their positions since others had organized this act. This follows from the official communique of the "Hoffman Correspondence," of November 10 in which the idea was advanced that Lossow and Seisser should be replaced by Hitler's Generals.

Herr Gademann further refers to a Military District VII Headquarters circular of January 10, 1924 which was directed towards the chairmen of the various officers' unions. Oddly enough, the circular contained prominent passages which completely matched the indictment. The letter was sent out in strict confidence in order to create a hostile mood toward the officers in the dock. Among other things, ambitious associates were mentioned in it. This can be compared with Forstrat Escherich's characterization of Lieutenant Colonel Kriebel as an upright man who always puts the matter at hand above personalities.

Herr Schramm asks inquires whether Kahr, Lossow, and Seisser shouldn't have mustered the courage, after they had changed their minds, to tell the defendants about their change of heart, without waiting for the arrival of the Reichswehr.

HERR KRIEBEL: They very easily could have done just that, for we were all set to go with them, not against them.

HERR SCHRAMM: Herr Kahr, Lossow, and Seisser not only failed to inform the defendants, but also, in pointed words, prevented an understanding from being reached? Didn't these gentlemen further state that they would have no truck with revolutionaries; that revolutionaries would be shot, and an example made of them?

HERR KRIEBEL: I only knew about the first.

In response to Herr Luetgebrune's question, Lieutenant Colonel Kriebel states that in military considerations General Ludendorff was held to be their spiritual leader because, on German Day in Nürnberg, he had sided absolutely with the nationalist ideals; but that Ludendorff had never had the power to give orders to the Kampfbund and had never exercised it either.

Herr Luetgebrune remarks that the indictment accuses General Ludendorff of commissioning the seizure of the Wehrkreiskommando. In response to counsel's question, Lieutenant Colonel Kriebel terms this accusation erroneous; the original intention had been to lure the Reichskriegsflagge, with music, from the Löwenbräukeller into the city and there to make propaganda. Only after, did the plan evolve into combining the march into the city with the march to the Wehrkreiskommando in order that the Reichskriegsflagge could act as an honor guard there. It could have been possible that the motorcycle messengers who had been sent to deliver the order had said that the Wehrkreiskommando was to be seized on General Ludendorff's orders.

HERR RODER: Is it true that Excellency Ludendorff first stated that he wanted to attack not on November 6, but on October 24?

HERR KRIEBEL: At the time, Excellency Ludendorff explained that there were three ways to proceed, and the first consisted of creating our own orders.

HERR RODER: Did Excellency Ludendorff state that the term "attack on Berlin" would have to be disguised by using another phrase?

HERR KRIEBEL: Yes, we mentioned disguising this word by using another.

HERR RODER: Is Lieutenant Colonel Kriebel aware that Excellency Ludendorff also spoke with Captain Göring about the assault, and that at that juncture Lossow stated he was ready to attack, but that he first wanted to see the facts so that he could fully orient himself?

HERR KRIEBEL: I had no thorough instructions about that; therefore I am not able to testify as to whether it happened like that or not.

Herr Roder notes that, pursuant to this, Captain Göring, one of our best aviation officers, had personally told him that.

HERR RODER: Would you have taken action against Seisser, an old friend, if you hadn't been convinced, from the beginning, that Seisser was in?

HERR KRIEBEL: I wouldn't have taken any action against my old friend. I was positively convinced that he was in.

In response to another question of counsel as to whether Herr Frick had been groomed from the outset to take over the office of Police President, or whether they assumed that he would be ready for such a position, Lieutenant Colonel Kriebel remarks that Dr. Frick was not informed beforehand. He (Kriebel) only knew that Frick stood in such good relation to Pöhner that if Pöhner accepted, then they could certainly count on Frick's acceptance as well.
Here Hitler requests permission to speak in order to correct an error which had crept into Kriebel's testimony. Kriebel

believed the purpose of the discussion with Kahr was to inform Kahr ahead of time of what was to come. He (Hitler) only wanted to submit a few questions to Kahr, however. The first one was to be: "Do you want to take action?" If Kahr had said: "We don't want to," then that would have been the end of that and there would have been no coup. If he had answered the first question affirmatively, then the second question to have been asked was: "When do you want to take action?" If Kahr had answered the first question, "I do," and the second question of when it should take place, with: "I can't say," then action would have been taken anyway, that evening, to make participation possible for the men who really wanted it but didn't have the nerve to make the leap.

Herr Holl asks Hitler, in connection with the intended conversation at Kommerzienrat Zentz's home, whether he had set up his plans so that he could call them off later?

HERR HITLER: I would have been able to rescind the orders until around 7:30.

After further explanation, he states that he could have recalled the orders only until 7:00 o'clock.

HERR GÖTZ: Do you remember, Lieutenant Colonel Kriebel, from the meetings you attended not only in October and September, but also in June and May, whether the topic of conversation concerned Herr Frick as the future Police President?

HERR KRIEBEL: No.

JUDGE NEITHARDT: That contradicts an affidavit which stated that he was proposed long before.

HERR KRIEBEL: The question was, "May and June."

HERR GÖTZ: We are concerned with the fact that the information reached Police Headquarters that Frick was contemplated for the post of Police President.

JUDGE NEITHARDT: That was in October.

HERR GÖTZ: On October 23, Regierungsrat Bernreuther and Oberregierungsrat Tenner said that at a meeting a commissioner from Division G reported on the future status of various positions. One of these gentlemen remembers distinctly that the

213

name "Frick" was mentioned. Now I would like to know, since we can't cross-examine the officials in question—these officials have not been released from their security clearances—whether firm agreements were revealed in these conversations?

HERR KRIEBEL: No firm agreements, but of course he was a useful man, in every respect.

HERR HITLER: The circle of members was small. It is obvious that such a circle can only be kept small under absolute mutual trust. The few men were bound by their word never to divulge anything to anyone without the consent of all the others. When I was with Pöhner, naturally I exacted the same promise from him not to impart one word to anyone without our knowledge. Of course Frick was proposed by me in the event of a new alignment. But, while we were at the drawing board, there was no need to notify a man whose attitudes we knew so well. We bear the responsibility. Everyone else that didn't need to know about the action wasn't informed about it. At the very least, the others were unconcerned that one individual—Frick—whose support was so apparent, would be badly received. It was clear to me that, in the end, Herr Frick would take up an influential position.

HERR HEMMETER: Does Lieutenant Colonel Kriebel remember that during the time the Kampfverbände still existed, the leaders were all in agreement that their implacable foe was Lieutenant Colonel von Berchem; and that all Lossow's resistance against them was the result of Berchem?

HERR KRIEBEL: I could not shake the suspicion that the source of these misunderstandings was none other than Herr Berchem. I would like to state explicitly that despite the very insulting remark made by Lieutenant Colonel Berchem, I have no personal quarrel with him in the proceedings. I consider him to be an officer who has acted—as he believes he must act—to the best of his knowledge and conscience. I only meant that he moved in other circles and, as a consequence, in spirit he could not approach our movement.

Herr Kohl asks Lieutenant Colonel Kriebel whether, when the first shot was fired at Odeonsplatz, the Landespolizei were either in an upright or a prone position when they opened fire.

HERR KRIEBEL: Many were standing, and a few were running.

HERR KOHL: Isn't it standard procedure that if one shoots into a crowd, that first a signal is given and then if there eventually is shooting, isn't it done from a prone position?

HERR KRIEBEL: I don't know about that last part. I know, from experience, about the former—that there is usually a warning given.

HERR KOHL: Did an officer come and say that if you marched any further they would commence firing?

HERR KRIEBEL: No.

HERR KOHL: Did they shoot from the armored car?

HERR KRIEBEL: I didn't see any shooting from there, but I was told about it later.

HERR KOHL: Are you aware of the identity of the men in the armored car?

HERR KRIEBEL: I have heard about it, but I wouldn't care to comment.

Herr Mayer asks if the parade could have been either stopped or turned around, in view of the narrowness of the street.

HERR KRIEBEL: That's hard to say. If we had been able to go another 50 meters, the parade probably would have stopped by itself. With all the clamor in the street, it was impossible to give the command to halt.

HERR ZEZSCHWITSCH: At the moment of the sudden attack, wasn't the song *Deutschland hoch in Ehren* being sung?

HERR KRIEBEL: Yes, sir.

HERR GÖTZ: Did you see how First Lieutenant von Godin snatched a carbine from a Green Policeman?

HERR KRIEBEL: I only saw him carrying it.

HERR EHARD: I have no cause to delve deeper into the tragic

occurrence in the Residenzstrasse. I only want to establish one thing, because the most serious charges are being leveled against the Landespolizei here. It is disputed that the other side fired on the Landespolizei. I would just like to verify that besides Captain Schrauth, several men of the Landespolizei died; they all were shot from the front. I ask you not to consider this statement as reason to incite debate over details. I do, however, want to establish one thing; namely, that if one is caught in the middle of such a situation, it is naturally difficult to render individual perceptions afterward. An example is in order. I believe it was Dr. Weber who said that First Lieutenant von Godin placed the barrel of the carbine to a standard bearer's temple or chest. Lieutenant Colonel Kriebel saw how First Lieutenant von Godin swung his carbine, butt first. I would like to call attention to both perceptions in order to show how unreliable such observations really are.

JUDGE NEITHARDT: That can also be reversed. I don't think we will be able to find the answer to this question, even if we summon 100 witnesses from one side and 100 witnesses from the other side. We would then probably get 200 different statements, and the Court would still be unable to establish who fired the first shot.

HERR KRIEBEL: I respect the dead on the other side just as I respect our own. The officials did their duty. I particularly regret the death of Captain von Schrauth because, as it was reported to me, he attempted to avert a bloodbath. What I must protest, however, is how First Lieutenant von Godin celebrated his personal victory. He should have had to do his duty with rage and with clenched teeth; never should he have boasted about it.

JUDGE NEITHARDT: Perhaps the Prosecutor will tell us whether proceedings have been instituted against him?

HERR STENGLEIN: The preliminary hearing is still pending. We have encountered extraordinary difficulties which have involved an extraordinary amount of time, but we are now approaching the conclusion.

Herr von Zezschwitsch expresses the opinion that it is of paramount importance not only to the defendants, but to the nation, to determine whether the first decisive shot was fired by the Landespolizei; or, at the least, whether it came from their direction. This determination, he feels, can be made.

HERR SCHRAMM: I don't want to leave unchallenged the impression that the death of Captain von Schrauth can be traced to a bullet from these people. The death of Captain von Schrauth has not yet been clarified! There is a great probability that the bullet came from the men under First Lieutenant Godin's command.

In passing, I would also like to mention that the prosecution has made such an "extraordinary effort" to determine who fired the first shot, why have they only heard the testimony of the Landespolizei?

HERR EHARD: I, personally, in the name of the District Attorney, requested official Police Headquarters to interrogate all civilians who either reported themselves, or could be rounded up, about the events on Odeonsplatz. We divided our work; one interrogated the civilians, the other the members of the Landespolizei, and so on. I wish to verify this in order to stop the rumor from spreading that the prosecution performed their duty in a one-sided fashion—i.e. did not do their duty.

HERR KOHL: The prosecution may well verify which order the commanding officer received, who had the men file out, and who gave the order. This verification is all the more necessary because the events at the Feldherrnhalle have to be called "murder," according to the feelings of our people.

HERR EHARD: Your letter to the bands permits the conclusion that you believe that, if requested by the legally constituted government, the Reichswehr and the Landespolizei would turn on the bands.

HERR KRIEBEL: I only wanted to tell the bands that we were all working together, and that we would not leave them stranded. A whole slew of such letters came from North Germany.

HERR KOHL: Is it true that the troops that liberated Munich on May 1, 1919 reminded the Communists, by distributing leaflets, that anyone who had a gun in his hand would be taken for an enemy and shot on sight? In the present case, the National Socialists took no such measure.

217

HERR KRIEBEL: At the time of Munich's liberation, I was in Spaa. But if the Communists were warned, one could have expected that this would happen more readily, in our case, in regard to Ludendorff.

HERR RODER: The impression that Captain von Schrauth was gunned down by the National Socialists should not be left unchallenged. One can learn from the files that he was killed by a bullet ricocheting off a wall. One also finds in the files that a heavy machine gun in the armored car sprayed the National Socialists with bullets.

HERR HEMMETER: The question is whether or not the use of force was ordered by Lossow, with Kahr's approval. When I was arrested on November 9 in Police Headquarters, I was told about 1:00 o'clock that I could only be released when a police action in progress was finished. I deduced from that that the order to fire in the barracks had been given, and that they wanted a military victory.

HERR EHARD: Herr Roder is grasping for straws. I have established only that officials of the Landespolizei were also killed, and that they were hit from the front. It will be proven that the marchers also fired. I haven't said one word about how Captain von Schrauth was hit.

HERR ZEZSCHWITSCH: On the afternoon of November 6, did Herr Lossow declare that he was going to proceed *"manu militari"*?

HERR KRIEBEL: Yes, sir. I said yesterday that the occupying troops who were to be at the telegraph office and the main train station were to be replaced by Munich police, at once. I did not oversee the payment of the troops; but only to their food and shelter.

At this point, the hearing is recessed.

—AFTERNOON SESSION—

As the trial resumes in the afternoon, amid great tension in the courtroom, General Ludendorff is called to the stand. With clear, striking sentences, he introduces his defense.

Testimony of General Ludendorff

HERR LUDENDORFF: My life lies before the world in history. Above all, it was work for the Fatherland, for the people, and for the dynasty. My friends and colleagues here wanted to honor me with a special cachet. I thank the gentlemen for it, but I stand here as a German man who does not desire any special status.

JUDGE NEITHARDT: May I ask you, Excellency, to explain your political persuasion?

HERR LUDENDORFF: On October 21 of last year, I was drawn into the undertaking which is now under judgment. On October 21, I underwent the oath of the Bavarian Reichswehr through the Bavarian State. I recognized the possibility of a mutiny, which would be a serious breach of the constitution. Even if I have no reason to defend the Weimar constitution, I must mention it here. I saw in it the beginning of the decadence and the debilitation of the Reich and the incipient potency of the aspirations which I pursued for a long time with the greatest concern. I must elucidate because the indictment also elucidates, concerning my whole orientation.

I have grown old under the monstrous burden which the war placed upon me, under the work which I have accomplished for the military preparedness of the people, and under the spiritual exertions which I incurred in wrestling with my own country. However, my heart is young; it beats yet with a glowing desire for the liberty of the people, and with the love of the people. I cannot express my sentiments like Hitler did in his wonderful speech in the closed session yesterday, but the same holds true for me. I see the downfall of our people, our land, the misfortune

219

of the Imperial and Royal House, the misfortune of the illustrious House of Wittelsbach caused not by external forces but by our own sins.

There can be no doubt left about my attitude towards the Marxist and Communist scheme of things. Before the war, the Marxist world of ideas declared itself against all armed forces. In Paris, before the war, Scheidemann said: "You are not the enemy; our common enemy lies elsewhere." I remember him saying that a German victory would be injurious to the interests of the Party. And again terrible words were uttered: "It is our will that Germany lower its flag forever without victoriously bringing it home one last time." It is inconceivable to me that people with this motivation could possibly bring us freedom again. As far as my hopes for the freedom of the people are concerned, I am against all harbingers of the Marxist and Communist ideas.

In close connection with this Marxist problem stands the Jewish problem. I learned all too well during the war the dangers of the Jews, and I have applied myself to this problem earnestly and diligently. For me, the Jewish problem is racial. The Jewish race is in contrast to our race. The Jew should exercise as little persuasive influence in our country as the English or French exercise. One cannot expect the people's liberation to come from him. Therefore, I am against him.

We are dealing here with great historical relations, but the World War interrupted historical thinking. Today we fancy our destiny to be a sound economy. We have been taught to think only in economic terms. In the end, however, the world will be controlled by intellectual forces and ideas. The men who follow the Jewish thought seek power, and then enter politics finally seizing the economy to fortify their position.

I must address myself to the Ultramontane problem. I predict that the press will reproach me for preaching *Kulturkampf*. I know that only the merger of denominations can bring us forward. I regard the blessings of the Catholic Church as highly as I do those of the Protestant Church. I know that the Catholic soldiers who died in battle wanted a strong Germany just as badly as the Protestant soldiers. The events here in Bavaria, when the German Reich was founded, are well known. I will tell you that not everything went as smoothly as people often believe. I served in Posen, in Silesia, and in Strasbourg. I sensed how centrist politics impeded the Germanization of those areas. Upper Silesia is now Polish, thanks to Centrist politics. Bismarck best expressed my view when he said that the policies of the Center were directed towards the destruction of the ungodly specter of a German Reich with an Evangelist sovereign. And then Bismarck said: "They are not enemies of the Reich, theoretically and absolutely, but the Reich as we know it does not suit them." And then, "Rome will consider an Evangelist church and dynasty, in any *modus vivendi*, as an anomaly and a disease whose cure must be brought about by the Church." Then, just as it began to appear that a German nation would appear, in its embryonic stage, the War broke out. The dynasty disappeared on the surface, but it remained deeply rooted—the German ideal—in the people's consciousness. That awful event, the World War, summoned it; but where would the leaders of our nation lead the people?

After my discharge in 1918, I was obliged to go to Sweden where I learned from a newspaper that Bavaria sought a separate peace. The *Bayerische Kurier* wrote, on November 26, 1918, number 329 under the heading—mark it well—"Seize the time: Herr President Eisner, aren't you letting the old Reich dominated by Prussia disappear like the German cockade?" And further on, "Renounce a Germany in which power-mad Prussia and Berlin always want to call the tune. Say it again, Herr Minister, Bavaria wants a separate peace. Everyone non-Prussian will join us." And: "Just as surely will finally come a German Federation without Berlin's chicanery and its beloved Prussia.... Herr Minister, I believe you think the same way. I say, 'Away with Prussia!' Create the constitutional People's State of Bavaria; petition for a separate peace. Only the Prussians, whom the Slavic admixture has tainted, will not have peace." A more pointed sermon of particularism and separatism could not be preached.

I stand here not as an accuser, but as a man who wants to show how he came to hold certain views which, in turn, caused him to embark upon the action of October 21. The article by Dr. Georg Heim in the November 30 and December 1, 1918, issues of *Bayerische Kurier* outlined a very real system of power politics and economic endeavors. I can't repeat the article word-for-word, although not one word in this essay should be lost. At the time, the situation in Bavaria was by no means promising. However, the situation in Munich, under Eisner, wasn't any better. It didn't give any justification for regarding the situation in the

North more unfavorably than that in the South. Dr. Heim wrote in the second segment about the future configuration of Germany:

> "Herr Eisner's ideal is to have a Social Democratic centralized State without interior boundaries. I come from a greater German family and I heard again and again from my father's lips about those sad times when customs posts in the Reich were the symbols of the saddest kind of particularism. But—please note—I come to the following conclusions as a realist because I accept the unalterable facts as they are. It is beyond question and indisputable that according to the new configuration of things in Austria, the Entente will not permit, under any circumstances, the annexation of 10 million German Austrians to the Old Germany, reduced by the separation of Alsace-Lorraine and the Polish East Provinces. I never doubted that for a moment. My information confirms this. Now we face the question of the future of the German Austrians. There are two alternatives: The first alternative is that the rest of Germany will remain a federation, as before.

General Ludendorff remarks here that it wasn't a "federation," but rather a Federal State.

HERR LUDENDORFF: German Austria remains a trunk state of itself. "The second alternative is that German Austria, or parts of German Austria, unite with parts of hitherto existing Germany. Considered from a Bavarian point of view, the latter alternative would be preferable."

Dr. Hein does not spell out what is to happen to the rest of Germany. The article continues:

> "From a Bavarian point of view, we must also produce an extremely tight alliance of Bavaria, Voranlberg, Tyrol, Styvia, and Oberösterreich. Besides common ancestry, the same national character, the same sensibilities, this grouping is extraordinarily felicitous from the Bavarian point of view. If it is certain that the Allies will never concede that the Old Germany has been enlarged by

Austria, then Bavaria has to choose between the two alternatives. Either it remains as a cog in the Old Reich, in which case it must renounce the glittering prospect; or it consummates and engineers the annexation.

Or, clearer still, it leaves the Old Reich.

"In my (Hein's) estimation only the latter course can be considered. But the tentative objections to this are: The new economic area—namely, Austro-Bavaria—has no access to the sea, no adequate iron ore, no coal mining facilities.... . But there would be a solution here with the expanded Old Rhine Union: Hannover, West Germany up to the Elbe, and South Germany with Austria. There also are other reasons for this. If the Austrians say: 'We want to wait until Vienna belongs to the Viennese again and has rid itself of international Bolshevism and its quagmires,' the same is valid for Berlin and North German industrial areas. Whoever recognizes the development of the situation in Berlin must share my opinion that such an alignment in Germany alone means rescue from the swamp."

The North German industrialized areas lie in the regions now claimed by the Rhine Union as its home.

"There will be a process of dissolution, accelerated by a corruption that has never been experienced even in the worst of capitalistic eras. The great peril of poverty is thereby united with the greater peril that foreigners will come into possession of our natural resources and economic strength. For this reason, Bavaria must absolutely secede with the hope of eventually reuniting."

Ludendorff mentions similar proclamations in Hessen, Baden, Württemberg, in the Rhine provinces, and in Hannover where they extended even into the ranks of the Social Democrats. That was 1918.

HERR LUDENDORFF: In the spring of 1919, the well-known meeting between Dr. Heims and French officers in Wiesbaden took place. In Wilson's memoirs and documents we read: "Now France wouldn't hear of any inclusion of Austria in a South German confederation." We learn about a meeting between Dr. Heim of Bavaria and Rhenish conspirators and various representatives in Wiesbaden, which Foch reported to the Council on May 19, 1919:

> "Heim spoke confidently about the secession of other important German states from Prussia and he talked about the formation of a new confederation to include German Austria under a 'protectorate,' mainly with regard to economic policies. He stressed that such a Catholic and conservative bloc would form a more effective barrier to Bolshevism than a Prussified Germany was ever able to form."

Not only am I familiar with all of Dr. Heim's statements in the press concerning this matter, I am also aware of the then-Reichskanzler Scheidemann's statement that only when he read Dr. Heim's statements in the papers did he realize what kind of plans Dr. Heim was pursuing. In any case, I was seriously engaged by the problem; my feelings that Dr. Heim's opinions in Wiesbaden were pernicious to Germany were intensified. They moved completely against the direction of his essay.

Dr. Heim particularly rebeled against the phrase "Catholic Conservative Bloc" which served only to provide for an eventuality. In my opinion, this eventuality was the situation that should have been dealt with. I have a very comprehensive correspondence between Dr. Heim and Count von Bothmer from the year 1920. Count Bothmer's relations with French circles should have been obvious to Dr. Heim.

The chronology becomes somewhat displaced here as the Federalist Germany steps to the foreground. I would like to go into more detail here to show what trains of thought were in play so that my apprehensions might be made clear—although personally I am against the Centralist Weimar constitution. On March 25, 1920, after the Kapp action which, as you know, brought Bavaria the Kahr administration, Count Bothmer wrote to Dr. Heim:

> "In Cologne, they were on the point of forming their own state government, fulfilling English hopes. Since I was able to dissuade the

Rheinish People's Union from taking such a premature position on the formation of the state, and since the interior annexation of the federalist organizations of the Rheinland to Bavaria came a step closer, the possibility now exists that a shrewd administration could exert for us useful and necessary influence from Bavaria on the political configurations in West and South Germany.

"I make the observation in passing, Herr Privy Councillor, that you are a man of trust and patience. I shall only verbally inform you about certain conversations that I have had. Once again, I have examined the activity of Dr. Dorten. If the Rhine remains a German waterway, we will have his clever and superior work to thank. The inconspicuous and intensive work of Dr. Dorten has succeeded in breaking down the Greater Rhine Movement into its components. Today, our goal is to unite the whole Hessian area, including Marburg and Giessen, with the Rheinish Republic; to anchor this on the right bank of the Rhine; to realize this with the support of a high percentage of the Evangelist populace so that the odium of being a tool of Church succession cannot be hung on this state. To give these ideas a certain form, I stopped over in Darnstadt for a few days to take counsel with the real policy-maker of Hessia, Prince Leopold von Ofenburg, and to discuss everything thoroughly with Brentano. Brentano is a shrewd party trustee and tactician, but he has a second-rate political intellect. We must allow for his vanities and ambitions because he'll accomplish some useful things for us."

Ludendorff continues:

HERR LUDENDORFF: Then Bothmer writes, on April 21, 1920: "Now I would like to say just a word or two about the association with Professor Förster." This is the Förster we know as the traitor to his country. "I believe that we may proceed harmoniously here, also. Professor Förster will be an important figure for us, not in an active, diplomatic role, but for the purpose on the one hand, of remaining French distrust regarding thoughts of revenge; and, on the other hand, of exploiting his good contacts with the Social Democratic groups in order to woo them from the Unitarian to the Federalist camp. If we succeed in placing Förster with the Social Democrats of the Rhineland and South German states, then he will be able to do a lot of good."

In his letter of May 4, 1920, Count Bothmer enumerates various jobs he has undertaken to expand the sphere of activities of Bavarian politics in the Rhineland. "What would Bavaria say if Prussia was active in, say, Franconia? I regard these actions as an offense against unwritten laws which must plunge Germany into disaster." The following is an excerpt from Bothmer's letters:

> "As a further addendum, I am giving you a letter from Prince Ofenburg in Darmstadt and a copy of a memorandum which the Prince sent on to me in Mainz along with a copy of your letter. You can see for yourself, Herr Privy Councillor, how efficiently and orderly my middle-men have been drilled and how they work according to a uniform principle."

I was shocked when I read that. It's not a letter to Fuchs or Machhaus, but to one of the most prominent leaders of the Bayerische Volkspartei, who signs his letter to Count Bothmer: "With cordial greetings, Your Dr. Heim." On April 21, 1920, after he confirmed that Dr. Heim had used a "Herr X" in negotiations with the French, Herr Bothmer writes: "I have prevented Herr X from going to Herr Kahr because (1) Herr X isn't the right man to mediate between the representatives of the French Government and the temporary State government; and (2) under all circumstances, he must be sworn to give you every piece of foreign policy traffic so that in your absence—which, under the circumstances, you would have to disavow—clumsy and poorly informed government officials do not take up an official position.

In a letter dated May 4, 1920, written by Count Bothmer, Dr. Heim, characterized as Bavaria's real statesman, will have full powers to marshal the changes in Germany's form of government. Dr. Heim takes the following position in a letter to Count Bothmer dated April 12, 1920: "France should declare: We will be happy to accommodate a Germany that places its main emphasis on the individual states!" He also adds: "How splendidly France could enhance her position in Western Europe; yet France ignores this historical moment. France is preparing her own putrefaction."

Just how Dr. Heim envisions the solution is apparent from a letter to Count Bothmer dated July 7, 1920, right after he had written a letter to the latter on July 3. It is noteworthy that Privy Councillor Dr. Heim speaks about a conversation in Mainz—perhaps, a second conversation with French agents. That time was the high point of the display of Bolshevik military force.

Dr. Heim protested the separation of Prussia's provinces east of the Elbe since these would be pushed to the bosom of Russia. For a military Russia would immediately follow a Bolshevik Russia and this would put the old Prussian militarism back on its feet. That was the German reasons of Herr Privy Councillor, Dr. Heim. It was too late for the tool which the Hohenzollerns used to create the German Reich and which alone gave Bismarck the basis for his lenient policies. Privy Councillor Heim then writes:

"There is a splendid method, which many could accept, to break the Prussian hegemony; the creation of a strictly sub-divided federalistic Germany with a centralized foreign policy, common economic policy, legal system, army and militia system, but having the power to give orders to the states and having far-reaching independence and autonomy in everything else, especially in officialdom and cultural questions. This is a program that a German can present. France would smash Prussia's hegemony for all times and it would see a thoroughly peaceful Germany across the border. I also stated that an overwhelming majority of Bavarians are disinclined to thoughts of revenge. I have spoken openly in this manner. I remember the speech I gave in April at the District Party Day in Regensburg. It contains the same train of thought. I have presented my trains of thought repeatedly in my Party and I find more and more acceptance of them."

227

And then, in another letter, "The Hannoverians are another story and you probably haven't been briefed very thoroughly concerning either personalities or conditions. The affair is no simple matter. You will hear from me in person on how things are with the Hannoverians. There is no reason to call ourselves a 'State Party' immediately, on account of the Hannoverians. I hope we can find a common ground with the Hannoverians, but a few things will have to be straightened out first."

Privy Councillor Heim then underlines his acquaintance with Herr von Tannenberg, the well-known leader of Hannover's secessionist movement which sought to break away from the Prussian hegemony. Yet another brief remark, from a letter of Dr. Heim, dated May 25, 1920: "I'm just now reading your letter to Privy Councillor Grauert. I must come back briefly to one thing. From your letter, I gather you labeled the Munich journalist Gessner of the *Kölnische Volkszeitung* a Protestant and thereby you obviously sought to make him suspicious. That is, by all accounts, unbelieveable.... Can the Party be made culpable for such tactlessness?"

In the meantime, the efforts to smash Prussia and reorganize the Reich were anchored in the Reich constitution—in Article XVIII of the Weimar Constitution. Article XVIII permits the creation of new states inside the Reich. The Bayerische Volkspartei drew this conclusion in the "Bamberger Resolutions" of Autumn, 1920. Naturally I doubt whether the resolutions were presented to Herr Dard, as is claimed. Such rumors, however, are symptomatic. Point 2 of the Resolutions demands acceleration of the process for creating new states constitutionally—the Weimar Constitution prescribes two years for such alterations of territory—too long for the Bayerische Volkspartei. I don't believe the Bayerische Volkspartei had their sights set on secessionist movements; it was, rather, mainly a matter of crushing Prussia.

The sixth demand required the right for individual states to sign treaties with other states in matters of their own constitutionally given authority and to appoint representatives in foreign states. It was the same policy the *Bayrischer Kurier* had propagated in the fall of 1918. This policy was also represented in the coterie around Herr Kahr. Again and again I heard the phrase, invoking Bismarck—"a strong State in a strong Reich"—instead of "healthy states in a strong Reich"!

When I moved here in 1920—not for political, but solely for

private reasons—I also came in contact with Herr Kahr. During Sanitätsrat Pittinger's campaign against Forstrat Escherich in the fall of 1921, it seemed desirable to have me as an auxiliary against Escherich. My relationship to Herr Kahr became closer and I was able to gain some insight into his thinking. Here, during the temporary separation of Bavaria from the Reich, the thought of the annexation of the German Austrian states without Niederösterreich and Vienna was discussed—not by Herr Kahr, but quite publicly—as if it was a foregone conclusion. The idea of leaving Niederösterreich and Vienna to their fate, so to speak, seemed un-German. In any case, Vienna simply could not be subjected to Czech influences. Concerning Bavarian influences in Austria, others could probably give better information than I can. I only mention the finalization of an agreement between Dr. Pittinger and Count von Soden, and Major Gömbös—i.e. between Bavarian circles and Hungary's strongman at the time—as proof of Bavaria's policies.

I regard the idea of temporary separation as high treason. I hailed the Deutsche Volkspartei in Bavaria when it announced— quite belatedly—in its proclamation of May 31, 1922: "We utterly reject, as high treason, the idea of even temporarily separating Bavaria from the Reich."

That is the position I have taken for years. I still remember the events of the summer of '22, the storming of the Lerchenfeld ministry, which had very serious repercussions. Perhaps Dr. Pittinger can give us more details. Otherwise, I am ready to testify. Repeatedly the Separatist movements appeared undisguised supported by the Deputy Dard and his agents. The "Politika" of March 1923 writes: "The goal of France and her agents was a Catholic, monarchist, Alpine empire under Crown Prince Rupprecht, consisting of Bavaria, Würtemberg, the Palatinate, and the Rhineland. In the neighborhood of 15 million Germans would thereby be separated from Prussia. It is evident from the preceding that this statement wasn't as nonsensical as it appeared on the surface. Harsh light was thrown on this by the Leoprechting trial in May of 1922 and, above all, by the traitorous activities of Fuchs-Machhaus-Kühles, the last being a brother-in-law of Count von Bothmer of whom I spoke previously. Reports reached my ears that something was underway, but they were so hazy and incomprehensible that I was at a loss. I only realized the treachery when on March 6

Rechtsrat Kühles, who had said he preferred the rear of a French-man to the front of a Prussian, shot himself. For me, it was alarming how this traitor was interred. At the time I said sarcastically to my wife: "If I should ever be buried here, I won't receive any such funeral." The fact that a Catholic clergyman, who supposedly has to harden his heart to any suicide, gave a graveside eulogy was characteristic of the feeling at this time, as far as I was concerned.

I discussed this case and the whole official treatment of this gigantic betrayal with Dr. Traubing at that time. He convinced me that other forces stood behind the traitors. I also never believed that the wiliest French agent, Lieutenant Colonel Richert, negotiated with Fuchs and Machhaus as private citizens. Herr Richert's offer included the partial annexation of Austria to Bavaria through the creation of a European Peoples' League under a French protectorate which stood at the Ruhr and now would grow to include Bavaria. Bavaria was supposed to be given cause to march into Middle Germany where the French would stir up a Bolshevik revolt. They were showing Bavaria how it could aggrandize itself.

At the time the French thought the Berlin government would offer active resistance in the Ruhr. It would be thwarted and the Reich would be humiliated anew. The whole affair made a strong impression on me. The deliberations had not yet begun when another incident claimed my attention.

In the beginning of May, the following statement by the Bavarian cabinet council was issued in the press: "Ministers von Knilling, Schweyer, and Matt want to advocate a merger with Austria. Only the question of whether a Bavarian or an Austrian prince ascends the throne remains open. Minister Schweyer discussed this with the French General de Metz on his trip to the Palatinate and he has received the General's approval. If the plan is realized, the Palatinate and North Bavaria will be separated. Cardinal Faulhaber and the Pope also want to back up this plan. The ministry specialists themselves are indignant about the conduct and attitude of all the ministers and are, by no means, in agreement with them." The *Bayerische Kurier* pleaded for a judicial ruling. The *Volkische Beobachter* expressed the expectation that this judicial way will never be trodden. And so it happened. The affair died away—or at least it didn't receive the only possible legal ruling.

The creation of such a powerless Germany by crushing

Protestant Prussia was an offshoot of Ultramontane policies which one can trace all the way back to the founding of the Reich in 1871. This idea first appeared during the World War and found its representative in the delegate Erzberger whose name, together with Count Czerny, will always be bound up with the Peace Resolution of July 19, 1917, the armistice, Versailles, and Weimar. The aforementioned Article XVIII of the Weimar Constitution, which permitted the Prussian territories a plebiscite— this was the heart of the matter—was Germany's tombstone for me, well-conceived by Germany's enemies and inserted into the Constitution. I do not understand any talk of a Centrist shift. Look at constitutional delegate Trimborn's speeches, which made a very strong impression on the committee at the time. In Germany's struggle, the Vatican wasn't neutral. It was anti-Germany. France was favored and honored. Since I esteem the benedictions and piety of the Catholic Church, it was painful for me to see how His Holiness the Pope last summer protested the acts of sabotage in the fight for the Ruhr and Rhine; how Marshall Foch received a sword of honor from the Jesuits during his trip to the United States; how Clemenceau received an honorary doctorate there. It seemed all these enemies of Germany worked for the Society of Jesus. I also remember the influences to which Kaiser Karl succumbed, his betrayal of Germany, and the inflammatory polemics of the Catholic clergy against Germany.

Equally painful were Cardinal Faulhaber's derogatory statements about Germany, which he made in America during the Fuchs-Machhaus trial. While the enemy Admiral Sims confirmed the validity of the sinking of the *Lusitania*, the Cardinal described it as contrary to International law. Also, he did not speak of the blame for the War in the way in which the overwhelming majority of the German people saw it. Also, here in Germany, a large segment of the press kept a discreet silence, thereby showing their true colors vis-a-vis the German Problem.

It was particularly noticeable how the Jews were increasingly defended by the higher clergy. This became more and more obvious, especially around November 8. I also don't consider it a coincidence that the Jew, Louis Hagen, and other Jews on the Rhine represent the Rhineland policies of Privy Councillor Dr. Heim and Adenauer, the Mayor of Cologne, the chairman of the Catholic Councils in Munich, and other Centrist Cabals, namely—may God punish them—in heavy industry circles.

231

Reich Chancellor Marx made himself the executor of these endeavors. The secessionist movements in Hannover, the intrigues in Hessia, and in the Rhine province were unsettling to the Reich's balance of power. I have outlined the cooperation with Bavarian circles. Economic controls were to cement the bonds of Vienna-Munich-Cologne. The formation of the Rhinebund, Dr. Heim's brainchild of 1918, seemed imminent. At that time, I was afraid. Today, the justification for my fear is obvious to the whole world. Even, for example, the *Kölnische Volkszeitung* openly supports separating the Rhine provinces not from the Reich, but from Prussia. Today the organs of the popular parties speak of movements that betray the country, while the *Volkszeitung* supports such traitorous notions. The outline of the constitution by the Bavarian government indicates where we will end up.

Bismarck's words seem to bear me out: "In the middle of sleepless nights, I cannot fight off the thought that perhaps one day our sons will once again sit at the round table of the Frankfurt Bundestag which I have known so well." And of course this can never be if a more serious loosening of the temporary separation from the Reich of Bavaria, in any form—or even secession— is attempted. Can you truly believe that the Ultramontanes are serious about rebuilding Bismarck's Reich if you read, for example, "No matter how lamentable the downfall of the Hohenzollerns may be, from a purely human and monarchist standpoint, from the standpoint of compensatory justice it is atonement for centuries of injustice on this earth."

It was difficult for me to reconcile the ties which I had supposed existed but which I now clearly recognize never existed, between Herr Kahr and legal councillor Class, the leader of the Alldeutscher Verband, the most powerful political organization in Germany, which had members in many high places. It may be clearly seen from reading the publications of the *Alldeutscher* press around October 21 that Herr Class was inclined to acquiesce most extensively to Herr Kahr's wishes to loosen Bavaria's relations to the Reich. But, on the other hand, Herr Class wanted to create the German Unified State by dissolving the states. He said to me, "from a people to a nation," exactly as it appeared on Herr Kahr's program announcement on November 8, 1923.

I could not see the will of the people in this idea; the people rejected such a solution. It was remarkable that a similar thought was expressed to me by a member of the Bayerische

Volkspartei shortly thereafter. Add to this idea the fact that it was tied to other designs and intents which, at the time, I regarded as anathema to the peace of Germany. That, however, only became evident later.

So many things were worrying me that naturally I was unable to disentangle the individual currents. But I saw no end to the things potentially harmful to Germany. I had that certain feeling that ruling Bavarian cliques, even when they spoke repeatedly: "in the sense of the Bismarck Constitution," wanted to destroy Bismarck's Germany or give it another form that had nothing in common with Bismarck's philosophy. While the name, "Bismarck," was misused, the word "Federalism" was given an interpretation that Bismarck had always detested. It meant the enduring enslavement of Germany by France, realized through the annihilation of Prussia! It was a struggle of weighty Bavarian cliques against a federal state.

I saw then, and continue to see a hazard here for the German Reich and the German people. I am not a Greater Prussian—this word has just been coined here—I am a German who wants a strong Germany; a Germany built on a Bismarckian foundation! I believe that the events of November 8 have opened many people's eyes—not to mention those of the Bavarian government. The undisguised objectives of the Bavarian Government are revealed in its memorandum concerning the constitution, together with the movements in the Rhineland and in Hannover and Hessen-Darnstadt. Naturally I was preoccupied and depressed by Germany's decline through our infelicitous policy of weakness within and without that ruined and killed our people. I don't want to go into this any further. I believe I may presume that my views are well known.

In addition to gaining insight into the events which I have just briefly outlined, it was also my duty to devise a plan of rescue. We had been fighting for the preservation of our Reich, on Bismarckian foundations, and our freedom, for four or more years; we couldn't let it be torn from us now and have our fate sealed as slaves forever. The World War and post-War phenomena had shown me which alien elements had brought about our defeat. I had become acquainted with the Internationalists, and their strong political desires. I was able to trace their activities that caused our nation to disintegrate. I had come to the conclusion—which I recently expressed—that the people must be made capable of resisting Internationalistic influences; that something new must be given to the people; something that could give substance to their life and wouldn't pamper them; rather, something that would keep them aggressive.

I recognized this in the *Völkische Freiheitsbewegung*. It became a deeply spiritual need and a matter of conscience for me. I had gained the unshakable conviction that this alone could help us over the rifts that weakened us. The movement alone tore workers from Marxist heresy and placed them on national ground. It also opened the heart of the employer to the social necessities of the employee. It smoothed over class differences as well as—more importantly—religious and traditional biases, as practical politics requires. It created Germans who rejected anything non-German, regardless of its origin. It wanted a strong, militant Germany. The "nefarious Prussian militarism" was no spectre for them. I thought that this movement had been called to meet the dangers I have already enumerated here. My love and obligation to the Fatherland left me no choice but to sponsor the movement with my name.

I met Herr Hitler who is a selfless man whose growth I was able to observe. He knew how to infuse the movement with substance the people could grasp instinctively. Here was something morally superior from which redemption could come. The nationalist movement did not consider itself an end in itself. It had—and still has—no affiliations. The movement considers itself a means to an end; and that end is to make the German man, the German Fatherland, and all the German people strong and free.

Politically speaking, the national movement, which joined the Deutscher Kampfbund in Nürnberg on September 1-2, 1923, set forth its program in the Nürnberg Proclamation. At this time this Proclamation was not attacked by any faction and has remained essentially the movement's creed. This movement was politically Greater German and regarded both denominations as entirely equal; but rejected Church political activity. It was nationalistically and militantly—i.e. tactically—oriented and, thus, anti-Jewish. It was regarded as an opponent by the Bayerische Volkspartei and, likewise—to its deep regret—by the important dignitaries of the Catholic Church. No explanation could be found for this.

Unfortunately, for personal reasons others also aligned themselves as opponents. The Greater German People's Program didn't suit these people because they pursued particular goals which we did not consider to be problems yet ripe for decision. Above all, I must mention the monarchy problem. I am a monarchist of the deepest convictions—even when it is called in question. I haven't forgotten the oath I swore to my Kaiser; but I believe the problem cannot be solved at this time. I have always held the view that the dynasty is not an end in itself—it exists for the people. If the people are there, they will solve the problem. I consider a premature solution, especially a unilateral solution in a single state, to be just another misfortune.

The Kampfbund had a loose military structure. It had set as its goal the maintenance of a military capability of the people, especially of the young people, a desperately needed substitute for compulsory military service—the surrender of which is the cause of our misery! I was closely connected with the Kampfbund and the nationalist movement. I never made any demands on them, and they regarded me as their leader not because of any formal agreement but, probably, because of my dedication to the business at hand. I enjoyed their trust and, as I said, claimed nothing more. I saw in them the possibility of effecting great gains for the Fatherland in the ideal direction and thus of banishing the perils of Germany which I have previously described.

Needless to say, another viscious campaign was started against me. The Jewish and Centrist press had always been against me. Now the Bayerische Volkspartei became especially unfriendly after my trip to Austria in February of 1923, which was an indication to me that I was disturbing their political circle. High officials have confirmed that I succeeded in doing just that. I am not at all surprised that even the German nationalist press turned on me when relations were opened between Excellency Lenz von Hergts and the Alldeutscher Verband and General von Seeckt. I hope the trial will also be able to shed some light on the various issues involved here.

When the Generalstaatskommissariat was created on September 27, 1923, there was no doubt in my mind that the first step had been taken toward the solution—a violent solution—to the German Problem. I was certain that Herr Kahr was in possession of the legal authority, in Bavaria—the legal armed forces of Bavaria—and even beyond that of the Reich armed forces, in the form of the 7th (Bavarian) Division. If I say the names Kahr, Lossow, and Seisser, I don't mean the private citizens, but rather the bearers of State and Police authority in

235

Bavaria and parts of the Reichswehr, which had already placed themselves at the disposal of the Bavarian State authority. These conditions constituted a double breach of the constitution: one committed by the Bavarian State, the other by General von Lossow and the officers who followed him—i.e. if one holds the view that obedience stops at high treason, high treason had been committed. It was not hurtled toward action. Otherwise, this high treason looked ridiculous in the eyes of the world and that turned out to be its eventual fate. So, at the time, I believed in action and I was looking forward to it all the more seriously when I heard of the designation of Pöhner as Staatskommissar for Saxony and Thuringia. This position was only hypothetical if the defending authority in Berlin still stood. Everything else was military misconduct.

I saw therein an attempt to expand, by force, Bavaria's dominance at the expense of other states because the Reich would never have ordered such an action against Thuringia the way conditions then stood just after the discord with Berlin. Direct action was possible only after a blatant transgression against the Reich Constitution or in self-defense. But that appeared completely unjustifiable in view of the situation in Thuringia, Saxony, and the Reich. I received more corroboration that summer when there was talk of Prussia's eventual annexation of the former Kingdom of Saxony. This also was felt by the Middle Party to be an injustice to Bavaria.

The collaboration of Bavarian officials and Erhardt, the military organizer of Herr Class, also paved the way in which the political trip might run. The establishment of a military tactical sub-section under Seisser at the Generalstaatskommissariat made a considerable impression on me. That was Kahr's Bavarian General Staff! I also remember ordinances to administrative areas, particularly to the finance and railroad areas. I have no doubt that the solution to the German Problem was to be solved in a manner seriously harmful to Germany because they battled Hitler, worked against him, and designated him as unnecessary. Colonel Banzer told his officers on or about October 8 that whoever would not fire on the National Socialists should take his leave.

Because of the pressure of the conflict surrounding General von Lossow, the official power brokers in Bavaria had to change their tone. The conflict on October 20 brought to a head the decision by the Bavarian State to bind the Bavarian Reichswehr

236

as the trustee of the Reich. I saw therein another slip on the precipitous road to the disintegration of the Reich. For the small Reichswehr had to remain under a single command. I was deeply distressed when I received the news early on the 20th. That day was Lieutenant Colonel von Grolmann's wedding day. He picked me up in his car. During the drive I expressed my serious misgivings. Therefore I was in a state of great suspense when I received, during the wedding feast, the news which said, in effect, that General von Lossow had called for me at my house again. He had urgently requested that I come to the Wehrkreiskommando. Lieutenant Erhardt passed this urgent request on to me.

As the meeting began, I was convinced it was held with the approval of the Generalstaatskommissar. I held the views of a General, not a private citizen. I left early. Later, General Lossow described to me how everything had gone. I mentioned my anxiety about Bavaria's posture. He rejoined that my anxiety was unnecessary. The Reichswehr is German and has only purely German interests at heart. It backed him to the man. The oath of allegiance also would be carried out without any friction. He wanted a development of intra-German relations in a Greater German, national sense; and he counted on Hitler's and my cooperation. I had the impression that Lossow was seeking a cover through me. Perhaps that is imputing too much, but he was moving in this direction. On this basis, I pledged my loyal cooperation. When I considered supporting General von Lossow with the authority of my name and by enlightening my friends of his desires, I reminded him that the new appeals were lacking in sincerity; that they heightened my fears! Lossow said that a dissatisfied Herr Knilling abruptly crossed off an outline, probably prepared by Colonel von Seisser.

I can only say that I was satisfied that my apprehensions about the structure of relationships in Germany at the time could be shelved and that I hoped for considerable progress in the convalescence of the Fatherland. I had complete confidence in General von Lossow. Even in the autumn of 1916 he had spoken to me of the necessity of unifying the German Army. I willingly placed myself at the disposal of General Lossow and the Bavarian Government, for I hoped to be able to serve the Fatherland.

I was never assailed by doubts that Herr Kahr and Herr Lossow wanted to radically influence the intra-German relations.

237

I always considered persuasion by using the Kampfverbände alone as misguided. No one in the Kampfbund ever harbored such thoughts. If the Bavarian State wanted to find the solution of the intra-German relations in a German national sense by using its armed forces, there could be no doubt of its success. There would be a mighty echo in the north if North Germany saw that it was happening in this manner—namely, together with the Bavarian State which was a prerequisite for my cooperation. My participation and my actions in the whole affair had been contingent upon the resolve of the Bavarian State, the Bavarian executive powers, and the Bavarian armed forces of the Reich in the form of the Bavarian Division.

When I spoke of such a political solution, I thought not of "rivers of blood," but of the pressure exerted upon the Reich government by the Bavarian State armed forces and by the Bavarian administration; both were buttressed by the patriotic bands. As the preliminary propaganda in Bavaria, and nominally in North Germany intensified, the pressure on Berlin increased. I told General Lossow that this propaganda had to be started by Hitler at once.

My depression in the morning gave way to peace of mind in the evening. In the next few days, with particular urgency, I listened to the radio announcements and declarations of the governments in Berlin and Munich, and the Generals von Seeckt and von Lossow, who left nothing to be desired in regard to clarity. They remembered the exchange of notes and telegram correspondence of two hostile powers before the beginning of the War. According to Lieutenant Colonel Kriebel, two periods had to be distinguished: the time before which the Reichswehr had been bound by oath; and the time after. In regard to the time before, I was kept almost completely in the dark. Afterwards, I received a certain orientation from General von Lossow.

I was also tensely watching the development of relations with the Infantry School. Here, the Bavarian officers had avoided the orders of the commandant of the Infantry School and had followed the orders of General von Lossow. The men were suspended from service, but then reinstated reluctantly a few days later. General von Lossow had acted out of patriotic concern. Thus, Berlin—without issuing official objections—had capitulated to Munich. I felt that a weighty step had been taken in the historical development of Germany; one that had to have a fateful effect if a counterbalance was not created in the German order. The fateful effect could only be avoided if the Bavarian State authorities also held fast to the goal that General von Lossow had fixed for me on October 21. Lossow's visit to me on the 23rd confirmed this feeling.

Once more I will note explicitly that my concern was not with questions concerning Dr. von Kahr, General von Lossow, or Colonel von Seisser—Excellency von Knilling knew them all—but, rather, about the sovereign power of Bavaria which was to be established with the assent of the Generalstaatskommissar and the cabinet, with the intention of solving the German Problem with the threat of force, if need be. It was made clear from various measures—from the establishment of a news station in Leipzig, and from the very cautious questionnaire this station received—that this was so. I would prefer not to delve deeper into all that, but I am prepared to discuss it if it is in any way doubted.

In general, Lossow's most important problem—or so he thought—was how the northern Reichswehr, particularly General von Seeckt, would react to the pressure. I was able to express my views to him. If General von Lossow, in his report, had told the public that I thought the Reichswehr stood behind me, that is totally incorrect. I never attempted that. I only implied that if pressure was exerted by the Bavarian administration with the Bavarian Reichswehr and the patriotic bands of Bavaria, then I—not my name alone, but rather the movement sponsored by Hitler—wouldn't create any resistance. Since large numbers of men who thought alike had been placed in the Reichswehr, then my name would assist in cutting off any action against a movement sponsored by the Bavarian administration. Also, General von Seeckt had tolerated the entry of the Marines in the Kapp days and rejected the armed intervention proposed by Reichswehr Minister Noske. I therefore believed that the Reich Government would resign under this pressure and that General von Seeckt would negotiate.

General von Lossow was quite skeptical. He told me that General von Seeckt would have to be persuaded to join us. I expressed the thought that he wouldn't suceed in this effort; that the only possible method was to force a decision on General von Seeckt's shoulders by an act of the Bavarian Government. That did not satisfy Lossow. He was of the opinion that if General von Seeckt could not be won over, that contact would have to be made with General von Behrendt. He mentioned this approximately two times on his visits; thus, I didn't bother about it any more.

I had always insisted on the necessity of giving Hitler a free rein for his propaganda work. I witnessed in the World War the power of propaganda. We were beaten by enemy propaganda. The mightier our spiritual movement, the greater the probability it would succeed in the Bavarian administration without delay. Even Lossow recognized that it was necessary not only to destroy Marxism with guns, but also to disseminate new ideas among the people. Unfortunately, nothing happened in the propaganda field. Only in the critical days around October 20-22 was Hitler permitted to hold a meeting—a welcoming party for Rossbach—a sign that the Bavarian Government needed these two men at the time. However, the rest of the time Hitler and his movement were being rejected—this was understandable in light of the character of the leading Bavarian officials, including the Generalstaatskommissar. I felt that this was the height of disloyalty, and I voiced this opinion to General Lossow. My belief in Lossow was so firm I thought he would do anything to surmount difficulties.

I must insert here an episode which has particularly preoccupied Prosecutor Dresse's time, in order to avoid interrupting the narrative later. It concerns the visit of a few officers from the Infantry School on November 4, at Rossbach's request. Rossbach had been in detention for months pending an investigation in Leipzig. He had allegedly attempted to disseminate provocative ideas. He was released in October and was to be taken into preventive arrest at once; just as we know it here. He found refuge in Munich, made a speech at the Generalstaatskommissariat, and received permission to move about freely here. A special welcoming party was permitted. Just after his arrival in Munich, Rossbach came to take tea with me. He thanked me for various favors during his imprisonment. We had been personally close since his well-known and much-discussed march from Thorn to the Baltic provinces. He always had shown himself to be a man of honor who always worked for the love of a cause and not for personal glory. What he has done here as an individual, I do not know.

When he asked me if I would care to receive several officers from the Infantry School, who would gladly listen to my opinion of the patriotic movement, I said—after repeated requests—that five or six gentlemen could come to tea on the afternoon of

November 4. Since the street was dark and unlit, I sent my son, First Lieutenant Pernet, to the train station to fetch the men: a calvary captain, two first lieutenants, one lieutenant. They were career officers, not cadets; there were two cadet lieutenants. That is how my son came into contact with these men. I welcomed the men and asked them what they were really after. I then spoke about my essay, "The Nationalist Movement," which I had published shortly before. The conversation with the men from the Infantry School was of a general nature. We spoke about current problems of the day. According to the indictment, I was supposed to have talked about a "white-blue danger." I have never even heard of this expression. This accusation must have been due to an error. I request the gentlemen to testify; I don't believe I said it. The colors are much too sacred to me.

Naturally I also spoke of the Greater German question. I also allegedly referred to the attitudes of certain circles in the Bayerische Volkspartei. Perhaps I spoke about the monarchy problem. It has been alleged that I said the monarchy will come when the people are ready for it. I am certain of that, even if my Party friends think differently. I only wish to say that what the indictment states on this point is not correct. I utterly refute the allegation that I spoke, in any way, of a "violent uprising," or a nationalist movement, or of anything of the kind particularly directed against the Bavarian State. In those days, I considered their solidarity with the Bavarian State an absolute certainty because of the messages which I continued to receive from General von Lossow. I said that the idea of the "Volk" would win out. At that time, I had considerably more time to phrase it. I am also supposed to have referred to the "terrible crisis." I was then working on an essay, "Cry of Warning," in which I ranked food distribution, along with compulsory military service, as vital necessities.

The Army will always be a product of the people. It was healthy in the War so long as it represented the people. If the people are attuned to the idea of "Volk," then the Army will reflect this. The duty of the officers is to look at the living problems that motivate the people with open eyes. The old Army was not involved in politics—thank God—but it loved its Fatherland and it was nationalistic and monarchistic. Such must the Reichswehr become, for it is the spirit that prevails in war, not the weapon.

I will now turn to the bigger connections. I was not

241

informed of the political negotiations and ties established by Kahr with gentlemen from North Germany—and particularly Herr Kahr's talks with Count Behr and Herr Knebel (Döberitz). Professor Martin Spahn later told me about it. He was quite surprised when I told him I hadn't been informed of this, and he said that was really strange. My curiosity was unusually aroused by the well-known article in the November 22nd issue of *Deutsche Zeitung* in which Herr Class of the Justice Ministry abandoned the idea of Prussian hegemony upon which the Bismarckian Reich rested and in which he referred to the Kaiser from the House of Wittelsbach. That gave me pause! If these questions were now being posed, a new schism would inevitably appear in the unity of the German people. This seemed to me to be extremely hazardous, not to mention the fact that I considered other things more advantageous to Germany. I welcomed the chance to involve myself in the events and I was determined to keep to the path which Lossow also said he wanted to follow on October 21. I directed all men who came to visit and wanted to discuss political issues to General von Lossow—i.e. Herr Kahr.

On October 25, General Director Minoux was brought to Munich by General von Seeckt—Minoux's separation from Stinnes was now complete—in order to drive to Berlin for discussions on the formation of a new government. If I must speak of it, I regret to say that General von Lossow—not I—drew this man to him. I have rarely met a man with such a tremendous intellect and such great love of the Fatherland. He and Colonel von Seisser drove out to my home that evening. Herr Minoux unfolded to us his political and economic views. His opinions were quite economics oriented, which was understandable. What I said, approximately, was: "My dear Minoux, I don't like your economic program." That statement apparently caused General von Lossow to go to my brother-in-law the following day and say that Ludendorff is a wild man; he's planning something underhanded; I can't understand it. In those days, Lieutenant Colonel Duesterberg (Halle) and Count Helldorff lived with me. Lieutenant Colonel Duesterberg informed me that Lossow had spoken with him about an "Angora Government." This circumstance, and the fact that General von Lossow had also written about it and had given me the essay shortly thereafter, seemed to me to be an invitation to explore it more fully.

General von Lossow wrote his discourse on the institution of an "Angora Government" for Germany, as his own answer to the demand of the Homeland in Bavaria. I understood Lossow to mean by the term, "Angora Government in Bavaria," a new government that would force an interior German recovery which would originate in Bavaria. General von Lossow arrived at the following conclusion: "There must be leaders outside Bavaria involved in the formation (of a government) with whom the leading men of the 'Angora Government' in Bavaria can agree and with whom they can take common action." We can see clearly from this that it was a matter of an "Angora Government in Bavaria" and not a "Reich Directory" in Berlin. "Leaders outside Bavaria (must be) involved" in the formation of an Angora Government; that is, either they should come here for the caucus or wait in North Germany in cooperation—always in cooperation—until Germany's recovery is forced by the Angora Government in Bavaria. General von Lossow closes his treatise with the following statement: "Nonetheless, a way must be found that does not lead to sure failure; rather, we seek a path similar to the Turkish Angora Government." It is noteworthy that General von Lossow recognized both "the frightening lack of bodies that can be considered for any political leadership" and "the necessity of giving the masses, from whom Marxist dogma and the like are to be taken, another substance for the intellectual orientation." I frequently told Lossow that this substance can only be Hitler's theories.

On November 2, Colonel von Seisser drove to Berlin. The result of this trip was a definite change in the views of the three men. I learned nothing about it, and held to my previous persuasions.

Now Admiral Scheer, as a deputy of Reich Chancellor Stresemann, visited Munich to study the Koburg situation and to familiarize himself with the prevailing intentions of the Munich leaders. I brought Scheer to Lossow and Kahr. I made no secret about the fact that I was for pressure directed at Berlin, in front of Scheer. Apparently Kahr and Lossow denied this, although on November 6, Major Vogts, as he himself says, drove to Berlin in order to pick up individuals from Berlin whose cooperation Kahr deemed imperative so that—as Major Vogts explains in his deposition—he could "intervene in the history of Germany" and "take action." At any rate, Scheer was not treated well by the three men. If I have spoken of the Reichswehr in connection with him, I really meant the Bavarian authorities.

243

On the afternoon of the 6th, Major Vogts came to me and made the statements I just mentioned. I told him I didn't believe any decision had been made by those three men. Major Vogts stayed with me and announced Lossow's visit the next morning. He himself would drive to Berlin and seek the men. He didn't tell me anything more. Then Lossow came and told me that, henceforth, the final decision to act would be against Berlin; that only a few gentlemen from the North had not yet joined the cause. The visit lasted from perhaps 9:30 to 10:30 a.m. Lossow wanted the arrival of the men from the North so desperately that I entrusted Herr Scheubner-Richter with the task of sending a man to Berlin who, among other things, would call on Herr Gräfe and ask him to come to talk with Herr Kahr soon, in Munich. In general, I doubted that anyone would come, with the exception of Herr Gräfe. It did seem important, however, to hear confirmation now also from Herr Kahr of Lossow's remarks because the Generalstaatskommissar, not General Lossow, represented the State of Bavaria. I wanted to reassure myself of his intentions. At the same time, I wanted to convey Hitler's discussion with Kahr which was initiated by Scheubner-Richter. I recommended a meeting that evening since the next day, presumably would be a full one since I was having guests for tea, and so forth. I made an appointment for Thursday, at 4:00 p.m. The meeting of Kahr and Hitler did not materialize.

In the course of our conversation, Scheubner-Richter mentioned the assembly that was to take place in the Bürgerbräukeller at 8:00 o'clock in the evening. I only know that at that time I felt a great distance between myself and Lossow and since I had attached a great political importance to the assembly and Lossow had said nothing to me about it—just as he had said little to me of the results of Seisser's trip to Berlin—and I had a need for some clarification from him. Nevertheless, in order to be absolutely sure, I asked him if an assembly was being held, and whether he planned to attend. My confidence in him was restored by his answer. I mention, in particular, that General von Lossow's official report places this call in the morning, and thus outside any context. This representation is a source of the gravest error and is quite prejudicial with regard to interrogation of the witnesses. This report says my son was at the War College in the afternoon to alert the squad leaders—not one word is true. This report, however, has appeared in all the newspapers. When the *Bayerischer Kurier* broke the story and attached a denial to it, the paper questioned its fairness. The presentation of the report constitutes a distortion of the facts which has caused my son and I a great deal of suffering.

Herr Gademann submits the report to the Court. General Ludendorff continues:

HERR LUDENDORFF: At the present time, after having studied certain documents, I have come to the conclusion that perhaps Scheubner-Richter actually did know of the plans for the evening of the 8th.

On the following morning, I had an interrogation at the Hall of Justice. It lasted until the noon hour, without coming to a close. I had to stop because I wanted to go home for lunch before I had a meeting with Herr Kahr at 4:00 o'clock. In setting a new deadline, I gathered from statements made by Herr Zezschwitsch that a faction had planned an action for a day in the not-too-distant future. As I departed, I discussed this with Herr Zezschwitsch. He then informed me that this was a false assumption. I am now explicitly stating that this was the first report I received that the gentlemen actually wanted to begin an action in the period between November 12-15—as we shall determine in the course of the hearing. This I can no longer doubt.

Around 3:00 o'clock, Count Helldorff visited me and gave me a report of his conversation with Lossow that morning. I received the same impressions I had gathered from conversations with Major Vogts on November 6, and General von Lossow on the 7th. Count Helldorff is scheduled to testify later, at which time I will return to this discussion. Count Helldorff drove with me into the city in a car provided by General von Lossow. Since Herr Kahr had taken such an active interest in the results of the talk, and since I couldn't continue to keep him waiting indefinitely, I met him in the only private dwelling I could find—that of Herr Scheubner-Richter. There is not very much to say of this conversation. Here, too, Herr Kahr was indignant that still no men had arrived from the North. He was probably aware that Herr Class and Herr Bang would be arriving Friday or early Saturday. I again mentioned briefly my suspicions that had been aroused that morning by Herr Zezschwitsch's statements, and that they had by no means been allayed. The gentlemen skipped over it. The assembly that evening wasn't brought up at all. I learned nothing new from the conversation and found only confirmation of General von Lossow's words that Kahr intended to act as soon as the men from the North arrived. No one promised to "call you from there," and no one said it to me. I drove from the Generalstaatskommissariat to Herr Scheubner-Richter's and told Count Helldorff that nothing had changed and that he might look around for people in Berlin, and then drove home.

Around 8:30 that evening—I didn't look at the clock—I was called to the telephone. The called said: "Your presence is urgently requested at the Bürgerbräukeller." I was asked to come there—a car would pick me up immediately. When I asked what was going on, I received the answer: "You will be informed." I do not remember whether Scheubner-Richter phoned me, or whether it was someone else. I waited for the car to arrive. Shortly thereafter, Scheubner-Richter arrived and told me the story. We discussed it for about 10 minutes, and then I climbed into the car and proceeded to the Bürgerbräukeller. When I arrived, Hitler greeted me and asked me to take over the office of Commander-in-Chief of the newly created National Army. As had Scheubner-Richter, Hitler briefly filled me in on the state of affairs. My most urgent question was: "How does the Bavarian Government stand, as embodied by the triumverate, on this?

I am not aware of the feelings of the other gentlemen, but I visualized the occurrences, at best, as the first step in the direction of their own chosen goals and I had absolutely no doubt that the men were inwardly firm in their resolve. When I entered the back room, I saw no weapon at the door nor at the window. Pöhner was in front of me in the room. I went up to him and asked him what he thought of the affair. He replied that Kahr had not yet made a decision. I didn't give a "public address." I then went over to Lossow. I have often been confronted with difficult decisions which I have had to own up to, and I did here also. I said to Lossow something like, "The stone has been rolled; this business cannot be stopped now." I related my belief that the goal of the Hitler undertaking was one and the same with the goal of the three gentlemen; that that goal would be endangered if the adopted course was not carried forth. Nevertheless, the condition was clearly understood that the Bavarian Government would collaborate. Lossow retorted to my remark that it was also his view that the undertaking had to be carried on. In response to my question as to whether he would accept the post offered to him, Pöhner told me he would have to discuss it with Excellency von Kahr. Kahr indicated to me that he couldn't make a decision; that he had been "led with a pistol," so to speak, into the back room; and that the men in the hall might believe he was being held here under duress.

In the meantime, Dr. Weber and Hitler confronted Kahr and, with hands folded, remonstrated with him. He finally gave in to the incessant requests in which I also took part. No coercion was used on the men in my presence. They didn't complain about force, either—I would like to have seen the one who would have hindered them! They made up their own minds as free men, both in giving their word and their hand, as representatives of the Bavarian Executive Branch which they had been commanding and would continue to lead. Power lay so securely in the hands of the three men that they didn't want to part with it. No one could take it from them! Had the men said "No," then I would have said, "No, not then."

When I approached General von Lossow, I assumed he had reached his decision; likewise, Colonel von Seisser. I didn't speak to either of these gentlemen. There was no reason to speak to them since I found no resistance among them. Yes! I addressed Herr Kahr. I thought it revolting that the national will should suffer injury.

The description in the official report is wrong. I know for certain that Lossow did not answer me with an acerbic tone, "Good." That doesn't fit in with "Put on an act," either! The declarations in the hall of the Bürgerbräukeller also seemed to me to be genuine. If Herr Seisser appeared disconcerted, as is alleged, the explanation for that is that he had never before given a speech in front of so large a gathering. At any rate, his words portrayed the situation exactly. I repeat, once again, that I continued to be convinced that these three men, who already controlled the Bavarian Government, had placed their authority openly behind the affair—which they themselves had planned. This, of course, was a precondition for my participation.

Furthermore, later on—on the 11th, as I recall—when Herr Lossow told members of the press: "If Ludendorff and Hitler had become dictators, the names Lossow and Seisser would have been mere trickery," I firmly state—and everyone in the assembly would have sensed it—I did not want to play tricks. I had every intention of keeping the promise I made to the two men. Besides, I believed the men had more confidence in their character which would have precluded trickery with them. I wanted them as "dummies"—it is claimed—to "inveigle" the Reichswehr and Landespolizei to join us—and yet didn't Lossow

247

want to use my name as a "dummy" when he asked for my support on October 21? I emphasize, in particular, that I didn't of my own accord want to become involved in Bavarian affairs of State and didn't want to get mixed up in them.

After the declaration in the main hall of the Bürgerbräukeller, I had a short meeting with both men in the back room. Our constitutional relationship to one another was still unclear. This confusion was supposed to be resolved at the Wehrkreiskommando. At this point it was my responsibility to prevent an incipient struggle in Bavaria from arising due to ignorance or misunderstanding, by immediately and quickly alerting all points—including the armed forces and the press. No decree of any kind was issued by me. I only asked the gentlemen to inform their staffs.

I wish to mention that Lieutenant Colonel Kriebel approached me with a request that left me with the impression that he didn't want any personal advantages arising from the success of the action. I asked him to accompany me temporarily. I didn't oversee the conditions in the Pioneer Barracks at all. I only heard from General von Aechter that friction existed between Bund Oberland and the Pioneer Battalion and that he feared it would develop into a clash which had to be avoided. I was not posted on the events at the Infantry School. The Infantry School reported to me in the Bürgerbräukeller because General von Lossow was no longer present. If use was made of my name here, it happened without my consent and certainly without my knowledge. I stand totally isolated from all those events and I learned the details only at the hearing and from the so-called "official" report.

Thus, I was quite surprised when the Infantry School reported to me. I asked Rossbach what General Tieschowitz had said. His answer was that he had declared his oath and had prohibited him from collaborating; but, that since the movement was at flood tide he didn't want to oppose it. Rossbach explained further, as I went with him to the Infantry School, that he was reporting to me in Lossow's absence. Also, he told me that he believed Lossow had driven past the Infantry School. I was greeted with a "Heil Germany," when I reviewed the formations of the Infantry School, and shook Rossbach's hands and told him that Lossow would give him instructions.

I then drove with Lieutenant Colonel Kriebel and Dr. Weber past Police Headquarters to the Wehrkreiskommando. Both men went into the building. I stayed behind since I had nothing to do there. Captain Röhm was inside the Wehrkreiskommando. He told me briefly that he had received orders to occupy the Wehrkreiskommando and that he wanted to welcome General Lossow with an honor guard. I was led to an office where I waited for Lossow. I refused to let myself be assigned a room since I didn't want to give the impression that I was the lord and master there. I was hoping for the speedy arrival of General von Lossow. I do not know when I arrived at the Wehrkreiskommando. In any case, it wasn't 1:00 o'clock, as the indictment states, but rather, considerably earlier—probably long before midnight. My efforts were directed toward getting in contact with Seisser and Lossow. The thought that they were encountering difficulties with their subordinates was firmly entrenched in my mind. I don't remember the details, exactly, but I finally reached Colonel von Seisser in the Generalstaatskommissariat. Attempts to reach Excellency von Kahr failed. I told Seisser I had received reports of dissension among the officers of the 19th Regiment. I don't remember where the rumor originated. I asked Seisser if he knew anything of this. He answered, "No," but he would make inquiries. He also told me he planned to visit the Wehrkreiskommando soon. I dispatched two messengers—one, Lieutenant Rainer, told me the same thing: that Colonel von Seisser will be there at once. The other messenger carried a written request and was not granted an audience with Seisser.

Chronologically, I can no longer keep events separated, but we got the impression that Kahr and Seisser were constrained by their decisions. In this connection, the order was given to the Infantry School to take custody of the Generalstaatskommissariat in order to have reliable troops at Seisser's disposal. I don't know whether I gave the order; however, I assume full responsibility for it. When I heard that Colonel von Seisser had said that the Landespolizei in the Generalstaatskommissariat wanted exactly what we did, I ordered the School to withdraw. I repeat, it was not possible to inform Colonel von Seisser of the situation because despite all our efforts telephone contact could not be maintained. We had no knowledge that a man we named as a witness had been dispatched from the Bürgerbräukeller. We became uneasy when the witness Neumann told us he hadn't received very favorable impressions at the Staatskommissariat. But then we were reassured again when Frick reported that the meeting with Pöhner, himself, and Excellency von Kahr had ended harmoniously. Kahr had released a radiogram: "A new government is formed. He has the governorship firmly in his hand."

And so our impressions fluctuated. For a long time we were not informed as to the whereabouts of General von Lossow. Attempts to come into telephone contact with the 19th Regiment met with failure. Then Lieutenant Rossmann came to relieve the guard. The main thing was to make inquiries about the situation, which Major Schönhärl did not control, as General von Lossow had not tipped him off. Lieutenant Colonel Kriebel wrote him a capsule description of the situation. He expressed the apprehension that a fight might break out. I explained we had no intention of firing on the Reichswehr; we didn't stand against them, we stood with them. I co-signed Kriebel's report and requested delivery of the document so that the parameters of the situation could be determined. We asked Rossmann to come back. He didn't. Shortly thereafter, Major Siry showed up, sent by Hitler at the 19th Regiment Headquarters to the Wehrkreiskommando. He didn't return either. I then sent Cavalry Marshall von Biberstein to Lieutenant Colonel Hoffmann in Ingolstadt with a request to come and lend me support. We didn't abandon hope that General von Lossow would overcome the forces threatening him.

Colonel Leupold had been with Lossow at around 3:00 o'clock. He told me that General von Lossow, since he had acted under the threat of force, did not consider his promise binding. After Lossow's exit, he had lain down to sleep and was roused from his bed by me. If he was supposed to make an official report to me, he would have come to me. If I hadn't fetched him, I wouldn't have received the information at all. I had the impression that Leupold was functioning as a mediator. I must acknowledge quietly the sad fact, which grieves me now as it grieved me then, that German men—German officers!—broke their promise and reneged on their word, without ever giving us any warning.

I left the Wehrkreiskommando at about 7:30 that morning, because I had given up hope that Lossow would come. I told Röhm to stay there. I didn't imagine and couldn't imagine that things would happen the way they did. It was a felony, a crime the like of which previous German history had not seen. I drove to the Bürgerbräukeller because I belonged with my friends in the movement. Hitler proposed to agitate the city through

250

propaganda in order to exert pressure on the three men. News from the city was favorable. That morning Major Hafelmayer came to the Bürgerbräukeller. He declaimed he knew nothing of Lossow's stance and wanted to mediate. We will hear later in this trial that Lossow had said he wouldn't negotiate with that "rabble."

I was forced to the conclusion that the national uprising, as planned on the evening before with the Bavarian administration, could have run aground. The uprising was impossible without the Bavarian Government—relying only on the Kampfbund organizations. I saw the spectre of danger to the Fatherland rear its head; I resolved to save the Nationalist Movement, not for the sake of the Movement, but for the sake of the Fatherland—for only the Nationalist Movement will save us. To withdraw from the movement now, as I was supposed to have done, would have been a breach of loyalty unworthy of a General Ludendorff. Until around noon reports from the city were that the propaganda was being received happily everywhere; the police were retreating. I knew nothing of any posters relating to the summons of Minister Matt. In contrast to Kriebel, I criticized the retreat to Rosenheim because it could either lead to a civil war or end only too easily in the dirt.

The March into the City

A demonstration march through the city seemed to me to be the only respectable and possible thing to do. It was a peaceful march. As a man of reason, naturally I was aware that there existed a slight possibility of criminal use of weapons occurring. Our rifles were unloaded—incidentally, a considerable number of them had no firing pins. We were surrounded by jubilant throngs at Marienplatz. We veered from Weinstrasse to Perusastrasse, then into Residenzstrasse. I cannot say why this direction was taken. I vanquished Tannenberg and the reasons for my tactics were understood only later. It was an instinctive action.

The Reichswehr sentries yielded just as they had at Ludwigsbrücke. The scene, however, changed abruptly and the following events occurred lightening fast. Landespolizei suddenly appeared at the foot of the Feldherrnhalle and began firing. The Residence Palace is still shot full of holes that came from the Feldherrnhalle. If Schrauth and his men were felled—it hurts me deeply—it was not the National Socialists' shooting, but rather shots that came from the Feldherrnhalle. I can still see the fire coming from the muzzles. The squads didn't attack; they fired bursts from the hip. Shots also came from the Residence Palace. I need not tell you the rest. At the Residence guard post I heard of the simultaneous events in front of the Wehrkreiskommando. I directed Captain Röhm to cease resistance.

Major Hafelmayer and Lieutenant Colonel Hoffmann informed me that the Seeckt dictatorship had been called forth in Berlin. As the Kapp action had brought a so-called "rightest government" to Munich, so might Hitler's action have acted as a catalyst in Berlin. At the time, we didn't understand the news; today I can only hint, Your Honor, at where the investigation will spread.

The hope that we nurtured for the recovery of the Fatherland on the evening of November 8 is now ashes because Herr Kahr, Lossow, and Seisser lost sight of the great goal. The great hour found Herr Kahr, Lossow, and Seisser to be little men. However, the most painful truth of all is that I have become convinced, judging from these events, that our leadership has proven to be incapable of instilling in the German people the will to be free. We have succeeded in rescuing the Nationalist Movement from perfidy, treason, and murder. It obtained fresh strength from the blood of martyrs. That is not the result desired by its enemies.

May the Nationalist Movement be able to fulfill the great task which history has thrust upon it! We don't want a Rhine League sanctioned by France. We don't want a State under Marxist, Jewish, or Ultramontane influence. We want a Germany that belongs only to the Germans! A strong Germany which is a treasure-trove of peace as in Bismarck's day!

JUDGE NEITHARDT: How did you propose to advance the movement if the three men hadn't "left the starting gate"?

HERR LUDENDORFF: Supported by what we heard yesterday, the movement would have become such a mighty demonstration that it could have accomplished its mission without violence.

HERR EHARD: The prosecution, as usual, endeavored to be as objective as possible in formulating the indictment, and to omit everything that might be construed as a personal insult. I concede that one passage in the indictment is not quite felicitous. I trust you will concede we have not been so insensitive as to impugn General Ludendorff's courage (this is regarding the reason General Ludendorff left the Wehrkreiskommando).

Was General Ludendorff aware that the action of November 8 was not only directed against the State of Bavaria, but also against the Reich Administration?

HERR LUDENDORFF: Only against the men in the government, not against the form of the government!

HERR EHART: You said, in the Bürgerbräukeller, "in my own right." How are we to understand these words?

HERR LUDENDORFF: In this case the feeling was that the assembly might have believed that I was Hitler's vassal. I wanted to say that I was not acting by virtue of Hitler's command; but from my own strength.

Whereupon, the hearing is recessed, to reconvene the next day.

THE FIFTH DAY, March 1, 1924

—*MORNING SESSION*—

Judge Neithardt discusses the postponement of examination of the first witnesses.

JUDGE NEITHARDT: I have had a number of witnesses summoned for yesterday and today. They were to give supplementary evidence. Due to the lengthy testimony, their testimony was postponed. One witness could not be delayed any longer. Colonel Etzel is to testify about the alert in Regensburg. His testimony, however, may hardly be necessary since it can hardly be disputed by Herr Hitler.

Judge Neithardt suggests waiving the testimony of this witness.

HERR RODER: I cannot waive this witness. I must ask him if he heard the same words from Lossow in a conversation in Munich as those that were established in the closed session. As long as these gentlemen refuse to admit that they wanted to march on Berlin, I cannot forego any witnesses.

JUDGE NEITHARDT: There is a multitude of witnesses on this affair.

Since Herr Roder will not forego the testimony of the witnesses, Colonel Etzel is called before the bench where the Judge advises him that he will not give testimony at this time but that he will receive another summons at a later date.

Defense Testimony of Herr Röhm

The Judge announces that Captain Röhm served in the entire World War, was wounded several times, and received numerous decorations including the Iron Cross, First Class. He also states that Captain Röhm participated in the action against

254

the insurgents in Munich and fought in the Ruhr with the Epp Brigade.

JUDGE NEITHARDT: Is that correct?

HERR RÖHM: Yes, sir.

JUDGE NEITHARDT: You may address the Court.

HERR RÖHM: Honored Tribunal! I must say that I still have difficulty conceiving of the fact that I must defend myself for a deed that is so essential to my nature that I wouldn't know how to act otherwise. I am an officer and a soldier and I request that my conduct be considered from this standpoint.

Captain Röhm testifies that he was in the Royal 10th Infantry Regiment which had a special relationship with King Ludwig III and he emphasizes that he still feels the obligation of this bond today. In describing his tour of duty in the field, Captain Röhm mentions the recognition he received from his superiors— he was a General Staff Officer—and states that more valuable than the recognition of his superiors was the recognition he received from his subordinates who displayed devotion, respect, and love for him even in the Stadelheim Prison. Captain Röhm then begins to speak about the revolution and testifies that he suffered from a bad case of influenza in the middle of October, 1918. It was the first time he had to take leave from the front because of sickness. In October, 1918, he still belonged to the incorrigibles who believed that we would win the War; that we would be victorious.

HERR RÖHM: To be sure, I gained this conviction not at home, but rather at the front, as a General Staff officer. After the English breakthrough in Flanders, I was sent to the front to find out where the command posts on the foremost lines were. The men who stood at the fore, the few heroes who had stuck it out, those men could win the War. One machine gun had put an English company to flight. In this frame of mind, that victory was an absolute certainty, I entered the field hospital near Brussels. There, for the first time, I met the forerunners of the revolution.

Captain Röhm saw these precursors in the unmilitary conduct of the hospital orderlies. Terrible news from home reached him in the hospital and, most terrible of all for him, news of Ludendorff's discharge. Captain Röhm further discloses that he only had one opportunity to meet the Quartermaster General in the field—when he was a representative of the 12th Bavarian Division. In their conversation at the time, Ludendorff said to Captain Röhm:

HERR RÖHM: Well, tell me about the valiant Bavarian Division.

Röhm expressed his desires thereafter and the very next day the Division had everything he had requested. Captain Röhm states that reverence for Ludendorff was a matter of course and that he had found him an especially good friend to the troops. The news that Captain Röhm received in the field hospital caused him to return to the front. After a brief stint, he suffered a relapse, collapsed and, on doctors orders, had to leave the troops.

HERR RÖHM: On our retreat we received the same hearty welcome in Alsace as we did in 1914; it wasn't as if the population was happy to be rid of us. In Munich, a staff sergeant with a red armband came up to me and demanded that I take off the tricolor cockade. I didn't do it—and I didn't put on the new cockade of the Reichswehr, either. I went into the War Ministry where I served as an adjutant of the Division of the Army, after my serious injury, in order to orient myself to the situation at home. The release from our oath of allegiance—which was passed on to the officers at the time—did not satisfy me at all. I found it demoralizing! I have never recognized it as having been given. Even now I consider myself bound to my oath to the present King. The head of the Press Department, Lieutenant Colonel von Sonnenburg, said to me: "For God's sake, you mustn't do anything; you must let everything run its course."

Then I received the opportunity to transfer to the 12th Division in Barmen-Elberfeld as an intelligence officer. In the place of the brave commander, Nagel, was another officer who had the nerve to say things to the Kaiser and to Hindenburg— things which I cannot repeat here. We demobilized in Landshut. On January 1, I reported for duty in Ingolstadt. There I met several hundred officers. Regrettably, we did not succeed in making bands out of the officers who would have been ready to fight. On the whole, there were only four officers who had the same philosophies. Among these men was Lieutenant Colonel Hoffmann who had already distinguished himself in the field as one of our bravest officers. I set about eliminating the drones. There was, for example, the court officer whom I caused, one day, to return to the forward lines. My activities in Ingolstadt were a three-fold battle: first, against the Bavarian 3rd Corps under Ewinger and Schneppenhorst; secondly, against the garrison soldiers' council; and, finally, against the Governor of the Fort to whom I once said: "We shall see who is right—you, with the Reds, or I, who rely on the Whites. If it's up to me, you'll go to hell."

On May 1, 1919, this came to pass. By chance, the brigade commander resigned. I took over leadership of the brigade and dissolved it. That was my first coup in the revolution. The soldiers' council wanted to complain to War Minister Rosshaupter and it traveled to Munich. But since Eisner was shot that day, it was not possible to meet Rosshaupter. I already had been in contact with North Germany and I heard of the establishment of a Freikorps in Ohrdruff by Epp. Accompanied by a liveryman and a secretary, I went there, and shortly thereafter, to Ulm with the Freikorps, to Starnbergersee, and finally under the tri-colored flag, into Munich. At the time, in the Stadthommandan-tur, my assignments included the dissolution of bands of revolu-tionaries, mustering a civil defense regiment, and establishing a Home Guard. I had some bad experiences in those days with a number of officers who discovered their bravery when Munich was already won and who only wanted valuable commissions.

When he had been installed as Police President, I made Pöhner's acquaintance. We then set up the civil defense regiment and the Munich Home Guard. For the latter goal, I sought to form a small, people's committee with whom I coordinated the whole affair. My opponent was then-Staatskommissar Dr. Ewinger who wanted to form a Home Guard whose arsenal was to be guarded by his Social Democratic comrades. It almost came to a clash, but I succeeded in arranging the matter the way I wanted. When Lieutenant Colonel Herrgott was replaced by Major Seisser, I requested a discharge because I had no desire to serve under a new municipal commandant.

I served further as chief of staff under Epp and my activities brought me into contact with the patriotic bands and the patriotic movement in general. Soon after its inception, I joined the National Socialist Workers Party. My relations with Kriebel, with whom I had worked in organizing the Home Guard, were not strained the whole time. At the beginning, I also worked closely with Escherich's successor, Dr. Pittinger. My activities left me in such a vulnerable position that the Reichswehr Ministry decided to remove me from my command at the end of 1922. Certain reports about me had been written by Herr Nimmerfall and Aver and sent to their fellow Party member, Ebert. Besides that, another report was delivered to the Commissioner on Public Order by a person who still lives at Schönfeldstrasse 7. Lossow had been apprised that this character had passed the report on to Berlin. In 1923, I separated from Dr. Pittinger. This was the starting point for the incorporation of the Kampfverbände into one organization. We were unable to admit the Blücherbund and other organizations because their leaders would not meet the stipulations we put forward.

In March or April, the Commander of the Reichswehr issued a decree prohibiting membership in the patriotic bands. At the request of Captain Heiss, I decided to found an Ortsgruppe of the Reichsflagge in Munich because I believed the Reichsflagge should serve as a link between the patriotic bands and between the Reichswehr and Landespolizei. Various members were also guests of the then-loyal bands. Even Kahr took part in the affairs. An all-encompassing friendly relationship had also developed. The various bodies guarded their loyalty, though I must state openly that the officers who joined the bands from the Reichswehr considered it more as participation in a benefit. They could go there, but they didn't want to be inconvenienced. If I express these bitter truisms here, I feel justified in doing so after what I have now experienced. I didn't understand how the whole Officers' Corps could approve a General's mutiny at the time. I did not hide my position from the men and I declared I would never take part in something injurious to Bavaria. I remember a whole slew of things from those days.

I want to raise one other issue in order to justify these bitter truisms. First Lieutenant Braun of the old Second Company of the Reichswehr's 19th Regiment, the man that Lieutenant Casella said on his death bed had shot him, remarked when he was called to account for the fact that the Reichswehr fired on the Patriotic Bands: "I don't care if the Reichskriegsflagge has two dead. I am a soldier and that's what I'm paid for."

Commotion in the courtroom.

HERR RÖHM: Today, Braun is still in the Reichswehr. I must mention this in order to make the Court realize that conflicts had to arise between my patriotic disposition and my duty as an officer of the Reichswehr. I resolved these conflicts by resigning my commission.

Captain Röhm now begins to speak about May 1, and discloses that he had already resigned the leadership of the Reichkreigsflagge because of his spiritual participation on May 1. He was transferred to Bayreuth as company commander, for disciplinary reasons. When his grievance had come to naught—he had refused to lodge a complaint in Berlin about his Bavarian Landeskommandant—he requested his discharge. Captain Röhm was then called before General von Lossow who made it clear to him there was no reason for his discharge. After lengthy discussion, Captain Röhm decided to withdraw his petition. In the meantime, however, someone in the Wehrkreiskommando had sent his petition to Berlin where Reichswehr Minister Dr. Gessler wired his acceptance of the resignation. General von Lossow did not recognize this and the discharge was withdrawn again. Then Captain Röhm began a three-month vacation. Since no decision had been reached as to his placement when he returned, he requested permission to participate in the Fall Maneuvers of the cavalry and artillery. On his return, he was informed he had been ordered to the Reichswehr Ministry in Berlin. Captain Röhm states:

HERR RÖHM: After things had developed so that I could not continue to serve in the Reichswehr—every hope of salvaging the situation disappeared in those days—I decided to make the final break. I then handed in my second resignation. I didn't know what to do with myself. I am, even today, still unsure what to do. I wanted to make myself completely free in order to be able to devote myself entirely to the patriotic movement. I found it particularly troublesome that there was no real political leader in the Kampfverbände. Therefore, I prevailed upon my two friends, Dr. Weber and Captain Heiss, to see to it that a political head be appointed.

At a meeting then, Adolf Hitler was appointed political leader of the Kampfbund by Heiss and Weber. The question of the appointment of Generalstaatskommissar arose and Hitler's position apropos this fact. Captain Heiss did not endorse this development; he felt he should side with Kahr. Then there was

259

an exchange between Hitler and Heiss in Bayreuth when Captain Heiss asked Hitler if he would like to expound his political views at the conference of State representatives of the Reichsflagge in Nürnberg. I then received various letters from Heiss in which he advised me that it was not necessary for Hitler to come. However, I considered it necessary. On October 2, Hitler drove to Nürnberg and wanted to speak there, but Heiss refused to allow him to speak.

Founding of the Reichskriegsflagge

I did not approve of this affront to Hitler and afterwards in an act of faith demanded by Captain Heiss, I denied him my confidence; consequently, I split with officers in South Bavaria who joined me to found the Reichskriegsflagge. This event took place in the first days of October. I was constantly in company with Hitler and also with Kriebel. I set up the Reichkriegsflagge as a military organization on a purely military basis. I was Commander-in-Chief and everyone was to obey unflinchingly. Therefore, it is quite impossible that any man of the Reichkreigsflagge could be held responsible in any way, since a precondition for his admission was absolute obedience to me. He could do nothing independently. I say this because a number of non-commissioned officers were hounded by the Prosecutor and clapped in jail unnecessarily. These men only did what I ordered. The rigidly martial orientation proceeded from the knowledge that other organizations were militarily useless.

Captain Röhm concludes that its military orientation was well recognized because the small band in the Wehrkreiskommando was surrounded by a large contingent of Reichswehr with mortars and Landespolizei. Captain Röhm was very proud of this fact. In his further exposition, Captain Röhm emphasizes that although he was continually in contact with Hitler and Kriebel, he never took part in decisive sessions. He asked Kriebel, who was also in the Reichkreigsflagge, to represent him militarily for he trusted him completely. Kriebel was not only Hitler's friend, but Röhm also placed such confidence in him that he asked him to release him from the eternal meetings.

HERR RÖHM: You need only say the word, and the Reichskreigsflagge will be at the Siegestor on the 10th. "You can depend on it."

Now Captain Röhm discusses the assembly of the Reichs-kriegsflagge in the Löwenbräukeller on the evening of November 8. The purpose of the assembly was to make a good impression upon the public. Captain Röhm states that the Reichskriegs-flagge, as was perfectly normal, was in uniform. At first, Captain Röhm had intended to invite Count der Moulin as the main speaker, but thought better of it and invited Hitler. He accepted and promised he would send another speaker in his place if he was prevented from coming; and so Esser came in his place.

Originally, the assembly was not especially large. Only later did a large number of bands show up. Captain Röhm states:

HERR RÖHM: The individual leaders of the bands reported to me as a matter of course. I would have been very offended if any leader had marched in with his troops without first reporting to me. At any rate, the assembly proceeded as usual. I spoke a few opening words which, naturally according to my whole tempera- ment and in view of the whole situation, called for action. Then Esser spoke. During this time, a man came to the table at which Major Hühnlein, Zeller, and Captain Seidel and others were sitting and gave me the news that a new government had been formed. The man, whose face I know but whose name escapes me, must have been a good acquaintance. Major Hühnlein and Zeller jumped up at me: "Is this true?" I ordered Captain Seidel to telephone and he brought me confirmation. I then went to the podium, interrupted Esser, and announced what had happened. At that, a gigantic celebration broke loose. The musicians danced around the stage and everyone sang *Deutschland, Deutschland Über Alles.* It was barely possible to speak. I created order with a few blasts of a trumpet and then said, "I order the assembly to march to the Bürgerbräukeller in honor of the new regime." The Reichswehr soldiers, who were there in large numbers, tore off the "misfortune" and believed that they were witnessing the revival of the tricolor.

The Events of November 8 and 9

Captain Röhm then describes the march to Odeonsplatz and states that a motorcyclist, who brought the order from the Bür-gerbräukeller that the Reichskreigsflagge should march into the Wehrkreiskommando in order to act as an honor guard for Lossow, came to the Odeon Bar. Captain Röhm did not know who gave the order. He later learned that it had come from Lieutenant Kriebel.

HERR RÖHM: In the Wehrkreiskommando, I informed the officer on duty that a new government was formed and that I was taking command until General Lossow arrived. In the preliminary investigation it was alleged that officers were placed under preventive arrest; that is not correct. I merely told the gentlemen they should not leave their offices. Even the Wehrkreiskommando, for its part, stated in the papers that the military conduct of the Reichskreigsflagge was above reproach. I tried to reach Lossow and telephoned, among other places, the Bürgerbräukeller with the appeal that it was crucial that General Lossow be sent over immediately because I was having difficulty with the troops. I learned that Lossow was at Municipal Headquarters; I received the order to report to Lossow as his adjutant. I was denied entry at Municipal Headquarters, which astounded me. When Ludendorff and Kriebel arrived later, I informed them of this affront. Ludendorff rejoined that it was impossible. He had discussed everything with Lossow and he was certain that Lossow would certainly be arriving soon. The Reichskriegsflagge, together with the Reichswehr, had taken over guard duty at the Wehrkreiskommando. I didn't get a clear perspective on the status that morning, either. However, those things which had appeared suspicious the night before and in the morning, were completely dispelled by the news in the morning papers, and especially by the report of the speeches of the men who had formed the new National Government. Only later did I receive an official communique saying that the Reichswehr was opposing us. I ordered the defense of the Wehrkreiskommando because the approach of armored cars was reported. We didn't know whether or not it was Reichswehr troops on the side of the old regime who would take action against the other Reichswehr. I took up the most dangerous position—Schönfeld-Ludwigstrasse—across from which the Reichswehr had set up a mortar.

As the morning progressed, Lieutenant Colonel Hörauf arrived—he was extraordinarily excited—and I told him I had orders to stay there and that I would make a stand there. After a short time, Epp came and then Lieutenant Colonel Hoffman arrived with a First Lieutenant. Perhaps they also had a white flag. At any rate, someone called: "Truce!" Epp said, "I can't stay here; I just can't fight the Reichswehr." I retorted, "The troops have orders not to shoot; if the other side doesn't shoot, nothing will happen." The emplacement of the Second Battalion of the 19th Regiment of the Reichswehr across from me in the Ludwigstrasse would have been impossible if I had wanted to prevent it. The entire front was covered with machine guns and no one could have moved without being spotted. So I let them, unmolested, scramble forward and take their positions. Lieutenant Colonel Hoffmann presented the matter from the other side. He said: "What do you want? You've already got what you want. We have a new government in Berlin."

We arranged a two-hour cease-fire because I was hoping to hear news from Ludendorff in the meantime. I transferred the command to my deputy. Epp guaranteed that the cease-fire would be upheld until I came back. I was led to the commander of the opposing troops. He claimed he was unauthorized and recommended that I go to General Danner at the Prinz Arnulf Barracks. General Danner wanted to speak with Lossow first, but I couldn't wait that long, so I returned to my troops. It was then reported to me that two men of the Reichskreigsflagge had been shot during the cease-fire. We were assured an honorable withdrawal upon the condition that we surrender our weapons to the Landespolizei. During the cease-fire, the Reichswehr had also scaled the wall and penetrated the Wehrkreiskommando. I subsequently reported to General von Danner and later turned myself in at Police Headquarters.

In response to the Presiding Judge's question, Herr Röhm reveals that he did receive news of his discharge from Stadelheim Prison around December 30. In response to another question, Captain Röhm clarifies information Hitler had given him concerning his meetings with Lossow and Seisser in October.

HERR RÖHM: I was less interested in the conversations with Seisser than in those with Lossow because I had been the original intermediary between Lossow and Hitler. I personally had always desired cooperation between Reichswehr and Kampfbund and had secretly discussed it with Lossow. I was overjoyed that a confidential relationship had been developed between Hitler and Lossow. Lossow also told me that he would always speak up for Hitler. Hitler informed me that he had persuaded Lossow that the Tricolor Affair must proceed and that action must be taken. Hitler was unusually optimistic.

On November 8, I beheld the conclusion of the whole development between Lossow and Hitler.

JUDGE NEITHARDT: There existed complete congruence of opinions between the men. Is that correct?

HERR RÖHM: Yes. The march on Berlin was explicitly discussed.

JUDGE NEITHARDT: Did you consider whether the matter was legal?

HERR RÖHM: No. My enthusiasm for the beginning of the national revolution was extraordinary.

Herr Röhm explains further that he was not present at the meeting of November 7. He then further concedes that he said he would defend the Wehrkreiskommando to the death; however that it would be incorrect to say that he gave orders to occupy the Generalstaatskommissariat.

HERR EHARD: Captain Röhm has given his presentation in such a way that various points may be said to be trenchant criticism of the Reichswehr. It is not my job to defend the Reichswehr. Nevertheless, I should like to refer to the remarks made by General Ludendorff yesterday concerning the Reichswehr. I am objective enough to realize that General Ludendorff has certain personal reasons to be angry with the Reichswehr; and it is precisely because of this that General Ludendorff's judgment is noteworthy. The negative side of Herr Röhm's criticism of the Reichswehr, in general, is therefore essentially superfluous.

HERR RÖHM: I feel that it is necessary to speak freely about certain officers, after the attacks we have sustained have appeared in public. Thus, the question will be raised as to whether, in all cases, a special concord of the Kampfbund representatives was considered necessary for political decisions.

HERR HITLER: The individual representatives must first give their approval to the fundamental determination of a certain course. I assumed the leadership on the condition that once a course was set, no individual could challenge it. That is why I fired Captain Heiss. It was a general guideline that was completely clear to all of us. I always advised Captain Röhm concerning the crucial negotiations with Lossow, as far as my impressions of them were concerned. Since I possessed Captain Röhm's political confidence, since Lieutenant Colonel Kriebel belonged to the Reichskreigsflagge, and since I heard at the first meeting in Munich that the Reichskriegsflagge had put itself into the action, it was completely superfluous to hear from another man.

HERR SCHRAMM: You gave explicit orders that in no case would the Reichswehr be fired upon? To whom did you give the order?

HERR RÖHM: To all the group commanders.

HERR SCHRAMM: The Reichskreigsflagge is accused of plundering the rations depot in the Wehrkreiskommando.

HERR RÖHM: There was absolutely no plundering.

JUDGE NEITHARDT: That is not the object of the hearings.

Herr Schramm asks if it is correct that when Captain Röhm went, during the night, to the Municipal Headquarters that he entrusted his command to Captain Kirschner of the Reichswehr.

HERR RÖHM: That is correct. I said to Captain Kirschner: "Be so good as to take over the troops in my absence." I considered the Reichswehr and the Reichskreisflagge as one.

HERR SCHRAMM: Did you also direct that joint sentries from the Reichswehr and Reichskriegsflagge were to be posted?

HERR RÖHM: Yes.

HERR SCHRAMM: Did you give the order to fetch people from outside?

HERR RÖHM: I saw in the files that Lieutenant Lembert had summoned people from Schongau. I hailed that because Lieutenant Lembert had most of his men stationed outside the area; we had seen but few of his men up to that time in Munich. I had spoken to Lieutenant Lembert several times about a "five-man battery." Possibly the men had been brought in because of this remark.

HERR SCHRAMM: When speaking of a "Lembert Battery," I would like to have verified the fact that Lembert was not even in the Wehrkreiskommando with any battery; that, in fact, there was no "battery" at all.

HERR RÖHM: The "Lembert Battery" was in Upper Silesia and retained its name.

As proof that the assembly in the Löwenbräukeller had no connection with the events in the Bürgerbräukeller, Captain Röhm replies to Herr Schramm's question that the assembly in the Löwenbräukeller had been originally planned for a different day.

HERR SCHRAMM: Night maneuvers were scheduled for the night of the 9th, as usual. Is it true that you invited General von Lossow to attend?

HERR RÖHM: I did not extend the invitation to him, but he was invited.

HERR SCHRAMM: Now, a military question: From a purely military standpoint, wasn't it absolutely necessary that you disengage from your opponent with your men in an orderly, military fashion?

HERR RÖHM: It would have been practically impossible for me to retreat and then say: "Okay, let's go home now." We wouldn't have been able to leave, anyway; we were completely surrounded.

In response to Herr Schramm's question, Captain Röhm declares that the conditions for withdrawal were not honored. He states that neither he nor his whole contingent were treated honorably by General von Danner.

HERR RÖHM: Withdrawal, with military honor, means that one displays military honors to the withdrawing troops. First Lieutenant Braun conducted himself in such an improper fashion that I had to restrain myself from knocking him down and chastising him.

Röhm replies to another question, that the Lieutenant even attempted to rip off officers' insignias.
Herr Hemmeter asks him if cadets of the Infantry School were members of the Reichsflagge.

HERR RÖHM: A number of Infantry School cadets were in the Reichsflagge earlier.

JUDGE NEITHARDT: "Earlier"?

HERR RÖHM: During the time we were still the Reichsflagge. I considered it unlikely, later.

In response to another question, Captain Röhm stresses that he has only now made Lieutenant Wagner's acquaintance.

Testimony of Herr Brückner

HERR BRÜCKNER: The decisive factor in shaping my attitude was the outbreak of the revolution. Shortly thereafter, Eisner came to Augsburg and gave an election speech. His brazen and cynical statements were the most absurd utterings I have ever heard. This speech ignited my fanatical hatred of those criminals who had ruined Germany. At that time I at least had the satisfaction of seeing the men in my company—who were also attending this meeting—spit in disgust. I participated in the liberation of Munich and was with the Second Rifle Regiment until the end of 1919. I later withdrew from the patriotic movement due to financial difficulties.

I was in the Home Guard, and when this was disbanded, my conviction grew that Hitler, through his ruthless battle against Marxism and through his nationalist and social orientations, was the one who could save Germany. It was significant to me that not only middle class people, officials, and students, but also large numbers of the working class, were members of his Party. Whoever had the eyes to see must have gained the conviction that liberation, in the end, depended on the nationalistic reeducation of the working class. I was especially proud that in the group I led, next to the officer, stood the student, the worker, the government official, and so on. In this group there existed a real comradly relationship—on-duty, a strict and unswerving obedience to superiors was stressed; off-duty, the relationship of man-to-man, comrade-to-comrade was exalted. Hitler was probably the first one to give our downtrodden, growing youth an ideal again: the ideal of a Greater German Reich. He awakened in us elders the hope for the future of Germany and the German people.

I have observed how those men appointed to government were incapable of putting a stop to the misery of the Fatherland. Those men with bleeding, tormented hearts who came to these men in power were told: "Everything is all right; just obey the law and keep order; don't do anything that could cause our bloodsuckers to crease their brows."

We were of another mind! We wanted and needed people who had with them an overflowing love of the Fatherland and a fanatical hatred for our enemies with a fanatical zeal for our diminished Fatherland—a Fatherland which is now surrounded by strong troops, and whose strength can only be counterbalanced by the national will of the people. For example, proof of this can be seen in the fact that the liberation of the Palantinate was not accomplished by endless protestations in parliament, but rather when men of hard cast crushed the traitor and scoundrel Heinz-Orbis.

Although I had the greatest confidence in my leaders before November 8 and 9, I must say that during the three months of my arrest this confidence has been strengthened even further. As military group commander, I had no knowledge of the meetings of November 8 and 9, nor was it necessary for me to know, since from the outset Hitler's great objective was clear to me. I heard only from my direct superior, Captain Göring, that Kahr, Lossow, and Seisser were willing to march on Berlin. In closed court session I have commented on what moved me to voice my supposition in front of my men.

On the morning of November 8, at 10:00, I received the orders for the Bürgerbräukeller. Previously none of my lieutenants knew what was planned for the evening. In spite of what is charged in the indictment, I must note that the orders to "tie down revolvers," if they were to be carried were issued so that our people would not come into collision somehow with security police or other police organs. After our arrival at the Bürgerbräukeller at about 8:00 that evening, I kept watch partly in the hall and partly with my officers. Captain Röhm came to me in the course of the evening with the report that the national government had been called forth. My perception is that an enthusiastic mood prevailed.

As for the attitude of the Pioneers, regarding the indictment I would like to mention that the national government corresponded to their wishes, too. They immediately tore off the "misfortune" from their caps and trampled on it. But, on Lossow's orders, they had to remove the tricolor cockade and put the "misfortune" back in its place.

The Presiding Judge censures this expression.

HERR BRÜCKNER: At 1:00 we were telephoned that looting was taking place in the "Bavaria" quarter, so I sent a company over there. They soon returned, however, saying that order had been restored. I was absolutely convinced, until the early hours, that everything was proceeding according to schedule and thus the information from the press only heightened this impression. If the indictment says there was "no doubt" that the Landespolizei refused to side with the Kampfbund, I would like to note that, actually, some doubt still exists in this regard. I, at least, didn't have the impression that the Landespolizei were absolutely opposing us. If one converses with the men of the Landespolizei, one doesn't stand in hostile opposition to them.

After my return from the inspection of the city, I met the parade with Hitler and Ludendorff marching at the head. I took my place in the parade. In reply to the indictment wherein it places special blame on me for this, I say it has always been my principle that where the soldier belongs, there also belongs the commander. If my men are marching into a city, I belong with them. I expressly avoided ordering my men to disarm the Landespolizei. I must also testify to the fact that the parade was joyously hailed by well-wishers on all sides. It was wonderful to see the tricolor and the swastika which had been unfurled at the Rathaus, for I can remember another day—the day King Ludwig III was laid to rest—when no sign of sympathy was to be seen at the Rathaus.

The parade marched through Dienerstrasse. Meanwhile, columns of four had swollen into columns of eight. In the vicinity of the Hoftheater-Restaurant, there stood a weak cordon of security police whose officer yelled something. I did not hear any calls to halt. At any rate, the cordon neither linked nor bunched up. The cordon let us pass through in such a manner that the impression was created that we could easily proceed. At the Residence Palace, likewise stood a weak cordon of security police. At the head stood a man who opened his mouth wide. Naturally we couldn't hear what he said. And to the witness, if there is any, who says there was a "disorderly row" in the parade, I can only say I don't know where the man was standing. In any case, I was singing the national anthem.

269

Brückner testifies that, at the beginning of the shooting, he had the impression that an irregular volley had been delivered. He considers it impossible that shots could have come from the rear of the column since the men in front would have been hit. Brückner contends that the theory of the bullet that killed Captain Schrauth first having hit the wall and then ricocheted into Captain Schrauth is a faulty one.

Brückner emphatically disputes the notion that those who threw themselves down did so out of cowardice:

HERR BRÜCKNER: I know, from my experience in the field, that if I am fired upon and I take cover, I won't be shot like a dog.

Brückner alleges that shots were fired from up on the Feldherrnhalle and he implies—contrary to the Prosecutor's statements on Friday—that the Landespolizei were hit by their own men. According to Brückner's testimony, the Landespolizei emerged from the great portal of the Residence Palace just as machine-gun fire opened up from the turret. Brückner cites bullet holes in the walls of the Residence as evidence.

Herr Roder produced a photograph of the bullet holes in the Residence. Brückner makes his presentation using this picture. Furthermore, Brückner thinks it would be very interesting to discover who was inside the armored car, and whether it opened fire. He had a curious experience in the days when he was still free. He wants to speak his mind on this subject later. He then continues his description of the events of the Residence Palace.

HERR BRÜCKNER: During the three months of my arrest, I had the opportunity to ponder everything. I must say I am proud, as a German, that I was an accomplice on the 8th and 9th. If I were in the same situation today, I would follow my leaders, Hitler and Ludendorff, in exactly the same way.

Brückner concludes with the declaration that he will answer for the orders he gave to his subordinates.

The Presiding Judge asks Brückner a series of questions.

JUDGE NEITHARDT: You were in the Löwenbräukeller? You were to wait there?

HERR BRÜCKNER: Yes, sir.

JUDGE NEITHARDT: Were you the go-between (for Lieutenant Kriebel)?

HERR BRÜCKNER: No, sir.

JUDGE NEITHARDT: You had orders to secure the bridges the next day?

HERR BRÜCKNER: Yes, sir.

JUDGE NEITHARDT: Did Göring give any reasons?

HERR BRÜCKNER: I can't remember.

JUDGE NEITHARDT: Against an enemy? You testified earlier that in the early morning hours a discussion centered around the fact that Lossow and Kahr were not acting as they did the night before. Considering Kahr's and Lossow's attitude, was this order really given?

HERR BRÜCKNER: Probably. I merely carried out the order.

The Presiding Judge asks pursuant to the disarmament on Ludwig Bridge:

JUDGE NEITHARDT: You testified earlier that, "In this situation I had the feeling, if the same scene was repeated, the guns would go off by themselves."

Brückner explains his words should be interpreted to mean that if someone takes aim at a retreat and a shot is fired, then the other guns will go off automatically.

In response to another question by the Judge, Brückner states that he gave no requisition order.

JUDGE NEITHARDT: You refused the command of a regiment?

HERR BRÜCKNER: Of course. I wanted to find the proper position for my age in the march on Berlin.

In response to a statement by the Prosecutor, Brückner replied to the Judge's question that he does not recognize the Weimar constitution.

JUDGE NEITHARDT: If the constitution were legitimate, would you have had to violate it?

HERR BRÜCKNER: I do not recognize it.

JUDGE NEITHARDT: You are free not to answer the question if you do not wish to.

HERR EHARD: At your first hearing, you testified that a man under you wore a loaded pistol.

HERR BRÜCKNER: No. He had it in his hand. I ordered the man: "Put it away and draw it only when you've been ordered to." He did this.

From time to time we demanded that the Communists, whom we had good reason to hate bitterly, either get away from us or they would be shot. We weren't warned! Probably some hysterical Pollyana gave the order to fire and then our men were killed.

HERR HEMMETER: Is the defendant aware that certain relations exist between what he has heard here and Lieutenant Wagner?

HERR BRÜCKNER: My acquaintance with Lieutenant Wagner dates from the Neudeck Prison.

Whereupon, the hearing is recessed, to reconvene March 3, 1924.

THE SIXTH DAY, March 3, 1924

—MORNING SESSION—

Testimony of Herrn Wagner, Frick, and Pernet

General Ludendorff delivers the following statement at the outset of the session:

HERR LUDENDORFF: I recently mentioned the name of Count Bothmer. I assumed the state of the Bothmer family was generally known. To my deep regret I have heard that a rumor is circulating that the Count Bothmer I named and the Senior General Count Bothmer are one and the same. I would like to establish, beyond any doubt, that I was not speaking of General Count Bothmer.

In order to counteract any inappropriate conclusions, Captain Röhm states that he wishes to verify that he is fully conscious of the significance of the serious charges he has made against individual officers of the Army. He states that he considered it advisable that, under the circumstances, officers be fully informed of the conduct of some of their comrades in order to be able to draw the necessary conclusions. He further declares that he was not issuing an outright condemnation of all non-commissioned officers and soldiers in the Army since there was no reason to criticize the spirit which manifested itself in their ranks; and that he was not offering a general reproach to the Reichswehr, at all.

HERR BAUER: Different parties have drawn to my attention the fact that the two Munich dailies—who for well-known reasons are not favorably disposed to the defendants or the defense attorneys—have undertaken a general attack on the defense counsels in editorials on the proceedings of February 28. Moreover, they have seen fit to mock me without, of course, mentioning me by name. The subject of discussion in that hearing was whether the public should be excluded from parts of the defendants' testimony. I stated, after the other attorneys had given their opinions on the motion, as First Lieutenant Pernet's council according to my duty, that I acquiesced in the motions and recommendations of my colleagues; that my client had a stake in having the proceedings made public; and, in particular, that the testimony of the defendants should be heard in public. The aforementioned papers said that my speech was highly superfluous and that I acted out of pomposity and personal ambition so as not to be outdone by the other attorneys. My friends know that such motives are totally alien to me; also, that I have no other ambition other than contribution to bringing the whole truth to light. Personally, this persecution leaves me cold. According to our judicial system, if a motion is made to exclude the public, the defendants or their counsel must be given the opportunity by the Court to make a statement; and that necessitated my statement.

HERR KOHL: In the course of the hearing I asked Lieutenant Colonel Kriebel if he could produce some information concerning the existing regulations relating to the use of weapons by the military. Lieutenant Colonel Kriebel did not answer the question in the way I had expected, but an officer of the Royal Bavarian Army informed me of the following regulation:

According to the *Regulations on the Use of Weapons*, cold steel is to be used first; and only if this proves to be inadequate are firearms then to be used. In both cases, three signals are to be given by a signalman, bugler, or dummer assigned to the troops. Following each signal a warning is to be given to the rebels, mutineers, and so on, by a district official or by a police officer, or by the ranking officer. After the last warning, the crowd is to be given time to disperse so they will not become victims of the violence. These regulations also exist today. In our case, the regulations were either insufficiently followed, or, in any case, they were not carried out; so that the military commanders-in-chief Lossow and Seisser, and the older subordinates, are answerable for the results. They, as German officers, should, at the very least, if they feared serious resistance, have felt an obligation to send out the white flag of truce and make copious use of the signalmen, especially after they became aware, or had to assume that the German Field Marshall Ludendorff faced them. But even this, either intentionally or through an oversight, was left undone on the long road from Ludwig Bridge to the Feldherrnhalle. We can attribute the outbreak of shooting and the large number of victims at Odeonsplatz to the fact that momentous reasons, unknown to the public, were at hand to bring about the shooting. The officer in question reminds me of the officer in the Fuchsmühl incident when, as you know, the Bavarian Army fired on Holzfrevler. It seems to me that if Holzfrevler was warned by signals, then it wouldn't have been asking too much to likewise have had signals prepared in the event that Ludendorff, a German Field Marshall, were marching at the head of the column.

I was further informed that the Landespolizei in Munich are divided into three sections: first, the inner city; second, west; and third, east perimeters of the city. In the case in question, section three was responsible for the area from the Bürgerbräu-keller up to Ludwig Bridge, and section one was in charge of the other stretch to Odeonsplatz. Each section was composed of 600 men. In an alert, three plainclothesmen would be dispatched from each 100-man team. Thus, there must have been 36 plain-clothes agents enroute with the march. They were to bring the Section Command up-to-date as to the direction, strength, and leadership of the march. The sectional commanders had to have known that the marchers intended no assault and that Luden-dorff was at the head of the column. If Section one headquarters put First Lieutenant von Godin into action without collecting information about the parade, then it is a case of gross negli-gence on the part of Section one headquarters. Every 100-man squad had painted signs with the inscription: "Halt! Or be shot!" Why weren't these signs distributed? Since the character of the parade was well known, it is incomprehensible that an officer wasn't sent to the leader of the march with instructions to detour the march.

Briefs, which will be withheld for the moment, are being prepared on the character of First Lieutenant von Godin. If the regulations I have just presented to the Court are correct, there can then be no doubt that the bloodshed—which the public has judged to be murder—must be charged to the accounts of Herr Kahr, Seisser, and Lossow; to Kahr, because full executive power had been transferred to him after the proclamation of the Bavarian State Government on September 27, 1923, and to the other men because of their positions in the military hierarchy.

I previously held the belief, and I do not want to abandon it,

275

that the prosecution is the most objective authority in the world. If this judgment is to have substance for posterity, as long as these regulations exist, the immediate arrests of Herr Kahr, Lossow, Seisser, and Godin are absolutely imperative. No blood sticks to the fingers of the accused and yet they have been under arrest pending investigation for three months and more while the men who are to blame for the bloodletting are still at large.

It will be necessary to arrange the interrogation of the entire Knilling Cabinet. I maintain that the entire Cabinet was taught by Kahr that the establishment of a dictatorship in the Reich was planned by an orthodox or unorthodox method. I petition to hear particularly what former Minister Wutzlhofer has to say about it. Privy Councillor Held's testimony is also absolutely necessary. Yesterday I read all of Kahr's speeches. It seems that Herr Kahr gave a presentation of the matter in a situation similar to the one that took place in the Bürgerbräukeller. This deviated so drastically from Held's formulation that I must believe there is either a remarkable forgetfulness or an extremely subjective presentation of the matter.

It will further be necessary to call Forstrat Escherich to the stand. He must be permitted to verify that Dr. von Kahr took a thoroughly conflicting attitude toward the question of disbanding the Home Guard. I also will present evidence of this through Kahr's speeches in Parliament and will therefore attempt to produce, from the years 1920 and 1921, stenographic reports concerning disbanding the Home Guard. We shall see that Kahr took a rather remarkable attitude for a statesman whom some have compared to Bismarck—Bismarck II—even called: Super-Bismarck.

And so I have already announced the motion to hear the witnesses so that Herr Held, Escherich, and the Ministers who are running for re-election are not obstructed in their campaigns.

HERR STENGLEIN: As I remarked previously, preliminary proceedings dealing with the incident at Odeonsplatz are pending. Questions surrounding the incident will be cleared up. The conjecture that criminal culpability for the bloodshed can be laid to Herr Kahr and Lossow has not been borne out. The inquiry is not yet closed and it will be carried out in all objectivity. The prosecution will fulfill its obligation to the best of its abilities. We need no admonition.

HERR LUETGEBRUNE: Privy Councillor Dr. Heim has

recently commented on the testimony of my client, General Ludendorff, in the *Münchener Neueste Nachrichten*. That, by itself, is his own business. However, in the article Dr. Heim addresses himself not only to Ludendorff's testimony here in the courtroom, but also to evidence produced by the defense not in the courtroom but in secret proceedings. Heim attributes this leak of the evidence to the opposing attorneys. It goes without saying that no information from court files may be passed on to private citizens. It also goes without saying that the defense is convinced that the tribunal did not give the evidence to Herr Dr. Heim. The defense didn't do it either. We can only conclude that Dr. Heim has committed an indiscretion. We request steps be taken to clarify the matter.

The Presiding Judge states that nothing has been released by the Tribunal

Herr Gademann cites an article in the Münchener Zeitung *where two sentences from Lieutenant Colonel Kriebel's presentation were plucked out of context arbitrarily and the conclusion reached that each defendant, without regard to the truth, was saying whatever he wanted. The defendants had to remain silent for four months. Attempts were made through statements in the press and secret propaganda, evidence of which he would submit, to prepare for the day when the defendants were free to speak. The defendants have spoken and have told the truth, word for word.*

Herr Mayer from Würzburg states in this connection that one could not impute to Kriebel on the basis of his testimony an active knowledge of illegality. He was not concerned with the juridical ramifications of his actions, but rather with advancing others to positions of authority. An active knowledge of illegality, regarding Kriebel, is most decidedly something to be argued.

There follows the testimony of Lieutenant Wagner.

Testimony of Lieutenant Wagner

The Presiding Judge reads from Court records that Wagner was a Lieutenant in the 14th Infantry Regiment Constance *and has attended the Infantry School in Munich since September 21, 1923. The moderator reads from his service record, signed by Colonel Leupold: "Wagner is an upright, very independent person, conscientious, stable, and animated by a burning love of his*

277

Fatherland. He has an ideal professional outlook, strives for the highest attainments, and holds fast with temerity to that which he believes just. His previous service was sterling."

Judge Neithardt further states that the defendant will now be given the opportunity to express his views. The defendant realizes that a number of military affairs will come into question which are not meant for the public. The defendant, therefore, must indicate when he can no longer conduct his defense in public.

HERR WAGNER: On November 2, 1918, when the nephew of the current Reich President, Staff Sergeant Ebert, roused the platoons to mutiny at Palenciennes and they gathered behind the front, I was assigned to lead the mutineers back to the front. A violent quarrel broke out between myself and Ebert. Ebert had aroused the troops to such a pitch that one of them threw a hand grenade at me and another put his rifle barrel to my chest. Ebert told me that the Regiment would fight no longer and would refuse to obey its superiors because the revolution was imminent. When I asked how he knew this, he said he had heard it from his uncle—the present President. Sergeant Ebert was secretary of the Social Democratic Party. I will remain silent about his actions towards me at the time of the retreat. In March, 1920, I had the same bitter experiences with the Social Democrats.

I had the most significant experiences in Meiningen and Thuringia. There, for patriotic reasons, I re-routed a considerable part of the weapons to be delivered outside the barracks. The Socialist Thuringian government got wind of it, confiscated the arms, detained me, and brought me before the State Court. The case was thrown out, at which time the cup of my bitterness overflowed. I realized then that liberation was impossible so long as there was one Socialist in Germany; for it had always been clear to me that it was not possible to liberate Germany from its domestic and foreign enemies by holding conferences. My bad experiences with Social Democracy opened my eyes to the Red danger to the people. So I became a dogged and resolute fighter for the nation. I never withheld my knowledge of the domestic situation in Germany from my soldiers. They were grateful for my openness. I also made no secret of my stance to my superiors. Even today, the troops that had pledged their allegiance still express their loyalty and gratitude in cards and letters.

In September, I presented a special squad to my regimental commander, Colonel von Brandenstein. This squad had been trained in a strongly nationalistic manner and it would not avoid battle with the enemy. Therein lies the great secret of my military training and the reason why my men clung to me with so much respect. At the end of September, I was ordered to the Infantry School in Munich. I followed this order with great joy. For years the attention of the Nationalists had been focused on the nationalistic development in Bavaria. They expected nothing more and nothing less than the liberation of the German people to come from Bavaria. Our hope seemed well founded.

Wagner remembers the Bavarian participation in putting down the revolt in the Ruhr and the battles in Upper Silesia; and states that the struggle in the Ruhr also blazed up in Bavaria. In particular, the Reichswehr expected the liberation from Bavaria.

HERR WAGNER: We non-Bavarians viewed the Bavarian Reichswehr with a certain envy. We believed that the Bavarian Reichswehr was always motivated by the nationalist and monarchist ideal. The Bavarian Reichswehr always openly expressed this. It was different with us. By the character of the Reich, the Reichswehr must have been motivated by the Republican-Pacifist-Internationalist ideal. Imagine such a Reichswehr!

JUDGE NEITHARDT: Is this to the point?

HERR WAGNER: Yes, sir! It was impossible for the Reichswehr to be motivated by such an ideal. The nebulous idea of a Fatherland does not suffice. The Reichswehr—its leaders and troops—wanted to know what was meant by the term, "Fatherland," whether it was the Versailles Germany, or Bismarck's Germany, or the Greater German Fatherland. They wanted to know whether it existed for the protection of the pacifist ideal or for the protection of the international banks and stock exchanges. And they were never clear about it.

Lieutenant Wagner then discloses that in October a large part of the cadets took part in the Rossbach celebration in the Löwenbräukeller, and he states that Lossow himself, as commander of the War College, required their attendance at Hitler's gatherings. He further points out that Colonel Leupold, commander of the second course, also ordered attendance at political meetings. "You must imagine," continues Wagner, "how great an inner salvation the nationalist spirit was from Jewish Berlin, Red Thuringia, Red Saxony, indifferent Baden, and so on."

HERR WAGNER: A few days later, the 7th Division separated from the Reichswehr. The commandant of the Infantry School granted the Bavarian men leave to join their troops. The entire Infantry School rejoiced over Lossow's act and saw in him the new Yorck. We reiterated this to our superior officers. Colonel Leupold was requested to inform General von Tieschowitz that the Infantry School stood solidly behind Lossow and the 7th Division. General von Tieschowitz was requested to tell Seeckt this fact. It goes without saying that Lossow, as was Seeckt, was well aware of the Infantry School's position. We would have looked like a miserable pack of dogs if we had put ourselves in opposition to the nationalist rebellion or had kept neutral. On the next day, Colonel Leupold drove to Berlin. When he returned, the cadets were reconvened. The Infantry School had not been liquidated as we had expected.

Our situation was this: On the one hand, Bavaria's open struggle with the Reich government and its constitution; on the other, the Reich's failure to act about it. Our premise was that the constitution no longer existed; no action took place to defend it. For this reason, the indictment's charge of high treason is indefensible. In the days that followed, the cadets took part in gatherings organized by Rossbach. Who convoked these meetings? I don't know. Staff officers of the Infantry School also participated in these meetings. The indictment is in error where it says the Kampfbund sought to gain influence over the Infantry School; rather, the Infantry School was pressing for clarification of the situation. Because of this need, Lieutenant Commander Erhardt was also asked to speak to the cadets. Erhardt said that Kahr wanted to march on Berlin. He regretted that Hitler and his followers were still on the sidelines and said that Kahr was waiting for Hitler to join in. In those days, it was public knowledge that Baron Auffess had thundered: "We don't want to be free of Berlin; we want to have at Berlin!" There was no doubt in our minds that a march on Berlin would follow the nationalist uprising in Bavaria.

In order to obtain some clarification, we attempted to arrange a visit with Excellency Ludendorff. Excellency Ludendorff flatly refused to speak before a large assembly of cadets, but declared himself ready to receive a delegation. During one visit, Excellency Ludendorff spoke of the goals of the Nationalist Movement. He spoke neither of a "White-Blue Peril"—as the indictment maintains—nor of Hitler's merits or those of the Reichswehr. He said, rather, that he would reserve judgment on the Reichswehr. It is out of the question that there was any influencing of the School concerning either the nationalist rebellion or encouraging disobedience to our superior officers.

Wagner requests that the participants in the reception be heard as witnesses.

HERR WAGNER: Excellency Ludendorff also said: "The people's movement should rally our people along nationalist lines. The present parties are unable to do this. The party spirit must be banished; the differences between the creeds must be bridged." Only the Nationalist Movement could do this. In response to our question as to when the Nationalist Movement would win out, Excellency Ludendorff replied that the Social Democrats needed 50 years, but that the Nationalist Movement would be victorious before long. What we wanted from Excellency Ludendorff was clarification of the objectives of the Nationalist Movement. That is what we got!

At the beginning of November, Colonel Leupold contacted General von Lossow. Lossow issued a written command in which he said the reintroduction of the tricolor was imminent and we must be patient. This order was posted on the bulletin board. I emphasize that Lossow gave this order behind the back of my commandant, General von Tieschowitz. On November 4, we participated in the War Memorial Service in front of the Army Museum. The cadets, as well as the patriotic bands, took part in the review for Lossow. We witnessed General von Lossow's last great military review before the action. And then November 8 was upon us. Between 12:00 and 1:00 in the afternoon, I was summoned to Schellingstrasse.

At this juncture, Herr Stenglein moves to exclude the public in the interests of national security.

Herr Hemmeter endorses the motion as it concerns the events in the Infantry School, which he says are a sorry spectacle. All the same, he is against a general exclusion of the public.

281

HERR HEMMETÈR: The business of November 8 must be dealt with in full view of the public. National security, in no way, will be compromised. The events have been portrayed one-sidedly—awkwardly—by the prosecution through the indictment, if I may say so, without casting aspersions.

Defense counsels request denial of the motion to exclude the public.

After the Tribunal briefly deliberates, the Presiding Judge hands down the following decision:

JUDGE NEITHARDT: The public is temporarily excluded, in the interests of national security. The persons named in the resolutions of February 26 and 28 are permitted to remain.

—SECRET SESSION—

Those present are directed to observe secrecy. They are informed that a violation of this injunction is punishable.

JUDGE NEITHARDT: A while ago you touched upon a question of weapons which should be kept secret. I could not interrupt you as otherwise attention would, of course, have been drawn to it all the more. I would have expected you to act somewhat more intelligently in this case. It has now come out and it was impossible to prevent it. You will, of course, be questioned about a number of facts which could actually have been discussed in public. In view of the error that occurred a moment ago, however, I have considered it advisable that you give your testimony in full here and that you later repeat those statements which can be made in public. Those are the points listed in the indictment. You are required to answer them publicly; it is expedient that you repeat them briefly.

HERR HEMMETER: The events touched upon are actually known. Legal proceedings were conducted and quashed.

JUDGE NEITHARDT: The events are known? That would excuse everything.

HERR WAGNER: I also expressly stated that the weapons were destroyed.

JUDGE NEITHARDT: I failed to notice that. We are now getting to the events of November 8.

HERR WAGNER: Between 11:00 and 1:00 in the afternoon, Pernet came to me and told me that Rossbach wanted to see me in the Schellingstrasse. In the Schellingstrasse, Rossbach asked me, first of all, for my word of honor that nobody was to learn anything about what I was about to hear.

JUDGE NEITHARDT: To the Oberkommando Schellingstrasse 39?

HERR WAGNER: Yes!

JUDGE NEITHARDT: Did Pernet tell you what you were supposed to do there?

HERR WAGNER: I asked Pernet: What am I supposed to do in the Schellingstrasse? He said he did not know. There were comrades around us, and I thought that was his reason for not telling me. But when I was with him on the tramway, I asked once more: What is going to happen? I could not imagine anything at all. He said: "I am very sorry, but I really don't know." I knew that that was the place where the Oberkommando was. So Rossbach took my word of honor that I would not talk about what I would hear until the proper time had come. Rossbach told me approximately the following:

> "At 8:30, the national Reichsregierung will be formed here in Munich under Kahr, Lossow, Seisser, Ludendorff, Hitler, Pöhner, Frick. The War College is to take up position at 8:30 and march under his command to the Bürgerbräukeller in order to present themselves to Lossow."

Upon my question as to whether Kahr, Lossow, Hitler, and so on, were in agreement, Rossbach answered that an agreement had been reached. Upon my question about what was to happen in the North, Rossbach told me that the national bands there would march on Berlin; the march would also proceed from Munich. I must mention here that we had already heard earlier of certain agreements between Lossow and other divisions. When Rossbach asked me whether I had any idea of how to alert the War College, I told him to leave that to me and my comrades.

Rossbach's instruction was confirmed to me by Göring. Around 3:00 p.m., I returned to the Infantry School. The first thing I did was to take my best comrades, about 5 or 6 officers, into my confidence. During the discussion, I confided in other officers and junior grade lieutenants so that until 8:30, approximately 20 men knew about the matter. We had no hesitations whatsoever on whether or not to go along.

After the action of Lossow, we had sided with the 7th Division and had informed all superiors, including Seeckt, about it. We also did not doubt that the instructions I received from Rossbach had come from Lossow. If Lossow had been able to have an order read directly to the cadets of the War College, circumventing the official channels and passing over my commander, Herr Tieschowitz, it never occurred to me that on November 8 he would not turn directly to the cadets themselves. By the way, I have not had these doubts until recently. At that time I did not hesitate at all, because it seemed to me absolutely beyond question that Lossow had prepared everything; that the Infantry School was to form a so-called "Storm Troop" composed only of cadets; while the resident officers would be assigned to their duties on the following day.

JUDGE NEITHARDT: Who told you that?

HERR WAGNER: Rossbach told me so. Those were the instructions I had received from Rossbach. Although there was no doubt in our minds that we had to join Lossow's national uprising unless we wanted to commit high treason against the national cause and national honor of our people, I would like to mention what might have happened had we decided to take a neutral position.

In the persons of Kahr, Lossow, and Seisser the legal means of authority of the State of Bavaria had been made available to the national uprising. With them, all Bavaria rose. According to Rossbach, the national bands in the North were to march on Berlin. There were to be agreements between Lossow and other divisions. Were we then supposed to become betrayers of that which for years we had been striving for with all our work and longing? Even if we had wanted to do so, we would have been forced, on the following day, to either go along or be disarmed. For us, it was a matter-of-course that, under the circumstances just described, the national uprising would be a success. We did not feel apprehensive about the legal or illegal method since we considered Lossow, our superior, to be our leader.

During the afternoon, the necessary preparations for the alert of the War College were made. At 8:15 the two groups of officers gathered here in this room. While the two groups of junior grade lieutenants met in a lecture hall, at the same time the cadets from the other side of the building took their places in the barrack square. I first informed the officers, then the junior grade officers, and finally the cadets about the situation. Everything went smoothly, as expected. They welcomed the planned national uprising with cheers. I instructed Lieutenant König to inquire within the 7th Division as to whether they stood behind the movement. The answer was affirmative. At about 9:00 in the evening, Captain Leuze told me that he had received a telephone call from the 7th Division informing him that the 7th Division was the chief supporter of the movement. If, at this moment, we had been told that the 7th Division was against the division we would, of course, not have reversed our position.

Simultaneously, some comrades—among them Lieutenant Block and Schrank—had assumed the task of informing Tieschowitz and the resident officers. The resident officers were for the uprising, heart and soul. Some of them offered their services right away; everything went as expected. Tieschowitz explained to Lieutenant Block that he had sworn an oath to the Berlin Government and, therefore, could do nothing. He dissolved the School and dismissed the cadets. Now we could do what we wanted. Tieschowitz also promised not to undertake anything against the movement.

The following took place in the Pioneer School: The commander of the School had the following message put on the blackboard: On orders from Tieschowitz, the Pioneer School is dissolved and the students are dismissed. Captain Löwer wrote under this order: I assume the command of the War College—of course for the national uprising. I quickly formed three companies of the School. Another company, the so-called "resident company," was added, which Lieutenant Hubrich was going to alert. At 8:45, Rossbach, with a platoon of his men, came and took over the guards and manned the telephones. The School, singing national songs, left for the Bürgerbräukeller under the black-white-red swastika flags and with swastika armbands.

They were greeted in the city with jubilation. It made a deep impression on me when I saw that the shouts of "Heil," rang loudest from the attics of the poorest apartments on the 4th floors. In the Marienplatz, the School saluted General von Lossow with a cheer. There, Herr Hitler also talked to us and explained the situation. Together with the crowds of people, we cheered Hitler and Ludendorff with shouts of "Heil." Then, a car full of officers passed us. Rossbach told me that Lossow was in the car. Rossbach wanted to report the School, but the car drove past too fast.

I am asking this now: When General von Lossow saw that a unit of his troops had marched to the Bürgerbräukeller, why didn't he think it necessary to order us to return to the War College? Why, at this moment, did General von Lossow not pay any attention to his troops and not order them to turn around? If, at this moment, we had received orders from the Landeskommandant, our highest superior here, to turn back, it would have been a matter-of-course for us to do so because it would have seemed insane to us to fight against the 7th Division and the Polizei—in fact, against the legal authority of the State and of the Reich.

In the Bürgerbräukeller, Rossbach and some escorting officers reported the College to Herr Ludendorff. Rossbach had intended to report to General von Lossow. As I mentioned, however, he had already left. Ludendorff then passed along the front of the four companies and welcomed the College. Afterwards, the College entered the Bürgerbräukeller. Towards midnight, I received orders from Rossbach to return to the College and check the guards. After having taken care of this, I was to go to the Generalstaatskommissariat since the College was intended as guards for the Generalstaatskommissar. I don't know the order that was given to the school then.

Upon arrival at the War College, I asked to see General von Tieschowitz. General von Tieschowitz said that the 7th Division would not go along. I replied that I could not believe that, judging from what had happened. Other officers, too, told me that the 7th Division did not go along; but at that time I could not yet imagine a general breaking his word. I arrived at the Generalstaatskommissariat at about 12:30. There, the closed unit of the War College stood face to face with the closed unit of the Polizei. I could not discern any hostility. Rossbach asked me to report the College to Herr Kahr or Colonel von Seisser and to ask for permission to enter the Generalstaatskommissariat. In the building, I was told by a First Lieutenant, whose name I did not know, that Kahr and Seisser were not there. I then told him that the College had come as a guard for Herr Kahr and that I wanted to report. The First Lieutenant answered that he had orders to put up guards and what he would do if we were to enter; he said he would not let us in. Then I asked him whether he was under the authority of the national government. He answered: "Yes, I am just as chauvinistic as you and I am under the new national government." I replied: "Then the service of the War College is no longer required; I shall inform my commanders and Rossbach of it."

When I came out into Maximilianstrasse, the War College had already left; it had sung songs as it marched away. When I got in touch with Rossbach, he told me that the school had received orders to occupy the railroad station. The order to act as guards for the Generalstaatskommissar had become void and had been a mistake since national troops or national polizei, respectively, had already put up the guards. Shortly before the station, we received orders to march to the War College. When we arrived at the College, some resident officers tried to convince the College that the 7th Division and General Lossow did not back the movement. A number of students believed it. In the meantime, an order had arrived stating that the College was again to march back to the Bürgerbräukeller, since many of my comrades had become irresolute, I brought the School together and told them that it was an insult to Lossow's reputation if they considered him capable of a breach of promise. We had no reason and no justification to assume a breach of promise of a German general who until now had been the chief supporter of the national movement. When I asked who wanted to stay behind, a number of cadets turned away; the great majority, however, marched to the Bürgerbräukeller.

In the Bürgerbräukeller, it was impossible for us to get any clear information about the situation. Around 10:00 in the morning, I saw an officer from the General Staff, I believe it was a major or a lieutenant colonel or a captain from the Bavarian units of the Reichswehr, standing in front of the cadets in the Bürgerbräukeller. I went to him and asked him about the situation. The General Staff officer told me that he himself did not know exactly what was going on. Upon my question what General Lossow and the 7th Division were doing, whether they intended to act against us and to shoot at us, the General Staff officer replied he did not think so. When I asked further what the War College was supposed to do, this General Staff officer told me they should stay where they were. After that, I had breakfast outside the Bürgerbräukeller.

When I returned, the College had already taken its place in the street at the end of the Kampfbund. The march into the city had been decided. Together with Rossbach, I went to the head of the College. In the city, our troops were greeted enthusiastically. Everywhere, the black-white-red flag appeared. Before we left, we had been ordered not to load our rifles. I told Rossbach and the leaders of the Kampfbund that we would not fight against the Reichswehr and the Polizei. Rossbach assured me that he would not lead us against the Reichswehr. After the unfortunate incident at the Feldherrnhalle, the College returned to the barracks. For us, that was the end of the action.

In summing up, I must emphasize that General von Lossow bears the moral responsibility for the march of the War College to the Bürgerbräukeller. I am not a man who shifts the blame to someone else. You can ask my comrades and superiors about it. But here, I definitely have no reason to take the blame for something caused entirely by General von Lossow. I must say this quite clearly; he tricked us into going into this venture; to use an image: he set us rolling, then suddenly stopped, and we rolled over him. He did not even consider it necessary to give us an order which we would, of course, have obeyed. I must reject the accusation that the action of the College was a breach of discipline, obedience, and loyalty, the value of which is much higher than that which the Reichswehr can possibly command. This proves that the charges against us are untenable.

Furthermore, we wanted to save our people because we considered this our duty as officers and soldiers; especially, we wanted to liberate them from the disgrace and shame of Versailles. We wanted the war of liberation. That, in fact, was the superior significance that this undertaking had for all of us. After all, we saw the preparations for a war; we saw the so-called black training and we participated in this training. I remember the activity in the garrisons. I had to be in charge of and to train two large training units there. I never thought that these people were trained in order to march to Berlin or to be employed within Germany; but, I did think that these men would be sent to the Ruhrgebiet against the external enemy. We, the men from the War College, also knew about the so-called preparations for mobilization, about the so-called fall maneuver 1923. It all came together; the result was our realization that something was in the offing which did not only concern internal politics, but which was directed against an external enemy. These are the terms in which we interpreted the action of November 8.

If today we are rebuked and the object of vicious accusations, then I say frankly that we, hundreds of officers and junior grade lieutenants, are proud to have wanted the national uprising and that we will rid ourselves of the filth of the accusations. I maintain that we are clean. I can see the day come which will justify our deeds. I also feel the need to tell you that the leaders of November 9, who put themselves at the head of the marchers, who defied death, have become saints to us. I have learned that many of my comrades bought pictures of Hitler and Ludendorff on their departure. I don't consider this a superficial act; rather, I believe that they carried the pictures of Hitler and Ludendorff in their hearts over into the Reichswehr.

It is not clear to me how one can determine the action of the War College to be high treason. Nor is it clear to me why I was held in prison for three months. If I am allowed to sit here in the prisoner's dock in the revered company of the best men of our people, I consider that an honor. I can only be grateful for the privilege to sit in this circle.

I must now discuss the indictment. It states here: "The Kampfbund tried for some time to exert its influence upon the members of the Infantry School." I think I have already refuted that. All we wanted was to be informed about what happened in Bavaria; this explains why we approached the Kampfbund, Rossbach, et cetera.

It has furthermore been said that Ludendorff had talked about the white-blue menace. That, too, I have sufficiently refuted. I request that witnesses be heard on this point.

I am supposed to have said the following: "At this moment, the Völkische government for Germany is proclaimed. At the same time, the Völkische revolution is going to break out in all of Germany. Völkische bands are already marching to Berlin from all directions!"

Wagner reads from page 14 of the Indictment.

I did not use, "already." I did not say, "Tomorrow, the march will begin from Munich."

As to the special accusation, I must call it completely untenable. There is no basis at all for it. I had no knowledge of the planned venture. I did not intend "to carry out the revolutionary act in conjunction with the other defendants." I did not know any of the other defendants, except for Ludendorff whom I knew fleetingly.

"The alert of the Infantry School (took place) behind the back of the superiors." The Infantry School was alerted, lined up in the square and marched off, under the eyes of its superiors. A great number of the resident officers offered their services immediately and as a matter-of-course.

290

Judge Neithardt announces the following resolution of the Court:

"Supplement to the resolution: Ministerialrat Dr. Denk, Prussian plenipotentiary, is permitted to be present."

JUDGE NEITHARDT: You said earlier that Rossbach had also mentioned to you the name of Frick when giving you the names of the new government?

HERR WAGNER: Perhaps I am mistaken. The name, Pöhner, was definitely mentioned. It is possible that the name, Frick, was not mentioned.

JUDGE NEITHARDT: Do you or don't you know?

HERR WAGNER: I don't remember exactly!

JUDGE NEITHARDT: What were your ideas about the formation of this new government?

HERR WAGNER: I never thought about it.

JUDGE NEITHARDT: But you are, after all, an intelligent person; you must have reflected about how this was to be accomplished!

HERR WAGNER: I did not think about it.

JUDGE NEITHARDT: You talked about an order which Lossow had given by passing over the commander of the Infantry School. That is not correct. We have a report from Tieschowitz stating that this order from Lossow had also gone to the Infantry School and had been handed down by the Commander of the Infantry School to the two course instructors for notification of the cadets. Hence, the order did go through Tieschowitz.

HERR WAGNER: Lieutenant Colonel Leupold came to us at the officers' mess and told us, literally: "Lossow has instructed me to read the following to you." If necessary, I can swear to this under oath at any time.

JUDGE NEITHARDT: Tieschowitz will confirm it as a witness.

Upon my question, you told me that you had not thought about whether the formation of a new government might constitute a violation of the constitution. Didn't you discuss this either?

HERR WAGNER: This was never discussed.

JUDGE NEITHARDT: You intended to make yourself available to the national movement?

HERR WAGNER: I did not say so; I considered it a matter-of-course.

JUDGE NEITHARDT: That's the way I interpreted it. You considered Lossow and Kahr as advocates?

HERR WAGNER: Yes.

JUDGE NEITHARDT: Was it your opinion that the formation of the Infantry School into Storm Troops was based on an indirect order by Lossow? Why did you think so?

HERR WAGNER: That was my definite opinion. I thought that until then Lossow was the chief supporter of the entire movement in Bavaria. We only looked at Lossow. All of us were firmly convinced that Lossow had sent us this order by circumventing Tieschowitz. Therefore, it was absolutely clear to us that Lossow would have to turn directly to us. Furthermore, Lossow knew that Tieschowitz opposed the Völkische uprising; he had expressed that in the preceding weeks.

JUDGE NEITHARDT: You told Lieutenant Wegmann that the method was legal because Kahr and Lossow had dictatorial power?

HERR WAGNER: To me, that was absolutely a foregone conclusion.

JUDGE NEITHARDT: You repeated that today. You are supposed to have stressed to Wegmann that all orders came from Lossow and that Lossow had also ordered the formation of the Infantry and Pioneer School into Storm Troops. Did you say that?

HERR WAGNER: Yes.

JUDGE NEITHARDT: That is not quite correct; there is no order. It is unusual for an order to be passed on through Rossbach. It should have gone through channels.

HERR WAGNER: Lossow tried every possible means to exert influence on the Reichswehr—

JUDGE NEITHARDT: At least that is your opinion. Whether it is correct is a different matter. You mentioned that a planned overthrow was not discussed.

HERR WAGNER: No!

JUDGE NEITHARDT: When marching into the city, you are supposed to have talked about emptying the rifles.

HERR WAGNER: We marched with empty rifles. I told Rossbach and someone else that the War College would never march with loaded rifles and would never participate in a battle against the Reichswehr and the Polizei.

JUDGE NEITHARDT: Did you at that time report to the War College to Ludendorff?

HERR WAGNER: No!

JUDGE NEITHARDT: Rossbach, and a resident officer?

HERR WAGNER: Yes!

JUDGE NEITHARDT: What position did the resident officers take in this entire matter? The resident officers saw how you lined up in the square and I read that many officers were in agreement with the movement, except for a small number. What was it like?

HERR WAGNER: Nobody in the War College took a position against the movement.

JUDGE NEITHARDT: But they did! Uhde is supposed to have opposed the movement.

HERR WAGNER: I am not aware of it. When the War College had taken its place in the square, the resident officers who lived in the barracks came immediately and offered their services, although they had been told expressly that they were not needed until the following day. May I state emphatically that we simply considered it natural that an officer would not oppose this national movement nor take a half-hearted, lax, neutral position. We never assumed anything; but we believed that things would move along smoothly.

JUDGE NEITHARDT: What was the conclusion you drew from

the behavior of the resident officers? How did it impress you?

HERR WAGNER: My conclusion was that one cannot defend what one has defended for amost five years.

JUDGE NEITHARDT: You or Lieutenant Block informed General Tieschowitz of your position. What was the content of this discussion?

HERR WAGNER: In the afternoon, when we sat together and talked about the alert, I asked Block to inform Tieschowitz, but not until 8:30. These were also my orders. Block was also to inform Captain Uhde. It was entirely up to him how, in which way he wanted to inform them, and he readily accepted the assignment. Other officers were also requested to inform the remaining resident officers. As far as I know, that was what happened.

JUDGE NEITHARDT: You say that you did not think about this change of the constitution, but rather, that all of you were overjoyed about the fact that things had finally come to this point, that you could take up your position for a national cause.

HERR WAGNER: May I even say that our misgivings were so insignificant that we did not think about it at all. We considered the matter legal since our superior, Lossow, was the chief supporter of the entire movement.

JUDGE NEITHARDT: Did you discuss this question at all with your comrades?

HERR WAGNER: No, that was absolutely not a matter of concern to us.

JUDGE NEITHARDT: Later, the doubts came. You learned that the 7th Division was not behind the affair. Why did you return once more to the Bürgerbräukeller?

HERR WAGNER: I explained that in detail awhile ago. At that time, as an officer, I could not imagine a German officer breaking his promise to Ludendorff. That to me is so atrocious and, if I had believed it, it would have appeared to me as an insult to Lossow. I just could not think in such terms. I had never experienced it.

Judge Neithardt submits the order from Lossow of October 23, 1923, concerning the reintroduction of the black-white-red cockade; he notes from the date of the order that the time mentioned by Herr Wagner is incorrect.

HERR HEMMETER: I request permission to ask those questions pertaining to matters discussed here which are of public relevance when the public is present. At this point, I shall limit my questions to those for which a closed session is appropriate. My questions are as follows: Wagner stated that the resident officers and the commanders of the School repeatedly expressed their wish to have the young officers of the Infantry School receive instruction about politics by attending meetings. Do you know whether these requests were passed on to the cadets in the form of military orders?

HERR WAGNER: I know that in the preceding course, General von Lossow, who at that time was the commander of the War College, had ordered the cadets to attend political meetings, Hitler meetings. I knew that because my comrades told me about it. I don't know how this was done. When Lieutenant Colonel Leupold renewed the request to attend Hitler meetings, he did so in the following way. We were having lunch here in the hall when Leupold came and told us that tonight—it was at the time when these 14 meetings were prohibited—Hitler would speak somewhere. He would consider it a matter-of-course that those officers who had to be informed politically would go there in order to be educated.

HERR HEMMETER: Judging from my former experience with the military, I personally would consider that an order. I did not know any other direction.

It was said that some resident officers had gone to bed early in the night from November 8 to November 9 so that they did not have to notice what was going on; they are supposed to have slept soundly so that they did not become aware of the departure of the Infantry School. Would you please tell me whether you can name one of these resident officers? Later, witnesses will be heard on this point.

HERR WAGNER: Yes. The man in question was the head of the first course, Lieutenant Colonel von Kretzschmar. He said that he heard that something special was going on; he thought, however, that it was a crazy party of the junior grade lieutenants or one of their drinking bouts. Hence, he did not feel that he had to check what it was.

HERR HEMMETER: Do you also know of a case in which one of the resident officers said he had had to put up curtains in his apartment in the afternoon; this had tired him so much that he had to lie down? I don't ask this question out of personal animosity; but, it is necessary for the defense to state that the small number of resident officers who could not decide to express their sympathy for the undertaking immediately—

JUDGE NEITHARDT: I consider these details irrelevant. We have a general idea of the fact that some resident officers sympathized with the movement, and that they did not hold back the Infantry cadets. That ought to be sufficient.

HERR HEMMETER: Do you know that the members of those units from which the individual cadets had been detached were sending letters to the cadets telling them that all of Germany, including the commanders, were waiting for the national movement to begin in Bavaria?

HERR WAGNER: Yes, I did. I can even say that all of us, without exception—we all, at least two to three officers or junior grade lieutenants, had gathered here from all arms of the German Reichswehr—agreed with Lossow's action in the Reichswehr. We found that everywhere, in all the units—I never heard the opposite—Lossow's action was welcomed enthusiastically and that they were only waiting for the moment of national uprising. I may add that on November 11, that is, three days after the collapse of the affair, I accidentally met here, in the city, delegations of troops who had come from Thuringia as observers. They told me: "What kind of nonsense is going on here? We are looking forward to your arrival, and now you are shooting each other?" An officer assured me: "We are still willing to go along, even today, if the operation is started once again." That approximately was the position of the North German Reichswehr.

HERR HEMMETER: When the infantry cadets and the resident officers discussed matters among themselves, did they mention that the chief of the 5th Reichswehr Division, General Müller, had the same national views as Lossow?

HERR WAGNER: Yes. We had learned that General Müller, First Lieutenant Müller, was with us; he was an eager and lively participant in the matter. We were never in doubt that the 4th Division would join the movement.

HERR HEMMETER: Is it true that the Infantry School was deeply impressed when, on Memorial Day, the flags of the old Army were carried by inactive soldiers and members of the Kampfverbände, and when the parade went past His Majesty the King and Crown Prince Ruprecht? Did the cadets talk about it?

HERR WAGNER: Yes. I emphasize the fact because we considered the parade as the last great show of the army before the action. All of us talked about it.

HERR HEMMETER: Were you aware of the fact that the fight against the external enemy was, above all, the goal of the movement which received its impetus in Munich on November 8 and 9? Did you know that the troops were expected to be able to turn left near Bitterfeld?

HERR WAGNER: Yes. I was not only aware of it, but it was our most sincere wish and, actually, our motivation.

Judge Neithardt asks Herr Wagner whether, in view of the fact that he had intended to ask for Göring's confirmation, the statements he made in the hearing of November 17, regarding Rossbach's information, were correct in their wording, except for one sentence which referred to the departure in company formation at 8:45 p.m. In a written explanation to the Court, Rossbach had written that this statement was incorrect.

HERR WAGNER: Yes.

HERR EHARD: I would like to make a brief remark here on behalf of the prosecution, and I think I am in agreement with Your Honor and the defense attorney of Herr Wagner. I would like to summarize briefly this observation as follows: Wagner is still an active officer. Just like the other Reichswehr officers, you have signed an oath to the constitution?

HERR WAGNER: Yes.

HERR EHARD: What actually is your attitude towards this oath?

HERR WAGNER: Naturally I kept in mind, until the last moment, my loyalty to this oath, and I have not broken the oath. As I have repeatedly stressed, the operation became legal as soon as Lossow became the chief supporter of this movement, and we had no scruples about the legal or illegal proceedings. To us, without a doubt, the operation would run its legal course at that moment when an active general who had signed the oath became its leader.

JUDGE NEITHARDT: You said before, in your opinion, that the constitution no longer existed, while the Prosecutor wanted to know (this) from you and told you that you had signed this oath.

HERR WAGNER: That is what I said; but, for that reason, the constitution did not have to be changed. Lossow can again acknowledge the same constitution. At least he does not have to violate its form, i.e. the republic. And Lossow did not intend to do that.

HERR EHARD: I would like to explain why I am asking this question in the secret session and why I do not intend to ask it in the public session. I must admit it makes a very poor impression on me if here an active officer of the Reichswehr, a very young active officer of the Reichswehr—this is not meant as a stab at you, Herr Wagner, but merely as a statement of fact—who has the audacity to pass judgment on the Reichswehr as a general instrument, as a constitutional instrument of a constitutional government, as a constitutional instrument composed of men who also know what duty, conscience, and national feeling are. After all, such judgments go far beyond those that are required for his defense. What must the entire nation, what must foreign nations think if a young officer permits himself here to make a general judgment about the Reichswehr for which he cannot possibly have a basis?

In this connection, I must especially direct your attention to the statement made by General Ludendorff: I also want to do this in closed session. I must stress especially—speaking for the prosecution—that General Ludendorff—I have mentioned here before, and I am objective enough to admit it—has more reason to be annoyed personally with the Reichswehr than Lieutenant Wagner; but, General von Ludendorff knew where to draw the line as far as the national interest is concerned. I must state here that he has not said a word which could damage (the nation) either internally or externally. I would like to make a special point of it; therefore, I also request, on behalf of the prosecution and in our common interest, to omit, at least in the public session, this sort of generalizing and incorrect criticism of the Reichswehr. Furthermore, in my opinion, in its general nature, it is not at all required for the defense. I especially object to the fact that Herr Wagner, as an officer, did not know where to draw the line, when to keep silent at the time when the public was not excluded.

JUDGE NEITHARDT: Was that a question or a reprimand?

HERR EHARD: I did not intend a reprimand. I know that the responsibility for the orderly conduct of the Court proceedings rests with you alone, Your Honor. I only thought I was justified to make this remark because you, yourself, have reacted to the statements by Herr Wagner in the same way as I have. I also know that it is usual to discuss such matters at length; but, I believe it is often good to say those things which have to be said with a few additional words. That is the only reason for my remark. I did not want the Court to take a certain position. I only wanted to underline that the prosecution shares the position which the Court has taken by excluding the public.

JUDGE NEITHARDT: I think that the remark of the Prosecutor is quite appropriate since there is a danger when Herr Wagner is further questioned that he might again express such general criticism which would be best left unsaid. I must, of course, let every defendant decide how far he should go in his defense. But, I must ask for a certain discretion.

HERR WAGNER: I believe the difference in age between me and the Second Prosecutor is not as great as it appears to be. It is not clear to me how the Prosecutor, as a non-active officer, thinks he can form a judgment on the Reichswehr. I regret to have to say that I have no answer for Herr Ehard.

HERR HEMMETER: I think that the statements of Herr Ehard are the result of his discussion with the representatives of the Reichswehr during the intermission. If you had not had cause, Herr Prosecutor, to take up the shield and to hold it over the Reichswehr, the Judge would have done so.

HERR EHARD: But it happened!

HERR HEMMETER: Not in this manner, because in the opinion of the Judge, it would not have been necessary; otherwise, he would have done it. I think Herr Ehard has put the situation in a different light when he spoke about a general criticism of the Reichswehr as inadmissable and unjustified.

HERR EHARD: Not necessary!

HERR HEMMETER: It must be left to the judgment of the defense attorney and Herr Wagner what is necessary for his defense, and it is the responsibility of the Judge to prevent such excesses. The Judge has noted that the statements by the Prosecutor were pleas or remarks which were not generally to be expected. I do not remember whether my client has permitted himself any form of criticism to which he was not entitled as a "young" officer of the Reichswehr. We all intend, if possible, to avoid in this trial anything that might be harmful; also, to avoid fictional ideas. I consider the Reichswehr to be a fictional idea since, if they have national feelings, its members are constantly in a conflict of conscience. The Prosecutor said that those gentlemen to whom the oath was sworn thought in the same national terms as we do. I refuse to accept that. If that were the case, we would not sit here. This is a point you must not touch. Its effect would be bitterness, and you would not achieve what you want to achieve.

It has been said that such a young active officer does not have the knowledge to make a judgment. Who, like I, has been a member of the Reichswehr until 1921, has acquainted himself with its origins, has observed its development? This person can say that only those who have grown up in it can make a judgment. We cannot deny this; those are facts. We shall attest to this without difficulty when the witnesses are heard. The fact that this was brought up is not Wagner's fault, nor that of the Court; but, it is entirely the fault of the prosecution who thought they had to bring Wagner into this trial. Now, they must bear the burden that that part of the Reichswehr who wants Wagner to be, so to speak, the sacrificial lamb, is told first of all: "You did the same thing;" and, secondly: "At that time, when you wanted to sacrifice the person of Wagner alone, you digressed from the principle of absolute justice."

In the course of the trial, we shall point out repeatedly that especially in the matter, "Infantry School and Wagner," things occurred on the part of the Infantry School which completely disregarded a just procedure and which cannot be reconciled with the general feeling of justice. The Judge was good enough to explain that it was not necessary to discuss further the fact that most of the resident officers wanted to go along. Whatever Wagner said is clear. Some gentlemen cleverly chose the better part and went to bed. If they intended to go along, they did go along, or at least, they did not oppose. If men in my battery had tried in any way to do something without me or against my will, I can state that an order—as I would have issued it—was never ordered. I can state that nothing was done on the part of the commanders of the Infantry School. On the contrary, the gentlemen showed great sympathy. It must rouse one's indignation, and one must say that it smells of foul play if one officer is put into prison for something that was also wanted and was to be executed knowingly and jointly by approximately 250 men who are not brought to trial. You cannot resent such feelings. It is my duty to express them here.

Later, in the presence of the public, I shall talk with as much moderation as possible about the fictional idea that the Reichswehr represents for me. I could not overlook the fact that I was not allowed to say: From the commander down to the youngest officer, an injustice has been committed when, without any proof at all, only one single man was picked out.

JUDGE NEITHARDT: I am just reminded of a small incident. You said that, in general, the resident officers had agreed with the national movement, or had not shown any opposition, but had let the Infantry cadets march out. There is the description of an incident in the documents according to which you are supposed to have said: "If you oppose the movement, I must arrest you."

HERR HEMMETER: That was in the Pioneer School. There, the situation for Herr Wagner was more favorable because the commander allowed the officers to do what they wanted to do. There, a resident officer of the Pioneer School was told that he would be arrested. I shall find the name of this officer in my papers. The commander's reply to that was: "That I would like to see."

HERR WAGNER: I am not aware of this incident.

HERR GÖTZ: I was not surprised by the attitude of the Prosecutor. I have, after all, noticed for some time how embarrassing this discussion must be for the representatives of the Reichswehr who are present here. May I say beforehand that I have the highest regard for the two gentlemen, whom I personally have known very well for a number of years. I do not at all consider it expedient, however, if one of the representatives—perhaps out of a sense of duty—expresses the rude surprises he receives with gestures, et cetera. Such manners must necessarily induce the Prosecutor to think it is his duty to intercede on their behalf.

I have listened attentively to the questioning of Wagner. From now on, I shall pay special attention to the discussion of military matters because I believe I have some expertise in this area. I must say I was surprised when I heard that the Reichswehr was supposed to have been attacked in a general and rude way. Who here has noticed such rude attacks on the Reichswehr? The representatives of the Reichswehr should be especially grateful that a finger is finally put in the wound. These are cancerous growths. Conditions have been disclosed which seemed impossible to me as an old officer. Just imagine the case of Lossow. One of the men says something, and I don't like it, and General Rüdt says: "I don't like what you are saying." Those are sores that must be cut out. I cannot see why—I am using the expression of the Prosecutor, 'this young officer'—the concept of the young officer is slightly tinged in times of peace. Therefore, I want to use this expression only to follow the Prosecutor. In reality, the young officer of former times is the one who does not care, who knows nothing, who drinks too much, of whom one doesn't take anything amiss. (I do not see) why this young officer cannot say here what has occupied his thoughts, no matter what his direction. It may very well be that he has received a very pitiful impression, just as I have. But we notice, after all, in the attitude Wagner had, this subjective element: this subjective element is of primary importance for the trial.

Whether or not this subjective position of Wagner was justified cannot be decided here. We are not the forum for it. Perhaps the Reichswehrministerium, if it was not too partial, is the forum for it. We do not have to make that decision; rather, we have to decide whether the dirt Wagner thinks he has observed may, perhaps, have generated in his heart sentiments which led him to the statements he made here. If the Prosecutor thinks he has to object to such statements in the interest of the State, I think such views must be left aside in favor of the principal right of the defendant which is to let us know and to give us an insight into his soul: Why did I act that way, and why did I have to act in the way I acted?

JUDGE NEITHARDT: I do not consider a continuation of this discussion necessary. Everybody in the courtroom is embarrassed by the debate of these conditions. It is painful to everyone, especially to the national-minded people. These things must be discussed to a certain extent; I am only requesting the defendants to exercise discretion before the public.

HERR RODER: I would like to mention one fact. In my opinion, the crux of the entire discussion is the following: Has Wagner committed something here which is not in order? Is he to be censured for it? In other words, is it a question of disorderly conduct? I believe it is the responsibility of Your Honor alone to keep order in the courtroom. Only you can or cannot reprimand any of the gentlemen. Until now, I and, perhaps, my colleagues, too, thought Your Honor had performed your duties above all the parties, in a high-minded and absolutely objectionable fashion. Now, there seems to be forces at work that presume to take over responsibility for keeping order in the courtroom. I myself did not see it, but Herr Hitler noticed that a representative of the Reichswehr, namely the second gentleman there from the left, tries to influence the Prosecutor, by gesturing and waving, to take the responsibility for order in the courtroom. I think if the Court is obliging enough to let the gentlemen from the Reichswehr be present, then these gentlemen ought to behave like any other listener; they must remain listeners and must not interfere with the conduct of the trial. If they persist, the Court has no other choice but to request the gentlemen to leave.

HERR STENGLEIN: I did not notice anything of the kind.

HERR SCHRAMM: I found it rather offensive to see the representative of the Reichswehrministerium second the remarks of the Prosecutor in a truly obvious and obtrusive way. I was very indignant that a man in his position, as the representative of this office, would display such arrogance in this serious trial. I would also like to say that our Bavarian Reichswehr is represented by His Excellency Lossow. The wrongs which burden Lossow affect our Reichswehr. Until now, I have not heard one word from the

Prosecutor as to whether he condemns the fact that Lossow did not obey an order by his supreme commander; that he, to say it in plain German, "mutinied"; that when he was reminded of his word of honor, he said: "You can call me a perjuring peasant." As long as our representative of the Reichswehr has not made the sacrifice of laying his uniform at the feet of the King, our Bavarian Reichswehr will also carry the blame for the mistakes made by this gentleman.

JUDGE NEITHARDT: We can no longer continue in this manner. Such general criticism must be withheld. We have been brought into an embarrassing situation. This kind of judgment and criticism calls, of course, for an answer. Persons who are present at this trial as guests are being embarrassed. They are brought into a position where they, too, will have to be heard, and that is not possible within the framework of this investigation. I therefore request you to restrain yourselves in the future.

HERR HEMMETER: I only want to say the following concerning the youth of Herr Wagner. It seems to have eluded the Prosecutor—and it was not mentioned when his personal data were recorded—that during the War he was at the front; that he was repeatedly wounded, and that he earned all the medals that can be earned in combat. I would like to underscore this because the way in which the concept of youth was used here by the Prosecutor might have been misleading. He is not a youngster who talks aggressively; rather, he is a serious, mature man who served on the front for years; Your Honor noted this at the beginning of this trial when you read from the certificate of good conduct issued by the appointed authorities. This man cannot be blamed for his youth.

HERR EHARD: May I make only one remark? Of course I did not intend to call Herr Wagner a youngster. But it cannot be an insult if I say that, within the Reichswehr, Lieutenant Wagner is a young officer. There is nothing insulting here.

In order to keep matters straight, I want only to remark briefly on the statements by Herr Götz. I think I have expressed myself clearly enough about the fact that I do not at all intend to limit the defense of Herr Wagner in any way. I only mentioned—and in that I followed, to be sure, the position Your Honor has taken as to the man who is responsible for an orderly conduct of the Court proceedings and with which Herr Hemmeter fully agreed and which he underlined—I only wanted to suggest whether it might not be useful to put aside certain matters and not to express such criticism in the public session. That is all I said. If I understand Herr Götz correctly, he agrees with me.

HERR HITLER: May I say something which, of course, concerns this matter, but which I do not want to say in the public session? It says in the indictment that the Infantry School was influenced by the Kampfbund, behind the backs of the officers. I myself gave a talk before the Infantry School, namely—I can no longer remember on which day—I believe it was in the Wurzerhof. Officers had invited me to come. The older gentlemen sat in the front rows; the resident officers, and the cadets were in the rear. As I do everywhere, I spoke frankly. When I had ended my speech—which took perhaps two hours—two resident officers, one was a Major or a Lieutenant Colonel and the other a Captain, came to me and expressed their appreciation on behalf of the Infantry School. This shows that one could actually not have influenced the Infantry School "behind the backs of the resident officers," since the officers themselves were present. Otherwise, the Infantry School was not influenced by us. Hence, I would like to say that this statement in the indictment is incorrect.

JUDGE NEITHARDT: One of the counselors considers it important to know what the relationship between resident officers and cadets was. Can you tell us briefly?

HERR WAGNER: It was nothing special; we were always together.

JUDGE NEITHARDT: I mean your official relationship.

HERR WAGNER: My designation was "student." There are teachers and students. The resident officers are the teachers, and the others the students.

HERR HEMMETER: One more remark. I was able to find in my papers the names of the witnesses for the question discussed earlier. They are Lieutenant Hubrich and Captain Grunemann who will attest that the discussion took place in a completely different form.

JUDGE NEITHARDT: Herr Pernet, as far as I know, you have

305

no statements to make with regard to this matter which has to be dealt with in secret session.

HERR BAUER: No.

JUDGE NEITHARDT: The public is to be readmitted.

At this time, the secret session is concluded and the hearing is again opened to the public.

After the resumption of the public proceedings, First Lieutenant Wagner asserts the allegations in the indictment do not pertain to him; specifically, that it is incorrect that he knew in advance of the action and that he wanted to expedite the action in collaboration with the other defendants. Prerequisite for this would be that he knew the other defendants personally. Besides Ludendorff, he knew not one of all the other defendants.

JUDGE NEITHARDT: You told us earlier that you interpreted everything Rossbach arranged as an indirect order, so to speak, from Lossow. You had gained the conviction that Kahr and Lossow, the men who possessed dictatorial authority, stood behind the affair. You believed the course they had set was legal. You were gratified that a new government would assume power and that no one spoke of an "overthrow." You did not count on a change in the constitution, but solely on the removal of unpopular persons. According to orders, you presented yourself at 8:45 p.m. and marched with the School to the Bürgerbräukeller. There, the cadets were presented to Ludendorff. Then an argument broke out over the occupation of the Executive Office Building. Then you went a second time to the Bürgerbräukeller. The parade was conducted with unloaded rifles?

HERR WAGNER: Yes, sir.

HERR HEMMETER: Were you of the opinion that Kahr's actions and preventive measures as dictator were justified if they were directed against the government? Did you also interpret Lossow's role as that of military dictator of Bavaria?

HERR WAGNER: Yes.

HERR HEMMETER: You were convinced, then, that if Kahr and Losssow went through with this prearranged plot, of which Rossbach had informed you, a legal action would have taken place?

HERR WAGNER: That's correct.

HERR HEMMETER: You were under the impression that the staff officers of the School were sympathetic to the School's march. It was intended to be a show of force for Lossow in the Bürgerbräukeller since they did nothing to stop it?

HERR WAGNER: I had the impression that the staff officers were overjoyed and keen on the idea.

HERR HEMMETER: Did you receive an official order from any superior officer to stay there, or withdraw?

HERR WAGNER: From neither an indirect nor a direct superior.

HERR HEMMETER: Didn't General von Tieschowitz state that he was bound by oath to the government in Berlin and was unable to do anything in the matter?

HERR WAGNER: I knew that.

HERR HEMMETER: Didn't he say, as a Bavarian, you obviously had to collaborate?

HERR WAGNER: I was aware he said it.

HERR HEMMETER: You have never advocated an act of aggression against the Reichswehr or Landespolizei, but rather stated that the cadets would never be drawn into a confrontation with the Reichswehr or Landespolizei?

Wagner answers affirmatively.

Wagner replies negatively to the defense attorney's question of whether the accused knew of any threat or any undisciplined conduct toward General von Tieschowitz. Likewise, he states that he cannot safely say whether individual officers of the Infantry School were held against their will in individual rooms.

HERR LUETGEBRUNE: If General Lossow had given the order to withdraw, this order would have been obeyed. Is that correct?

HERR WAGNER: Yes, of course we would have turned back.

HERR LUETGEBRUNE: Then if I understand you correctly,

General Lossow's conduct was the decisive factor for the behavior of the Infantry School?

HERR WAGNER: Certainly; I have emphasized that clearly.

Now Herr Heinrich Bauer, First Lieutenant Pernet's counsel, directs a series of questions at Lieutenant Wagner. The first question refers to whether Pernet made attempts to promote better relations between the Kampfbund and the Infantry School. Wagner answers that he is convinced that Pernet had no idea what the score was.

HERR BAUER: Pernet is also accused of taking part in Infantry School meetings. Was there something unusual about his participation?

HERR WAGNER: I only saw Pernet twice at meetings, including the Rossbach celebration at the Löwenbräukeller. Pernet was not politically active, nor did he attempt to exert influence on the Infantry School.

HERR BAUER: Pernet is also accused of arranging the Infantry School's visit to General Ludendorff.

HERR WAGNER: I did not know who supplied the impetus here. I once heard it was supposed to have been a staff officer.

HERR BAUER: Now, concerning the transmission of the alert order to the Infantry School, Lieutenant Wagner has stated that on the morning of November 8 Pernet came alone in order to ask him to go to Schellingstrasse. Did Pernet go with you to Schellingstrasse?

HERR WAGNER: Yes; we went there by streetcar. On the way, I again asked Pernet why I was supposed to go to Schellingstrasse and what was going on. Pernet replied that he was sorry, but he didn't know. I am convinced to this day that Pernet didn't know why he was ordered there.

HERR BAUER: Did Pernet go with you into the room on Schellingstrasse, or did he take his leave beforehand?

HERR WAGNER: When we stepped into the corridor, we saw a number of uniforms of the old Army—Reichswehr uniforms—and people in street clothes, too. Pernet disappeared in the crowd. Rossbach grabbed me by the arm and pulled me into the room. From that moment on, I didn't see Pernet again.

In response to Herr Ehard's question, Wagner announces that a section of the Infantry School disengaged from the parade because several staff officers had disseminated the rumor that General Lossow supported only the 7th Division, not the entire movement.

HERR EHARD: You loaded your weapons when the Landespolizei refused to let you through. Is that correct?

HERR WAGNER: I don't know if that's correct. I came later.

Whereupon, a luncheon recess is taken.

—AFTERNOON SESSION—

As the afternoon session begins, Herr Kohl hands over a written summary of the oral request for evidence he made in the morning session, regarding military use of weapons during riots and preceding warnings. He moves to call Major Freiherr Theodor von Tautphoeus as an expert witness in this matter. It would be, he states, desirable to have criminal proceedings instituted pursuant to this case as hastily as they have been instituted against the accused. Herr Kohl also moves to call the entire Knilling Cabinet, including erstwhile Minister of Agriculture Wutzlhofer, as witnesses to prove that they had been officially informed before November 8 that a Reich dictatorship, with Dr. von Kahr at its head, was to be established by fair or foul means; that the professional politicians and personalities were to vanish; and that the time was ripe to remove parliamentarism. Herr Kohl refers to a speech, particularly its last sentence, about Parliamentarians and politicians, given by Dr. von Kahr on November 8, 1923, in the Bürgerbräukeller. It came as no surprise to the cabinet ministers in attendance that they were momentarily arrested because they had to figure that they, if Herr Kahr's general dictatorship came into being, would be pushed aside momentarily.

Herr Kohl also moves to summon Privy Councillor Dr. Held. Dr. Held can verify that in Kahr's portrayal of the events that led to his resignation as Minister President, Kahr made striking deviations from the truth; that he is guilty of an incredibly subjective presentation of the facts; that he spoke of "unbelievable pressure" with reference to an undisclosed witness although such a witness is out of the question; that Kahr further refused, on grounds of physical impossibility, to make a statement to the Finance Committee although he knew Held could do this as his plenipotentiary. This request for evidence is extremely important for the execution of these proceedings because it constitutes a complement to the events in the Bürgerbräukeller; for, while Kahr declared during the Cabinet crisis that tentative force and pressure was exerted upon him, Privy

Councillor Dr. Held states this was out of the question. Even Kahr's refusal to make a statement to the Finance Committee itself has a bearing on the events in the Bürgerbräukeller.

In conclusion, Herr Kohl petitions to hear Forstrat Escherich testify that Herr Kahr opposed publicly, in the strongest terms and in the holiest fervor, the dissolution of the Home Guard; however, when the law was passed to disarm the Home Guard, he endorsed it with the same holy fervor. Herr Kohl also terms the stenographic reports from the Landtag of 1920 and 1921 as evidence of the content of Kahr's speeches.

The Presiding Judge then reads an amicus curiae from First Lieutenant Bruno Ritter von Hausenschild; he wishes to state that the allegation—i.e. the possibility that Captain Schrauth was felled by shots from the armored car—is untrue since not one shot was fired from the armored car on November 9.

Herr Kohl then cites the bulletin of the Christian Bavarian News Service which says that it is incorrect that Catholic student organizations stood behind Kahr. Herr Kohl observes that as a matter of fact witnesses informed him that representatives of Catholic student organizations made a statement favorable to Kahr. He is extraordinarily pleased with the Christian Bavarian News Service's statement for he sees in it the Catholic students' realization that it is improper to stand behind Kahr—behind a man who instituted disloyalty as a requisite for a German statesman.

Testimony of Herr Pernet

Now First Lieutenant (Ret.) Heinz Pernet, the stepson of General Ludendorff, will give testimony. The Presiding Judge verifies that Pernet served as an aviator until March, 1916; that he joined the 18th "Hussar" Regiment as a Lieutenant in February, 1919; that he took part in the riots in Berlin, the liberation of Munich, and the conflicts in the Ruhr; that upon the creation of the Reichswehr, he joined the 15th Cavalry Regiment as a Lieutenant. On March 1, 1923, after promotion to First Lieutenant, he was discharged. He then settled in Munich with his stepfather and mother, was active in architecture, and attended the necessary courses at the Technical Institute. Since the end of 1923, he has been a registered member of the National Socialist Party without any particular function.

JUDGE NEITHARDT: On the morning of November 7, around

10:00 a.m. or so, you met Dr. von Scheubner-Richter by chance in the street. Herr Scheubner-Richter, whom you knew slightly and who knew that acquaintances of yours were cadets, said you should go to the Infantry School and ask Lieutenant Wagner to come to the High Command on Schellingstrasse on the afternoon of the 8th, between 12:00 and 1:00.

HERR PERNET: That's correct.

JUDGE NEITHARDT: He didn't tell you why?

HERR PERNET: No

JUDGE NEITHARDT: You complied with his request, yet you didn't know what it was about?

HERR PERNET: He didn't tell me anything.

JUDGE NEITHARDT: You didn't have any idea?

HERR PERNET: No.

JUDGE NEITHARDT: Did you know something was going to happen on the 8th?

HERR PERNET: I read about the assembly in the Bürgerbräu-keller in the newspaper. The Prosecutor disputes that, but it was published in the *Augsburger Abendzeitung.*

JUDGE NEITHARDT: You weren't told whom Wagner was to see?

HERR PERNET: No. I went to the house with him and spoke with him. I thought nothing of it and then went home.

JUDGE NEITHARDT: You didn't find out what was discussed with Wagner, or with whom he spoke?

HERR PERNET: No.

JUDGE NEITHARDT: You met Dr. von Scheubner-Richter on the way to the Technical Institute?

HERR PERNET: That's correct.

JUDGE NEITHARDT: You didn't tell the truth, earlier?

HERR PERNET: I retracted that. I didn't want to implicate anyone.

The Presiding Judge asks Pernet why he went to the assembly in the Bürgerbräukeller in uniform. Pernet states that no one demanded he do so. He frequently dressed in uniform and if the Generalstaatskommissar was speaking, a certain formality was to be observed.

JUDGE NEITHARDT: You had no knowledge of what was planned?

HERR PERNET: No. I was taken by surprise.

JUDGE NEITHARDT: You witnessed the events. Tell us what you saw and heard.

HERR PERNET: The hall was very full. Suddenly the doors were thrown open, a machine gun was emplaced, and Hitler entered the hall. I behaved peacefully like the others.

JUDGE NEITHARDT: Did you see how the three men were invited outside?

HERR PERNET: Yes, I did.

Herr Pernet goes on to relate how, at Dr. Scheubner-Richter's demand, he went with him, his aide, and General Ludendorff's aide to pick up the General in a car. The trip out lasted 12-15 minutes, as did the trip back. The conversation and time for the General to dress lasted about 10 minutes.

JUDGE NEITHARDT: What did your stepfather say?

HERR PERNET: He only said that he had intended something different. In the car he asked me if I knew anything about this. I said, "No."

JUDGE NEITHARDT: You also testified that your stepfather was "pretty amazed"?

HERR PERNET: That's correct; he was unprepared.

JUDGE NEITHARDT: Earlier, you wouldn't admit you had been in the car.

HERR PERNET: Because I saw that Prosecutor Dresse would not speak well of my father.

314

JUDGE NEITHARDT: You didn't want to get involved?

HERR PERNET: That's correct.

In response to the Presiding Judge's questioning, Pernet testifies that he was engaged in checking passes and in quartering the troops. He signed the receipt for the 14.6 billion marks that had been requisitioned from Parcus.

JUDGE NEITHARDT: You also distributed the money?

HERR PERNET: I received the order to.

JUDGE NEITHARDT: From whom?

HERR PERNET: From Hitler.

JUDGE NEITHARDT: You distributed the money to the individual organizations? You no longer have the lists?

HERR PERNET: The list was destroyed. The military officers didn't receive anything.

Herr Pernet answers the Judge's remark that he testified earlier that, between 7:00 and 8:00, people already knew Kahr and Lossow had changed their minds by saying that that had only been a rumor.

JUDGE NEITHARDT: In any case, you felt justified in disposing of the money?

HERR PERNET: That's correct.

JUDGE NEITHARDT: You took nothing for yourself?

HERR PERNET: No.

JUDGE NEITHARDT: What were you thinking about during the incident? Did you think these events were constitutional, or unconstitutional?

HERR PERNET: I thought that if the Generalstaatskommissar, Lossow, and Seisser made speeches before my very eyes, and General Ludendorff and Hitler were operating in conjunction with the Bavarian Government, then it was legal.

JUDGE NEITHARDT: I assume that at first you didn't think

anything at all, and only later were you conscious that it wasn't quite so simple. Is that correct?

HERR PERNET: Yes.

JUDGE NEITHARDT: Did you transmit the invitation from Wagner and the other men at the Infantry School to Excellency Ludendorff?

HERR PERNET: No. I only picked up the men at the train station because the street was dark. The expression "White-Blue Peril" was not used in the conversation.

JUDGE NEITHARDT: Were you present at the conversation?

HERR PERNET: Yes. The conversation went as the Herr General said, and also as Lieutenant Wagner described it.

In answer to the Judge's question, Pernet testifies that that night, after 11:00, Dr. von Scheubner-Richter asked him to drive to Erhardt's home and pick him up. He was to apprise Erhardt of the situation. The trip was a failure.

JUDGE NEITHARDT: Do you have anything else to say?

HERR PERNET: No.

Herr Bauer refers to First Lieutenant Rossbach's affidavit, which is in the Court record. Rossbach says he had no knowledge on the 7th of what was planned for the 8th. Also, that on the 7th he ordered that Wagner be brought to Schellingstrasse by a middle man on the 8th. Rossbach further states in the affidavit that he received the order from an eminent person, but not General Ludendorff, to alert the Infantry School on the 8th.

JUDGE NEITHARDT: We can't question Rossbach because he is at large.

HERR BAUER: Rossbach's testimony also is supported by what Hitler and Lieutenant Colonel Kriebel have said.

Prosecutor Ehard asks the defendant if he can explain why it was Lieutenant Wagner who was chosen from the Infantry School.

HERR PERNET: It could just as well have been anyone.

Lieutenant Wagner states, in answer to the Judge's question, that he can't explain why he was chosen.

Dr. Frick's testimony begins:

Testimony of Herr Frick

HERR FRICK: For as long as I have thought in political terms, it has been clear to me—and the history of my homeland, the Palatinate, bears me out—that the essence of the State is power: power at home and abroad. Without power, a State has no authority, no dignity, no respect, and no political direction. This fundamental proposition has always been the guideline of my political thoughts and deeds. Never in my life have I been led astray by Marxist, pacifist, or democratic apologetics! Thanks to the achievements of the Revolution, the essence of the new German Reich is impotence! At home, its motley governments are the exponents and playthings of an ungodly party system; abroad, they stagger from one hostile kick to another and exhaust themselves in pitiable fits of whining for enemy or alien succor; and, in feeble, therefore ridiculous, protests.

From 1907 to 1917, I served as a county assessor in Pirmasens in the same office building where now only the burnt-out walls stand as a symbol of French and Separatist despotism. The Pirmasens office, in peace-time, was considered as one of the most difficult and demanding posts in the Kingdom because of the rapid, almost American growth that the shoe industry achieved there and because of the great masses of workers who crowded the city and the county. In war-time, these difficulties multiplied. The director and the second assessor enlisted in August and September, respectively. And since I was unfit for service, I inherited the task of administering the office from 1914 to 1917. The difficulties of providing food in the first two winters of the War were enormous because of the large worker population and the weak emphasis on farming. Nevertheless, the people managed to hang on. It was the worker population who, early on, proved by manly deeds—when they got rid of the tyranny of the bloodsuckers—that they had their German hearts in the right place.

This deed should be a model for us in dealing with traitors. We will help the people of the Palatinate not with beautiful words, not with pretty newspaper articles about loyalty for loyalty's sake, not with cash outlays like the financing of the Ruhr struggle, but with manly, resolute, and liberating acts.

On August 1, 1917, I came to Police Headquarters in Munich to assume command of the official War Profiteering Department. I was simultaneously the Department's specialist. During the days of the Soviets in April, 1919, I incurred the special goodwill of the Communist authorities who had set up camp in the Police Headquarters. I had the honor of being placed on the list of hostages to be detained. At the beginning of May, Pöhner took over as Chief of Police and by the middle of May he appointed me head of the Political Section, which since the Revolution had sunk to a miserable state. I inherited the task of rebuilding this section. For months we had our hands full reconciling thousands of crimes that the Soviet Republicans and heroes of the Red Army had committed. By that time I had become acquainted with all manner of officials—Reichswehr, Polizeiwehr, Home Guard—and other organizations and their leaders with whom I later came in contact.

Thanks to the concerted efforts of the aforementioned organs, we succeeded in removing the Marxist rule in Bavaria for the first time since the Kapp days in 1920. At that time I was very close to Herr Kahr who played a prominent role. I can still remember vividly how Herr Kahr, who was constantly present at Police Headquarters, expressed himself in violent terms about the Parliament and party system and how he was determined to remedy these abuses.

On March 16, 1920, Dr. Heim sat near Dr. von Kahr in the conference room. Kahr gave in. Half an hour later, he made his way to the Landtag and disappointed his standard bearers by lowering himself to become a tool, an executive mechanism, for parliamentarianism. Never again did he have a cabinet of efficient experts. This was the result of Kahr's rising star. The whole party system found expression in a cabinet of bosses in which every minister was a leader of the ruling parties. It is well known that, in forming his government, Herr Kahr invited the Marxists, but that these gentlemen graciously declined. Herr Kahr's second capitulation was the Home Guard question. The third disappointment was his deplorable exit in September, 1921. After these experiences, it was hard to retain one's confidence in Herr Kahr.

It was impossible for Herr Pöhner to continue to head up Police Headquarters after Herr von Kahr's resignation because the assistance Herr Kahr had given him—which was more in the line of tolerance than active help—had evaporated. Since Pöhner did not want to undertake a change of convictions—that is, of replacing Kahr as the leader of Bavarian politics—he asked for his discharge. I asked for a new position as his first political advisor. I became Director of Section III at Headquarters.

Great differences arose in the handling of national questions, particularly those concerning the burgeoning Nationalist Movement, embodied by Hitler's National Socialist Party. We saw in this movement, which then was still small and would have been easy to suppress, the germ of Germany's revival. From the beginning we were convinced that this movement was suited to gaining a firm footing in the Marxist-contaminated-ranks of the workers, and leading them back into the nationalist camp. Therefore, we held our sheltering hand over the National Socialist Party and Hitler.

At the time, the exceptional circumstances dictated that Police Headquarters would censor posters, but approve gatherings. I still remember well how the censorship of posters always caused violent confrontations in the Landtag and in government. We probably eliminated the large obstacles, but for such a young movement that had to make propaganda, it was naturally inevitable that we allowed them certain liberties.

On the same day, Kahr finally took his leave as Minister President. Secretary of State Schweyer summoned us to the Landtag and, in a very ungracious speech, apprised us of his dissenting opinion on the handling of the racial problem, particularly the Jewish problem.

After this, it was clear that it was impossible to continue our work as before. I am an upright man and it was beyond my strength—those strengths I considered necessary for Germany—to keep a low profile. Therefore I asked Herr Pöhner for a new position. My relations with President Pöhner at Police Headquarters during the two and one-half years of our collaboration in very difficult situations—I mention only the Kapp period—were highly confidential. I found that President Pöhner and I shared, to a great extent, similar political views so that the relations that we had made during my official service persisted even after he had stepped down.

The year 1922 brought another split in the patriotic movement. Herr Kahr had retained the honorary chairmanship of the Home Guard and its successor, Bayern und Reich, and he still remained active in the patriotic movement. I still maintained relations with Herr Kahr. He commissioned me to outline a new

Reich constitution—a task I did not take up because I had promised myself not to become involved until conditions had changed.

My contacts with Herr Kahr became fewer as the patriotic movement was further broken up. Slowly the two positions crystallized: on the one hand, Bayern und Reich, with Sanitätsrat Dr. Pittinger and Herr Kahr; on the other side, the nationalist-activist elements embodied by the Storm Troops, Bund Oberland, and Reichsflagge. My inclination was always toward the nationalist-activist side. I always considered them the one patriotic organization that most clearly recognized that Germany's salvation, from all national and economic woes, was possible only through creation of a new army and a renewed willingness to fight, and through the bands who, realizing this, were determined not only to talk, but also to act. I never tried to hide my sympathy for the Kampfbund. I still maintain today that only a policy of activism can help us—if we can be helped at all.

Conditions grew worse and worse. When Pöhner left Police Headquarters, what I had feared would happen, happened. The close contact between Police Headquarters and the patriotic movement became looser and looser. There were certain excesses committed by the National Socialist Party which were to be expected from a movement that always wanted to cause a breakthrough of a nationalist movement through its primordial strength.

Hitler always sympathized with my objections to these excesses and agreed to eliminate them. Under Pöhner, just as we laid great stress on keeping in touch with the National Socialist Party and its leader, Hitler, we had good relations with the Home Guard in order to bridle the movement and to exercise a certain influence. Hitler's immortal service was the propaganda he brought to the masses which is now beginning to have an effect in the effort to smash the Marxist reign of terror. After Pöhner's departure, the close contact with the National Socialists became more and more tenuous. The contrast became ever sharper; the Party went its own way. On May 1, 1923, the well-known incident at Oberwiesenfeld took place. On account of its inadequate contact with the Nationalist Movement, the government didn't emerge from the affair with a boost in prestige.

On the afternoon of September 26, 1923, Herr Kahr was appointed Generalstaatskommissar by the Council of Ministers.

Two hours later I received a phone call from him and went to him. He invited me to join his staff. He said he wanted to use me in his Office of the Press.

I told him: "I consider my profitable assistance possible only if the Kampfbund supports you," for I had the feeling the appointment of a Generalstaatskommissar was directed towards crushing the Nationalist Movement. The day before, 14 Hitler gatherings had been announced; the government was apparently anxious about these gatherings and hoped to prevent them by establishing a Generalstaatskommissariat. I could not and would not dishonor my prior commitment. I would not deliver the Nationalist Movement over to extinction! I asked Herr Kahr for a parley with Herr Pöhner before a final decision was made.

At the same time, I remonstrated that the people expected a complete dictatorship and that the Generalstaatskommissariat bore no resemblance to this whatsoever. Who would rule the people? Herr Kahr, or the government and parliament? Herr Kahr didn't know how to answer that one. He only said that he had set up an economic advisory council. When I asked Herr Pöhner his opinion, he stated he didn't believe the Kampfbund would unconditionally back up Kahr.

The next morning, when I went back to Herr Kahr, in the anteroom I met representatives of the Patriotic Bands: Dr. Pittinger, Professor Bauer, Herr Kühner, and also Dr. Scheubner-Richter for the Kampfbund. I listened as Professor Bauer told Dr. Pittinger that the 14 gatherings had already been prohibited. Kühner said to me: "Then it's all over. The purpose of the representatives gathered here was to reach an unconditional agreement for the Patriotic Bands and the Kampfbund to stand behind Herr Kahr."

I had to agree with him. I then told Herr Kahr that, under the circumstances, I was unable to accept the position he had offered me. Herr Kahr expressed his regrets. I assured him of my personal loyalty, for my goal was to unite the entire Nationalist Movement behind Herr Kahr. I remained active in this sense for the next few days.

At Pöhner's, I met Lieutenant Colonel Hofmann from Ingolstadt, who wanted to know the position the Kampfbund was taking. We wanted to try to bring about this unification and we went to Schellingstrasse to speak with Hitler. It was proposed that the unification be accomplished by placing Pöhner in a leading position under Kahr, perhaps as Governor of South Bavaria.

Nothing came of this proposal, however, because Kahr had no authorization to delegate such power; that had not been provided for in the Emergency Act. Later, however, it happened that such authorization was transferred not to Kahr but to the Minister President.

A second attempt at unification took place when Erhardt visited Pöhner; there I also met Lieutenant Colonel Kriebel and Lieutenant Commander Kautter on September 29. Next, I went again to Kahr and explained that now the struggle with Berlin was certain; for, in the meantime, Kahr had inhibited the enactment of the "Defense of the Republic" law for Bavaria. I explained that he would be fighting on three fronts simultaneously—Berlin, the Marxists, the Nationalists. There was a real possibility that battle lines could be drawn with the last. Herr Kahr agreed, in principle. I informed him of the conversation with Erhardt and asked him to speak with Pöhner. He arranged the meeting for the following morning, a Sunday. I informed Pöhner and, accompanied by Kriebel, we went to Herr Kahr where we also found Seisser. The conversation ran on the way Pöhner and Kriebel have already described it. With that, attempts at unification were finished. At the end of October, by coincidence, I met Herr Kahr again at the Hoftheater. I spoke to him of the economic troubles which were getting bigger and bigger. Herr Kahr answered: "Well, my dear fellow, our economic distress will last at least another three years. Hundreds of thousands of people will starve. Herr Minoux, who paid me a visit three days ago, told me so."

Then came November 8. Herr Zentz invited officials from Police Headquarters to the assembly at the Bürgerbräukeller. Days earlier the word was out that Hitler would come to the gathering, probably resulting in an alliance between Kahr and Hitler. A meeting at Police Headquarters, in which President Mantel also participated, lasted until 6:30 in the evening. Afterwards, I went to a neighboring office of Section 6, where I ran into Regierungsrat Balss. We discussed the goals Kahr had aimed for, then Regierungsrat Werberger joined us, and the remark was made that it was time to govern differently. I myself was undecided whether or not to go to the assembly, for I had listened to enough pretty speeches and didn't anticipate any great revelation. However, I finally decided to go to the Bürgerbräukeller. I was about to go through my office to the duty room to report that I was going to the Bürgerbräukeller when I saw

322

the evening newspaper laying in my office, and I stopped to read it. Then I said to myself: now it's too late to go, and I remained in my office to work on some documents. Shortly after 9:00, my telephone rang. A voice asked, "Is Oberamtmann Frick there?" When I said, "Yes," the caller stated: "The dictatorship of Hitler and Kahr has been acclaimed with the unanimous approval of the assembly." Before I could ask who the caller was, the connection was cut off. I went into the duty room and asked the officer of the day, Oberkommissar Haberl, what he knew about this event. He told me a mob of armed National Socialists had blocked off access to the Bürgerbräukeller with machine guns and the security team had been ejected. I instructed an official to connected me at once with the head of the Criminal Division, Oberkommissar Kiefer. I say in advance that I assumed the caller was a police official, because regulations demanded that all officials must notify the head of Section I in all serious violations of security. When I reached Oberkommissar Kiefer, he told me what Oberkommissar Haberl had already said; namely, that the security team had been ejected. I asked: "How many men are there?" As far as I can recall, he said: "15 men." He declared he couldn't do anything against hundreds of men armed with machine guns. I agreed, and told him: "You can't do anything there. First off, just limit yourself to maintaining order on the street."

After this conversation, I went immediately to the officer of the day, Captain Stumpf. There is a special line from the duty room to the officer of the day. I called and said I would be right up. I met Captain Stumpf and asked him: "Do you have any news from the Bürgerbräukeller?" He replied that he already had reports here. I asked him if he had troops ready. Stumpf replied: "A 100-man squad at the old *Schwere Reiter* barracks." I told him I thought it was advisable to deploy the team immediately because we didn't know yet what was happening and because it seemed to me that one squad was too weak to intervene successfully and avoid senseless bloodshed. Captain Stumpf agreed. I gave him no authorization to do anything. We were agreed that it was impractical to send in the squad. Then—this was around 9:15—I went to the duty room immediately. There was a great commotion there and the switchboard was flooded with inquiries. There was a lot to do. I remember telephone inquiries from First Lieutenant Berchem and Ministerialrat Zettlmeier and I gave them the news that I had.

At 9:30, Commissioner Reithmeier rushed in, breathless, from the Löwenbräukeller and told me what had been announced there: The government has fallen; a new government has been proclaimed at the Bürgerbräukeller; and people are forming a parade at Stiglmaierplatz. They intended to march to the Feldherrnhalle and dedicate the new regime there. Let me say in advance that the duty room was subordinate to the head of Section 1, but I did not take command. The official was in command. I stayed there, giving instructions and disseminating information. The official on duty remained responsible. I ordered fortification of the duty room. A few able officials from Internal Affairs, such as Police Secretary Rau and several inspectors from the Political Division, were supposed to be rounded up and a telephone service set up—the telephone service is closed down at 8:00 at Headquarters. Around this time, Secretary Appel of the Security Squad came and alerted the Landespolizei. I deduced that the officer of the day had ordered the alerting of the Security Squad and the Landespolizei. Once again I went to the officer of the day, but found his room empty. So I went to the neighboring room where I met Major Imhoff. He expressed his reservations—nothing new had been announced—whether the affair would work in the North.

Then I went back to the duty room. The first people from the Bürgerbräukeller arrived around 10:00. Police Secretary Rau arrived from the assembly and filed a report on the incident. Now we received news, particularly about Kahr's, Lossow's, and Seisser's speeches. Shortly thereafter, Ministerialsrat Zetlmeier entered the duty room. He listened to Rau's report with us. Rau also said: "And you, Herr Oberamtmann Frick, are supposed to become Police President. Your name, too, Herr Ministerialsrat, was announced; you are to be arrested." Zetlmeier shook his head at the news. It was well known that cabinet ministers had been taken into custody. Ministerial Advisor Zetlmeier said: "Well, we can't do anything more; they aren't a responsible government. I don't know who to turn to." With that, he left the Police building.

I went to Major Imhoff to inform him. I met with Major Imhoff, and with General von Danner, who was bent over a desk apparently still busy with the alert. I saw that a certain mistrust existed; at least General von Danner abruptly took his leave. I shared what I knew with Major Imhoff and went into the duty room. I stayed there until 10:30 p.m. Then someone came into the duty room and asked if I would come to the executive office, that Pöhner wanted to speak to me. I went up and met Pöhner, who told me he had been named Minister President at the assembly. He asked me—in the name of Excellency Kahr, also—to take charge of the Police Presidium. I immediately objected, saying that I was ready to accept this commission not as Police President but, perhaps in my present condition, for as long as Police President Mantel was absent—it had already been revealed that Mantel had been taken into protective custody. But I immediately declared that it was necessary to drive to Excellency von Kahr's to speak with him.

As we stood in the executive office, Regierungsrat Balss came in and said, as I recall: "Herr President, I believe Herr Balss could best lead the Political Sections," and Herr Pöhner said, "Yes, Herr Balss, you take charge of the Political Section." No one else from the Political Section was there. Regierungsrat Bernreuther was under preventive arrest and Regierungsrat Obermayer came later. Then Colonel Banzer came into the foyer of the Presidium with First Lieutenant Prosch. We had just come out. Colonel Banzer said to Herr Pöhner, "Send Herr Prosch away, he was sent with me as a custodial guard from the Bürgerbräukeller." Herr Pöhner complied, at once, and said, "First Lieutenant, you may go." Colonel Banzer then went into the executive office with Major Imhoff. They struck an official tone—why, I don't know. Herr Pöhner said he had become Minister President and I was to head up the Police Presidium. Both of them, with beaming faces, congratulated us. I said not a word.

In the meantime, members of the press had entered the library. I believe they had already been summoned to the Bürgerbräukeller. I cautioned Herr Pöhner that it would be necessary to drive to Excellency von Kahr before making a statement to the press. At 11:00 we went down and were on our way to Excellency von Kahr's. When we were down in the passage, Oberregierungsrat Tenner, I believe, was coming from a play and asked me, as he was going up: "What kind of stories are you spreading, anyway? What's going on?" I replied: "Just go on up to Balss, he'll tell you." Shortly after 11:00, we were driving to Excellency von Kahr's.

As we approached, I saw a crowd of Blue and Green Police in front of the building. We went up to His Excellency. Herr Kahr made us wait a good half-hour. We imagined all kinds of reasons for his keeping us waiting. We supposed that Excellency von Kahr might still be so worked up over the incident at the Bürgerbräukeller that he had to relax a bit. At around 11:30, he cheerfully and briskly entered the room, greeted us warmly, and apologized for the long delay. He explained that he had been speaking with Minister Matt and that that was why it had taken him so long. Excellency von Kahr made several laudatory remarks about Minister Matt—about the splendid qualities he possessed. Herr Kahr, in reference to the incident at the Bürgerbräukeller, declared that Hitler's action affected him adversely, even "embittered" him—I remember this word exactly—but that he had put up with it.

Then we came to the business at hand. Excellency von Kahr said the press should be briefed as little as possible. In response to the question of whether the State authorities and party leaders were to be notified, Excellency von Kahr said, "Yes, I have already released a wireless message to the authorities." He pulled out a slip of paper from his vest pocket—apparently Herr Pöhner had forgotten it—and read aloud: "As deputy, I have the government of Bavaria firmly in hand." That was, literally, the message he wanted to have sent out. I asked if that was to be made public. He said, "Yes." In response to my question, Excellency von Kahr stated that Hitler had charge of the proclamation to the people and that he didn't want to interfere. At the conclusion, Pöhner asked Kahr when he could meet with him to discuss the formation of a cabinet. Excellency von Kahr replied, "Tomorrow at 9:30." Then, as at the beginning, he bade us a farewell with a cordial handshake.

It was past 12:00 midnight when we arrived at Police Headquarters. Here the meeting with the press, which included the editors-in-chief of the Munich and the National Press, took place. We briefed them along the same lines we had discussed with Excellency von Kahr. We discussed the utility of releasing a few passages of the speeches in the Bürgerbräukeller.

Lossow's Countermove

After we had arrived at Police Headquarters, several news reports reached us. One, for example, was from Nürnberg that the Reichswehr was on stand-by alert and had been ordered to Munich; and, that the Reichswehr in Passau had been alerted. These reports disconcerted me. On top of that, we discovered that it was impossible to contact Lossow and Seisser. These efforts were begun the moment we returned to Police Headquarters. Especially after the press conference, I repeatedly tried to reach Lossow and Seisser. The story was that Lossow was with the 19th Regiment. I called and asked if I could speak to Lossow. Someone answered, "He'll be right there." I waited on the phone and asked if he were there. In return, someone asked me, "Who's there?" Then someone said, "His Excellency will be here presently." Five minutes later, I got the same run-around. I hung on the line for 15 minutes and finally they said, "Excellency has gone." I realized that they were lying for Lossow and that he didn't want to come to the phone. I instructed all telephone operators to notify me at once if Lossow or Seisser turned up.

Various reports were coming in indicating that the *Münchener Post* had been broken into and that the presses had been destroyed. Detectives were sent there immediately to investigate. We received a report that a throng was gathering in front of Auer's house. Detectives were dispatched immediately to head off any vandalism. Another report came in that at the Bavaria Circle, Jews were being yanked from their homes. The Landespolizei were ordered out there. Hitler was notified by Pöhner to tell his men to avoid such excesses. Colonel Banzer informed me that there was a threat of armed conflict in front of the Generalstaatskommissariat, between the Landespolizei and the National Socialists and other armed men who wanted to disarm the Landespolizei. Dr. Weber, who was on the scene, was sent to the Executive Offices Building to persuade the men—we later learned they were cadets—to retreat.

It is apparent from all these orders that it was never my intention to count on a conflict with the Reichswehr and the Landespolizei and the organizations; but, that rather we worked hand in hand with the Reichswehr, Landespolizei, and the other organizations. Later, things were calmer and there was enthusiasm everywhere for the new government.

Pöhner went home. I discharged all the officials for the night because I assumed that the dance would begin in the morning, at which time we would have to deal with either a general strike or radical leftist demonstrations. The telephones were still manned. At 3:00 in the morning, I went home to get a little rest.

I hadn't been home long when the telephone rang. I learned that Colonel Seisser had had a conversation with Colonel Banzer.

I went at once to Colonel Banzer; when I met him he was involved in a discussion with Major Imhoff. I asked him if something was wrong. The men said no. It struck me that Major Imhoff, in particular, manifested a somewhat reserved demeanor. I asked Banzer what Colonel Seisser had said, and Banzer retorted that he hadn't spoken with Seisser.

As I turned to the door, Major Imhoff turned the key and said in a kind voice, "My dear Frick, I'm terribly sorry. Colonel, do your duty!"

Colonel Banzer said, "In the name of the legally constituted government, you are hereby under arrest."

I asked, "Who is the legally constituted government?" The answer: "Minister Matt."

I didn't say anything to that, but I knew that Matt wasn't authorized to issue such orders; that Kahr had united all the executive power into his hands. I was reluctant to accept the fact that the man, with whom just four hours ago I had had an extremely cordial conversation in which he had pledged to me his full cooperation, could give such an order. I remained there in the room in the presence of the two officers. It seemed that it was to be avoided at all costs to have it become known that I had disappeared there. At 7:30 the next morning, I was able to call to our maid—who was serving coffee to the Green Police located behind a machine gun nest—to bring me some coffee, also. That is how my family learned where I was. Since that time, for four months, I have been sitting in jail.

JUDGE NEITHARDT: As you know, the indictment presumes that you had prior knowledge of the action planned for November 8.

HERR FRICK: I must most decidedly deny that.

JUDGE NEITHARDT: This has been deduced from a number of facts. Your name had already been mentioned as the future head of the Police Presidium.

HERR FRICK: That was an informer's report. I don't know whether or not it's true, but I had no knowledge of it. My political philosophy was generally well known, especially in chauvinist circles. Pöhner's name, dating from his activity as Police President, signified a political problem and, since I was his political advisor, it's easy to see how my name was linked with his.

JUDGE NEITHARDT: We must take into account the well-known note pad that was found at Kriebel's: "Frick, 26,868, Chief Hofmann, first report to Frick, 'successfully delivered,' Löwenbräukeller." The digits are your telephone number at your office. It is assumed that there is a code word which you also knew.

HERR FRICK: I can only say that it didn't reach me, and I didn't agree to it, either.

JUDGE NEITHARDT: Captain Göring remarked to the Chief of the Blue Police that he wanted to wait until 8:40, "then Frick would come."

HERR FRICK: Perhaps he assumed I was going out. I didn't arrange anything; and I don't know how he came to that conclusion.

JUDGE NEITHARDT: Scheubner-Richter supposedly said, to Lieutenant Commander Hofmann, "Drive directly to Police Headquarters and tell Frick to take charge of Police Headquarters." Berchtold commented to a police sergeant in the Löwenbräukeller: "The police are safely in Frick hands." At this time, everything was still up in the air. It was before the new men were called forth.

HERR FRICK: I know nothing about that, either.

JUDGE NEITHARDT: It is significant for the indictment that you told your wife you were going to the Bürgerbräukeller, but instead went to your office to read newspapers. It implies an agreement that you were to be called not at home but at your office, at 9:00.

HERR FRICK: I frequently went next door to the office to work after dinner.

JUDGE NEITHARDT: You are accused of neglecting to alert the Landespolizei or the Security Police, although a distinct possibility existed that the affair might get out of hand.

HERR FRICK: When I was detained, I was thoroughly in the dark about the basis for the accusation of high treason. I was directed to the press release which was, of course, inspired by

Kahr, which said: "The particular cunning behind these incidents is apparent in that an accomplice of Hitler who occupied an influential position at Police Headquarters delayed Landespolizei and Reichswehr intervention on behalf of the Generalstaatskommissar by giving false information." That kind of libel has been repeated to the public for four months.

JUDGE NEITHARDT: That expression is not proper here.

HERR FRICK: Whoever disseminated this information has committed libels! The indictment hasn't adopted any such accusations. It accuses me of neglecting both to alert all the Landespolizei and Reichswehr and to go to the Police President's deputy, Oberregierungsrat Tenner. It is completely omitted that 15 men were to attack the Bürgerbräukeller. There was unanimity that it would serve no purpose to send in one squad because it was too small. In the conversation with Captain Stumpf, the question of whether to send in the troops was at issue. At that point in time there was no talk of alerting the Landespolizei. Moreover, only the officer of the day could give the alert. Major Imhoff did not personally order the alert of the Landespolizei; he did so only at the direction of the Generalstaatskommissariat. If I have betrayed my country, then Captain Stumpf and Major Imhoff also must be accused of high treason. Everything took place inside of five minutes. Fifteen minutes after talking with Captain Stumpf, I learned of the alert. It could not have affected any change at the Bürgerbräukeller assembly.

JUDGE NEITHARDT: If you knew of the plans for that evening beforehand and yet did not take precautions in time, then you are guilty of negligence which, of course, is punishable.

HERR FRICK: I deny I had any knowledge thereof.

JUDGE NEITHARDT: You stated earlier that you didn't give the alert because you didn't think of it.

HERR FRICK: I just wanted to say that at that moment, when I was conferring with Captain Stumpf, the question of an alert was not raised. I was thinking only of sending in troops. In regard to not notifying the Police President's deputy, the officer of the day was in charge. It was incumbent upon him to notify the Police President's deputy. I wasn't constantly in the duty room. I went to the Landespolizei three times; and I had telephone messages to convey. Also, people came into the duty room and I had to speak with them. I assumed the officer of the day had already given the notification.

In response to the Presiding Judge's question of whether when he later learned of the power relationships he hadn't usurped the office of Police President, or exercised the power of such an office, Frick replies:

HERR FRICK: When President Pöhner called me into the executive office and told me I might take over the office of Police President, I refused; and the whole night I did not refer to myself as Police President. In the numerous telephone conversations I had, I always identified myself as Oberamtmann Frick. Naturally I couldn't prevent some members of the press from addressing me as "Police President." When Herr Pöhner told me that Excellency von Kahr had given me this commission, and Excellency von Kahr was unconditionally authorized as the holder of the executive power, then he could confer on me the interim regulation of the Police President. I didn't interpret it as anything but that. I left the question unresolved as to whether the new government already had this legal authority or not.

JUDGE NEITHARDT: You appointed Regierungsrat Balss Chief of the Political Division. As senior official, did you feel justified in ordering this transfer?

HERR FRICK: Certainly. Balss was the only one there.

JUDGE NEITHARDT: You saw to it that police authority was handed back to the police, and that it wasn't left to the Kampf-bund. Is that correct?

HERR FRICK: Certainly.

JUDGE NEITHARDT: You also said to Regierungsrat Werber that foodstuff provisions had to be secured. Is that another aspect?

HERR FRICK: I can't remember anymore, exactly. I probably thought the situation could become more difficult, through a general strike or something of that nature; or perhaps the thought of plundering food warehouses occurred to me. I can't recall any definite agreement now.

331

JUDGE NEITHARDT: You also directed that the press could write about the new government, but could not sabotage it?

HERR FRICK: That was said at the press conference, which was mainly conducted by Pöhner.

In response to questioning concerning the threatened conflict in front of the Generalstaatskommissariat, between the Infantry School and the Landespolizei, Frick states:

HERR FRICK: Colonel Banzer came to me and said there would be shooting in front of the Executive Offices Building if the Infantry School did not withdraw immediately. I then sent word that the Infantry School was to withdraw at once.

JUDGE NEITHARDT: Then you deny emphatically having had prior knowledge of the action, and having committed the crime of negligence?

HERR FRICK: I certainly do. Even if I were in the same position today, under the given circumstances I could not act any differently. My motive was to prevent the bloodshed of patriotic men. If I really contributed to preventing that, then I would be proud of it. I do not envy those gentlemen responsible for the death of 23 patriots.

In conclusion, I would like to add one more thing. The statement which Herr Roder released to the public on December 10, at Hitler's, Pöhner's, and my request—the first statement the defendants were able to make publicly—read: "Herr Oberstlandesgerichtsrat Pöhner and Dr. Frick reported to Kahr on November 8 at 11:00 at the Executive Offices Building. The gentlemen had to wait a half an hour because Minister Matt was with Kahr." The Generalstaatskommissar comments: "Cabinet Minister Matt did not set foot in the Executive Offices Building or in Kahr's dwelling on the night of November 8." I would note that Dr. Matt was on the phone with Kahr. This denial, then, is not wholly true. Herr Roder's statement also reads: "From 11:30 to 12:00 midnight, Kahr conferred with Pöhner and Frick. He greeted them cordially and was in good spirits. He revealed that he had released an appropriate message to all governmental authorities via radio. Their parting was equally cordial." In the comments of the Generalstaatskommissariat, it states: "See above for the real radiogram." The situation is characterized by the inference that as the conversation was taking place, Hitler's troops were advancing on the Executive Offices Building. I must dispute that Kahr could have known that Hitler's troops were advancing on the Executive Offices Building because, according to the indictment itself, the order went out to Hitler's troops to advance on the Executive Offices Building between 12:00 and 1:00 a.m.

In response to the Judge's question concerning the radio message, Frick states:

HERR FRICK: Pöhner told me that he had asked Kahr whether the contents of the message should be released to the press. He received express consent to do so. If only Kahr had merely implied that the affair couldn't go on like this, the tragedy of November 9 could still have been averted at that point.

Whereupon Hitler requests permission to comment on the statement that a session on October 23, in which he supposedly took part, did not take place. With the admonition of the Judge that Major Huber and the chemist Strasser will be testifying as to the fact of this session, Hitler states that he has done some research and found that a military session, not a political session, took place on October 23; there, he had made only a salutatory speech.

JUDGE NEITHARDT: You are supposed to have said that the time had come for the entire nation to rise up against the Jewish tyranny in Berlin.

HERR HITLER: I have been saying that ceaselessly for about four years now. We first mentioned Frick's name when Kahr forced Count Lerchenfeld's resignation in mid-summer, 1922. When Pöhner was brought in, he emphasized that it was a natural thing that if he was ever to be expected to cooperate, his former colleague Frick had to be with him. It went without saying that Oberamtmann Frick was to be involved in any solution. I never mentioned Frick by name. It was enough, for me, that Frick was in on the affair.

In response to Herr Götz's question, Frick states he has never belonged to a political party.

HERR GÖTZ: When he announced the police measures he had taken to Herr Balss, did Oberamtmann Frick hold the conviction that the measures not directed by him were to be sufficient, at the time?

HERR FRICK: Yes. The preparations which made available a squad of Green Police, and an appropriate number of Security Police, were entirely appropriate and were similar to those made for assemblies of that kind. To order more troops was unfeasible, because that would finally lead to keeping the Landespolizei on emergency alert for every assembly. The police can't be blamed for negligence. The only thing one might think about would be the political news service's breakdown—but then there were only a very few people who knew what was happening.

Herr Götz asks what the relationship of the Green Police is to the Blue Police.

HERR FRICK: Since the Green Police have come to the Police building—they had come thanks to me and Pöhner—a certain discord has materialized. Relations between the Green and Blue Police aren't particularly good.

In response to another question, Frick remarks that first of all the officer of the day is authorized to sound an alert, but that the official of the day has the right to request the officer of the day to give the alert.

HERR RODER: If you had known then that a revolution was breaking out, and if you had wanted to collaborate, couldn't you have exercised a different kind of influence on Police Headquarters and intervened actively in a different way?

HERR FRICK: Certainly. It is inexplicable why they even bothered to notify me, after 9:00. What was I supposed to do? Everything had already happened. After 9:00 there were already 600-1,000 armed men in front of the Bürgerbräukeller.

JUDGE NEITHARDT: In other words, you could have made appropriate preparations if you had known beforehand?

HERR FRICK: Certainly, if I had known. In any case, I believe that any other official could have instituted the measures I took.

HERR GADEMANN: Did Kahr tell you that his radio message had already been sent to the radio stations?

HERR FRICK: Kahr didn't say that he wanted to let the message go out. Instead, he told us that telegrams had already been sent, not just to the President but to all the officials of the State.

Herr Gademann remarks that the defense has a report from one station that received the message.

Finally, defense counsel moves for the hearing of General von Hildebrand as a witness for the defense this week.

The Court is adjourned until Tuesday morning at 8:30.

THE SEVENTH DAY, March 4, 1924

—MORNING SESSION—

Testimony of the Witnesses

The proceedings on Tuesday morning begin with the testimony of the witnesses. After the roll-call of the witnesses summoned for today—including numerous Reichswehr officers—Herr Roder begins an oration in the name of the defense.

HERR RODER: Today marks the beginning of the witnesses' testimony. May it please the Court, on behalf of all defense counsels, I wish to declare a brief statement that the witnesses have already been influenced to a most extraordinary degree. This influencing took various forms. In the first place, the truth has been suppressed and shunted to the side. The newspapers were generally advised not to publish any conflicting statements. Thus, the truth was suppressed; at which point, untruths were actively and positively spread among the people. So-called "official" or "authentic" accounts of the trial have been forwarded to the press. Also, messages have been sent to those persons scheduled to give uninfluenced and non-partisan testimony. General von Lossow has readied a few hundred copies of a so-called "official account." I believe there are 400 of them. These were delivered to individual senior officers and troop commanders.

All this elaborate staging was set up to prepare the witnesses for influencing and prejudicing the Court. The High Tribunal has already received a copy from me. You will find the notation on the pamphlet, "Secret!" "Confidential!" You will find a passage on the first page which reads: "With regard to the pending judicial hearings, the Wehrkreiskommando requests careful handling of this confidential matter. Copies of any kind, including excerpts, are prohibited." We can clearly see here the guilty conscience of the author that something will be done with the papers—something under-handed. If a true, objective statement of the facts was to be given, then all this business about "confidentiality" would have been unnecessary. General von Lossow was not the only one to work in this fashion; another side developed schemes along the same lines.

In any case, this white and blue pamphlet I have here is well known to the High Tribunal. It contains no statements from which one could deduce that Kahr, Lossow, or Seisser published it or caused it to be written. However, there are other means to trace the author. I have taken it upon myself to compare various pages of the manuscript with the witnesses' depositions. In doing so, I found that Herr Seisser's deposition is almost identical to this manuscript—page-for-page, nearly word-for-word.

As evidence, Herr Roder reads out a lengthy passage from Seisser's deposition and a passage from the pamphlet, one after the other.

HERR RODER: Thus we conclude that the booklet has been copied. The author, or whoever commissioned it, must be one and the same person. That can only be Herr Seisser, or another, in the event that Seisser himself did not compose the booklet.

JUDGE NEITHARDT: I would consider it more appropriate if these charges were made in the presence of the witnesses.

HERR RODER: The Court must know beforehand what has taken place to influence the witnesses so that it can be in the position to ask each witness whether he has received Lossow's report, or the white and blue booklet. I ask the Court to institute this procedure at the outset for all witnesses.

The attorney further declares that the white and blue booklet can only have been written by Herr Seisser, or one of his lackeys. This is already patently obvious because every contrary opinion of Hitler's has been suppressed. If the pamphlet had not come from the other side, it would have been seized and confiscated. The defender terms this the second proof of influencing witnesses. Herr Roder then refers to a memorandum from the government in Upper Bavaria to its officials "regarding political enlightenment" in which one-sided opinions were expressed in order to create solidarity.

HERR RODER: These men didn't stop at influencing witnesses; they went so far as to jointly compose their depositions. In the documents themselves, I see a couple of air-tight examples. The law requires that every witness give his deposition individually and independently. But what has happened here? In the first place, it is odd that Herr Kahr, Lossow, and Seisser were interrogated at the very end. It gives the appearance that all the material was made available to them beforehand. In the second place, each of these men procured the deposition of the other, studied it, and based his own on the others'. There are several pieces of evidence to corroborate this. You find many passages that are identical, word-for-word. You also find several identical passages that are false and untrue; for example, the allegation that Pöhner came to the Bürgerbräukeller after Ludendorff.

I have another striking piece of evidence. Lossow's deposition about November 6 in the Court records reads: "Preceding this are the depositions of Kahr and Seisser, with whose testimony I am in complete agreement." We see that General von Lossow illicitly did give his deposition, not in an impartial, objective fashion, but rather they all put their heads together and he gave his deposition jointly with them. And so we read later in the deposition, as General Lossow writes of November 8: "I am in complete agreement with the testimony of Excellency von Kahr and Seisser." Once again the same convincing evidence exists.

The attorney remarks that the book was made available to approximately 400 military personnel and that the addressors conveyed the contents of the manuscript to the other witnesses. In his opinion, then, there are to be only a couple of witnesses appearing before the Court who have not been prejudiced. He moves for the reading of General Lossow's report.

HERR RODER: It will be seen from this reading that: one, those who received the report have been unilaterally influenced; two, the report contains so many blatant falsehoods that witnesses have been influenced in terms of falsification of the truth; and, three, passages from this report have been implanted, word-for-word, in the indictment or vice-versa. The total impression here is that the truth, on one side, has been suppressed to an unbelievable degree; and on the other side, untruths have been spread and a large segment of the public has been unduly prejudiced.

JUDGE NEITHARDT: At this time, the reading of the report is uncalled for.

HERR RODER: I don't know if every witness has seen this.

JUDGE NEITHARDT: Well, we can ask them. We shall read out the report when the time is right.

Herr Roder holds his petition aloft.

Herr von Zezschwitsch supports the motion, but requests that the prosecution be asked, in the meantime, to see to it— in the event the Court decides differently—that the memoranda sent from the Wehrkreiskommando Staff to individual commanders and from them to their subordinates, be produced. Likewise, that such action should also be taken in regard to the Landespolizei.

Herr von Zezschwitsch also states that unmistakable similarities exist between the indictment and Lossow's secret report.

HERR ZEZSCHWITSCH: When the Chief Prosecutor states that he doesn't know of any secret report, he must emphasize that another person in the prosecution has been active. Many— yes, the majority—of the documents carry the stamp of Prosecutor Dresse, the driving force behind the indictment. Even if Herr Dresse perhaps does not know of the secret report, we stand fast in our conviction that the witnesses have been prejudiced by the secret report.

Herr Holl remarks that if he had been there Monday—Herr Holl was prevented from attending because of his mother's funeral—he certainly would have opposed certain motions. He wouldn't want to awaken the impression that Herr Kahr, Lossow, and Seisser should be punished for high treason; his concern is for the release of his client so that his client may devote himself to the Nationalist Movement. For him, it is not a question of who fired the first shot at the Feldherrnhalle. The question of who fired the first shot at the Feldherrnhalle has no bearing on the matter at hand—namely, whether or not high treason has been committed. Herr Holl then adds a message from the Technical Institute that Cardinal Schulte had declared from his pulpit in Cologne that he took issue with Ludendorff's statements.

HERR HOLL: I just want to say that I would consider it a sacrilege if the pulpit was to be placed in the service of this affair. We see the methods the other side uses in this struggle.

The Nationalist Movement does not oppose religion. It opposes those leaders who want to drag religion into the machinery of politics and political parties. I share the opinion that the report must be read out, in its entirety. It is highly striking that the report and the depositions are identical, word-for-word. Your Honor, that must be verified publicly. I am positive a few of the witnesses received this report. So that no shadow of a doubt remains that the copy of the report is correct, I submit a photographic copy of this report.

HERR KOHL: The differences of opinion exist solely as to the timing of the reading. When Herr Gademann surrendered the report, the Judge wanted to read it out. This has not been done. As soon as the report is entered in the record, it must also be brought to the attention of the entire Court.

Herr Schramm submits to proof that shortly after the Bür-gerbräukeller assembly, the "joyful news" was given by Colonel von Seisser to a captain that he was Minister of Reichspolizei, but that later he was warned he would suffer the consequences if he made use of the news. Also, according to Kriebel's testimony, the interrogating Prosecutor immediately went to the Wehrkreiskommando and discussed the deposition in front of the officers gathered there.

HERR GADEMANN: The report which I handed over during Ludendorff's speech was not read out, so as not to interrupt His Excellency for a length of time, but it was intended to be read out. After my client was interrogated on January 19, 1924, and on the very day he made serious charges, Herr Dresse at once drove from Neudeck to the Wehrkreiskommando with the manuscript, where a lengthy, agitated meeting took place. This fact alone would suffice to prove the necessity of reading out the report at once.

HERR STENGLEIN: The prosecution has no connection with the report. If individual passages of the report share the same wording as the indictment, it can only be because the indictment is based on the same witnesses whose expressions and wording have perhaps been utilized in the report. Nor has the prosecution delivered any material for this report. On behalf of Herr Dresse, whom I esteem as a colleague and upon whose objectivity I rely, I must state explicitly that it is inconceivable that he has done anything which would overstep the boundaries of his duty in objectively clearing up the matter. If he did drive to the Wehrkreiskommando after taking Kriebel's deposition—I was unaware of this—it can only have been for the permissible purpose of obtaining statements warranted by Lieutenant Colonel Kriebel's testimony as soon as possible from certain men. That is not to say that witnesses' statements were made illegally. I leave it to the Court to decide on the motion to read out the report.

HERR LUETGEBRUNE: Herr Stenglein has confirmed the peculiar fact that the indictment is essentially identical to the memorandum. I do not believe the prosecution gave the authors of the memo the depositions for their records. I must reiterate, however, that the primary concern is that the memo was sent; we are justified in our conclusion that certain witnesses made use of it. That must be generally established. Therefore I definitely support my colleagues' petition.

HERR ZEZSCHWITSCH: The memo was read in officers' circles at the end of November.

HERR GADEMANN: The Chairman of the Officers' Club of the Munich Field Artillery Regiment had an original of the manuscript from the records now before the Court, which by itself is of no consequence; but which, in unauthorized hands, can be a weapon against the defendants. The gentleman has given his word of honor not to say where he got the document. That is also similar to what Herr Roder was condemning before, and should be cleared up by the motion.

HERR HEMMETER: I endorse Roder's motion because it has been proven that the first deposition by a commission of *ad usum delphini* resulted in a form that must have been extremely strange. It had witnesses who gave testimony favorable to Lieutenant Wagner standing at attention for five hours during the time they were interrogated. Every military man knows that situations like that do not favorably influence a deposition. It knew how to phrase the questioning—staff officers were shut out. I move that we read this pamphlet—that's what I call the memo. It had no purpose other than to give biased information to subordinate officers. The results of the one-sided information have already become important in individual depositions.

341

JUDGE NEITHARDT: The memorandum went out on January 10.

The defense counsels object.

HERR HOLL: The memo went through three stages. The first description was given out on November 24, 1923, to ranking officers and regimental commanders for transmittal to their officers. The same description was forwarded to the Chief of the Landespolizei on December 12, and finally to chairmen of the Officers' Clubs on January 10. We can see how important it is to read the memo from the second and third paragraphs of the cover letter.

> "The memo, which briefly describes the actual course of events, should serve to combat distortions of fact and erroneous rumors which abound. The Wehrkreiskommando considers it especially desirable that the officers of the Old Army are able to familiarize themselves with the incidents and events contained in the official account. Your Excellencies are requested to disclose the contents of the document to the officers of the club in a suitable form."

JUDGE NEITHARDT: The depositions were already taken at the Infantry School on November 9 and 10.

HERR HEMMETER: And on November 12!

HERR BAUER: Lieutenant Pernet was placed under arrest, pending investigation, on the basis of the allegations in the memorandum.

HERR STENGLEIN: As far as I can remember, the reason for his arrest was the receipt of the confiscated money.

HERR BAUER: They were found much later.

HERR GADEMANN: I request clarification: When were Herr Kahr, Lossow, and Seisser interrogated? Before, or after the other witnesses?

JUDGE NEITHARDT: Kahr's interrogation was on December 4; Seisser's was on December 4; and Lossow's was on December 6.

342

After secret deliberations, the Court passes the resolution that the reading of the memo will take place at a later time to be determined by the Presiding Judge.

HERR ZEZSCHWITSCH: Since the presence of the military inspectors may disrupt the witnesses' testimony, I wish to be the first to urge these gentlemen to retire from the courtroom for the duration of the following military witnesses' testimony.

CAPTAIN SPECK: Since basic concerns of the Reich Army are at stake, I request permission to remain in the hall as a delegate from the Reichswehr Ministry.

HERR GÖTZ: I support the motion of Herr Zezschwitsch wholly and completely. Several diligent officers have already been suddenly robbed of their existence. I don't want those officers who must testify here—the Berlin office, General Seeckt, and the officers whom he has drawn to himself, alone have the final say on life or death—to come into the conflict of either telling the truth, or reading in the next official gazette or in the famous blue letter that they are expendable. Both these men, whom I personally regard highly, must either report to Berlin—and then the one who says something they don't want to hear flies out the door--or they don't report, in which case I don't see why they're here.

Herr Kohl says that the gentlemen from the Reichswehr Ministry and the Wehrkreiskommando, recognized by their behavior at the hearing on Monday, could not have failed to influence at least the prosecution.

HERR STENGLEIN: I only want to remark that the prosecution has not been influenced. Also, I had no inkling that such an attempt was made by the two men.

The Court now recesses to discuss a resolution. After the conference, the Presiding Judge passes the following resolution:

JUDGE NEITHARDT: During the testimony of the witnesses summoned for this morning, the public will be excluded because a public hearing may constitute a danger to national security. Attendance is permitted to those persons named in the resolutions of February 26 and 27, with the exception of the representatives of the Reichswehr Ministry and Wehrkreiskommando Number 7.

At 10:00 the Court begins the secret hearings.

The First Witnesses

*Witnesses summoned for the morning are: General von Ties-
chowitz, Lieutenant Colonel Leupold, Lieutenant Colonel Dümlein, Captain Leuze, Captain Loepper, Lieutenants Block, Weckmann, König, Mahler, Hubrich, and Fähnrich Engelte.*

*Of the witnesses called in connection with the events at the
Infantry School, only General von Tieschowitz and Colonel Leupold will be cross-examined. The other witnesses are not questioned pursuant to this area.*

Hans Tieschowitz von Tieschowa,

*Fifty-eight years of age, Evangelical, married, Commander of
the Infantry School at Munich, not related by blood or by
marriage to the defendants, having been duly sworn, testifies as
follows:*

HERR TIESCHOWITZ: I was a subordinate of General Ludendorff for a long time, and since I held a special position of trust,
I find it extremely painful to have to appear here as a witness
against him; but I must do so in the interest of my cadets. I
have no statements to make which might implicate His Excellency. I can only say that his name will be remembered along
with that of very great men, no matter what happens. As to the
connections I have to one of the defendants—

JUDGE NEITHARDT: What can you tell us about the events,
and what do you know about the happenings in the Infantry
School on November 8?

HERR TIESCHOWITZ: I must specifically emphasize two facts
which were significant for the entire intellectual attitude of the
cadets—an attitude which was the whole foundation for these
events. One was the conduct of General von Lossow towards
General Seeckt which, without question, deeply affected the disciplinary principles of my cadets. The second reason is the secret

344

propaganda made by Rossbach. In this propaganda, the name of Ludendorff, as he himself said here recently, was greatly abused without his knowledge. Actually, the cadets were led to believe that Ludendorff was behind the entire Rossbach propaganda, a fact that was of extreme importance.

Also, in the orders received by Wagner on November 8 at noon, and in the evening, the name of Ludendorff was abused in a very special way. For instance, one order said that Ludendorff ordered the School to leave at once. Also, another said that the School would immediately be transformed into a "Ludendorff Regiment." Furthermore, they stated that Ludendorff wanted to see the resident officers the next morning. The implication in all these orders was that they had been issued by Ludendorff, and that he was our leader. This idea had a decisive influence on the cadets.

Ludendorff has already said that his name had been misused and that it had been done against his will. This abuse of the name of Ludendorff makes Rossbach, who had close relations with Ludendorff, appear in a very ominous light. Thus, he brought the name of Ludendorff into this conspiracy—as it was understood at the time in the School. I would like to say openly that, among the cadets, Rossbach at first exerted a decisive influence as a demagogue on the night of November 8 to 9. Later, however, he bitterly disappointed them when he acted as a leader during this night. I speak the truth when I say that this was at least the impression he made, as the School report confirms. I express this here, even though the man concerned cannot defend himself here.

I would like to offer my opinion on two points, since in his speech on Friday afternoon Ludendorff mentioned a few things that concerned me, but that contained some mistakes. Since they have reached the public, I would appreciate it if my statements, too, were to be made public.

JUDGE NEITHARDT: It was resolved to exclude the public from this session.

HERR TIESCHOWITZ: According to newspaper reports to which I had access, Ludendorff said:

> "I observed the development of the situa-
> tion at the Infantry School with apprehen-
> sion. Here the Bavarian officers followed the

345

order of the commander of the Infantry
School. The latter suspended them, only to
reinstate them a few days later when he regretted his action. He said General von Lossow had acted for patriotic reasons. Berlin
had capitulated before Munich."

The events did not actually take place exactly as he
described. The truth is that after Lossow had declared that he
would take a stand against Seeckt—and after Seeckt had sharply
protested—I informed the Bavarian officers that I no longer
regretted that I was able to cooperate with them if they were to
swear an oath to the Bavarian government. Later, Lossow, however, refrained from demanding this oath from the Bavarian
members of the Infantry School. They never actually swore an
oath. Hence, the matter became completely void; the gentlemen
resumed their duties; and there was neither capitulation nor
contrite reinstatement on my part. The voiding of the matter
was a consequence of the fact that the men had not sworn the
oath.

The second point concerns me personally. Ludendorff said:

"To my surprise, the Infantry School reported to me in the Bürgerbräukeller. I asked
Rossbach what General von Tieschowitz had
said. His reply was that Tieschowitz had said
his oath prohibited him from going along;
since, however, the movement had begun to
progress, he did not want to oppose it."

My comments are as follows: The events in the Infantry School
happened like a surprise attack; both the resident officers and I
were presented with *faits accomplis*. We did not have the power
to interfere effectively. I then said to those who brought the
news: "Since I have no means at my disposal, I no longer have
the power to take steps against a movement which has
progressed this far. I shall remain faithful to my oath."

Those are the words I used. They have not been repeated
correctly here. That was all I wanted to say so that my position
would not be distorted.

JUDGE NEITHARDT: I would like to ask, in this context,
whether you may have said: "I cannot reconcile it with my oath,
but go away!" You are supposed to have said it like that.

HERR TIESCHOWITZ: No. I did not say that. I only said: "I

346

cannot do anything against the movement." That was to Lieutenant Block and to Lieutenant Seck.

JUDGE NEITHARDT: Perhaps you can tell us in this connection: What was the cadets' opinion of the events which were to take place on November 8?

HERR TIESCHOWITZ: They thought that a great national action, with Ludendorff, Lossow, Kahr, and Seisser at the head, had begun to move and that the main parts of North Germany had also joined the movement. They actually would not have to answer this question, they would simply have to go along.

JUDGE NEITHARDT: What was their final goal?

HERR TIESCHOWITZ: The final goal was probably to form a national government. I don't really believe that they thought about it a great deal since Ludendorff, Lossow, and Kahr were there. They thought that those were the leaders and they had to go along; they probably considered it an obligation. In my opinion, no cadets were aware of the fact that they had somehow become guilty of a serious crime against the State.

JUDGE NEITHARDT: A change of the constitution?

HERR TIESCHOWITZ: Nobody thought of that. I am firmly convinced of it. They were all enthusiastic about the national idea; they were enthusiastic about the idealistic goals of the Völkische movement which is quite understandable; and that to act under those leaders who, to them, had always seemed to be the perfect leaders was their highest duty.

JUDGE NEITHARDT: Do you know Lossow's division order of October 23 about the question of cockades?

HERR TIESCHOWITZ: This order has been interpreted in a completely wrong way. This order was supposed to mean something different. Whatever we read in the papers was not quite correct. Lossow made this statement because he wanted to make clear that the black-white-red cockade could not yet be worn. As soon as the Reichswehr had sworn its oath to Bavaria, there was a note recommending the black-white-red cockade. Lossow was requested to give this order to the entire Bavarian Reichswehr. He did not comply, however, because he did not want to increase the discord between North and South. He issued the order: "The cockade is not to be worn." He hoped, however, that the time would not be far when we could wear the black-white-red cockade again. To wear this cockade again, with which the War had been fought, is the hope of every Reichswehr soldier. It is natural that everyone strikes to wear this cockade again. No one has any doubts about it.

JUDGE NEITHARDT: When Block was informed, it was stressed that the 7th Division stood behind the uprising.

HERR TIESCHOWITZ: No cadet would have moved a finger if the 7th Division had not gone along.

JUDGE NEITHARDT: But you made inquiries with the Wehrkreiskommando?

HERR TIESCHOWITZ: Yes, inquiries were immediately made; but, they took a very long time.

JUDGE NEITHARDT: The men were away; then, they returned. When did you find out about what was really going on?

HERR TIESCHOWITZ: After midnight, we received definite information about the situation; we immediately took steps to inform the cadets. It was, however, not quite possible (to do that) because they had not yet returned. Even after they had returned, a number of officers were prevented from telling the people what the situation really was. Rossbach prevented it. Still, we succeeded in convincing quite a few cadets not to go along. Rossbach alerted the remaining cadets when he noticed that the men were to be informed. Then, he marched off with them.

JUDGE NEITHARDT: After the cadets had returned, did you again make official inquiries with the Wehrkreiskommando?

HERR TIESCHOWITZ: No.

JUDGE NEITHARDT: The cadets are supposed to have been told: "You are not to ask any further; the order is here, you are once again to march to the Bürgerbräukeller." Don't you know about this?

HERR TIESCHOWITZ: No.

JUDGE NEITHARDT: What position did the resident officers take?

HERR TIESCHOWITZ: They felt like I did. They had been completely taken by surprise. The others had selected a time when the resident officers were not there, partly during the night. The building was occupied by Rossbach. The cadets were over-enthusiastic about the action and could no longer be restrained. Any active participation of the resident officers is out of the question.

JUDGE NEITHARDT: Nevertheless, the resident officers did not hold back the cadets?

HERR TIESCHOWITZ: Well, it is very difficult to decide how far that would have been possible. Some of the resident officers intervened; then came the order from Ludendorff and Lossow. The men did not really know the nature of the situation either. They told themselves that if all Bavaria rises, the few of us cannot do anything.

JUDGE NEITHARDT: What you are saying is very important. It was therefore said that there was an order from Ludendorff and Lossow?

HERR TIESCHOWITZ: Yes, of course. With his great name, Ludendorff exerted quite an influence on the people. Ludendorff, Lossow, Seisser, and Kahr—those were men who belonged together; and if their names were heard together, everything seemed to go smoothly.

JUDGE NEITHARDT: Did Lieutenant Wagner play an important role?

HERR TIESCHOWITZ: On that evening? Or when?

JUDGE NEITHARDT: On that evening.

HERR TIESCHOWITZ: Yes, he did play a role since he was the mediator. But otherwise, for instance, as a leader he played no greater role than many others.

JUDGE NEITHARDT: You, General, are supposed to have made a remark to Captain Leuze which you now deny. You are supposed to have said: "For you, as a Bavarian, everything is quite clear. Lieutenant Dümlein has just telephoned the Wehr-kreiskommando and was told that Lossow is behind the action with the 7th Division."

HERR TIESCHOWITZ: This was how the incident happened: A few days after the Bavarian officers had not sworn the oath to the Bavarian Government, Colonel Leupold, as the oldest Ba-varian officer, came to me and told me that the Bavarian officers had not sworn the oath, but that they would inwardly take Lossow's side if they should have to make that decision. They told each other, if Lossow should call—as it seemed imminent at the time—we will stand behind our Landeskommandant. Those were their views. And in my opinion, these views were absolutely comprehensible. If I had been a Bavarian, I would definitely have stood behind the commander of the Division.

JUDGE NEITHARDT: Were the views you just described the general views? Perhaps you will be good enough to tell us what Lieutenant Block told you—namely, that the national govern-ment of the Reich was to be proclaimed in Munich, and so on?

HERR TIESCHOWITZ: Yes, he told me that the national government was to be proclaimed; that General Ludendorff would not force the resident officers to make a decision tonight, but that he would make the decision tomorrow. When the Lieu-tenant asked me about my position on this matter, I replied I would remain faithful to my oath, but that I did not have the means to prevent the uprising at this point.

JUDGE NEITHARDT: Were the questions you discussed with the men purely military?

HERR TIESCHOWITZ: The men did not, in any way, violate discipline. Only the manner in which they appeared was some-what peculiar. Four armed cadets dressed for combat came to me. To me, this meant that if I had attempted to prevent it the men would have asked me to leave the room. Also, the corridors outside my room were occupied by Rossbach's people. The whole thing probably had an appearance of violence; there is no doubt about it. But nobody actually used any violence against me.

JUDGE NEITHARDT: You had no complaints about First Lieutenant Wagner's behavior?

HERR TIESCHOWITZ: No. I had no close contact with Wagner. I talked to him only once; that was after I had received information that the division would not participate. I happened to hear that he was in the building. I asked him to see me. I then told him about it; he answered: "That does not change my decision." In any case, my impression of Lieutenant Wagner was quite favorable. I do not think he is any more guilty than the other cadets. He undoubtedly acted with the best of intentions. The only problem is he stuck to the cause afterwards, and said: "I have made myself available to the cause, and I shall stay with it." I don't believe he was aware of the fact that in so doing he committed a crime against the authority of the State. I cannot possibly lay any blame upon him.

JUDGE NEITHARDT: What are the reasons that attracted the cadets to the uprising?

HERR TIESCHOWITZ: The young men were virtually possessed by a spiritual epidemic. One must realize that. The men did not ask themselves what they had done or what they wanted to do. They saw the great national uprising and they thought they could not deprive themselves of participating in it. Compared with this, any other reasons and considerations carried no weight.

JUDGE NEITHARDT: And they had waited day by day for the rise of the national movement?

HERR TIESCHOWITZ: Yes, because preparations for it were constantly going on. It was a chapter about which they spoke incessantly.

JUDGE NEITHARDT: Do you know that Lossow is supposed to have requested—to have ordered the cadets to attend political meetings?

HERR TIESCHOWITZ: I don't believe it. I discussed this with General Lindemann and he told me that the order did not say so—at least not as an intention on Lossow's part. We have a military regulation that we are not to be involved in politics. I also told that to the cadets. But there is no doubt, either, that General Lossow did not issue a counter-order. He may have modified somewhat the regulation that we were not to involve ourselves in politics. He told the men that now people had to be national-minded and patriotic, but this was expected especially of our young soldiers. He may have said: "Very well, go to such meetings." He thought in reference to those meetings which, in his opinion, would further national feelings. Anyhow, this would not in any way violate the existing orders. That would be a wrong assumption. I read this false assumption in the paper.

JUDGE NEITHARDT: General, didn't you know that the young men were attending the meetings?

HERR TIESCHOWITZ: I did not know that. In my opinion, the men in question were only those of the second course. I think only Colonel Leupold has given definite directives in regard to this matter. Otherwise, I was not aware of anything that might indicate an abuse.

JUDGE NEITHARDT: Are there any other questions to be directed to the General?

HERR HEMMETER: Did you, General, know that the Bavarian Infantry cadets would put themselves behind Lossow?

HERR TIESCHOWITZ: The Infantry cadets did not do that.

HERR HEMMETER: Not even some gentlemen of the Infantry School?

HERR TIESCHOWITZ: I know that they did not take the oath to Lossow and the Bavarian Government. Only shortly before November 8, was I informed by Colonel Leupold that they felt a moral obligation to stand behind Lossow if necessary. As Leupold told me, they had not made an official pledge.

HERR HEMMETER: General, I am only interested in one thing. It is said that you, General, had gone to Berlin and had there taken care of highly personal matters.

HERR TIESCHOWITZ: I went to Berlin after Lossow had bound by oath the Bavarian officers and men. Since in the long run this had to create an untenable situation, I wanted to interrupt the course. For this reason, I went to Berlin and reported the state of things. At that time I was given the order to interrupt the course. Then came the telephone call from Herr Lossow that he had withdrawn from demanding the oath. That meant we could continue our work. Later I reconsidered dissolving the

Infantry School when I heard of the agitation by Rossbach which could not be prevented. I therefore went to interrupt the course again, but that was prevented by Berlin.

HERR HEMMETER: General, you returned from Berlin and stated in a speech here in Munich that His Excellency Seeckt wanted the same (good) as Lossow.

HERR TIESCHOWITZ: No. It was like this. There is no doubt that General Seeckt has the same goals as General Ludendorff. He, too, is no friend of the present form of the State. This is what I approximately said. I also mentioned the fact that Seeckt pursues the same goal as General Ludendorff.

HERR LUDENDORFF: No!

HERR TIESCHOWITZ: In general, Seeckt pursues the same goals as General Ludendorff.

HERR LUDENDORFF: No!

Laughter.

HERR TIESCHOWITZ: Yes, Your Excellency wants to go a different way. Well, in any case, if His Excellency Ludendorff does not agree, I cannot say anything against him. At least I have said that the goals of General Seeckt were just as nationalistic as ours. We all want an upright German Fatherland again. That is what I told the cadets. I think that most of them did not know about it. I explained to the men that when he took up office, General Seeckt had said he was a convinced monarchist. Yet, he would take this position in the Republic because he would not refuse to serve his Fatherland. I told the men this to make them understand that General Seeckt, too, was a nationalistic minded, not socialistic minded, as many perhaps thought.

HERR HEMMETER: I have asked you this question, General, because it is important to me to ascertain that the young officers had reason to believe that, in the end, General Seeckt, too, would participate in the national uprising.

HERR TIESCHOWITZ: No. I did not mean to say that. I wanted to bring General Seeckt somewhat closer to the men by saying that he was a nationalist.

HERR HEMMETER: I only think that the young men could come to the conclusion that—

HERR TIESCHOWITZ: I don't think they could derive this conclusion from my speech. To be sure, the reports of the cadets led me to believe that a number of them were convinced that, within a short time, a national uprising would come. It was also rumored that large sections of the Reichswehr were going along. Of course, that could generate the opinion that General Seeckt was behind them. They could not conclude this from my speech; it had a completely different purpose.

JUDGE NEITHARDT: But didn't the fact that you, the General, and the other resident officers were certain that this movement was actually considered legal as long as Lossow, Kahr, and Seisser were supporters of the movement? Didn't this explain why the General's resident officers did not attempt to interfere with the development at the Infantry School by issuing an order?

HERR TIESCHOWITZ: We were no longer in a position to give orders because the situation had moved beyond us. This is how the situation should be interpreted. To be sure, we also told ourselves: as long as Kahr, Lossow, and Seisser are behind it, there is no use at all to do anything; after all, we cannot go against all Bavaria. There was, however, a feeling: We must above all keep discipline! And that is the most painful aspect—that the principle of discipline was violated.

HERR HEMMETER: May I say that you, General, did not give the direct order to stay?

HERR TIESCHOWITZ: It was not given.

HERR HEMMETER: And it is not known whether any of the resident officers gave such an order?

HERR TIESCHOWITZ: Not generally. In some cases, the gentlemen interfered when they inspected; but a unified order was not given.

HERR HEMMETER: A detailed report was made by the General on November 13. According to the statements made today by the General, I must assume that, under today's circumstances, the General would no longer make his report in the form

354

in which he did. The general himself admitted that these young officers acted in the best of faith and that the idea of any violations—

HERR TIESCHOWITZ: Here I would like to repeat what has already been said.

HERR HEMMETER: In that report, Lieutenant Wagner was described as the chief ringleader. According to what you said today, General, there seems to be a difference of opinion, in that these previous views no longer correspond with your present views.

HERR TIESCHOWITZ: As far as I can see, no longer to that degree.

HERR HEMMETER: I don't consider this very important. I do not believe that Lieutenant Wagner did more than the others. That was my concern.

May I ask you something else? Is it true that the news that Lossow and Kahr would no longer go along first appeared as a rumor?

HERR TIESCHOWITZ: First as a rumor; then I received the news through the officer whom I had sent and who reported affirmatively—at night, between 12:00 and 1:00.

HERR HEMMETER: At that time, the Infantry School had not yet returned?

HERR TIESCHOWITZ: It had not yet returned.

HERR HEMMETER: Quite true. Lieutenant Colonel Dümlein of the Pioneer School said: "The Division actually stands behind the movement."

HERR TIESCHOWITZ: That was much earlier, perhaps at 9:00. I had made a telephone call, but had talked only with the officer on duty who knew nothing about the matter. He had no connection with Lossow. Therefore, we had to be satisfied with entirely noncommittal news from which we could not draw exact conclusions.

HERR HEMMETER: It is surprising that Dümlein and Captain Leuze then requested and received permission from the General to leave the Infantry School.

355

HERR TIESCHOWITZ: That was only for the purpose of defense because we did not see matters clearly.

HERR HEMMETER: Is the General aware of the fact that Lieutenant Ochsner also took an oath to the Bavarian Government?

HERR TIESCHOWITZ: I am not aware of it.

HERR HEMMETER: There are supposed to be a few others.

HERR TIESCHOWITZ: As cadets? I don't know about that. It is possible that, by accident, some of the gentlemen could no longer be informed.

HERR WAGNER: I know that Ochsner took the oath.

HERR TIESCHOWITZ: That may have been accidental; this is not to be taken as a general rule.

HERR LUDENDORFF: I would like to say why I thought that the Bavarian officers had actually taken an oath. On Sunday, October 21, Lossow informed me of the order which he had issued under number I-A-793 that the troops and military posts of the Munich District, including those at the Infantry and Pioneer Schools, had to be sworn in by the commander. Through this discussion I formed the opinion I stated.

Today, I heard for the first time that the swearing-in did not take place. This was not explained to me by Lossow. I thought, however, that it would have to be considered as one of the worst blows to be dealt to the young Reichswehr if the Government of the Reich did not act against this oath-taking. But I did not consider it a capitulation.

HERR LUETGEBRUNE: A moment ago you said that Rossbach had had close connections with Ludendorff. Do you personally know that there were connections between Rossbach and Ludendorff?

HERR TIESCHOWITZ: I know only what His Excellency said in his speech. That was only a conclusion I drew.

HERR LUETGEBRUNE: In reality, their entire relations consisted of one meeting—once Rossbach had had tea with Ludendorff.

HERR TIESCHOWITZ: I was not informed about it.

HERR LUETGEBRUNE: I would like to ask you whether you ever talked to Rossbach himself, or whether you ever heard that he was active in the School?

HERR TIESCHOWITZ: I never spoke with Rossbach personally; only later did I hear unofficially of the contents of his discussions with the cadets.

HERR LUETGEBRUNE: As you know, the Wehrkreiskommando issued a memorandum which is supposed to be an authentic report of the events of November 8 and 9—to be sure—from the point of view of the Wehrkreiskommando. Do you know this memorandum?

HERR TIESCHOWITZ: We officially received it. I suppose this was a certain clarification of the situation for the high authorities and that it was also sent to other officers.

HERR LUETGEBRUNE: When did you receive this memorandum?

HERR TIESCHOWITZ: That was perhaps at the beginning of December, a few weeks after the event had taken place.

HERR KOHL: How did Seeckt and North Germany feel generally about the oath-taking of the 7th Division to Bavaria?

HERR TIESCHOWITZ: It was considered a serious violation of discipline which shook the entire foundation of our military. I, too, felt that way about it. I think that was the most shocking thing of all the events. The uprising would not have progressed that far if it had not been for this oath.

HERR KOHL: Hence it was not only considered a breakdown of discipline, but as the beginning of a punishable act?

HERR TIESCHOWITZ: At least I told myself: If he does that, then the next step, the march on Berlin, is completely clear. Therefore, when I received the news I had no doubt whatsoever that Lossow and Ludendorff stood together.

HERR KOHL: In your whole statement, I found one point somewhat painful. You stated that in that night Rossbach, as the leader, did not behave as one could have and should have expected. Does the General know that there are indications that he behaved very correctly and energetically?

HERR TIESCHOWITZ: I can refer only to the reports of the cadets, especially to one of them who is still to be questioned. I can read a report here which says that Rossbach was a great disappointment to the cadets.

JUDGE NEITHARDT: Please, no details!

HERR TIESCHOWITZ: It says that at first he had told the biggest lies, and then when the cadets wanted to attack the buildings of the Bavarian Government, he was missing—as always during this night—when there was danger that shooting might occur.

That is a serious charge. In any case, he made a very unpleasant impression as a leader. He was not a leader.

HERR KOHL: The reason for this accusation is, perhaps, that some men maintain that, at a given moment, he had been at a different spot from where they had expected him to be. To me, it is important because Rossbach has been accused and is possibly to be tried later. This would play a significant role. The General will admit that the individual man can never judge why a leader happens to be in this or that place. At that moment, Rossbach had—

HERR TIESCHOWITZ: I don't know Rossbach at all. I only know of this from the report.

HERR KOHL: Do you know that on other occasions Rossbach has proved to be very vigorous?

HERR TIESCHOWITZ: I never became acquainted with his personal courage; he probably displayed it at the front. Nobody can blame me if I personally do not think of him with pleasure. I do not know him myself and I personally don't know anything about him.

HERR KOHL: Rossbach had been in prison in Leipzig for seven months pending investigation. From the papers we know he, with a masked face, was led before the Judge. If he had failed with regard to his personal courage, this might be explained by the fact that he had just spent a long time in prison.

HERR TIESCHOWITZ: I emphasize that I consider all the propaganda which he carried out in the name of Ludendorff, and the way in which he exploited him, indecent. It can be said that there are other means to reach a goal. Other officers of mine also found it offensive.

HERR KOHL: The General said that sympathies are not important.

HERR LUDENDORFF: I had the impression from the statements by the General that I was supposed to have cooperated directly with Lossow in the matter of oath-taking.

HERR HITLER: May I ask the General, as an officer, to tell us whether in his opinion, after Lossow's refusal to obey, if there was any other way for Lossow but to fight the battle until the end, or to resign? Does the General believe that after such a—let us say—"refusal to obey," a "reconciliation," so to speak, would have been possible, from a military or disciplinary point of view?

HERR TIESCHOWITZ: I don't believe so. The only possible way would have been resignation or continuation.

HERR HOLL: You know that Seeckt described the action of the gentlemen in Munich as "mutiny"; but you probably also know that afterwards, whether in reality or in appearance, Seeckt gave in to the Munich gentlemen. Now I would like to know whether you know anything about the reasons for the General's attitude. Why did Seeckt not draw the consequences from Lossow's behavior? For what reasons did he not do it?

HERR TIESCHOWITZ: I cannot tell you.

HERR HOLL: You do not know anything at all about it?

HERR TIESCHOWITZ: I am not informed about it. He has not said a word about it. I spoke with him only once—that was in November—but this matter was not discussed. He said only that Lossow was now resigning; but he did not mention anything about his own goals.

HERR HOLL: You did not hear anything from anywhere else?

HERR TIESCHOWITZ: I have not heard anything.

HERR RODER: How would you have judged the further development of events if Kahr, Lossow, and Seisser had seriously participated; if the Bavarian Reichswehr and Polizei had actually participated; and if in North Germany sections of the Reichswehr, and at the very least, many patriotic bands had participated? How would you have judged the further developments?

HERR TIESCHOWITZ: That is hard to say.

HERR RODER: Was it insane, or was it possible?

HERR TIESCHOWITZ: It was this way: Everything would have depended on whether and how the North German Reichswehr would have been deployed. I don't have enough information about it. If the North German Reichswehr had gone along, the action would probably have been successful. But whether this would generally have been the case, I cannot say; I am not informed about it.

HERR RODER: Don't you know that some generals up North were in favor of the uprising?

HERR TIESCHOWITZ: I cannot say that. I did not speak about it with anyone.

HERR RODER: That is, it is said that an action was planned for November 12.

HERR TIESCHOWITZ: I read it in the newspapers—it was absolutely new to me—I didn't know anything about it until then.

HERR RODER: Let us suppose the other side had planned something for November 12. Would you, General, not think that this action would have been successful?

HERR TIESCHOWITZ: It is very difficult to prophesize the future; I really cannot say that.

HERR RODER: General, do you consider it possible that a General, armed and in uniform, who declares: "I am going along!" will later say it was only a pretense; it is not valid?

HERR TIESCHOWITZ: We all know it.

HERR RODER: And we, too, all know it.

Laughter.

360

HERR RODER: Do you not think it is necessary that the one who has given his word to Ludendorff, even if he was only pretending and no longer considers it to be valid, should have at least told Ludendorff that, "My declaration was a pretense, I am not going along"? Don't you think that this was a serious omission on Lossow's part?

HERR TIESCHOWITZ: Yes, yes, definitely.

HERR RODER: Do you think it was a grave offense by Lossow that he did not let Leupold return to Ludendorff to report Lossow's revised attitude?

HERR TIESCHOWITZ: Certainly I think that Leupold should have returned to Ludendorff. I believe Leupold should have reported Lossow's attitude. That was, of course, a private matter. Lossow's step was not an official one, but I interpreted it as official notification by Colonel Leupold.

HERR RODER: One last question, General. After Grossmann and Leupold had informed Lossow of the fact that Hitler and Ludendorff had no intention of using arms, that they did not want to shoot, don't you consider it improper that Lossow did not notify the gentlemen of his intention to use arms?

HERR TIESCHOWITZ: At the very least, I don't consider it fair.

HERR ZEZSCHWITSCH: Did Colonel Leupold tell you there were other officers present whose views differed fundamentally from those of General Lossow—e.g., the Generals Kress and Ruith, when he heard that Lossow had reversed himself? Are you aware of that?

HERR TIESCHOWITZ: No, I am not aware of it.

HERR ZEZSCHWITSCH: That is of great significance—of essential significance. If the gentlemen were present when Lossow informed Colonel Leupold, he might have done so under pressure from Herrn Kress and Ruith.

HERR TIESCHOWITZ: We were notified of Lossow's position at the same time. There was nobody else present.

HERR RODER: Do you know that the Reichswehr was supposed to be used against Bavaria?

HERR TIESCHOWITZ: No, I don't know anything about that. I heard only of orders which already had come from Berlin during the night and which concerned the border guards against Bavaria. I don't know anything else.

HERR RODER: The Reichswehr is said to have been employed. Lossow is supposed to have learned of this. This is to have been the reason for his turnabout.

HERR TIESCHOWITZ: I am not aware of these events. I don't know the reason for Lossow's turnabout. That one would have to hear from Lossow himself.

HERR SCHRAMM: General Lossow and Colonel von Seisser maintained they had been bullied with a pistol into giving their word. General, do you consider it possible that an officer lets himself be bullied by a civilian into giving his word?

JUDGE NEITHARDT: Herr Schramm, this question has nothing to do with the observations of this witness.

HERR TIESCHOWITZ: That is very hard to say. It simply depends on the personalities. That is terribly hard to say.

HERR SCHRAMM: Perhaps you, General, can answer the question in this way: Would you have given your word of honor, without intending to keep it?

HERR TIESCHOWITZ: At the very least, it is so much against my feelings that I believe I would not have done it.

HERR GADEMANN: General, did you—the General was, as I heard, in Berlin at the time—during the period in which Lossow's mutiny took place, ever hear anything to the effect that the Reichsregierung or the Reichswehrminister intended to take action against Bavaria?

HERR TIESCHOWITZ: According to what I heard in Berlin, this was not intended.

HERR GADEMANN: According to what you heard in Berlin, this was not intended?

HERR TIESCHOWITZ: I had, of course, no official information. I heard this only from friends. Let us say that I had the impression that an action was not intended.

HERR BAUER: General, were you informed on the evening of November 8 that First Lieutenant Pernet was supposed to have brought the order for the alert of the Infantry School to Lieutenant Wagner?

HERR TIESCHOWITZ: I was informed of it through the reports of the cadets. According to these reports, First Lieutenant Pernet was at the Infantry School to pick up Lieutenant Wagner. That is all I know about the activity of First Lieutenant Pernet.

HERR HITLER: Does the General know the regulations about the so-called "Fall Maneuver"?

HERR TIESCHOWITZ: No, I do not know them. I only heard about them through the investigation.

JUDGE NEITHARDT: If there are no more questions to be asked of the witness, the matter is settled.
General, you are dismissed.

Herr Ludwig Leupold,

Fifty-five years of age, married, a Colonel in the Infantry School, not related by blood or by marriage to the defendants, having been duly sworn, testifies as follows:

JUDGE NEITHARDT: Colonel, do you want to give us a description of the events which occurred on November 8th and 9th, as they relate to the Infantry School?

HERR LEUPOLD: Only those events relating to the Infantry School?

JUDGE NEITHARDT: Yes—at least for now.

HERR LEUPOLD: Yes. On November 8, shortly after 12:00 midnight, I returned to the Infantry School from a Police Club. There had been a meeting at the club of the Regiment Association. When I approached the School, I was surprised to see guards from Rossbach's people standing at the entrance; and, that the building in which my course was accomodated—as well as the place in which I live—was occupied by, I think, approximately 100 of Rossbach's men. The only cadet I saw in there was Lieutenant Mai, one of my students. I asked him what was going on. He told me the Infantry School had already marched

363

to the Bürgerbräukeller, around 9:00. I asked him who ordered the march. He said that Rossbach had been there and had led the men to the Bürgerbräukeller on orders from His Excellency Ludendorff. I asked: "Why wasn't I told about it? I did not leave the school until about 8:20 p.m." He then told me the resident officers, on orders from His Excellency, were to receive their assignments at 10:00 on the following day at the Infantry School. At around 8:30, there had been several gentlemen to see me to inform me of the plans but, unfortunately, I had not been there.

I then went over to the Commander of the School, General von Tieschowitz of the Cadet Corps, to receive orders and to report what I knew and had heard during the night. While we talked—it may have been between 12:00 and 1:00—Captain Ottenbacher of Course I, who had been sent out to get in touch with Lossow, returned and brought the following news from Lossow: Herrn Lossow, Kahr, and Seisser did not consider themselves bound by the promise in the Bürgerbräukeller because they felt they had been forced to make it and now they were taking countermeasures; and that caution would be necessary if orders were to arrive which appeared to have come from Lossow.

The Commander of the School then gave orders that our cadets were to be brought back. We discussed how best to go about this. Everybody else who was still in the School—resident officers, resident personnel, clerks, and so forth—were to be assembled and brought into the barracks of I 19, where Herrn Kahr, Lossow, and Seisser were waiting. I was supposed to make contact with the 7th Division. When I was just about to walk over there to speak with General Lossow, I met Major Fischer who told me the cadets were to return soon because he had prepared quarters. I then said: It goes without saying that we shall stay here and make sure the cadets are informed.

Afterwards, since the General had already left, I did not meet with him. Shortly after 3:00 a.m., Rossbach returned with the cadets. I had left orders that Rossbach was to see me as soon as he returned with the men. He let me know that he was back, but that he had no time to meet with me. I then went to him. At that time, I met him for the first time. I explained to him that it was my duty, as the senior officer of the School, to clarify matters. He told me I would need permission from His Excellency Ludendorff. I said to him: "Get it!" He went to the telephone and returned a few minutes later saying, "His Excellency did not give his permission." Rossbach then again put the School on alert. From that moment on, I was constantly accompanied by Rossbach's men, one on my right and one on my left. I was told to abstain from attempting to exert any influence on the cadets. Junior grade lieutenants were also led away after they attempted to brief the men.

Nevertheless, I still succeeded in speaking briefly with eight or ten officers. I told them that things were different than they had been presented; that the 7th Division and the Landespolizei opposed the uprising. The result was that approximately more than half the cadets stayed in the Infantry School. One officer then informed me he would march along in order to inform the cadets of this opposition. I actually wanted to occupy the Infantry School with our men, but they were not in the mood to do so. They were so depressed that the best thing then was to allow them to go to their rooms.

I then went to I 19, to General Lossow as well as to Tieschowitz, to report on the situation at the School and on my orders. At the same time, I asked for further orders. Lossow ordered the immediate occupation of the School; that any further rapprochement with the Kampfbund was to be prevented—if necessary, by force.

I returned to the School and ordered its defense, inasmuch as I could get the men together. The Rossbach men had left this building, but were still in the Cadet Corps building. I then ordered that they be compelled, without force, to leave. We succeeded in that about half an hour later. When I stood in the corridor, Major Hühnlein came to me and said he had been sent by His Excellency Ludendorff; that Ludendorff wished to see me—that was a different matter. A guard came in to me and said that Major Hühnlein was there; he would like to talk to me, and to ask me whether he had safe-conduct. I said: "Of course." He entered and I said: "What do you want?" He replied: "Ludendorff is at the Wehrkreiskommando and requests that you come there." I replied, "For what purpose?" He answered that he did not know. I attempted to telephone Lossow to secure his permission, but was not able to reach him. I therefore said: "I will just go there with you; maybe I can accomplish something good."

I was received by Ludendorff shortly after 5:00. His Excellency went with Hitler and I into an adjacent room. There were no other witnesses. His Excellency informed me that last night he had been suddenly asked to come to the Bürgerbräukeller where Kahr was going to speak; and that he had been very much surprised by the situation he found there. He told me he had taken over command of the National Army after the other gentlemen had agreed to take the positions that were assigned to them.

Now he had been here at the Wehrkreiskommando since 11:00 and was waiting for Lossow; but he was not coming. I then said: "I can explain that. He will not come—for we had received the news I mentioned earlier, between 12:00 and 1:00." Now he stated that Lossow having been "forced" was out of the question; that as long as he had been there, no force had been used. I replied that I had heard in conversations with General Hemmer regarding Seisser and Lossow that pistols were used quite a lot. Ludendorff replied that he did not know anything about it; nothing had happened in his presence. I had been told that Herr Hitler had seized an officer's holster and had threatened one of his men with the pistol; but that he had then apologized. Furthermore, I said, I had received confirmation of this first information at the Wehrkreiskommando; and, that between 12:00 and 1:00 I had been told that the gentlemen were not supporting the affair and that troops had been sent to Munich. At that, Ludendorff asked, with great surprise, "What does he want with that?" Then I said: "I do not know it either; I think he wants to restore order."

Now Ludendorff concluded that I was to ask Lossow once again about his views; that I was to tell him Ludendorff was counting on his word of honor; and that I should ask him to come there. The use of force would be out of the question. The National Movement was progressing beautifully and, if he were to oppose it, the entire Movement would be finished.

I told him I did not believe Lossow would change his mind since orders had already gone out to the troops. Hitler then made a long speech, after which he said: You know that I am an idealist and have done nothing else for the past four years but work for the national cause, in the interest of the people. You know I want nothing at all for myself, and that I have done everything only for our people." Naturally, I confirmed at once that I, too, was convinced of this.

I have known Hitler for almost five years. I think it was in the fall of 1919 when he entered my Regiment 41 as a private first class and got a job in the office of the Regiment. I can still remember this period very well. I know that not only was he an exemplary soldier—thus he had a favorable influence on his comrades—but he also gradually helped to bring an excellent spirit into the Regiment, through his patriotic speeches he made before his comrades. At that time, that was not easy, since 500 to 600 officers and students, who served in the Regiment as soldiers, had to be dismissed; and, since the people who stayed were not as hardened against attacks from the left as perhaps they now are. I can certainly say that since that time I have had the most grateful regard for him.

Hitler then continued: "If they destroy my work for which I have lived these four years, then I am also determined to fight for my cause. You know I am not a coward. I have the most enthusiastic people. I wish to impress that upon Lossow. I have expressed my regret—but I do not believe a violent conflict will occur." Furthermore, he said, "If the gentlemen are going to destroy my work, they no longer have a reason for existence." I was to give them this message. I then took my leave and said I would return if I was ordered to do so.

First of all, I went to the School and, between 6:00 and 7:00, I went to Lossow and reported to him. When I had concluded, I asked him whether he had any message. I received the answer: "No." I was then led to Kahr who was in a different room. I also informed him of the main points I had heard during the discussion in the Wehrkreiskommando.

JUDGE NEITHARDT: I would like to return to the events in the Infantry School. What was the general attitude of the cadets regarding this movement?

HERR LEUPOLD: They were very much in favor of the movement and thought that this was the great day of which one had talked and read so much.

JUDGE NEITHARDT: Was this generally expressed?

HERR LEUPOLD: Yes. It was expressed when the conflict between Berlin and Munich between Seeckt and Lossow broke out. At that time I was off on Sundays. The outbreak occurred on a Saturday or Sunday. When I returned on Monday morning, the Commander of the School had spoken with the cadets. Some of them stood in my office and said they were willing to take an oath to the Bavarian Government. Those were non-Bavarians.

I said: "It does not concern you." I then calmed the men

down and reported the matter to the General. The men said they did not see it as a personal conflict, nor as disobedience to Lossow; but, rather, the open expression of deeper conflicts and of differences in their Weltanschauung. Some of the men put on black-white-red cockades. I stopped them for disciplinary reasons, and told them that the time had not yet come when individual men could act on their own. I also told them I had a formal note from Lossow in which he said that, at this point, this act could not yet be accomplished but that he hoped the time would soon come when it could. I informed the cadets of this note in order to calm them down.

JUDGE NEITHARDT: Is Lieutenant Wagner a member of your course? Did you state that in your official report? Didn't you interrogate him?

HERR LEUPOLD: No.

JUDGE NIETHARDT: What do you know of his personal attitude? Did you talk to him?

HERR LEUPOLD: I spoke with him about it afterwards.

JUDGE NEITHARDT: Did you explain to the men that it would mean a change of the constitution if they were to go to the Bürgerbräukeller?

HERR LEUPOLD: I did not know anything about the march to the Bürgerbräukeller.

JUDGE NEITHARDT: Did you find out about it later?

HERR LEUPOLD: I did not talk about it then.

JUDGE NEITHARDT: That is, you had no official order from Lossow to side with him?

HERR LEUPOLD: No.

JUDGE NEITHARDT: He had clearly stated it?

HERR LEUPOLD: It was absolutely clear to me.

JUDGE NEITHARDT: Can you tell us the words Lossow used when speaking to you?

HERR LEUPOLD: He only listened to me. He did not say anything. In the end, I asked him: "Can I report anything? Because I had promised to return." He said: "No."

JUDGE NEITHARDT: Did you tell him what was happening in the Bürgerbräukeller?

HERR LEUPOLD: All the gentlemen who were outside frequently interrupted my report by expressing their disgust about the manner in which he had been treated and about the person who had treated him like that.

JUDGE NEITHARDT: Did he expressly state that he did not go along?

HERR LEUPOLD: He was not going along.

HERR HITLER: May I, perhaps, state that the gentleman who was threatened by me with a pistol was Major Hunglinger. He put his hands in his pocket and I had to assume he wanted to shoot at me. I then threatened him with a pistol myself. Later I said to my other men: "He is the only officer whom I respect." I also said I had no respect for the others. They had acted pitifully; in the end they had broken their word. He was the only officer for whom I had any respect because he stood up against me.

HERR HEMMETER: The Colonel knows that he was liked very much by his cadets. Hence, he was the man who enjoyed, to a certain degree, the general confidence of his subordinates. The Colonel knows that he himself was to be informed. But since you were not there, it could not be done.

In view of the events since the Seeckt-Lossow conflict and because of the orders and intentions expressed by General von Seeckt, of which these young men were aware, don't you think that the Bavarians at the Infantry School had to be convinced that it would not take long until the national uprising would begin in Bavaria and advance from there?

HERR LEUPOLD: Yes, ever since the conflict between Seeckt and Lossow had broken out. Of course—myself included—we only waited for the moment when things would begin to move.

I would like to add something to this. When the Bavarian

officers, in my presence, declared their willingness at the Wehr-kreiskommando to follow Lossow in opposition to the Chief Commander of the Army, we emphasized that this was not to be a Bavarian matter, but a German matter. If it was not to become a German matter, we would not go along. I said we could not limit ourselves to be on the defensive; if a line was to be drawn between Bavaria and the rest of the Reich, we would lose and our role would end. Those were exactly my words—"that we would have to be on the offensive." Nobody said that we would have to march in. I asked: Do we have any connections there? Do we carry on any propaganda?

HERR STENGLEIN: Where was that?

HERR LEUPOLD: That was in a meeting of the senior officers of the District.

Objection by the First Prosecutor.

HERR LEUPOLD: There are two meetings in which I was present. This was during the first meeting.

HERR HEMMETER: That was at the first meeting in October.

HERR LEUPOLD: That was when we declared we would follow Lossow.

HERR HEMMETER: Colonel, are you still convinced that General Lossow was determined, at that time, to take such a step which would have to be considered as a continuation of the policy that began with an act of disobedience?

HERR LEUPOLD: Yes, I am still convinced of it. The abnormal way was also mentioned on November 7th. They said that if the normal way could no longer be taken, one would have to choose the abnormal way. It was also said, however, that the time would be determined not by the Verbände, but by His Excellency von Lossow.

HERR HEMMETER: As long as the Colonel thought that Kahr, Lossow, and Seisser were in agreement with the Kampf-bund leaders, was there any doubt that this was a legal operation?

HERR LEUPOLD: No doubt.

HERR HEMMETER: When you, Colonel, were at the Infantry School, did you ever notice any of the officers showing you any disrespect or disobedience?

HERR LEUPOLD: Never; neither the officers, nor the junior grade officers, nor Rossbach's men. All of them were alike in displaying military discipline.

HERR HEMMETER: There seems to me to be no doubt that, in view of the sympathies enjoyed by you, Colonel, the men would have followed your orders without hesitation. But, so long as you thought Lossow, Kahr, and Seisser were backing the movement, there would have been no need for that.

HERR LEUPOLD: I would have interfered. I would have immediately said that under no circumstances would I permit the Infantry School to be led away by First Lieutenant Rossbach; that my course (cadets) remain under my command; that I am going to look into the situation.

HERR HEMMETER: It is said that during the night, between 12:00 and 1:00, Lieutenant Weckmann came here and met with you, Colonel. Nevertheless, you did not order him to stay; rather, you simply asked: "Well, why wasn't I informed?" You did not order a single cadet to stay until you had received clarifying information?

HERR LEUPOLD: I wasn't even there until then. I could not have given any clarifying information. There was nobody else but First Lieutenant Mai.

HERR HEMMETER: Colonel, I am sure you know that the resident officers had the same views as the cadets; and, that they said that if Lossow began the National Movement in Bavaria, we will go along.

HERR RODER: Colonel, you also mentioned the meeting of November 7?

HERR LEUPOLD: Yes. The meeting of November 6 was discussed at this meeting of November 7.

HERR RODER: His Excellency von Lossow gave you a report about the meeting with Kahr on November 6. Would you please answer the following question: Is it correct, approximately, that

371

Lossow is said to have made the following statements—I am following the statements made by Lieutenant Colonel Pflügel, page 124 of the Court documents—that he was willing to support a right-wing dictatorship; that a coup d'etat in the Reich would have to be undertaken by those who had authority; that it was doubtful whether General Seeckt would find that way; that we, too, aimed for the great goal; however, not under the dictatorship of Hitler, but under a more prospective one? Do you remember some of these words?

HERR LEUPOLD: I think this matter is of such significance that other men should be questioned—the men who took notes of Lossow's statements, because they wanted to discuss it with their officers. That was not necessary for me. I only got into the Infantry School because I was the oldest Bavarian. I did not write anything down. I remember only His Excellency Lossow saying one would have to choose the abnormal way if the normal way could not be taken.

HERR RODER: Lossow is supposed to have said that Kahr had told him on the day before that his views were to the right and that he would demand a Reichsregierung, without a parliament—a Reich dictatorship. Don't you know anything about this, either? Then we shall probably have to go back to Witness Pflügel.

During the first meeting of October 24, His Excellency von Lossow is supposed to have talked about the march to Berlin, but that this plan was to remain secret and hidden under the concept of "inner unrest," or "Fall Maneuver 23." Do you, perhaps, remember that?

HERR LEUPOLD: I would have remembered that. But I don't know the cover words.

HERR RODER: That has been confirmed by someone else.

HERR ZEZSCHWITSCH: Do you remember whether you informed General Tieschowitz about the meeting of November 24, which you just mentioned?

HERR LEUPOLD: Yes, I reported to the General what had been discussed.

HERR ZEZSCHWITSCH: Colonel, did you also take an oath in accordance with Lossow's decree of October 21 and 22?

372

HERR LEUPOLD: No, my course (cadets) did not take an oath, and neither did I.

HERR SCHRAMM: One of the phrases used by the Colonel struck me. That is, when he asked Lossow, he said: "Can I report anything? Because I said I would return." Colonel, when asking His Excellency von Lossow this question, did you in any way indicate that you would go once again to the Wehrkreis-kommando?

HERR LEUPOLD: No, I indicated that.

HERR SCHRAMM: Is it a fact that your Infantry School was also under the control of Lossow? Did the Infantry School ever receive any "Fall Maneuver 23" order?

HERR LEUPOLD: I did not receive it.

HERR SCHRAMM: Colonel, were you at all informed of matters which had to do with the "Fall Maneuver 23"?

HERR LEUPOLD: From talks.

HERR SCHRAMM: Didn't it strike you as odd that the Infantry School did not receive this order?

HERR LEUPOLD: I thought our Commander had received this order.

HERR SCHRAMM: Can one possibly see a connection between the fact that the Infantry School did not receive the "Fall Maneuver 23" order, and the fact that it did not have to take the oath? Doesn't this point to a certain contradiction between the Infantry School and the rest of the Bavarian Army?

HERR LEUPOLD: The Infantry School was not put under oath because it—

HERR SCHRAMM: It is, after all, strange that the Infantry School was not put under oath to the Bavarian Government, nor did it receive the "Fall Maneuver 23" order.

HERR LEUPOLD: I did not consider it strange that I did not receive the order. I assumed that the commander had received it. I probably did not receive many things that the Commander of the School received.

HERR GADEMANN: I would like to ask the witness whether, after the mutiny of Lossow, he ever heard anything—officially or privately—that those in authority thought action would be taken by Berlin against Bavaria? Did anyone ever express any fears with regard to this question?

HERR LEUPOLD: In conversations, such fears were expressed. Officially, I was not informed of it. They did not think that such an event would occur.

HERR KRIEBEL: I would like to make a brief statement. The cover word, "inner unrest," was mentioned in a meeting at which the Colonel was not present. That was the meeting of October 24, to which Lossow had been invited along with his closest staff and the military leaders of the patriotic bands. The Colonel could not give any information about it because he was not present at the time.

HERR LUETGEBRUNE: Is it correct to say that as a result of your talk with Ludendorff you were to drive out to General Lossow and to negotiate with him?

HERR LEUPOLD: Not to "negotiate" with him; but to report to him what I had heard. I considered myself a middleman, a messenger, a carrier of orders.

HERR LUETGEBRUNE: Captain Kürschner says he had spoken with you and you had said you would drive to Lossow and negotiate with him. The question is whether Ludendorff was led to expect that he could hear something definite concerning Lossow's attitude.

HERR LEUPOLD: I expected to be able to bring back a decision.

HERR LUETGEBRUNE: You would definitely have returned to Ludendorff if, upon your report, you had not received such a clear "no," from Lossow?

HERR LUDENDORFF: The Colonel probably remembers me telling him I would not shoot. I also remember that at exactly that moment you promised to tell Lossow that we did not want to shoot. When you told me that Lossow was assembling Reichswehr from outside, I said I did not find that very nice, since

General Lossow knew that we did not want to fight or to shoot. I don't know—do you still recall that?

HERR LEUPOLD: Yes.

HERR LUDENDORFF: In any case, I think you received the impression that any use of force was out of the question.

Colonel, you just said that Rossbach had mentioned an order from me. You did not talk to me about the Infantry School at all. If Rossbach had discussed this with me, I could have easily said this discussion did not take place; nor do I think Rossbach will testify that he had called me up but had not received my permission.

HERR LEUPOLD: I think Rossbach abused the name of Your Excellency. I said that when I asked the gentlemen in the barracks—that was between 3:00 and 4:00; the staff was sitting at their desks working—"What is going to happen now? Will any measures be taken against the Wehrkreiskommando?" I was told, "No, since His Excellency Ludendorff is not going to shoot." I reported this to Your Excellency. Your Excellency then replied—I can recall this very well—"In that case, it is not logical if he assembles the troops now. What are the troops supposed to do?"

HERR ZEZSCHWITSCH: As far as I know, Colonel, you are part of the 8th Infantry Regiment. In the evening, from November 8 to November 9, a closed meeting took place of former members of the 8th Infantry Regiment. You were present when General von Hemmer appeared. Did General Hemmer report about the events, saying he was happy that the operation was now taking place?

HERR LEUPOLD: Yes. He came at about 10:30 with fresh impressions from the Bürgerbräukeller. He was still somewhat dazed by the whole thing and just very quickly briefed me. He asked me what I would do if I were in Lossow's place. I said I would have waited for this moment. Now things had finally begun to roll—even though the bomb had exploded a little too early. In any case, it would be impossible to oppose it now.

HERR HOLL: Do you know anything about the decree of the Reichswehrministerium prohibiting any cooperation of the Reichswehr with the so-called "illegal Verbände"?

HERR LEUPOLD: I don't know anything about it.

HERR HOLL: Then I direct my question to General von Tieschowitz.

HERR TIESCHOWITZ: I also know nothing of it. I never received anything.

HERR LEUPOLD: We did not take this matter seriously at all.

JUDGE NEITHARDT: I think the position of the cadets has been sufficiently explained by these two witnesses. I believe the matter is completely clear. It would be a waste of time to interrogate further witnesses. In my opinion, we can do without all the other witnesses.

HERR HEMMETER: I agree, but the witnesses we have questioned are witnesses for the prosecution.

JUDGE NEITHARDT: The Prosecutor would like to see Witness Block.

HERR HEMMETER: I would like to delay the testimony of Witness Block, not because of the Infantry School, but for other reasons. I suppose the Prosecutor wants the questioning of Witness Block with regard to the visit of Ludendorff. I would refrain from questioning the witness at all. I do not need him for the Infantry School.

JUDGE NEITHARDT: I think we can let it go at that. It would only introduce a number of details which I do not consider necessary. I would abstain, if the prosecution abstains.

HERR LUDENDORFF: Block said that I had spoken of a blue-white danger. That is my special concern. Other than that, I have no questions. If the decision of the Court is firm, I have no other wishes.

JUDGE NEITHARDT: I do not consider it necessary.

HERR LUDENDORFF: Then I am not interested in it, either.

HERR STENGLEIN: I thought it was not only the visit with Ludendorff that was of interest — I personally wanted to find out which position the Infantry School had taken towards the Generalstaatskommissariat. It is my understanding that Block was present.

HERR HEMMETER: I do not support this interrogation. It is insignificant in view of the fact that it has been previously determined that Wagner did not participate in it. If the Court considers it necessary to receive proof of it, it may question the witness; it is meaningless for Wagner.

JUDGE NEITHARDT: I think it is absolutely superfluous.

HERR STENGLEIN: The prosecution abstains.

JUDGE NEITHARDT: Do you abstain from hearing other witnesses, too?

Affirmed.

JUDGE NEITHARDT: I then request the witnesses to enter the courtroom.

The witnesses enter.

JUDGE NEITHARDT: I would like to inform the witnesses that both the prosecution and the defense have abstained from interrogating them.

The hearing of the witnesses, for this morning, has been concluded. I suggest we continue this afternoon at 2:30 p.m.

Whereupon, at 11:36 a.m., the hearing is recessed, to reconvene at 2:30 p.m., the same day.

—AFTERNOON SESSION—

At the afternoon session, the witnesses will be called in connection with the case of Dr. Frick.

Beforehand, Herr Holl begins a statement in which he notes that according to the testimony of Captain Röhm, Lieutenant Casella said, before he died, that he had been shot by First Lieutenant Braun. Now we read in No. 31 of the Grossdeutsche Zeitung *that on March 3, 1924, Lieutenant Berchem gave a speech to his Battalion in which he spoke of Braun as an excellent officer, and that he defended him from the charges raised by Captain Röhm. Berchem claimed that until his death Casella never used the word "Braun." Berchem also added that he wanted Röhm known as a common liar, until he retracted his slander. The soldiers were also encouraged to slap any civilian across the face if he slandered Braun; then, he would think twice before making such a statement again.*

Herr Schramm remarks, in connection with this article, that he considers this depiction so monstrous that he would like to assume, for Lieutenant Colonel von Berchem's sake, that the description in this form is untrue.

HERR SCHRAMM: But, if it is true, then it can't be condemned enough. There exists but one witness who heard the words from the dying Casella's lips, which Röhm has repeated. This witness is a member of the Reichskreigsflagge. Casella died neither in Lieutenant Colonel von Berchem's, nor in Braun's arms, nor in the arms of a member of the Reichskreigsflagge. There is no way Lieutenant Colonel von Berchem can know whether Röhm's assertion is true. It is incomprehensible how Berchem comes to the conclusion that Captain Röhm's claim is not only objectively untrue, but also brands him with the reproach, "common liar." I expect that Lieutenant Colonel von Berchem will hastily deny this description of the facts. If he neglects to recognize the truth of this description, then Captain Röhm will know how to obtain satisfaction from Lieutenant

Colonel Berchem in the way most fitting for him. Besides that, an article has appeared in the *Augsburger Zeitung* in which a rifleman, Hans Kappler, feels it is his duty to shield First Lieutenant Braun. Captain Röhm doesn't feel compelled to comment on these statements.

Hereupon, Judge Neithardt reveals a letter which Colonel Hitzelsberger of the 19th Infantry Regiment sent to the Tribunal.

JUDGE NEITHARDT: Basically, it reads:

> "As Commandant of the 19th Infantry Regiment, I wish to address myself to the defense of my subordinate officer, First Lieutenant Braun. Lieutenant Casella did not die at the hands of First Lieutenant Braun. Braun did not fire one shot. Nor did he say, 'I am a soldier; that's what I'm paid for.' A number of witnesses can verify what was actually said. Professor Adolph Schmidt, who stood by Lieutenant Casella a quarter-hour before his death, confirmed that Lieutenant Casella did not mention Braun's name to him. First Lieutenant Braun fought in the World War from beginning to end, distinguished himself as an excellent, courageous officer, and was wounded five times."

Testimony of Oberregierungsrat Tenner

The first witness, Supreme Councillor of State Tenner of Police Headquarters, is questioned regarding the character of Oberamtmann Frick and the nature of his political persuasions. The witness cites his long relationship with Frick since they both belong to the same organization. From conversations with Frick, he had gotten the impression that Frick stood on the Right, and that he knew the leading lights of the German Nationalist Movement, as a result of his activities in the Political Division. From political talks he had with Frick, Tenner never got the impression that Frick would join a movement which was working toward a violent overthrow of the constitution; nor did he have any indication that Frick had prior knowledge that a putsch had been planned for November 8.

HERR TENNER: I have already testified that in the latter half of October the Police President informed me he had learned from the Political Division that a certain report had been discussed. The report detailed which men should become leaders of the Movement, in the event of a political upheaval, and in the course of the discussion the viewpoint was expressed: Herr Frick would be considered for the post of Police President; or he had already declared himself ready to assume that position. Police President Mantel said this information had not been verified and thus he would not undertake anything on the basis of hearsay. He couldn't believe Frick was capable of such an action which he termed "hostile," to him.

President Mantel wanted to gather more information, beyond this session, and only then would he call Frick to his office.

JUDGE NEITHARDT: You did not obtain more evidence that could be corroborated in this regard?

HERR TENNER: No.

Herr Tenner states that he learned nothing more about security measures planned for the Bürgerbräukeller assembly. He himself was at a theater. When he came home, his wife told him Police Secretary Rau had called to say that Hitler's revolution had broken out at the Bürgerbräukeller. The witness then called Police Headquarters where Herr Rau gave him a brief synopsis of the events in the Bürgerbräukeller and said that Pöhner had been appointed Minister President, and Dr. Frick, Police President. The witness then reports on a meeting with Pöhner and Frick in the passageway at Headquarters, immediately before their nocturnal trip to Kahr's. The witness divulges his knowledge of the press conference at Police Headquarters, and testifies that he was called to Headquarters the next morning, at 6:00, where he was informed that Pöhner and Frick had been arrested on the orders of the Generalstaatskommissar. In response to a question, Herr Tenner answers that Herr Rau filled him in about 10:00 at night.

JUDGE NEITHARDT: In your estimation, would Frick have been obliged to inform you since you are a representative of the Police President?

HERR TENNER: In my opinion, yes. It is customary to inform the deputy, if the Director is not in.

JUDGE NEITHARDT: Who would do this?

HERR TENNER: Whoever found out first.

JUDGE NEITHARDT: You have no grounds to believe that Dr. Frick obtained prior knowledge of the action?

HERR TENNER: No.

HERR RODER: If Herr Frick and the duty official are in a room at the same time, and people come in and report that such-and-such has happened, who is obliged to notify your superior—the duty official, or Herr Frick, who just happens to be there?

HERR TENNER: One can't really speak of "accidentally being there," if it is the Chief of Police. He is in charge of the duty assignments. He is superior to the duty official. The functions of the duty official are transferred to the Chief of Police, if he is present.

The Witness further states, in response to Herr Roder's question, that the expert takes over the business of the duty official only insofar as he gets involved with the duties of the official. If the duty official knows that a police specialist has learned of events of great import, then the official can assume that the specialists will take charge of the matter. Herr Tenner also remarks that it can't be said that the duty official is released from his obligation to inform the proper authorities nor is the specialist absolved of his duty. The Witness emphasizes:

HERR TENNER: I don't view the fact that Herr Frick did not notify me as positive proof that he didn't want to notify me, or that he wanted to keep me in the dark. Sometimes, in one's haste, one overlooks the obvious.

HERR RODER: Herr Frick went to Captain Stumpf and probably left the telephone calls to a subordinate official. If one knows this, one can then speak of dereliction of duty because he didn't notify you?

HERR TENNER: It is a general question of official protocol that one notifies one's superior. I can't answer the question of whether we are dealing with dereliction of duty. He could have assumed I would be informed by another party; in fact, that is what happened.

HERR RODER: Would the course of events have been altered if Herr Frick had notified you? You were not there?

HERR TENNER: No.

Testimony of Regierungsrat Bernreuther

State Councillor Bernreuther, Chief of the Political Division, is questioned as the next witness.

JUDGE NEITHARDT: Perhaps you can tell us something about Herr Frick's political persuasion?

HERR BERNREUTHER: As far as I know, Oberamtmann Frick did not belong to any political party during the time we worked together—that would be from February 20 to September 21—but I knew he was a staunch Rightist and that he actively disliked Parliamentarianism. His relations with the National Socialists dated from that time. Hitler visited him two or three times.

JUDGE NEITHARDT: At the end of October, a message was forwarded to you that Herr Frick was to be appointed Police President at an assembly in the event of a coup d'etat?

HERR BERNREUTHER: There was a meeting of the Kampfbund on Schellingstrasse. At the conference, individual men were nominated in case there was an overthrow by the Right. As far as I recall, Pöhner was nominated for Minister of the Interior and Frick for Police President. The report was passed on to the Police President. He ordered a check on the report. For certain reasons which I refuse to reveal, this could not occur.

JUDGE NEITHARDT: Do you know anything about Herr Frick's dereliction of duty?

HERR BERNREUTHER: I was kept in the dark and only subsequently heard about those things. I was seized after the ministers in the Bürgerbräukeller. The matter is: If a police official receives such a report, it is his duty to do everything that can be done. In this case, I would have alerted the Green Police, but I wouldn't have sent them in. I would then have alerted the Municipal Commandant on account of the Reichswehr. Of course I would have alerted the Security Squad and the personnel of Internal Affairs as far as that was possible. What happened, in fact, I do not know.

In response to another question by the Judge, the Witness states he considered it right and proper that Herr Balss carried on the business of the Political Division. Then the Witness describes his impressions in the Bürgerbräukeller up to his arrest:

HERR BERNREUTHER: We were guarded by four, later six men armed with rifles and automatic weapons. We were told we would be taken out during the night. We were requested to write down our addresses so our immediate families could be notified. This last order only partially took place.

I got into a car with Minister Wutzlhofer. We drove out on Rosenheimerstrasse to the Lehmann villa on Holzkirchnerstrasse. Each man was shown to a separate room. First, I went into Herr Lehmann's bedroom; then his library; and later to Herr Hühn's room. I received a reclining chair and a sleeping bag for the night. We were treated well. Herr Lehmann gave us tea in the evening, breakfast in the morning, and lunch. That afternoon, Herr Lehmann, with a mien heavy with worry, told me: there had been a setback; the Reichswehr had fired upon a parade through the city; Ludendorff was dead; Hitler had been shot in the head; Ludendorff's stepson and Dr. Weber had been decapitated by machine-gune fire. That afternoon, the villa was fortified for a last stand. Herr Lehmann said, after our whereabouts were discovered, the Reichswehr would free us. That afternoon we were herded into one room; we were able to drink coffee together. At 5:30, the lights went out not only in our room, but also on the street. We heard people in the garden. Herr Lehmann came up to our room and said he would now take steps to let us out—we only had to be careful of the sentry. After a while, several police officials arrived and let us out. Herr Lehmann revealed to us that the sentry had left his post over an hour ago—but an hour had not passed between our last conversation with him and our rescue. We then went to the nearest police station.

JUDGE NEITHARDT: Do you have reason to believe that Herr Frick had prior knowledge of the events of the evening of November 8?

HERR BERNREUTHER: I can't say, exactly. That afternoon he was in Section VI and asked if we were going to the assembly. We said we were.

In response to Herr Götz's question, Herr Bernreuther states that Frick had asked Balss, in the course of the evening, about the security measures and asked whether necessary preparations had been made.

HERR GÖTZ: Was this inquiry something out of the ordinary?

HERR BERNREUTHER: It frequently happened that someone would inquire as to whether this or that action had been taken.

HERR RODER: Did you sense something behind Frick's question about whether you were going to the Bürgerbräukeller?

HERR BERNREUTHER: I didn't suspect anything. It was a perfectly normal question. There had been a lot of talk about the assembly.

HERR RODER: Where did the information that Frick was prospective Police President come from?

HERR BERNREUTHER: It was a message from the Police News Agency where we receive a certain amount of news.

HERR RODER: Then it was an informant's tip?

HERR BERNREUTHER: I don't like to use that expression. It wasn't an official bulletin.

HERR RODER: Then it came from an outsider. It was impossible to check its veracity?

HERR BERNREUTHER: No.

HERR RODER: In your opinion, did Frick exert influence on the Police News Agency that evening?

HERR BERNREUTHER: No.

HERR RODER: Did he influence the preparations and preventive measures?

HERR BERNREUTHER: No.

HERR KOHL: Would it have been possible for the prosecution eventually to learn from you Erhardt's whereabouts?

HERR BERNREUTHER: No.

HERR KOHL: Have you been acquainted with the person who sent the aforementioned message for a long time?

HERR BERNREUTHER: I refuse to answer that because I have not been released from my security clearance.

HERR KOHL: Then the supposition that it was a Herr Weber is not totally insupportable?

HERR ZEZSCHWITSCH: Money that was earmarked by General Ludendorff for charities was simply taken away. Did the order come from the Police or from the Generalstaatskommissariat?

HERR BERNREUTHER: The supervision was ordered by the Generalstaatskommissariat and carried out by the Police. All money earmarked for the National Socialist Party was to be forfeited. This money has been confiscated, but not forfeited.

HERR ZEZSCHWITSCH: Do you know that a check for over $250 for the Schlageter Memorial Fund is being withheld?

HERR BERNREUTHER: This sum is still at Police Headquarters.

HERR ZEZSCHWITSCH: Why wasn't it returned?

HERR BERNREUTHER: That escapes me.

HERR EHARD: Is the Witness aware that in the circles which later united into the Kampfbund there were efforts to expedite a violent action against the government, long before September?

HERR BERNREUTHER: I don't know about "long before September," but I do know in September documents were found in the course of a search of papers at the Party Bureau, or at the *Völkischer Beobachter*, alluding to it.

HERR HITLER: Are you aware of the reasons for the formation of the Generalstaatskommissariat?

HERR BERNREUTHER: Not all of them. The Staatskommissariat was formed in due course on account of the threat of a rightest putsch as early as September.

HERR HITLER: Is the Witness aware that Minister President

Knilling later declared that the reason was fear of a putsch arising from the 14 assemblies?

HERR BERNREUTHER: No. Scheubner-Richter was asked at the Generalstaatskommissariat: "If it comes to a putsch as a result of these 14 assemblies, what then?" Scheubner-Richter assured them there would be no putsch. If, however, something did develop out of the assemblies, they wouldn't oppose it; they'd join it.

HERR HITLER: Were there any precautionary measures that would go into effect if the assemblies had resulted in a putsch?

HERR BERNREUTHER: Of course an attempt could have been made, but I do believe it would have been suppressed.

HERR HITLER: Do you think that important men such as Herr Kahr, or the Police President, would have been present at these 14 assemblies?

HERR BERNREUTHER: I can't say, but I don't think so.

Herr Holl asks the Witness whether he remembers that he (Holl) had spoken at an assembly of the District Patriotic Leagues and emphasized that if the Red wave crests over North Germany, Bavaria would not capsize? The Witness states this is possible, and acknowledges in response to another question that Herr Kahr also participated in this assembly.

Regierungsrat Werberger

Councillor of State Werberger, of Police Headquarters, states that Herr Frick, in the course of a meeting which Regierungsrat Balss also attended, inquired about the security measures that had been taken for that evening at the Bürgerbräukeller assembly. Herr Balss replied that, since nothing out of the ordinary was anticipated, a 100-man detachment had been dispatched. The subject of taking stiffer action against usurers was also debated. There was no talk of a putsch. In response to the Judge's question of whether he has reason to believe Frick had prior knowledge of the overthrow attempt, the witness says he does not know; there was nothing unusual about him.

HERR RODER: How did you perceive the formation of the new government in the Bürgerbräukeller? Did you think everything had transpired legally?

HERR WERBERGER: I had the impression that after the Generalstaatskommissar, who essentially controlled all executive power, had cast his lot with Hitler, I had no reason to stay on the sidelines.

The Witness states further that he can't remember whether the appointment of Frick as Police President was mentioned at all at an assembly on October 23. Only once was there a so-called "rap-session" in which role assignation was discussed. He cannot remember with any certainty whether Frick was to get a leading position.

HERR HITLER: Were you informed that, by reason of our 14 assemblies, we were on the brink of a putsch?

HERR WERBERGER: I can only remember that the question of banning the assemblies was discussed and that we made adjustments for the possibility that the assemblies could be used to disrupt order.

In reply to another question, whether the danger seemed so great that it necessitated the establishment of the Generalstaats-kommissariat, the Witness disclaims his competence to answer that.

Testimony of Regierungsrat Balss

The next Witness, Councillor of State Balss, Specialist in the Political Division at Police Headquarters, states:

HERR BALSS: I was at the Bürgerbräukeller on the evening of November 8. Before I left for the assembly, Herr Frick came up to me and we discussed whether he was going. He asked me who was attending from Section VI. We had decided earlier that all the specialists would attend the assembly. Herr Frick asked me: "What do you think of this evening's assembly?" Herr Kahr was in the process of giving his speech. I said, "I think very little will be achieved with this speech." Frick said: "I don't know if I'll go." Then we talked generally about the state of the nation, about the general dissatisfaction.

Herr Balss states he has nothing to contribute to the description of events at the assembly in the Bürgerbräukeller as they have appeared in the press. According to him, the atmosphere was very tense right from the start, when Hitler forced his way in, since no one knew what Hitler had in mind and whether this entrance was aimed at the assembly or Excellency von Kahr. As he recalls, Balss thinks he said to Pöhner: "Herr Pöhner, you are well known; it will be easy for you to create order."

Then the Witness Balss saw how the Cabinet Ministers, the Police President, and Herr Bernreuther were led from the hall. The Witness testifies that, in the hall, he didn't see anyone of an opposing opinion or who didn't join in the jubilation—at least not around him. The first thing he did when he was able to leave the hall was to return to Police Headquarters. As a specialist in Section VI, he knew for certain that there was much to do that night. And so he went with Lieutenant Colonel Schlichtegroll to Police Headquarters.

The Witness reports on the following events.

HERR BALSS: The office was already open. I went at once to the Presidium to see who was there. When I entered, I saw Herr Pöhner and Herr Frick. I can still remember—I forget the exact words he used—Herr Pöhner saying to Herr Frick something like: From now on, you are in charge of the Police Presidium. I do this in accord with, or in the name of—I can't remember which—Excellency von Kahr. I looked Herr Frick right in the eye and noticed that he was startled at this transfer of power. I don't know what his rejoinder was but, in any case, I do remember he expressed his joy. I have already mentioned his astonishment. He disclaimed feeling like the Police President. I vaguely remember Herr Frick saying President Mantel had been arrested, but that he would return; if Pöhner and Kahr so wished, he would do it.

In any case, the Witness did not get the impression that Herr Frick considered his appointment a beneficence.

HERR BALSS: Neither in the evening, nor in the early morning, as long as we were together did he bill himself as Police President; nor did he permit himself to be addressed as such. I always called him "Herr Oberamtmann," never "Herr President." Frick then asked me, "Where is Bernreuther?" Whereupon, I explained that he had been arrested. One of the two men—I believe it was Supreme Court Councillor Pöhner—replied, "Good, then take him to Section VI." I said that that was why I had come; my duty had obliged me to. I still remember, when he arrived in the foyer, Colonel Banzer's extreme agitation and his words to Herr Pöhner: "Release me at once from the custody of this man!" Pöhner thereupon looked sharply at Colonel Banzer and the other officer and asked the Colonel: "Can I rely on you and your men without fail?" Banzer snapped to attention and said, as he shook Pöhner's hand: "Herr President, absolutely and unconditionally!" Then Pöhner winked at the First Lieutenant and said, "You can go!"

JUDGE NEITHARDT: What time was that?

HERR BALSS: Right at the beginning. It seems to me I arrived at Police Headquarters around the same time Herr Pöhner and Frick did, because I would assume that Pöhner's first act would have been to ask Herr Frick to take over the Police Presidium. Next, either Herr Pöhner or Herr Frick—I can't recall which one—commissioned me to assemble the members of the press; they wanted to inform the press of the sudden change and to warn them to write only what the government would approve, no criticism or sarcastic comments.

The Witness mentions Pöhner's and Frick's trip to Kahr and reports on the press conference.

HERR BALSS: While Pöhner and Frick were with Kahr, I received a call from the Nürnberg Police. My colleague, Herr Schachinger, was on the line and I related to him what had happened. To which he said: "That's strange, because our Reichswehr is prepared to march to Munich." I could say only that everything was just the way I had told him.

In the meantime, I telephoned the Generalstaatskommissariat. Major Döhla answered the phone. When I told him about the report from Nürnberg, he evasively said: "No, they're coming from Passau." I asked him why, and the connection was broken off. At that point, I didn't have any suspicions that something was going on behind the scenes. Later, however, I informed Frick and Pöhner of this development. It was only in connection with the fruitless search for General von Lossow and von Seisser that I mentioned the information concerning the fact that the Nürnberg conversation and the missing men seemed strange. At that, Herr Pöhner, I believe, said: "What? Are you beginning to have doubts? Excellency von Kahr has given his word." I thought nothing more of it.

Various reports about the looting and vandalism at the

389

Münchener Post, the events in the Bavaria Quarter, and of some other disturbances came in during the night. There was a lot to do. By this time it was 3:00. I drove home in a police car. I had just gotten home when the phone rang. Commissioner Herrmann asked me whether Kahr's proclamation should be posted. I remembered, from the press conference, that Kahr did not plan to post any proclamation. I therefore said: "Are you sure it's from Kahr? Who signed it?" Herrmann answered: "Kahr himself." Since I knew Kahr used only German script, I asked: "German or Latin letters?" Herrmann said: "Latin." So, I replied: "This isn't right. Try to reach Herr Pöhner or Herr Frick." Herrmann called me back to say he was able to locate Pöhner—in the Wehrkreiskommando, I think—and Pöhner had said that the proclamation must not be posted. Herrmann pleaded with me to come at once; he was now completely lost as to what to do. When I arrived I was immediately informed that Pöhner and Frick had been arrested. Since I was present at the Bürgerbräukeller and since I had thought—there was no doubt in my mind—that the gentlemen's declarations were sincere, this news naturally shook me deeply.

HERR RODER: You considered Pöhner and Kahr to be the bearers of actual legal power?

HERR BALSS: Yes.

HERR HITLER: Was a report sent by the Polizei to the government stating that the 14 assemblies were to be used for a putsch and that therefore the establishment of a Generalstaatskommissariat was necessary?

HERR BALSS: I know nothing of that.

HERR HITLER: Wouldn't you have had to see it if a report regarding an imminent putsch had gone to the government?

HERR BALSS: Undoubtedly. The formation of a Generalstaatskommissariat does not dispose of a threatened putsch.

HERR HITLER: In the event the Polizei were absolutely positive that a political leader wanted to foment a coup d'etat in the form of a putsch, this leader would be arrested. Would that be correct?

The Witness affirms this.

HERR RODER: Frick went to Captain Stumpf. Do you consider that a higher priority than telephoning?

HERR BALSS: Certainly. I believe what Frick didn't do is meritorious. I must say: "Thank God, Frick didn't sound the alarm," otherwise, there would undoubtedly have been a bloodbath.

HERR HEMMETER: You are probably aware that extremely cordial relations had existed between Pöhner and Kahr since 1920. When you arrived at Police Headquarters on the evening of November 8, would you have thought it possible that Kahr could find it in himself to deceive his long-standing friend and coworker by having told him nothing of his change of heart?

HERR BALSS: When two men have cooperated so intensively and intimately as Pöhner and Kahr, then of course I consider it unexpected. I noticed at the press conference that Herr Pöhner and Herr Frick appeared to be very satisfied upon their return from the meeting with Kahr. Pöhner discounted my tentative hint that a connection could possibly exist between the troop alert in Nürnberg and the fact that Lossow and Seisser could not be located; and that, consequently, we might deduce from that that something just might be wrong.

In response to Herr Ehard's question, the Witness testifies:

HERR BALSS: The Bürgerbräukeller was surrounded by members of the Kampfbund. If a weak force in the form of a 100-man detachment had advanced, then either they would have been disarmed or they would have broken through, or a gun would have gone off and a gunfight would have been started. If a larger contingent had been sent out that night, the situation then could have and would have developed into a bloodbath. The Bürgerbräukeller was jam-packed with people. If they had heard shooting outside, the panic would have been horrible.

HERR EHARD: If I understand you correctly, you are saying you considered it proper not to send in the mustered forces. Were you of the opinion that an alarm should not have been given at all?

HERR BALSS: That is something entirely different—but I never would have done it alone. I would have conferred with the duty officer.

391

HERR EHARD: You heard the declarations at the Bürgerbräu-keller. Did you assume that Hitler was to take over the post of Reich Chancellor? Or that he wanted only to be the "drummer" of some movement?

HERR BALSS: That he wanted to become Reich Chancellor, no. In patriotic circles the word was that it would be nice if Kahr would accept Hitler as the "drummer." I also thought he should beat the drum for the movement; obviously, he didn't.

HERR HITLER: In the first hour of these proceedings I stated that we were dealing with a struggle; and I will assume the leadership in this struggle. The squaring of accounts with the November criminals remains a proviso for me, if not now then in the near future, Herr Prosecutor.

Stirring in the courtroom.

HERR KOHL: Did you or did you not assume Kahr was with the Movement?

HERR BALSS: One must differentiate two sets of circum-stances. If it is reported to me that squads are advancing on the Bürgerbräukeller, and I am uninformed as to what's afoot, then I have an obligation to see what I can do to divert these people who may have something up their sleeves. If, on the other hand, I know that Kahr, Lossow, and Seisser have joined them, then I wouldn't do anything at all. I have then only to apprise the traffic police and order them to let the streetcars run, and so forth. The rest wouldn't bother me; the moment I learned that the highest bearer of executive power was cooperating, then it goes without saying that I would obey. I said right away to Herr Frick: "If you want to stop the Polizei, then your first task is to see that the Polizei are directed by Police Headquarters, and no one else. If Ludendorff reorganizes the Army, then the soldiers belong in the barracks and not running around with unslung rifles as they did during the Soviet period." The men agreed with me and declared they would countermand that.

In response to another question from Herr Kohl, Balss states he does not know where Erhardt is. Amid gales of laughter in the courtroom, Herr Kohl himself answers.

HERR KOHL: Erhardt is on the fourth floor of the Ring Hotel.

The Witness explains that of course the Polizei would have had to look him up if the prosecution had issued a warrant.

In response to Herr Luetgebrune's question, Herr Balss states, once again, that he thought when Hitler stormed into the hall, a crippling fear settled over the assembly.

HERR BALSS: If Herr Kahr, after this business was over, had declared: "I won't do it," they might have abducted him and the rest of the Cabinet Ministers, but nothing would have happened. Later it was revealed to me that Lossow and Seisser lectured the officers gathered in Munich on November 6 and 7. To what end I do not know. I always thought that if the organs of power—the Polizei and the Reichswehr—were instructed to act along certain lines, then it would not matter if the Generalstaatskommissar was arrested as a civilian. Then the organs of power would have done the right thing. Only one thing strikes me as strange: The Generalstaatskommissar did not send for the presidents from Munich and from Nürnberg and did not inform them of the situation. Kahr could then have let himself be arrested. If Kahr had been adamant, I can't see how there could have been a bloodbath.

HERR HEMMETER: Were you personally surprised by the speeches made by the three men, or did you recognize in them the keystone of their prior conduct? Were you aware that these men also intended to march on Berlin?

HERR BALSS: Kahr was doing something there that bound the Bavarian Reichswehr, by oath, to Bavaria; this led me to believe that other actions would take place—otherwise this act would have been pointless. When I went to the Bürgerbräukeller, and Hitler stormed in, I didn't get the impression that the three gentlemen were taking the final logical steps that their previous behavior had dictated. Later, however, when the men gave their speeches, I said to myself: Now this is an extension of the commitment they took in pledging the Bavarian Reichswehr.

HERR HOLL: Did you know that the Reich Court issued a warrant for the arrests of Lieutenant Commanders Erhardt, Rossbach, and Heiss? Do you know who refused to carry out, or uphold the execution of this order? Was it the Generalstaatskommissar, the Minister of the Interior, or both? Did the Polizei know about it?

HERR BALSS: I must refuse to answer that.

HERR HOLL: Now I know it was not inhibited by the Polizei but, rather, by a higher office.

Testimony of Oberkommissar Kiefer

The Witness, Police Commissioner Kiefer, who gave orders to the 30 guards at the Bürgerbräukeller, describes in detail the observations he made there. He testifies that, after Hitler's troops arrived at the hall—which he had been checking out—he tried in vain to return to his squad at the entrance. When he asked, in the foyer, what was going on, he was told: "Just wait a few moments; you'll see soon enough. The Nationalist Government will be proclaimed."

HERR KIEFER: I noticed that something wasn't right; something wasn't on the program. I went back to the coat-room and was about to enter the kitchen to notify the Polizei by telephone, but the kitchen was locked. I went back to the exit where the ranks of armed men were swelling. I presented my credentials as a police official to a man near me, and called to his attention that I was there on official business. I said they should let me out so I could get in touch with my security team. This man told me I should direct my request to the man in uniform just then walking by, Captain Göring. I presented my request to Captain Göring. He listened to me quietly and then said: "Wait until 8:40, then Frick will be here."

I had absolutely no idea what was going on. Another gentleman, in civilian clothes, pulled out his watch and said it was already 8:40. I was able to make my way to the exit, and from the station at Weissenburgerplatz, I tried to telephone Section VI at Police Headquarters. I was finally connected with the duty room and I asked Commissioner Haberl if, indeed, the Polizei already knew of the incident. He replied that no one knew anything there. Then I was able to speak with Herr Frick, who countered my questions with his questions about the size of the security team and the kind of weapons the men had at the Bürgerbräukeller. At the end of the conversation, he said to me: "You really won't be able to do anything." I told him I was completely powerless; I could not cross through their lines again, and I was cut off from the security team. I didn't learn of anything else.

Testimony of Wachtmeister Bücks

The Witness, Police Sergeant Bücks, who attended the assembly as a private citizen and reached as far as the foyer, was able to observe how the ministers were abducted. He testifies that he and three other people, including two police officials in street clothes, were ordered not to leave the foyer or else they would face dire consequences.

HERR BÜCKS: We went up to a Major in the Green Police and requested permission to withdraw from the foyer. On this occasion, I heard the startling news: "The City is in safe hands; the Polizei, too." When I asked whose hands—I asked because I had also seen Police President Mantel being taken away—he rejoined: "Herr Frick is in charge of the Police Presidium."

When Judge Neithardt asks what he has to say about this, or previous testimony, Herr Frick remarks that the witnesses so far seem to be convinced that he would obey the call.

Testimony of Herr Hoffmann

Sales Representative Matthäus Hoffmann, former Sergeant at Police Headquarters, was questioned on the assumption that he conveyed the telephone message, "successfully delivered," to Herr Frick from the Löwenbräukeller. He denies this and states that just because the name, "Hoffmann," was there, it doesn't mean he was the midwife of everything. He has never made a secret of his affiliation with the National Socialists; because of this he has incurred many disadvantages in the service; but he didn't sign a commitment to the Republic. He ripped it up, because he could swear only one oath, the one that he had made to his King.

HERR KRIEBEL: I would just like to state that this gentleman is not "Report Chief Hofmann."

HERR HOFFMANN: I accompanied Hitler all through the night, and from my observations it is obvious that there was absolutely no intention of offering any resistance whatsoever against the government. At the Wehrkreiskommando, I could hear through the thin door how Hitler, Pöhner, and Ludendorff were discussing only propaganda in the next room. In the morning, I was at Ludwig Bridge. As the Landespolizei marched up on the other side, an overzealous junior officer jumped out at Göring and Brückner and shouted: "Are we going to fire?" Brückner replied: "For God's sake, if they advance, we'll retreat slowly."

In response to Herr Schramm's question of whether First Lieutenant von Godin said: "There's going to be a battle royal; every shot must count," the Witness states he heard that from a police official who, in turn, heard it from someone else.

Testimony of Kriminalkommissar Werner

The Witness, Crime Commissioner Werner, reports on the Reichskreigsflagge assembly at the Löwenbräukeller on November 8, to which he and his son, a member of the Reichskreigsflagge, were invited. After Esser had embarked on one of his speech's many digressions, a chauffeur burst in from the rear and whispered to the men sitting at the speaker's table. Werner sat at a nearby table and he strained to listen. Röhm and his staff got to their feet. Hoffmann heard that the government had been deposed and a new government set up. He turned to the merchant, Zeller, and said: "If you let me borrow your car, I'll try to find out what's going on." Röhm agreed. As Werner made ready to go to the car, someone called out to him to stay there for they had already received confirmation. Because of the news of the formation of the new government, a prolonged, massive celebration broke out in the hall. While the march was being organized, Werner made his way to the taproom and attempted to contact Police Headquarters. The line was busy so he took the shortest route to Police Headquarters.

JUDGE NEITHARDT: You testified earlier: "My impressions in the Löwenbräukeller lead me to the firm opinion that Captain Röhm and his staff had no prior knowledge of the incident." Moreover, the witness spoke of Röhm's "excitement" and the perplexity of his staff, in his earlier testimony.

HERR WERNER: On that night, I was convinced that Captain Röhm and his staff knew nothing of the putsch. It was real consternation I saw. I had the impression that Captain Röhm and his staff had no prior knowledge of the events. At first they didn't know what to do. Esser's plan for such a grandiose speech also drove me to this conclusion. I said to my son: "This speech will last two hours, at least."

HERR SCHRAMM: Did you hear Captain Röhm say: "I don't believe it! That's impossible! They should have told me.'"?

HERR WERNER: I don't know. I saw only how Captain Röhm shook his head and was overcome by genuine bewilderment.

HERR SCHRAMM: Did you hear Captain Röhm attach the comment, "to dedicate the new government," to the summons to the Bürgerbräukeller?

HERR WERNER: I don't recall it.

The Witness Hoffmann is recalled to the stand. He remarks that he read in a newspaper that Hitler's star was on the rise. He discloses that Hitler ordered him to have posters printed to advertise the 14 assemblies in Munich on Friday evening and an immense national proclamation Sunday at Königsplatz. Hitler was to speak everywhere. This fact is proof that Hitler didn't want to play regent; instead he wanted to make propaganda for the Nationalist Government. The Witness also mentions the attack on the Israelite restaurant. According to him, he notified Hitler that this would give the Party a bad reputation and it would be extremely embarrassing for the Polizei. By chance, the culprit, a young lieutenant, was there. Hitler called him in and took him to task. The man protested that he hadn't worn the Party insignia. Hitler told the man he had announced that his actions had nothing to do with the Party by removing the Party insignia. Hitler expelled the lieutenant and his entire squad from the Party saying: "I will see to it that you find no refuge in any Nationalist Kampfbund." That is how Hitler condemned excesses. Moreover, remarks Herr Hoffmann, it has been mentioned many times that Hitler, like so many other Party bigwigs, was out for personal gain. Herr Hitler would not hold it against him if he reveals that Hitler made a brief excursion last Easter. He (Hoffmann) himself had seen how Hitler borrowed pocket money from Captain Göring.

Herr Luetgebrune states that of course Privy Council Heim did not receive any information from the prosecution concerning an incident at the secret session.

HERR STENGLEIN: This morning, certain charges were made against Prosecutor Dresse whereby it was alleged that immediately after Kriebel's interrogation, he drove to the Wehrkreiskommando, where an emergency conference took place.

Herr Dresse declares that this allegation is incorrect. After Kriebel's interrogation, he went to his office at the Hall of Justice with his stenographer. Then he betook himself to the Wehrkreiskommando on January 28, to compare Lossow's statements with Kriebel's, insofar as these were new. The minutes of the January 28 meeting are in the Court records in their original form.

After a brief consultation, Judge Neithardt hands down the decision that the public will be excluded for the duration of the examination of Witnesses Huber and Strasser. Permission to remain is granted to individuals previously named, under imposition of an oath of secrecy.

Testimony of Witness Huber

JUDGE NEITHARDT: I have already recorded your personal data: Major Eduard Huber, 38 years of age, married, Bayreuth, no connection to the defendants.

First of all, I want to question you unsworn, because there may have been a certain degree of participation.

This concerns the meeting of October 23, 1923, which has been designated as a meeting of the military command of the National Socialists—Schellingstrasse 39. Do you know of this meeting and of its substance? Would you tell us briefly what was discussed? I shall help you out if you have forgotten this or that detail.

HERR HUBER: The meeting of October 23 was a purely military meeting, which had been called by the military leaders of the National Socialists and the Kampfbund, to be held in the Schellingstrasse. Hitler did not attend this meeting. He appeared only at the beginning of the meeting, probably because so many leaders of the Kampfbund had come from far away. He welcomed the leaders with a short speech. I don't know whether you would like me to reiterate the contents of this speech.

JUDGE NEITHARDT: If you can remember it!

HERR HUBER: The ideas were, approximately, the following: Hitler said to us that the National Movement is progressing vigorously. It will not be long before the national spirit of the German people will rise. The foundation for this national uprising has been laid. An independent action on the part of the troops of the Kampfbund was impossible, and out of the question. The national uprising could occur only in closest association with the Bavarian Reichswehr and the Landespolizei.

Then Hitler said, approximately, the following: The establishment of a national dictatorship from Munich was an absolute necessity—also the creation of a National Army. The only man in a position to do this job was the reorganizer of our future army, His Excellency von Ludendorff.

I don't quite remember whether the things I am about to say were Hitler's words, or those of the military leaders, but I think Hitler also mentioned that the National Army would have to work in the closest possible cooperation with the professional army. That was the meaning of the speech. It lasted for about 10 minutes.

Then came the actual military discussion. Here we discussed only questions of the organization of the Kampfbund, as well as organizational problems for the creation of a National Army, which had been called an absolute necessity—that is, the question of selecting the leaders; the question of equipment and of weaponry. I would like to mention, regarding the arms problem, that I indicated—which is why I remember it so clearly—that we in Upper Franconia had very few arms, compared to other national bands. I was told: "This problem should not worry you at all. We will receive weapons from the supplies of the Reichswehr and the Landespolizei, with whom an agreement has already been made in the Wehrkreiskommando." Furthermore, we discussed in the meeting the training of parts of our combat troops by the Reichswehr, which had been planned in close collaboration with the Munich Reichswehrkommando, and the formation of special units, which had at least been planned, in theory, in conjunction with the Reichswehrkommando but which then could not be realized because of the events that followed.

JUDGE NEITHARDT: You told us essentially what went on. Three possibilities have been indicated. The first one is that Bavaria had separatist intentions and would secede from the Reich, and so forth. Göring chaired the discussion; and there were representatives from Landshut, Ingolstadt, Oesterreich, Württemberg, Baden, and North Germany present. Hitler said his task was over as soon as the people had been made to arise. Can you remember that?

HERR HUBER: Yes.

JUDGE NEITHARDT: Ludendorff was mentioned. Seisser was supposed to have been won over to the cause. Roth and Pöhner were also being discussed. Can you remember that?

HERR HUBER: I vaguely remember that Hitler said: "The

400

establishment of a national dictatorship, from Munich, is an absolute necessity. Men like Lossow and Seisser are to be considered for positions of leadership."

JUDGE NEITHARDT: Do you remember that Herr Frick's name was mentioned for the position of Police President?

HERR HUBER: I am quite sure it was not mentioned.

HERR HITLER: During the German Day in Bayreuth, I had a brief meeting with the leaders at the Hotel Anker. Do you remember that, at that time, I opposed the Ehrhardt Brigade and said a march with the Freikorps, to Thuringia and Saxony, would be insane; it would collapse 5 kilometers behind the border. If a march was to be undertaken, it could be done only with military power so that the enemy troops would be immediately disarmed by a certain moral effect. Furthermore, that only a big and well-organized army, with the black-white-red flag, headed by the best leaders of the War—only an army such as that could guarantee the absence of resistance; and possibly that the opposing troops would surrender without shooting. Do you remember that I then demanded a break with the Ehrhardt Brigade since there was a danger they might proceed on their own and that we would be drawn into an unfortunate situation?

HERR HUBER: That is correct.

HERR RODER: You said that, at the time, Hitler had never applied for a post in the new cabinet; that, on the contrary, he had declared that his work would be finished just as soon as the people had been led to the national uprising.

HERR HUBER: That is true.

HERR RODER: You also said Hitler stated the National Socialists would never undertake a coup; and that he could only visualize an action jointly with the Reichswehr and the Landespolizei.

HERR HUBER: Yes.

JUDGE NEITHARDT: A statement is alleged to have been made to the effect that Lossow and Hitler were in complete agreement.

HERR HITLER: It was then that we agreed.

HERR HUBER: In earlier meetings of the leaders, we always received such reports from our top leaders.

JUDGE NEITHARDT: Simultaneously with the establishment of a Reich dictatorship, a proclamation was to be made to form a National Army. The proclamation had already been sent out.

HERR HUBER: We were told that when the national revolution would break out, proclamations would be printed and sent to us. I never saw them.

HERR SCHRAMM: Do you know Captain Röhm?

HERR HUBER: I don't know him.

HERR SCHRAMM: If I tell you now that he is the gentleman next to me, would you recall that he was present?

HERR HUBER: I would definitely remember.

HERR SCHRAMM: I consider the remark that he was not present important.

JUDGE NEITHARDT: I did not say that.

HERR HOLL: Since Herr Hitler mentioned the Ehrhardt Brigade, I would like to state on behalf of Dr. Weber that in the second half of October, Ehrhardt also approached Dr. Weber— this was after Kahr, Lossow, and Seisser had been procrastinating—he was asked to take action independently, to be sure without these three men. It was Dr. Weber who, like Herr Hitler, told Ehrhardt he definitely rejected such nonsense. He said: "We carry out such an uprising only in accord with the Reichswehr and the Landespolizei."

Testimony of Gregor Strasser

Personal data are stated. The Witness is not related to the defendants either by blood or by marriage.

JUDGE NEITHARDT: For the time being, you will be questioned without oath.

You were present on October 23 at the meeting of the National Socialist leaders in the Schellingstrasse. Would you please tell us as much as you can remember?

HERR STRASSER: I would like to begin by saying that I am unable to remember the exact details of the meeting. At the time I did not know I would ever be questioned about it.

The discussion itself was a purely military discussion. Only the district chiefs were present. I don't know many of their names because the gentlemen changed frequently. I knew many gentlemen by sight, but not by name.

The purpose of this meeting was to formulate organizational measures for the Storm Troops. Captain Göring, the head of the Storm Troops, reported about them. The main points of the discussion concerned the distribution, the question of a national uprising, the formation of the National Army, and the association with the professional army—this last point appeared to me to be the most important one. I remember it well because the expression was used with emphasis. The expression was used several times. Göring, too, pointed out how the integration of the Storm Troops and the Kampfbund troops into the National Army, which was to be formed, was to be accomplished once the national uprising in Germany had begun.

I wish to stress, again, that they always used the expression, "in association with the professional army." Furthermore, we discussed how to begin the propaganda work, where to assign those who wanted to enlist in the National Army; the question of the Kampfbund troops was no longer mentioned.

When the problem of arms arose, I interjected a question because I knew of an arsenal in Lower Bavaria which contained many weapons, although they were in bad condition. I then told Göring: "These weapons are useless in their present condition. You cannot shoot with rusty rifles." Thereupon, I received orders to take these weapons to the Reichswehr. Thus, on November 8 at 3:30 in the afternoon, after discussion with Lieutenant Colonel Hoffmann of the Reichswehr, I delivered to them approximately 700 arms. Hoffmann, upon his word of honor, promised to clear the arms, store them in a separate room, and return them to me whenever I had need of them.

I say this only because on the next day, after November 9, the Lieutenant Colonel called me a scoundrel and a traitor in several speeches he made before his men. Concerning the question of training which may be of interest here, I don't know—

JUDGE NEITHARDT: We don't need the information right now.

HERR STRASSER: The general theme of the discussion was the formation of a National Army and the integration of the Storm Troops. These groups, which were to be increased through propaganda, were to form the nucleus of the National Army. That was the main point. This discussion was, for me, perhaps the most beautiful moment since 1918, because from that moment on I thought things would change. During the discussion, it was indicated several times that we would proceed in association with the professional army. It was expressed in a positive way. We did not want to be so foolish as to consider doing anything without the Landespolizei and the Reichswehr. We could only guess the political implications. Nothing was said about them, but I definitely gathered, from the entire discussion, that here agreements had been made which did not and could not interest us as the military leaders who were second in command.

My views were corroborated when I received an order immediately after the meeting requesting me to transfer to the Reichswehr—i.e. to the Reichswehr Training Battalion 19, at Landshut—a company of men who had formerly served in my Battalion. I had sent the Storm Troops to Lower Bavaria. I went directly to Lieutenant Colonel Hoffmann. He had the same order. I was still speaking to him at that time. I said: "That's right; you get the order and I get the order that we are to transfer 150 men to you. That corresponds with other things I have heard. Now it won't take much longer." I had to give him the names of 150 men. They were to be combined with the Reichswehr as a closed company. I also had to provide the names of the commanders and the non-commissioned officers. They wanted the information immediately about the people, and I verified it. They could not tell me yet when the men would be called in. It might take 8 days, 10 days—I don't remember exactly; but I don't think I am wrong if I say the code word was to be "sunrise." Meanwhile, it was November 9th.

JUDGE NEITHARDT: You do not have to answer the question I am about to ask you now, because it might incriminate you. You received orders, and you went to Freising on November 8, around midnight?

HERR STRASSER: On the 7th.

JUDGE NEITHARDT: Then you received orders to march off to Munich?

HERR STRASSER: That must have been on the 7th, because I had already left on the 7th.

JUDGE NEITHARDT: "On the 8th around midnight," may have been my mistake. It was probably on the 7th around midnight. Then you were ordered to go to Munich, and you received orders to occupy the Wittelsbach Bridge.

HERR STRASSER: Yes. That was on the 8th. I arrived in Freising; around 12:00 a messenger from the new government arrived with the order to move from Freising to Munich.

JUDGE NEITHARDT: That is all we need to know. I want to inform you that you may refuse to answer this question if you wish to do so. Were certain names mentioned? Do you recall the names of those people who were to be members of the new government?

HERR STRASSER: No.

JUDGE NEITHARDT: New men?

HERR STRASSER: I even found it strange. I talked about it with one of my friends. I thought it was the right thing to do. We were told, in a purely military fashion, what was to be done. It sounded like an order.

JUDGE NEITHARDT: Who told you?

HERR STRASSER: Captain Göring.

JUDGE NEITHARDT: Captain Göring told you? You don't have anything else to say?

HERR STRASSER: I have nothing else to say.

JUDGE NEITHARDT: Hitler, too, made a brief speech.

HERR STRASSER: Hitler only welcomed us. That had happened before. He only came in. We always were happy to see him. Hitler simply greeted us briefly.

JUDGE NEITHARDT: And he made a speech?

HERR STRASSER: He made a speech, I believe, of at most 10 minutes. I don't know the exact time any more.

JUDGE NEITHARDT: And the content of the speech?

HERR STRASSER: The content of the speech! How can I explain that?

JUDGE NEITHARDT: Did he also emphasize the joint action with the Reichswehr and Landespolizei?

HERR STRASSER: I can even remember that Hitler said—he used the expression which I used a moment ago—"I am not such an idiot that I would go against the Reichswehr and Landespolizei." I think this expression came from Hitler.

HERR RODER: You thought that now the march against Berlin would begin? Or that the march against Thuringia would begin? What were your thoughts?

HERR STRASSER: With regard to what?

HERR RODER: With regard to the Fall Maneuver 1923, when these orders arrived.

HERR STRASSER: We always cooperate with the Reichswehr.

HERR RODER: Did you think the march to Berlin would begin?

HERR STRASSER: Naturally.

HERR RODER: Was this also expressed by the gentlemen from the Reichswehr?

HERR STRASSER: I had had quite an argument earlier with Lieutenant Colonel Hoffmann because he thought I did not sign the oath fast enough. I had asked for assurances from our leadership. When they came, Hoffmann said: "Finally we are going to work together. Thank goodness. Now times will also change." In my opinion we were definitely going to march to that place where the present situation can be changed—Berlin.

HERR RODER: Of course! Don't you recall whether the gentlemen of the Reichswehr had indicated that the march was to go to Berlin?

HERR STRASSER: I cannot say that because I am no longer certain—perhaps because Lieutenant Colonel Hoffmann was especially cautious in that regard. For instance, he expressed himself in an extraordinarily diplomatic way in the so-called Lossow case. He told me he was suffering terribly because of this conflict. For this reason, he may have been very cautious, even towards me. Nevertheless, at the time, he congratulated me saying, "Thank God, any obstacles which may have existed between us because of the 1st of May are now, I think, removed. Now we are going to work together, and I am looking forward to this cooperation. Now the day will finally come when we will be freed from the disgrace of 1918."

HERR RODER: That is clear enough.

HERR LUDENDORFF: General Lossow says in his testimony that he had given me the information which the First Prosecutor has just read—this matter of the 23rd—when he visited me on November 7th in the morning. I did not quite understand, at that time, this note because I did not know of these events.

Today I am looking at this matter from a somewhat different perspective. This discussion of the 23rd of October preceded the discussion of the 24th. If I might be permitted to ask this question, I would like to know when you were asked to come to this meeting of October 23? When did you receive your orders to come on the 23rd?

HERR STRASSER: If I remember correctly, the evening before, or in the course of the night, I was told very briefly by Göring that I was to come to Munich, under any circumstances.

HERR LUDENDORFF: Until now I actually had been under the impression that this whole affair of October 23 had been arranged on Kriebel's order of the 16th, since the notes read by the Prosecutor contain references to the formation of the Freikorps. On October 24th, however, it was decided—and you have confirmed it—that the Freikorps, or rather shall we say, "these organizations," were to be integrated into the Reichswehr. You yourself said you were later to integrate a company into the Reichswehr?

HERR STRASSER: Yes, the designation was "as a reinforcement of the 7th Division."

HERR LUDENDORFF: When did this discussion with Lieutenant Colonel Hoffmann take place?

HERR STRASSER: Immediately afterwards. The meeting was on the 23rd. I suppose I received the order of the Supreme Command to make the men available from Göring on the 24th in the afternoon. This was at 8:00 in the evening. In order to clarify the sometimes-troubled relationship between the Lieutenant Colonel and myself, and to tell him my views, I went to the barracks and asked the aide to bring the Lieutenant Colonel downstairs. I then began by saying: "The last remnants of distrust and doubts which you have had against us have now been removed. I have here the order to support you with a company." He replied, "I also received it. The matter is now clear to me, as well." Previously I had had a rather sharp dispute with him. He then said, "I am sorry I was so harsh at that time."

HERR LUDENDORFF: You also mentioned the word, "sunrise."

HERR STRASSER: I think I remember it quite clearly. Nevertheless, I wouldn't want to make a definite statement—when I considered the statement about the password, I had my doubts.

I then told him I was also interested in the outlying areas—Passau, et cetera. He said: "My aide will leave you a note with a password—a motto—in case you should not be there." I might not be very much mistaken, but I don't want to say so with certainty that it was "sunrise."

HERR LUDENDORFF: It was the same word, we know, which was read by Herr Gademann.

Now, the last matter: The Fall Maneuver 1923. I mention this because I did not understand the note left by General Lossow. Lossow had told me at the time that the Reichswehr would be tripled. This actually happened through Order I A 800. This triplication could be achieved only through the integration of patriotic bands in the Reichswehr.

Now, in this order of the 23rd, there again are references to the Freikorps. That is why I did not understand it. I think the order of the 23rd, on which Lossow puts so much weight and on which he presents this as a disloyal act, is incorrectly dated in view of Kriebel's agreement with Lossow of the 24th. I mention this because I now understand it. At that time I did not understand why Lossow considered the order of the 23rd to be disloyal—after all, on the 24th, Kriebel had very loyally put himself and his men at Lossow's disposal. That this agreement was followed is proven, for instance, by the case of the company.

JUDGE NEITHARDT: How often did these meetings of the National Socialist leaders take place?

HERR STRASSER: The intervals were rather long. This was the first one in which important problems were discussed.

HERR HITLER: Before the formation of the Generalstaatskommissariat—or rather before the swearing-in of the Bavarian Reichswehr to the Bavarian Government, did you ever hear from us that we intended to march on Berlin?

HERR STRASSER: No. As I have already indicated, important matters were discussed for the first time during the meeting of the 23rd. The matter to be discussed, at that time, was the transformation of the Storm Troops from a purely protective force into company and battalion units of a more militaristic and disciplined character.

JUDGE NEITHARDT: Since you had been assigned to occupy the bridges, we will abstain from binding you by oath.

HERR KOHL: Just a brief remark regarding the oathtaking. When the Witness entered the courtroom, Your Honor immediately said, "For the time being, you will be questioned without an oath." I quite agree with this procedure, since I am certain that if this Witness is questioned unsworn, Witnesses Lossow, Kahr, and so on, can definitely not take an oath. Therefore, let us accept the ruling of Your Honor.

JUDGE NEITHARDT: I already mentioned that the Witness had orders to occupy the bridges. This means implication. Therefore he cannot take an oath here.

HERR KOHL: Lossow had the order to march on Berlin.

JUDGE NEITHARDT: I do not think it important whether the Witness is under oath or not. His statements will be believed even if he is not under oath.

As far as the Witness Glaser is concerned, we were of the opinion that he, too, would have something to say on this matter. That was incorrect. I don't think we need him. Herr Glaser will not be able to add very much.

HERR RODER: He is the head of the department which has these agents under its jurisdiction.

JUDGE NEITHARDT: He cannot talk about this, in any case, because he has not been released from his oath of office; and I would not permit that, either. I think it is in the best interests of all concerned if we abstain from hearing this Witness.

There are no further objections.

Whereupon, at 3:53 p.m., the secret session is ended.

410